D1452078

THE PEOPLE'S BUDGET 1909/10

THE PEOPLE'S BUDGET 1909/10: LLOYD GEORGE AND LIBERAL POLITICS

by
BRUCE K. MURRAY

CLARENDON PRESS OXFORD
1980

Oxford University Press, Walton Street, Oxford OX2 6DP

OXFORD   LONDON   GLASGOW
NEW YORK   TORONTO   MELBOURNE   WELLINGTON
KUALA LUMPUR   SINGAPORE   JAKARTA   HONG KONG   TOKYO
DELHI   BOMBAY   CALCUTTA   MADRAS   KARACHI
NAIROBI   DAR ES SALAAM   CAPE TOWN

Published in the United States by Oxford University Press, New York

© Bruce K. Murray 1980

LMS

British Library Cataloguing in Publication Data

Murray, Bruce K
    The People's Budget 1909/10.
    1. Taxation — Great Britain — History — 20th century
    2. Fiscal policy — Great Britain — History — 20th century
    3. Great Britain — Politics and government — 1901—1910
    I. Title
    336.2'00941   HJ2619   80—40901

    ISBN 0—19—822626—8

Typeset by Express Litho Service (Oxford).
Printed in Great Britain by Lowe and Brydone Ltd., Thetford.

TO MY MOTHER AND
IN MEMORY OF MY FATHER

Preface

The question of the decline and downfall of the Liberal party
and the rise of Labour as the party of social reform and the
working classes has exercised a strong fascination for historians of twentieth-century Britain. Much of the debate has
come to centre on whether the Edwardian Liberal party was
fighting a winning or a losing battle in its efforts to avert a
fundamental erosion of its support to the Unionists on the
right and the new Labour party on the left. This monograph
looks at the Liberal party in the Edwardian period, and
through the prism of Liberal fiscal policy, as encompassed in
Lloyd George's celebrated 'People's Budget' of 1909/10,
seeks to indicate how, and with what success, the Liberals
attempted to hold themselves together as a party of both the
middle and the working classes at a juncture when the 'social
question' was advancing to the centre of the political stage,
and with it the very fundamental question of how policies
of social reform were to be financed, when class interests
were becoming increasingly important in determining
political allegiances, and when the Liberals were confronted
with an altogether new threat on the left with the advent
of the Labour party.

This study is considerably indebted to many persons and
institutions. I wish to acknowledge, in the first instance, my
gratitude to Professor Aldon Bell, who supervised my post-
graduate degree work on Lloyd George and Edwardian
politics. I owe an enormous debt of gratitude to Dr Kenneth
O. Morgan for the invaluable advice and support he gave me
in the preparation of this monograph. I am also most grateful
to Dr Neal Blewett and Mr Graham Neame for their reading
of earlier drafts and their many useful suggestions. I would
like to thank Professor A. J. A. Morris for generously providing me with some of the material he had collected for his
biography of C. P. Trevelyan, and Mr Brian Cleave for helping
me to secure access to hitherto unavailable records in
Somerset House.

For permission to use or quote from private manuscript material I wish to acknowledge my gratitude to Lady Burke, the Hon. Mark Bonham Carter, Baron Gainford, the late Viscount Harcourt, Brigadier A. W. A. Llewellen Palmer, the Hon. Mrs H. B. Pease, and Mr A. J. P. Taylor and the Beaverbrook Foundation.

To Mr D. S. Porter and the staff of the Bodleian Library, Oxford, and to the staffs of the old Beaverbrook Library, the British Library, the Nuffield College Library, Oxford, the Public Record Office, the Library of the University of the Witwatersrand, Johannesburg, and the numerous other libraries and record offices which have assisted me in my research, I owe a considerable debt of gratitude.

I would finally like to express my gratitude to the Council of the University of the Witwatersrand, Johannesburg, and the British Council for their generous financial assistance in helping to make this study possible.

Bruce Murray

University of the Witwatersrand, Johannesburg,
June 1979.

Contents

I.	Introduction	1
II.	Public Finance and Liberal Politics	17
III.	Asquith's Inheritance	51
IV.	Lloyd George at the Treasury	76
V.	Preparation of the Budget	112
VI.	The Budget in the Cabinet	148
VII.	The Budget in the Commons and the Country	172
VIII.	Rejection	209
IX.	The Budget Election	236
X.	The Passage of the Budget	261
XI.	Impact of the Budget	290
	Abbreviations	315
	Notes	317
	Bibliography	336
	Index	343

I. Introduction

The question of public finance, as several recent studies have underlined, was of central significance to the politics of the Edwardian era. The period between the Anglo-Boer War and the outbreak of World War I witnessed a marked upswing in government expenditure, notably for social reform and national defence, and the question of how this new expenditure was to be financed proved a major point of debate within parties and of cleavage between parties.

P. F. Clarke, in his study of *Lancashire and the New Liberalism,* describes the question of how social reform was to be financed as nothing less than 'the core of the argument' between the Liberal and Unionist parties by 1909/10. As he points out, the Unionists looked to a 'broadening of the basis of taxation' by way of new tariffs, and the Liberals to increases in direct taxation. In the Budget for 1909/10, Lloyd George's celebrated 'People's Budget', he asserts that the Liberal Government made the 'deliberate decision to opt for direct taxation'. The difference between indirect and direct taxation, he quotes Winston Churchill as declaring in 1909, was 'the difference between the taxation of wages and the taxation of wealth'. As presented by Liberal politicians, and by Clarke, what was at issue in the contest over the 'People's Budget', including its rejection by the Unionist-dominated House of Lords, was whether wealth and large incomes were to make a larger contribution to the financing of social reform, and national defence, than wages.[1] What was at issue with regard to social reform particularly, in other words, was whether measures such as non-contributory old-age pensions, introduced in 1908, were to have the effect of partially redistributing income between classes or whether they were to be paid for by the working classes themselves in the form of tariff duties on articles of general consumption.

The focus of this study is on the Liberal party, traditionally the party of 'economy' in government, and the strategy it

1

developed when in office after December 1905 to finance new measures of social reform, and the general increase in government expenditure, along lines that might enable it to retain the bulk of its middle-class support and rally working-class voters. In 1909, in a period of declining trade, the Liberal Government sought to raise the revenue for both old-age pensions and increased naval expenditure. The fiscal strategy adopted by the Government in that year, and the responses which that strategy elicited from within the party and in the country, bore directly on the question of what sort of party the Liberals saw themselves as becoming, and where they considered their main support to reside.

It is Clarke's contention that by the two general elections of 1910 the Liberals, in a working 'progressive' alliance with the new Labour party, had succeeded in adapting to the arrival of class-based politics and in securing, at least in industrial conurbations like Lancashire and London, a distinctive working-class support. By 1910 the Liberals had become the party of social reform, and had consequently succeeded in engaging the support of the working classes, though at the loss, as instanced in Lancashire, of considerable support among capitalist employers.[2] In his study of the general elections of January and December 1910, Neal Blewett confirms that in England the Liberals were highly successful in rallying working-class support but with losses in suburbia being 'in part the cost of the operation'.[3] It is, however, the contention of D. A. Hamer, H. V. Emy, and Bentley Gilbert, that the Liberals had no certain long-term future as a party of social reform precisely because its traditional middle-class support had no interest in or was positively antagonistic towards costly programmes of social reform for the benefit of the working classes. In Hamer's argument, it is quite clear that after 1905 it was the traditional Liberal causes — 'opposition to imperialism and militarism, Home Rule, temperance, the agitation against the landowners, and so forth' — that aroused the enthusiasm of the Liberal party's middle-class rank and file, which provided the party with its local leadership and parliamentary representation, rather than social reform, which was the work and the passion of the great 'outsiders' such as Lloyd George and

Winston Churchill, neither of whom fitted comfortably into the established order of Liberal politics. Divorced from its 'sectional' interests and enthusiasms the Liberal party had no real life or meaning for its traditional middle-class adherents: '[T]he distinctive Liberal rationale for social reform, that it was needed in order to avert class conflict and "socialism", could just as well be expressed in that defensive, protective reaction which was causing the middle classes to desert Liberalism for Conservatism, especially when the existence of a Labour party was polarizing politics along class lines.'[4] The thrust of Emy's study is that while the Liberal party came to possess 'a sufficient theoretical commitment' to social and economic change, and that while shifts in the composition of the party's parliamentary representation, especially after 1906, gave a new voice to advanced reformers in the party's ranks, the resistance of orthodox and 'business' Liberals to state intervention in the market economy, and to the Liberal Government's financial policies, caused major strains within the party, and ultimately rendered it 'unable to accommodate itself to becoming a party of the left or of the right'. [5] Bentley Gilbert draws the lines rather more firmly. The revolt by a section of 'influential' Liberal MPs against the Budget for 1914, and the Government's retreat in the face of that revolt, indicated that by 1914 the New Liberalism had effectively run its course. The limits of the Liberal party's 'tolerance for social and economic change' had been reached.[6]

This study points to the positive enthusiasm which existed for social reform within the Liberal ranks, an enthusiasm that was to be successfully tapped by the 'People's Budget', as well as investigating the constraints which acted upon social reformers in the Liberal party, particularly with regard to the financing of social reform. By 1914 these constraints had by no means succeeded in stifling the New Liberalism.

The point is sometimes made that, in fact, the adoption by the Liberal Governments of 1905–14 of several major social welfare measures, including old-age pensions and health and unemployment insurance, provoked remarkably little resistance within the party. The measures that did occasion

some overt resistance in the party were the Budgets for 1909
and 1914, which provided for the taxes to help finance new
measures of reform as well as large increases in naval expenditure. It was, in other words, over the questions of the cost
and financing of social reform that the main debate over
social reform was waged within the Liberal party. The
concern of certain Liberals was that the taxes adopted by
the Government in 1909 and 1914 would have the effect of
eroding and ultimately destroying the party's support among
classes other than the urban working class, and consequently
divorce the party from its traditional sources of regular
support.

   The particular concern of this study is the Budget for
1909/10, the taxation strategy that it adopted for financing
social reform and increased naval expenditure, and the
political implications of that strategy. At a time when the
Liberal Government's attempts to satisfy its minority
'sectional' interests were being frustrated by the obstructionism of the Lords, and its hold over its working-class
support was being challenged by both the Tariff Reformers
in the Unionist party and by assertive elements in the Labour
ranks, and when also the Government was confronted by a
large prospective deficit caused by the adoption of old age
pensions and increased naval construction, the Budget for
1909/10 represented a multi-pronged attempt to employ
finance in the effort to hold the Liberal party's middle-
and working-class support together in a 'progressive' coalition for reform. The primary emphasis that Lloyd George
gave to the Budget in his speech introducing it in the
Commons on 29 April 1909 was that it was designed to raise
the revenue for social reform, and that it did so by resorting
mainly to direct taxation. In these respects, its main appeal
was directed at the working classes, but by avoiding direct
taxes that would substantially increase the burden of taxation
for the large majority of income tax payers it endeavoured to
reassure the bulk of the party's middle-class support, that
might otherwise be attracted to new tariffs as a source of
revenue. By its resort to massive new licence duties and to land
value taxes, it sought to arouse the positive enthusiasm of
middle-class temperance and land reformers, who had hitherto

found their programmes blocked by the obstructionism of the Lords.

The taxation strategy adopted by the 'People's Budget' represented no sudden innovation. Much of the groundwork for it had already been prepared by H. H. Asquith during his tenure as Chancellor of the Exchequer from 1905 to 1908, and almost all its direct taxes, including the supertax, the land value duties and increased licence duties, had been actively campaigned for within the Liberal party. The truly striking feature about the Budget for 1909/10 was that it incorporated within a single measure virtually the entire fiscal strategy towards which Liberalism had been moving. None the less, as this study seeks to demonstrate, the Budget for 1909/10 was essentially the personal initiative of Lloyd George. He had to fight long and hard to get his proposals past a Treasury still strongly attached to Gladstonian orthodoxy, and through a Cabinet alarmed by the boldness of the Budget and fearful that its provisions might serve to frighten off middle-class support from the party.

As this study intends to show, the 'People's Budget', as it emerged from the Cabinet, was in fact carefully designed to avoid directly antagonizing the bulk of the middle classes. The increases in direct taxation were aimed mainly at the wealthy, and at unearned sources of income. They were specifically intended to avoid foisting large new tax demands on small traders, white-collar workers, most professionals, and indeed the large majority of the income tax paying class. As the *Liberal Magazine* for May 1909 put it, 'the middle class who work for the incomes which are taxed are most gently treated; the "rentier" middle class rather less gently'. The Government's purpose, and the purpose of the 'People's Budget', was that Liberal social reform and Liberal finance should in fact promote the welding together of a 'progressive' coalition for reform that encompassed both the middle and working classes.

In the social reform policies adopted in 1908 and after, the Liberal Government sought to consolidate its support among the working classes in response to the challenge to that support from both the Tariff Reformers in the Unionist party and the new Labour party. To a very considerable extent, as this study intends to show, it was the campaign mounted by the Tariff Reformers, after their set-back in the Liberal 'landslide' victory in the general election of January 1906, to give tariff reform a genuine social appeal, by means of promising more work and the protection of jobs and by promising to finance social reform out of the revenue from tariffs, that impelled the Liberal Government to focus more on social reform and the maintenance of its support among the working classes. The latter, as C. F. G. Masterman diagnosed in early 1908, were by no means 'entirely certain' in their attachment to the Liberal policy of free trade and were likely to be greatly influenced by the condition of trade.[7] In 1907 trade began to turn downwards, which offered the Tariff Reformers new opportunities. The Liberal party was simultaneously exposed on its left flank to possible inroads by the Labour party should it fail to cater at all effectively for the interests of its working-class support. Both these considerations, in short, virtually compelled the Liberal Government to look to its working-class support, and provided the advocates of a New Liberalism of social reform and progressive direct taxation with their opportunity to steer official Liberalism into the policies of the New Liberalism.

The achievement of the New Liberal theorists of the late nineteenth and early twentieth centuries in providing Liberalism with an ideology of social reform has already been comprehensively examined by H. V. Emy and Michael Freeden.[8] Both stress Liberalism's own internal dynamic towards social reform, and the emphasis placed by the New Liberalism on the notion of community and of a shared responsibility for social reforms directed at promoting the common interest. Both consequently attach much importance to the principles advanced by the New Liberals for using finance as an essential weapon of reform by means of taxes and expenditures that employed the resources of the community for the benefit of the community. The New Liberals advocated progressive graduated taxation, levied in accordance with ability to pay, in order to finance 'productive social investment by the state'. They advanced the idea of a fund of capital and income that was created by the action of the community itself to which the state should secure access, by way of direct taxation, for the financing of social reform.

Freeden makes the point that, whereas the gulf between the ideas and policies of official Liberalism and the New Liberals was often immense during the Liberal Administrations of 1905-14, finance was the one field of reform in which official Liberalism did not appear to be 'lagging too far behind its theorists'. Lloyd George's Budget of 1909/10 was acclaimed by leading theorists of the New Liberalism for its 'audacity', and it is Freeden's opinion that, both in its details and in its general conception, the Budget 'was firmly based on the new Liberal perception of society'. It was based on the assumption that the resources of the community belonged to the community, and it was directed towards the effective and equitable employment of those resources for the regenerative function of social reform.[9]

In presenting his Budget to the Commons, Lloyd George emphasized that it was designed to provide the revenue for social reform, that it sought, through its licence duties, to tax to better advantage property values created by the state itself, and through its land-value duties, property values created by the community. In its general design its exactions were intended to ensure that all classes of the community contributed their fair share to the requirements of the community. But if the 'People's Budget' reflected the taxation principles of the New Liberalism, the point emphasized in this study is that it reflected even more accurately a political concern to combine an appeal to the working classes with reassurances to the bulk of the middle classes. The appeal to the working classes lay in the Budget's promise to finance social reform to a large extent out of direct taxation, in contrast to the resort of the Tariff Reformers to taxation of the food of the people; its reassurance to the middle classes lay in the fact that it exempted the great majority of them from the main thrust of increased direct taxation. Liberal fiscal strategy between 1906 and 1914, and notably the strategy of the 'People's Budget', was carefully designed to increase the proportion of direct to indirect taxation by means that would still protect the bulk of middle-class income tax payers.

Lloyd George's Budget was to prove enormously popular among a large segment of the Liberal rank and file. It was seen by 'advanced' Liberals as an effective rejoinder to the contention of the Tariff Reformers that the resources of free trade finance were virtually exhausted, and as an effective response to the obstructionism of the Lords to the Government's earlier measures for land and licensing reform. Above all, the Budget seemed to them to move the Government and the party along the path they wanted to see Liberalism adopt. It was a proclamation that the Liberal party was to be the party of social-democratic reform and progressive taxation. Right wing Liberals, for their part, were disturbed by the fiscal strategy encompassed in the Budget, while many cautious Liberals, while perhaps approving the over-all strategy, were alarmed by Lloyd George's boldness in incorporating the entire strategy in a single Budget. For these very reasons Lloyd George's proposals encountered distinct resistance among Liberals in Parliament and in the country as well as within the Cabinet.

What troubled right-wing and many 'moderate' Liberals about the 'People's Budget' was that it seemed to constitute an attack on wealth and property, and as such they feared that it was likely to drive not only wealth and property from the party but also many of the intermediate and lower middle classes who were often seen as inclined to identify more with the classes above them than those below them. They feared, in other words, that the 'People's Budget' would promote rather than postpone the arrival of class-based politics, and that the politics of class would mean the ultimate demise of the Liberal party, or at least of the Liberal party as they knew it.

The attitude of Lloyd George and the 'advanced' Liberals was that Liberalism could not for ever wait upon the reservations of the party's right-wing, and the hesitations of its cautious centre, if Liberalism was to survive as a living creed capable of making a genuine appeal to the working classes. In the Edwardian period it became for Lloyd George, and for 'advanced' Liberals generally, a fundamental article of faith that what had destroyed organized Liberalism on the continent was its divorce from the working classes, and that if the Liberal party in Britain was to avoid a similar fate it had at all costs to cater effectively for working-class needs and interests, particularly since the advent of a separate Labour party.[10]

Lloyd George always accepted that his Budget was bound to drive some wealthy members from the party, and that it would lose the party most of the gains it had made in 1906 among the middle classes in the South of England.[11] Otherwise, he trusted that the Budget would be accepted by wealthy and 'business' Liberals as the necessary price to be paid for the preservation of free trade on the one hand, and the prevention of the further rise of the Labour party on the other, and with it the prospect of a more 'confiscatory' mode of taxation. For the rest, the Budget sought to reassure the bulk of the middle-class taxpayers and to make a positive appeal to the Liberal party's traditional supporters through the taxation of licences and land, which struck against two traditional enemies of middle-class Liberalism — 'the trade' and the landowners. By mounting a campaign against the landowners, indeed, Lloyd George sought to promote an identity of interest between the party's middle- and working-class support, for both, in conventional Liberal demonology, had a deep-seated grievance against the extortionate demands of the narrow class that monopolized the land.

In the event, the 'People's Budget', and the campaigns and contests it gave rise to, proved noticeably more successful in consolidating the Liberal party's hold on urban working-class voters than it did in preserving middle-class support for the party, notably in England. In the general election of January 1910 the 'Celtic fringe' held firm for the Liberal party. In England, however, as Neal Blewett has demonstrated, politics tended to polarize along class lines, with the Liberal party holding most of its representation in urban working-class areas, and successfully containing the Labour party, but suffering major losses to the Unionists in suburbia and in rural areas.[12] 'It is the abiding problem of Liberal statesmanship to arouse the enthusiasm of the working-classes without frightening the middle-classes', Herbert Samuel commented in the midst of the general election of January 1910. 'It can be done; but it has not been done this time.'[13]

The outcome of the general election of January 1910, which deprived the Liberal Government of its absolute majority in the House of Commons and placed it in a position of dependence on the support of the Irish Nationalist and Labour parties, virtually forced the Government to determine whether its priority was to restore its appeal among the 'moderate' middle classes by adopting a cautious policy, notably in immediate terms in regard to the question of the Lords, or whether it should proceed with more radical policies. In the final analysis, the Liberal Government, after much agonizing, accepted the outcome of the January 1910 general election, not least because of pressure from its own back benches, and gave priority to the attempt to satisfy those groups that had actively supported it in the general election or on whose support in the Commons the Government depended for its continuation in office. The result was the Parliament Act of 1911, which deprived the House of Lords of its absolute veto; the introduction of payment of MPs; the National Insurance Act of 1911, which established health and unemployment insurance; and the introduction of bills for Irish Home Rule and Welsh Disestablishment. In terms of parliamentary time, these latter measures diverted the Liberal Government away from social reform, but as Emy has pointed out the Liberal concern for social politics never really diminished.[14] Lloyd George's Budget for 1914, which sought to build on the foundations laid by the 'People's Budget', indicated this continuing concern, and went even further than its predecessor in focusing on direct taxation. The Budget for 1914 provided for substantial increases in taxation, the first since 1909, partly with a view to reorganizing and extending Exchequer grants in relief of rates, for the benefit of both middle-class and working-class ratepayers; these increases were all in direct taxation. In 1909 Lloyd George had resorted to significant increases in the taxes on tobacco and spirits, in part so as to avoid increasing the income tax on earned incomes under £2,000; in 1914 he increased the income tax for all incomes over £1,000, as well as greatly increasing taxation of 'the rich', and avoided any increases in indirect taxation.

Despite its reliance entirely on increased direct taxation, the Budget for 1914 none the less indicated that the Government was still anxious to protect and reassure the majority of income tax payers. The large proportion of income tax payers, in fact, earned under £1,000 per annum, and as rate-payers they would benefit from the new Exchequer grants to local authorities and, supposedly, from Lloyd George's scheme to establish site value rating. Even more so than the 'People's Budget', the Budget for 1914 was directed at 'the rich'. From first reactions to it in the Commons Churchill got the impression that 'No one seems to care a rap for the rich.'[15] He was soon proved mistaken, and in the face of a 'cave' of wealthy Liberals against the Budget the Government retreated in its plans for reorganizing local finance and taxation. But it was a strategic retreat, not a capitulation or a decisive set-back for the New Liberalism. The Liberal Government and party had by 1914 moved too far along the road of social politics to allow them to turn back, though the Government remained anxious to minimize losses to the party among its traditional supporters outside the working classes.

There is no evidence by 1914 that advanced reformers among the Liberals were seriously contemplating abandoning the party as an instrument for the attainment of social reform. After World War I, C. P. Trevelyan, who had now joined the Labour party, commented that 'The Labour party exists to reorganize economic society. The Liberal party does it against the grain. That is why all social reformers are bound to gravitate, as I have done, to Labour.'[16] That was not an attitude that prevailed among 'advanced' Liberals before the war. They were, to be sure, highly conscious of the fact that they had to wage an almost continuous battle to get the Liberal Government to follow their lead, but the 'People's Budget', and the Government's subsequent actions and policies had gone far to maintain their faith in the reform possibilities of Liberalism and the Liberal party. Official Liberalism was cautious and hesitant in moving forward, but it was moving in the right direction, and Lloyd George and his 'People's Budget' had played a crucial role in steering it in that direction.

The 'People's Budget' likewise had a significant impact on Unionist politics and policies. In November 1909 the Unionists adopted the extreme course of securing the rejection of the Budget by the House of Lords in defiance of the constitutional convention that the Commons possessed sole control over the provision of finance. The result was to be a disaster for much of what the Unionist party supposedly represented. The Unionist defeat in the general election of January 1910 was to prove a decisive set-back for tariff reform, while the party's defeat in the general election of December of the same year sealed the fate of the House of Lords. The Parliament Act of 1911, by depriving the Lords of its absolute veto, removed the Lords as a permanent obstacle to Home Rule for Ireland, and thereby brought the Union itself into jeopardy. The Unionists had gambled heavily in having the Budget rejected by the Lords, and had lost.

The prolonged and often bitter struggle to which Lloyd George's Budget proposals gave rise was without precedent in the annals of British budgetary history. As this study shows, the resistance that Lloyd George's proposals encountered from their inception to their final enactment in law, and even thereafter, was quite extraordinary. In the preparation of the Budget Lloyd George had to contend with the hostility of the majority of his senior officials, including Sir George Murray, the Permanent Secretary to the Treasury, and of his own junior minister, Charles Hobhouse, the Financial Secretary to the Treasury. In the Cabinet his proposals were subjected to the closest scrutiny. More often than not they were opposed and criticized on points of principle and detail. In the Commons they aroused the wrath of the Unionists, antagonized the Irish Nationalists, and prompted the formation of a Liberal 'cave' against the land value duties. It required seventy parliamentary days and 554 divisions to secure the passage of the Budget through the Commons, a record for any finance measure. The Budget was then rejected by the House of Lords, and subjected to the buffeting of a general election. The Liberal Government's dependence on Irish Nationalist support in the new Parliament, and Irish antagonism to the Budget, meant that even after the election the Budget's passage into law was by no means ensured. It required months of tense negotiation, on the policy the Government intended to adopt towards the Lords and on the content of the Budget itself, before it became possible for the Government to reintroduce the Budget in the Commons basically unchanged and secure its passage into law.

On 29 April 1910, a year after Lloyd George had introduced his Budget in the Commons, and over eighteen months after he had begun its active preparation, the 'People's Budget' finally became law. Thereafter resistance to its provisions continued in the organized protests of the 'interests' affected and, notably in the instance of the land value duties, in the form of litigation. In the evidence that Percy Thompson, a commissioner of the Inland Revenue, gave to the Select Committee on Land Values in 1919 as to why the valuation and collection of taxes under the land value clauses of the 'People's Budget' had run into so many complications, he explained that 'The smooth administration of taxation must to a great extent depend upon the consent of the public to bear the taxes imposed upon it. In the case of the Land Value Duties such consent has never been apparent on the part of the bulk of taxpayers affected.'[17]

Different groups and 'interests' opposed and criticized the 'People's Budget' for different reasons. But what has to be explained is why the Unionist party should have gone to the length of securing the rejection of the Budget in the House of Lords, particularly when the Unionist leaders, A. J. Balfour in the Commons and Lansdowne in the Lords, recognized that their party could hardly expect to win a general election caused by the rejection of the Budget. The explanation is to be found in the fury among Unionists at what they saw as the calculated unfairness of the Budget in striking at 'the rich' and the 'interests' opposed to the Liberal Government, in the Unionist claim that the enactment of the Budget would mark a beginning of 'Socialism' and confiscatory' taxation, and in the rare tenacity with which the Unionists contested the Budget in the Commons. They sensed that to allow it a free passage through the Lords would represent a desertion of the 'interests' that supported them as well as a humiliating retreat for their party and the Lords. But above all the explanation of the Unionist reaction is to be found in the opposition of the Tariff Reformers to the Budget. The Budget was represented by Lloyd George, and accepted by the Tariff Reformers, as a challenge to tariff reform. The conclusion reached by the militant Tariff Reformers was that the enactment of the Budget might constitute a decisive set-back for tariff reform by removing the revenue motive for new tariffs. Balfour, who had for long equivocated over tariff reform, recognized by the late summer of 1909 that the prospects for promoting a consensus in his party for rejection were far greater than for any other course of action; in this sense he capitulated to the militants. What is stressed in this study is that, while he appreciated that his party would probably lose a general election caused by the rejection of the Budget, he calculated that the Liberal Government would be reduced to a dependence on the Irish Nationalists and he calculated also on a second general election on the issue of the Lords. With Home Rule as an additional aid to the Unionists, he hoped for a Unionist victory in this second election.

Some historians have suggested that the contest between the Liberals and the Unionists over the 'People's Budget', including its rejection by the House of Lords, was more the product of a partisan temper than of fundamental policy differences, notably on the question of taxation. J. R. Hay, in his studies of Liberal finance in the Edwardian era, concludes that: 'In practice the differences between the parties, both on the principles of income redistribution and the methods of finance, may have been somewhat less than the fury of contemporary debate, and some historical comments, have suggested.' He finds that by 1914 the poor were still taxed as heavily as the rich, and that taxpayers still contributed in proportion to income rather than in proportion to ability. Moreover, the Government's resort to the insurance principle for financing its health and unemployment measures was simply an alternative method to tariffs for getting the working classes themselves to pay for social reform.[18] The contention of S. J. Hurwitz, in his study of state intervention in Britain, is that the 'People's Budget' itself was basically a fraud. The novel imposts of the Budget, notably the land value duties, were largely 'theatrical', and its most exacting provisions were in the increases in indirect taxation, which affected the working classes particularly and made their lot decidedly harder than before. 'Liquor and tobacco taxes,' he comments, 'levied on commodities which the average male adult in Britain ranked as "necessaries", yielded a greater percentage of the total revenue in the 1909 Budget than in any other Budget since the war Budget of 1900.'[19]

Such assessments fail to appreciate the undoubted significance which the 'People's Budget' had for contemporaries. At a critical juncture, when through tariff reform a sustained attempt was being mounted to perpetuate the regressive features of British taxation, the 'People's Budget' signified the Liberal Government's preparedness to ensure that direct taxes should be responsible for a measurably larger share of taxation than regressive indirect taxes. It ensured this by methods designed to increase very considerably the rate of taxation for the wealthy and simultaneously protect the white-collar, small-business, and professional middle classes from bearing the real burden of increased direct taxation. Partly because it was the wealthy who most obviously escaped most lightly from taxation by any progressive standards, and partly for the political reason that the Liberal Government was anxious not to alienate the white-collar, small-business, and professional middle classes, the 'People's Budget' directed its main thrust at the wealthy, and even resorted to substantial increases in indirect taxation so as to protect the ordinary middle-class income tax payer. Its immediate aims for redistributing the burden of taxation were consequently limited, but none the less it did seek to destroy the defences that had hitherto protected large and unearned incomes from progressive taxation, and for that very reason provoked fierce hostility. The 'People's Budget' aroused furious opposition on the Unionist side not so much because of its immediate impositions, but precisely because its principles threatened large and unearned incomes, because it seemed to undercut the revenue argument for tariffs, and because it threatened to bypass the veto of the House of Lords on the issues of land valuation and public house licensing.

The 'People's Budget' occupies an important place in the history of British taxation. Together with Sir William Harcourt's famous Death Duties Budget of 1894, and

Asquith's Budget of 1907 which differentiated between earned and unearned income, it provided the basic structure for the establishment of modern 'democratic' or progressive taxation in Britain. It constituted a distinct break from the previously entrenched principle that taxation was to be imposed for revenue purposes only. The 'People's Budget' was founded on the new principle that taxation should serve as a major instrument of long-term social policy.

What is evident from the statistics provided by Herbert Samuel, a member of the Liberal Cabinet from June 1909, in a presidential address delivered before the Royal Statistical Society in 1919 on 'The Taxation of the Various Classes of the People', and also from the Colwyn Committee of 1927 on National Debt and Taxation, is that it was the holders of large and primarily unearned incomes who felt the main brunt of the taxation demands of Liberal finance between 1906 and 1914, and particularly of the taxes imposed by the 'People's Budget'. The rate of taxation in proportion to income was considerably increased for these groups. It is also evident from the statistics given by Samuel and the Colwyn Committee that the working classes and the middle classes with earned incomes under £2,000 positively benefited from Liberal taxation policy between 1906 and 1914. These groups, largely as a consequence of the concessions and changes made by Asquith during his tenure as Chancellor of the Exchequer, experienced a positive decline in the burden of their imperial taxes in relation to earned income, and the decline was most marked for the middle classes with earned incomes under £2,000.[20] Liberal fiscal strategy, while designed to help finance social reform and rally working-class support to the party, was conditioned throughout by a powerful concern to protect and reassure the large majority of middle-class income tax payers.

II. Public Finance and Liberal Politics

I

One of the most formidable problems that confronted the Liberal party in the Edwardian era was that of how to finance social reform without resorting to tariffs and without destroying middle-class support for the party. For raising the revenue for social reform, and other new government expenditure, out of taxation, Liberals looked more to direct than to indirect taxation, and shunned the notion of resorting to tariff duties. Indirect taxation was regarded by Liberals as regressive, as bearing hardest on the poorer sections of society, and the party was committed to the maintenance of free trade finance in opposition to Joseph Chamberlain's campaign for tariff reform. The fundamental problem was that of how to raise large new revenues from direct taxation, and promote some degree of income redistribution, without simultaneously frightening off the party's middle-class support.

Advanced social reformers in the Liberal party were always prepared to accept that part of the price that the party would have to pay for becoming a major instrument of social progress, and retaining its working-class support, would be the shedding of some of its more conservative-minded support, but no Liberal of consequence was prepared to contemplate a wholesale withdrawal of middle-class support from the party.

Winston Churchill once described the Liberal Government formed in December 1905 as 'a government representative of and resting on the middle and working classes, a government supported by nonconformists and trade unions'.[1] As seen by C. F. G. Masterman, in an article in January 1908 on 'Politics in Transition', the Liberal party that swept to the 'landslide' victory in the general election of January 1906 included relatively few rich men, but a considerable number who were extraordinarily susceptible to the influence of the wealthier classes; a minority only of the professional classes in England, though perhaps a greater proportion in Wales and Scotland; the large proportion, outside London, of the middle classes generally, including small tradesmen and the bulk of the Nonconformists, from which groups the Liberal party derived its 'permanent fighting staff in the constituencies'; and finally 'large masses of the industrial populations'. The main difficulty confronting the Liberal Government, as Masterman saw it, was that of catering for all the interests of so wide a range of support, particularly when 'the interests of each section are generally diverse and often contradictory'. The Government's middle-class supporters demanded free trade, education legislation to satisfy Nonconformist interests, temperance legislation to reduce facilities for drink, and retrenchment, especially in the army and navy, so as to limit taxation and avoid 'the fostering of a military and truculent spirit'. Its working-class supporters, by contrast, were probably more interested in prosperous trade than in the principle of free trade. They cared nothing at all about religious teaching in schools, had a distinct aversion to temperance legislation, cared little for retrenchment on armaments, and desired some direct betterment of their own condition in the form of provisions for old age and unemployed labour, better houses at less rent, less work for more wages, the removal of sweating, the reform of the Poor Law, and improved chances for their children. The neglect of either of these two programmes, Masterman commented, would mean the shedding of large bodies of support, either to the right of the party or to its left.

As Masterman appreciated, it was not merely the neglect of programmes, but their active pursuance, that might serve to disrupt the broad coalition that supported the Liberal Government and party in 1906. Working-class supporters of the Liberals in 1906 were likely to be positively antagonized by temperance legislation and retrenchment on armaments that entailed the loss of jobs in dockyards and arsenals, and social reform required charting a 'dim and perilous way' between 'the defiant rights of property' and 'the equally defiant rights of personality'. The fundamental question for Masterman, as a committed

social reformer, was whether the Liberal Government could
in fact pursue a positive programme of social reform without
driving wealth and middle-class support out of the party.
As he presented the Liberal dilemma:

Will the Liberal party continue to hold within its embrace all these
diverse elements? Can it retain, for example, its few men of wealth,
without losing those adherents who demand direct taxation of that
wealth in the interests of social reform? Can it continue to bridge over
that wide chasm of interest which exists to-day between the lower
middle class and the working class, which leads the former always to
associate itself in interest with the classes above, and alternatively to
fear and despise the classes below; which is causing in that middle class
a violent revolt to-day at the pampering of the working man and a
vague fear of an advancing social revolution.[2]

It was vital to the Liberal party that it should continue to
act as a bridge between the middle and working classes,
particularly after the emergence of a separate Labour party.
As a good many contemporaries perceived the situation,
should the Liberal party cease to provide such a bridge, and
should the main line of cleavage in politics cut between the
middle and working classes, that would entail not only a
defeat for the Liberal notion of community, embodied in the
slogan 'masses vs. classes', but also the destruction of the
Liberal party as a major party. On the Liberal side H. H.
Fowler dreaded the prospect of 'the disruption of the Liberal
party and the ultimate division of parties into the Haves and
the Have-nots'. For the Unionists, George Wyndham looked
forward to the day when that 'blatant, lower-middle-class,
fraud, called Liberalism' had been destroyed and the ring
cleared for a 'fight to the finish' between Labour and Imperialism.[3]

The Liberal dilemma over social reform and its financing
was heightened by several other considerations and developments, all of which helped to make finance a central question
not only for Liberals, but in British politics generally. To a
very considerable extent, indeed, British politics in the
Edwardian era were about public finance.

In addition to the question of financing social reform four
other factors served to establish finance in a central position
in the politics of the period — the growth in public expendi-

ture, both imperial and local; a general concern at the performance of the British economy; Joseph Chamberlain's challenge in 1903 to free trade; and in 1908 the political sense that emerged in Liberal circles that finance offered a Liberal government the only means by which it might achieve some of its reform goals against the wishes of the House of Lords.

II

In the period from the eve of the Anglo-Boer War to the eve of World War I, expenditure by government rose dramatically. Sharp increases in government expenditure were imposed for the army and navy, education, economic services, social reforms, and general administration. As calculated by Peacock and Wiseman, in their study of the growth of public expenditure in the United Kingdom, total government expenditure jumped from £156,800,000 in 1895 to £305,400,000 by 1913. In other words, it virtually doubled in less than a generation. Allowing for inflation, the increase was still in the order of 60 per cent. At 1900 prices, total government expenditure rose between 1895 and 1913 from £172,300,000 to £284,200,000.[4]

Such an increase marked a distinct break from the Victorian doctrine of retrenchment, and the development of new attitudes to government spending. In the Edwardian era, public debate on the extent of government expenditure was still a very live one, but it was no longer conditioned by a sense that government spending was necessarily unproductive. When Liberals preached 'retrenchment and reform' in the campaign for the general election of January 1906, they specifically meant that they wanted to secure a cut-back in 'wasteful' expenditure on armaments so as to release funds for more 'productive' expenditure on social reform. Until 1908 the Liberal Government was able to pursue a policy of 'retrenchment' on armaments; thereafter the intensification of Anglo-German naval rivalry, and fears for British security in the world, obliged it to accept a large programme of naval construction. At the same time it did not abandon its policies of social reform. The outcome was that the Liberals and the majority of the Unionists were henceforward generally agreed on the need for substantial new expenditure for defence and social reform; where they diverged most fundamentally was on the question of how to raise the revenue necessary to meet the enlarged government expenditure. The Liberals had become committed to extending and graduating direct taxation; the Unionists to 'broadening the basis of taxation' by way of new tariff duties.

By the late nineteenth century the Victorian doctrine of retrenchment was already in retreat. 'Economy' had been the watchword of Gladstonian finance; as Chancellor of the Exchequer, Gladstone had steadfastly insisted that government expediture should be kept to an absolute minimum, and that the state should refrain from providing anything more than essential services. This attachment to retrenchment was rooted in a suspicion that government expenditure, unless severely scrutinized 'to save what are meant by candle-ends', naturally tended to extravagance and waste, and in the twin conviction that all taxation acted in restraint of trade and industry, and that the individual knew better than the state how best to employ his own resources. The late nineteenth century witnessed the development of new ideas and attitudes about the efficacy and desirability of state action, and even about the ability of government spending to stimulate economic growth. As a consequence the doctrine of retrenchment lost ground, and debate came to focus more on the notion of taxable capacity, both of the country as a whole and of particular groups of taxpayers. It was considerations of taxable capacity, in relation to the country's productive capacity and to levels of tolerance, that increasingly came to serve as the major restraint on government expenditure. In 1895 Sir William Harcourt, the Liberal Chancellor of the Exchequer, declared that 'in the growth of the expenditure of the country you have very nearly reached the limits of tolerable taxation'.[5]

The period of the Anglo-Boer War inevitably resulted in a sharp increase in government expenditure, and with it in levels of taxation, despite the fact that the Unionist Government of Lord Salisbury resorted to large-scale borrowing to help finance the war. Expenditure by the national government, including subsidies to local government, leapt from £117,600,000 in 1898/9 to £205,200,000 in 1901/2, and Exchequer revenue from £117,800,000 in 1898/9 to £161,300,000 in 1902/3. Income tax was raised in stages from 8*d*. in the £ to 1*s*. 3*d*., additions were made to the charges on beer and spirits, the duties on tobacco and tea were increased, and three former taxes were revived, an import duty on sugar, an export duty on coal, and a registration duty on imported corn and flour.

The increases in the number of indirect taxes, and the intimations of Sir Michael Hicks-Beach, the Unionist Chancellor of the Exchequer, that his formidable deficits stemmed in no small measure from increases in ordinary expenditure, gave a new urgency to the debate over the country's taxable capacity, and brought into focus the crucial question of where permanent new sources of revenue might be found. The main thrust of Hicks-Beach's Budget speech of 18 April 1901 was that the country's fiscal system had to contend not only with a war deficit, but also with a steadily increasing ordinary expenditure that had effectively outgrown the capacity of the existing basis of taxation. He repeated the warnings made by George Goschen, the Unionist Chancellor of the Exchequer from 1887 to 1892, that the country's basis of taxation had become dangerously narrow, and that it was essential to broaden the basis if revenue was to keep pace with the rise in ordinary expenditure.

What the period of the Anglo-Boer War produced was a general recognition that the level of normal government expenditure would inevitably be very much higher after the war than before. In the calculation of Sir Robert Giffen, a recognized statistical expert, in a series of letters to *The Times* in January 1902, the age of a normal national government expenditure of about £160,000,000 had already dawned. The point he stressed was that it was within the country's capacity to finance such an expenditure.

A growing concern at the beginning of the twentieth century at the apparent weakness of the British economy, and the slowing down in the rate of economic growth, which coincided with the beginning of the period of rapid growth in government expenditure, served to highlight the question of how far Britain could afford to sustain a substantially larger government expenditure. Giffen's point was that in the 1860s Britain had succeeded in maintaining, without straining the resources of the country, a level of government expenditure that was, in proportion to the wealth of the country and individual incomes, as high as the level of expenditure he expected for the 1900s. The country, he pointed out, was 'not unprosperous in the sixties'. Since the 1860s the wealth of the country had doubled and was quite sufficient to sustain a normal government expenditure of £160,000,000. What Giffen urged was that the additional revenue required to meet the higher level of government expenditure should be raised by indirect rather than by direct taxation. High levels of direct taxation would hinder the capital accumulation and investment required for the future growth of the economy, but increases in indirect taxation could be so diffused as to be hardly felt at all. Indeed, for Giffen, the real cause of the country's financial difficulties stemmed not from any fundamental lack of taxable capacity, but from the 'wanton sacrifice' of indirect revenue since the Gladstone ministry of 1869–74. He consequently recommended that all new regular revenues should be raised by indirect taxation, reserving increases in direct taxation for emergencies.[6]

Liberal theorists, by contrast, were beginning by the turn of the century to explore the notion that progressive direct taxation and government expenditure on social welfare measures might in fact prove capable of helping to offset cyclical depressions and to regenerate economic activity by promoting income redistribution and with it consumption. At the same time, Liberal politicians were also exploring the potential capacity of direct taxation to meet higher new levels of government expenditure, and were investigating the possibilities for reforming the system of direct taxation so as to render it more productive of revenue, particularly the income tax. 'I am not sure', R. B. Haldane put it to the House of Commons in 1902, 'we have exhausted the resources of civilization in respect of the income tax.'[7]

In so far as the Anglo-Boer War was financed out of taxation, Hicks-Beach scrupulously sought to ensure that increases in direct and indirect taxation roughly balanced one another, and a fair equilibrium was maintained between the amounts raised by the two 'sisters', as Gladstone had referred to them. In point of fact, for the first time in British history, slightly more was raised by direct rather than indirect taxation in the years 1901/2 and 1902/3. None the less, the further fact that Hicks-Beach kept well away from any proposals for the reform of direct taxation, that he spoke, even as a committed free trader, of the need to find additional taxes that everybody would pay, and that he imposed new indirect taxes, all suggested that he was looking for permanent new forms of indirect taxation. The promise for some, and the threat and challenge to others, was that Unionist finance was becoming committed to containing direct taxation, and to extending the area and even the proportion of indirect taxation. Since Peel's budgets of the 1840s, the whole trend in taxation had been to reduce the proportion paid by indirect taxes until, by the Anglo-Boer War, an approximately equal share of Exchequer revenue was raised from direct and indirect taxation. The questions that were now highlighted were whether direct taxation was to become the primary instrument of imperial finance, or whether the balance between the two kinds of taxation was to be maintained, or whether Victorian trends were to be positively reversed and a new emphasis given to indirect taxation. On these questions politicians and parties divided in the Edwardian era.

III

What served to give a dramatic new intensity to the debate over taxation, and to crystallize the opposing positions, was Joseph Chamberlain's campaign for tariff reform, launched in 1903. Tariff reform immediately became the most divisive single issue in British politics, shattering the unity of the Unionist party and making the defence of free trade the Liberal rallying point for the creation of a new anti-Unionist coalition.

Chamberlain's campaign, in its timing at least, was a direct outgrowth of the debate over taxation, and the

Unionist concern to 'broaden the basis' of indirect taxation. As Colonial Secretary, Chamberlain's own primary concern was to tighten the bonds of Empire through a system of imperial preference; he was an imperialist before he was ever a protectionist or an advocate of the virtues of indirect taxation. Under the impact of war, new tariff duties had been imposed for revenue purposes, and Unionist finance was moving in the direction of finding lucrative new sources of indirect revenue, thereby creating the political opportunity to construct an entirely new system of tariffs that might do very much more than raise revenue. It might also offer some protection against foreign competition to hard-pressed British industries and lead, through preferences granted to the colonies, to a closer economic, and perhaps even political, unity of the Empire.

In late 1902 Chamberlain persuaded A. J. Balfour, Salisbury's successor as Prime Minister, and the majority in his Cabinet to remit in favour of the self-governing colonies the registration duty on imported corn, and in so doing establish the principle of imperial preference. In the preparation of the Budget for the next year C. T. Ritchie, Hicks-Beach's successor at the Exchequer, deliberately sabotaged the plan, and secured, in Chamberlain's absence in South Africa, the abolition of the corn duty. On 15 May 1903, in his famous speech in the Birmingham town hall, Chamberlain countered by publicly challenging the sanctity of free trade, and urged the case for promoting the economic and political unity of the Empire through preferential tariffs. On 6 October, after having resigned as Colonial Secretary, Chamberlain launched his popular crusade for tariff reform in a speech at Glasgow. The scheme he recommended was a duty of 2s. a quarter on foreign corn, excluding maize, and a corresponding tax on flour; a 5 per cent tax on foreign meat and dairy produce, excluding bacon; and an average duty of 10 per cent on manufactured goods entering Britain. From all these duties the colonies would be exempt.[8]

The content and emphases of the tariff reform campaign proved fluid rather than fixed. This was a fluidity that derived from Chamberlain's own imprecision on matters of detail and his own shifting judgements, from the uneasiness of the

relation between the imperialists and the outright protec-
tionists within the tariff reform movement, and from prag-
matic responses to political, economic, and fiscal developments.

Initially, Chamberlain had expected that his campaign
for tariff reform would appeal to labour, but he was to be
disappointed. Labour as well as Liberalism rejected his
proposed food taxes. By his own admission, Chamberlain
had gravely underestimated the extent and the solidity of
the opposition to the food duties, or the 'stomach taxes'
as they were rapidly dubbed. Any scheme of imperial preference necessarily involved taxes on raw materials or food
or both. Duties on raw materials Chamberlain ruled out
because raw materials were 'a necessity of our manufacturing
trade'. That left food. 'I make hon. Gentlemen opposite a
present of that', Chamberlain conceded, amid Liberal cheers,
in the Commons on 28 May 1903.

To counter the charge that his tariff scheme would inevitably bring about an increase in the cost of living, especially
for the poorer sections of the community, Chamberlain
proposed at Glasgow to remit three-quarters of the existing
duty on tea, half the duty on sugar, and corresponding
amounts on cocoa and coffee, so that over-all his proposals
would involve 'no addition to the cost of living, but only a
transfer of taxation from one item to another'. Furthermore
he held out the prospect that the yield of about £9,000,000
annually from the duty on manufactured goods might be
used 'for the further reduction both of taxes on food and
also of some other taxes which press most hardly on different sections of the community'.

In suggesting the remission of taxation out of funds
collected from the duty on manufactured goods, Chamberlain
was beating something of a strategic retreat from his earlier
proposals in the Commons. On 22, and again on 28 May,
Chamberlain had stated in the House that the surplus revenue
collected from the new tariffs should be devoted to financing
old-age pensions and other social reforms that had previously
been beyond the reach of 'immediate practical politics'.
Tariff reform, he had then contended, would provide the
hitherto unobtainable revenue for advanced social reform.

But, convinced that the Liberals were already making 'unscrupulous' use of the 'dear bread' cry against his proposals for imperial preference, Chamberlain chose at Glasgow to subordinate his ideas for financing social reform to the needs of his argument that the tariffs he envisaged would not result in a higher cost of living.[9] Thereafter he based his 'social' argument for tariffs not on their ability to underwrite social reform but rather on the need for them to protect and create jobs for the working men of Britain.

In his study of the genesis and evolution of Chamberlain's campaign for tariff reform, Julian Amery has queried the wisdom of Chamberlain jettisoning his reference to old-age pensions. By so doing, in Amery's opinion, Chamberlain lost 'the golden chance to put a great social reform in the forefront of his programme'. Chamberlain himself seems to have appreciated this after the devastating defeat of the Unionists, and the first major political breakthrough of Labour, in the general election of January 1906, and in his speeches thereafter he returned to the notion of financing social reform by means of tariffs. 'I need not argue the question now,' he told the 1900 Club on 25 June 1906, 'but it is clear that, if great extension is to be given to social reform, the money can only be found by an extension of the basis of our taxation. It seems to me that it cannot be found in a less burden upon the people, a less interference with trade than by the moderate suggestions which the Unionist party have made.'[10]

The Tariff Reformers possessed fewer prejudices against large-scale government expenditure than any other political group in Edwardian Britain. They were not frightened by the prospect of rapidly escalating government expenditure; if anything, they welcomed it. The attainment of their objectives positively required massive government spending. As 'constructive imperialists' their concerns were to promote the unity and security of the Empire, and the efficiency of the British peoples, and they accepted that vast public spending would be required to maintain the Empire's defences and to provide essential social reforms at home. From their standpoint, moreover, increased government expenditure was to be welcomed in itself in so far as it would force the country to look increasingly to tariffs for revenue.

For the Unionist party, Chamberlain's 'raging, tearing' campaign for tariff reform brought only dissension, division, and defeat. In response to Chamberlain's challenge to fiscal orthodoxy, the party promptly splintered into three factions — the Chamberlainite Tariff Reformers or 'whole hoggers', the Balfourite moderates or 'little piggers', and the outright Free Traders or 'free fooders'. Balfour's Cabinet itself was deprived of five of its members in the shake-up of September/October 1903. Chamberlain resigned as Colonial Secretary to go forth and preach tariff reform to the people, and out of the Cabinet went also the four Free Trade ministers, Ritchie, Lord Balfour of Burleigh, Lord George Hamilton, and the Duke of Devonshire.

Even before the Cabinet resignations, the Tariff Reform and Unionist Free Food Leagues had been formed by the rival factions, and after them party divisions rapidly solidified. The Unionist Free Traders, numbering in 1903 between sixty and seventy MPs in a total Unionist contingent in the Commons of nearly 400, resorted to an uncompromising opposition to tariff reform, even to the extent of advising their supporters to co-operate with Liberals when necessary to ensure the defeat of Chamberlainite candidates at by-elections. This hostility towards Chamberlain and his proposals fed on a variety of attitudes and outlooks — on an antipathy to Chamberlain himself, and his methods; on a sense that Chamberlain was challenging the existing power structure of the party, and threatening to establish the dominance of industrial and 'democratic' Birmingham over the old landed and patrician leadership; on a concern that the traditional interests of the Unionist party might be sacrificed to the needs of tariff reform; and on a fear that high food prices would drive the working classes to Socialism. As the studies of Blewett and Rempel have indicated, the Unionist Free Traders were also, with only very few exceptions, extremely conservative in regard to social reform, and were reluctant to contemplate large expenditures in that direction.[11] Basically, they were Gladstonians in their opposition to increasing state interventionism and to 'profligate finance'.

In placing himself on the fence between the whole hoggers

and the free fooders, Balfour, while he remained Prime Minister, never came to any firm conclusions one way or the other on the fiscal issue. For temperamental as well as political reasons, he sat tight on the fence. Sceptical of the continued viability for Britain of the prevailing system of free trade, and equally sceptical of the panacea offered by Chamberlain, Balfour got no further in his own thinking than the formula he advanced in 1903 for retaliation. He was willing to revise the country's tariff policies so as to enable Britain to regain her liberty of fiscal negotiation and retaliate against those nations that imposed unwarranted tariffs on British goods, but he failed to develop even this proposal systematically. His mind, Lord Hugh Cecil, Balfour's cousin and a Free Trader, explained to Devonshire, was 'not that of a leader, but of a diplomatist'.[12] It was a mind that simply lacked conviction, one way or the other, on the tariff issue. Where Balfour was resolute was in his determination to preserve his party, his leadership, and, for so long as was possible, his Government. To these ends, he made a political virtue out of his own absence of conviction, deliberately resorting to a strategy of ambiguity, equivocation, and simple evasion on the tariff issue.

In this Balfour met with a real measure of success. Although he could not control the feuding factions within the party, and although individual free fooders, notably J. E. B. Seely and Winston Churchill, defected to the Liberals, the Unionist party survived largely intact. The Government managed to prolong its existence until December 1905. What assisted Balfour in holding out against the blandishments of Chamberlain was the fact that tariff reform fared very badly at the polls in 1904 and 1905, thereby seeming to confirm the assessment made in August 1903 by Sir Alexander Acland-Hood, the Conservative Chief Whip, that the country was indifferent about preferential tariffs, but actively hostile to taxing bread and meat.[13] This latter consideration weighed heavily with Balfour. 'The prejudice against a small tax on food', he reminded Chamberlain in February 1905, 'is not the fad of a few imperfectly informed theorists: it is a deep-rooted prejudice affecting the large mass of voters, especially the poorest class, which it will be a matter of extreme difficulty to overcome.'[14]

Balfour's Government was finally brought to an end after Chamberlain, anxious to force a general election, had made it clear in November 1905 that he could no longer tolerate the Prime Minister's fiscal sophistries and his reluctance to move nearer to the Chamberlainite camp. Balfour's continuance in office had now been made impossible. The Chamberlainites had gradually been building up their power base in the party, capturing the Liberal Unionist organization and gaining effective control of the National Union Conference; they constituted by far the largest group among Unionist MPs; and it was out of the question that Balfour should continue to govern in defiance of them. On 4 December he resigned, trusting that the suggestions of a new feud in the Liberal party over Home Rule might serve to embarrass Sir Henry Campbell-Bannerman in the formation of a Liberal Government.

Whatever the success of Balfour's stratagems in 1904/5, a high price was ultimately paid in the disastrous election defeat of his party in January 1906. 'You cannot reason with a pendulum', Balfour protested before the general election, but it is at least arguable that his delaying tactics and persistence in office accentuated the pendulum's swing when it finally came. That, at any rate, had been Chamberlain's foreboding; the longer a general election was delayed, he had predicted in March 1904, 'the worse will be the result'.[15] What is certain is that, torn by dissension, and without a clear lead from the centre, the Unionist party, in the words of A. K. Russell, the historian of the 1906 general election, could 'neither attract support nor organise effectively for action'.[16]

IV

Thoroughly divisive in its impact upon the Unionist party, Chamberlain's attack on free trade performed the miracle of bringing all Liberals together in a truly united front. The Liberals, out of office since 1895, had been badly divided by the Anglo-Boer War. The Liberal Imperialists, gathered around Lord Rosebery, had come out firmly in favour of the war, the Radicals firmly in opposition to it, with the 'moderates', including Campbell-Bannerman, the Liberal leader in the Commons, occupying various positions in between, though later moving nearer to the Radicals in their criticism of the 'methods of barbarism' with which the war came to be waged. In 1903 all wings of the party, including the Liberal Imperialists, rallied to the defence of free trade. So far from rushing to join Chamberlain's crusade for imperial unity, the leading Liberal Imperialists went 'bald-headed for J. C. and his swindle of a zollverein'.[17]

The point is often made that the Liberal revival of 1903—5 was the result less of advances in Liberal thinking and activity than the collapse of the Unionist alliance, and that the 'landslide' Liberal victory in the general election of January 1906 was due far more to Unionist difficulties than to any positive new appeal made by the Liberal party.[18]

It is true that many of the social reforms that the last Liberal governments were to carry were barely fore-shadowed in the campaigning for the 1906 general election, but it is none the less a mistake to underestimate the advances in Liberal thinking by 1906, and it is certainly a mistake to suggest that the Liberals 'showed no interest in social reform legislation' during the election campaign.[19] As Russell has demonstrated, Liberal pledges to social reform 'amounted to a recognisable and extensive commitment'. Slightly more than two-thirds of the Liberal candidates incorporated in their election addresses proposals for social reform that went beyond the traditional Nonconformist issues, such as licensing. These proposals commonly included poor law reform and old age pensions, state-sponsored development schemes to combat unemployment, land reform and the taxation of land values, and the reform of trade union law so as to protect trade union funds against damages for strike action, an issue made pressing by the Taff Vale decision of the Lords in 1901.[20]

The Liberals cannot be said to have presented to the electorate a definite programme of social reform. Certainly, the ministers in the new Liberal Government formed by Campbell-Bannerman in December 1905 were exceptionally cautious on the score of social reform, stressing that what the new Government might or might not accomplish rested very heavily on finance. Asquith, the new Chancellor of the Exchequer, insisted in private and in public that it was essential to restore sound finance before reform could proceed. His Liberal Imperialist associate, Haldane, bluntly told his constituents on 10 January that the Liberal Government 'could not make great promises because they had . . . [first] to pay off a load of debt'.[21] The promise that Campbell-Bannerman and other leading Liberals did make was that the new Government would seek to cut down on wasteful military expenditure, and in so doing release funds for domestic reform. In short, the Liberals held out the prospect of a combination of retrenchment and reform; they managed to combine a commitment to fiscal orthodoxy with pledges to promote constructive social reform. They also made it clear that, against Unionist attempts to 'broaden the basis' of indirect taxation, they favoured new forms of direct taxation as a means of placing public finance on a sound basis, and ensuring an equitable distribution of the burden of taxation.

There is no question that between the Khaki Election of October 1900 and the general election of January 1906, thinking among Liberals on social issues had advanced enormously. It did so in response primarily to the experience of the Anglo-Boer War and to the challenge of Joseph Chamberlain's campaign for tariff reform. The experience of the war encouraged a sharper concern for social problems within the Liberal ranks, most notably among the Liberal Imperialists, who were alarmed at the distressing physical condition of working-class recruits to the army, and Chamberlain's challenge to free trade did even more to force Liberals to focus on the whole 'condition of the people' question; they were literally driven by Chamberlain's 'squalid argument' to contemplate constructive alternatives to tariff reform. Even so traditional a Gladstonian as Campbell-Bannerman was made to realize that a mere defence of free trade was insufficient to meet Chamberlain's challenge, and that it was necessary for Liberals to evolve new and constructive policies of social reform.

The outcome was that the ideas of a New Liberalism, which provided Liberals with an ideology of social reform and which had been pioneered since the early 1890s by a new generation of Liberal theorists, headed by J. A. Hobson and L. T. Hobhouse, began to penetrate the thinking of the Liberal leaders and, even more dramatically, to capture the imagination of a younger generation of Liberal politicians.[22] Integral to this New Liberalism was a theory of taxation which justified the taxation of one class for the immediate benefit of another, on the grounds that the ultimate beneficiary would be the community as a whole. Social reform was to be financed, in part, by taxing the superfluities of the wealthy.

By 1906 three sets of considerations were leading Liberals in the direction of furthering progressive direct taxation. The first was the considerable growth in government expenditure, local as well as imperial, which seemed to demand the reform of the system of taxation so as to make it both more efficient and more equitable. The second was Chamberlain's campaign for tariff reform, and the imperialist and social democratic guise it sought to provide for the restoration of long unfashionable indirect taxes. The third was the development of Liberal social and economic theory, and the growing Liberal commitment to social reforms that would have the effect of redistributing income.

As against the Unionist movement towards extending indirect taxation by way of tariffs on imported manufactured goods and commodities of general consumption, the Liberals clung to traditional nineteenth-century notions which sought to limit tariffs and the extent of indirect taxation. For Liberals, tariffs would hinder the free flow of trade, artificially divert resources from their most productive use, increase the cost of living, and throw an even greater part of the burden of taxation on the lower income groups. From the Liberal standpoint, direct taxes were less likely to disrupt trade, enterprise, and production, were more certain and efficient in raising revenue, and offered more possibilities for ensuring an equitable distribution of the burden of taxation.[23]

A feature of the proposals that advanced Liberals developed for new forms of direct taxation, notably the graduation of the income tax and differentiation between earned and unearned incomes, the increase and graduation of the death duties, and the taxation of land values, was that they were fundamentally as radical as those advocated by contemporary Socialist groups. The Fabian programme for restructuring the British system of taxation, as put forward by Sidney Webb in the *Star* in 1888 and by J. F. Oakeshott in Fabian Tract No. 39 of 1892, entitled 'A Democratic Budget', was in its main outline entirely acceptable to advanced Liberals. What the Fabians recommended was the abolition of all food taxes, and a corresponding extension of direct taxation through graduation and increases in the death duties and income tax, and the taxation of land values.[24]

The basic similarity between the fiscal proposals of the Fabians and the New Liberalism did not necessarily mean that the latter was 'permeated' by the former. On the contrary, as Michael Freeden has indicated, the fiscal ideas of the New Liberalism constituted a natural development from traditional Liberal tenets on taxation, including equality of sacrifice and the distinction between earned and unearned income.[25] What the concurrent advocacy of these ideas by Socialist groups meant was that Liberal policies on taxation, once they embodied the suggestions of the New Liberalism, would come to enjoy wide support on the left.

By the early twentieth century Liberals had already progressed a long way in reinterpreting John Stuart Mill's maxim of equality of sacrifice in taxation to justify progressive as against proportional taxation. Advanced Liberals no longer equated fairness in taxation with arithmetical equality, after allowances had been made for subsistence, but had gone on to interpret equality of sacrifice as meaning that citizens should be taxed in relation to their ability to pay. If burdens were to be put on a more equal footing, a larger percentage would have to be taken in taxes from higher incomes than from lower, and earned incomes, which were precarious, would need to be taxed more lightly than unearned incomes, which were considered permanent.[26] As presented in academic terms by F. Y. Edgeworth, in a series of articles in the *Economic Journal* in 1897, the declining marginal utility of income increments justified differential taxation.[27]

Liberal theory did not stop at seeking to render more equitable the burden of taxes required for the needs of the state. What the New Liberalism promised was that public finance would become a major instrument for redressing social inequalities; it looked to taxation and government programmes of social reform as the means by which income might be redistributed between classes. Taxation for such purposes was justified by advanced Liberals not only on grounds of social justice but also on the grounds that it would ultimately benefit the entire community. Hobson's under-consumptionist thesis attributed the cyclical crises in the economy to the maldistribution of income; the way out of these crises, the way to revive production and employment, was to promote consumption by the labouring classes by means of the redistribution of income.[28] More generally, advanced Liberals reasoned that schemes of social improvement would raise the health and efficiency of large sections of society, thereby benefiting the society as a whole. In short, public expenditure on social reform was ultimately to the benefit of the entire community, and as such should be financed by all sections of the community, including the rich and the well-to-do, in accordance with their ability to pay. In crude terms, the rich migh be taxed to help finance social reforms for the immediate benefit of the poorer sections of the community, but the end product was the greater benefit of the entire community in accordance with ability to pay. As put by Herbert Samuel in *Liberalism,* published in 1902: '. . . all expenditure which succeeds in improving the part benefits, not that part alone, but the whole of the community, and this is why all sections may justly be called upon to share the cost of measures which in their direct and immediate application touch only the well-being of the poorer'.[29]

In 1894, in his celebrated Death Duties Budget, the Liberal Chancellor of the Exchequer, Sir William Harcourt, had taken the first effective step in introducing progressive graduation into British taxation when he provided for the simplification, consolidation, and also graduation of the death duties. He had also contemplated inaugurating a graduated 'income surcharge' on incomes over £5,000, but had desisted in the face of vehement opposition from Sir Alfred Milner, chairman of the Board of Inland Revenue. What Harcourt did achieve by way of income tax reform was to relieve 'a large and most deserving class' among income tax payers by raising the limit of total exemption to incomes up to £160, as against the previous limit of £150, and by extending the range of abatements.[30]

In essentials, Harcourt's Budget of 1894/5 anticipated the main thrust of Liberal taxation policy in the Edwardian era. It expanded the area and over-all proportion of direct taxation by way of progressive graduation, and equally as important it provided relief for income tax payers at the bottom end of the scale. Liberal fiscal strategy in the Edwardian era was never directed simply at increasing the proportion of direct taxation and at raising the levels of taxation on large incomes and accumulations of wealth; one of its primary purposes was also positively to ease the burden of direct taxation on the small business, professional, and salaried middle classes.

In looking to finance new schemes of social reform, Liberal politicians in the Edwardian period showed themselves anxious to avoid alienating the mass of the middle classes by obliging the ordinary middle-class taxpayer and voter to foot the bill for social reform. In so far as the Liberal party was prepared to promote a redistribution of income, this was not to be at the expense of the small business, professional and lower middle classes; on the contrary, these classes were to be protected and reassured.

As Liberals generally came to appreciate, particularly from 1903 onwards, the manner in which they handled the financing of social reform would prove crucial both to the future of their party and the survival of free trade. Major increases in direct taxation affecting the entire income tax paying class would conceivably destroy middle-class support for the Liberal party and free trade.

In contemporary estimates of the incidence of taxation, it was commonly accepted that the overwhelming proportion of direct taxation was paid by members of the income tax paying class. In 1905, when the Liberals came to office, the number of income tax payers was generally reckoned around 1 million, and by the census of 1911 it was generally estimated to have grown to around 1,100,000. The number of voters on the register for the general election of January 1906 was 7,200,000, including about 600,000 plural voters, and for the general elections of 1910 it was 7,700,000.[31]

At £160 per annum, the income level at which income tax was paid in Edwardian Britain was high, and it exempted the majority of the middle classes. In the memorandum Bernard Mallet prepared at the Inland Revenue in 1902 on the 'Incidence of Public Burdens', he calculated the income tax paying families at 900,000, the 'intermediate' class at 1,528,000 families, and the manual labour class at 6,500,000 families.[32] The income tax paying class comprised land-owners, employers in industry, commerce, and finance, higher professionals, and the top brackets of the white collar, lower professional, independent worker, and farmer occupational groups, as well apparently as a smattering of wage-earners.[33] The large majority in the lower-middle-class groups did not pay income tax. On the basis of the 1911 census and Inland Revenue report for 1911, Professor A. L. Bowley estimated the number of salaried males in the United Kingdom at 1,120,000, of whom 385,000 paid income tax, and the number of farmers at 580,000, of whom only 30,000 paid income tax.[34]

Politically, it was the concern of Liberals to protect the bulk of the middle classes, income tax paying and non-income tax paying alike, against substantial new taxation. Retrenchment in certain areas, and the diversion of funds from armaments to social reform, was one expedient whereby this might be achieved: progressive graduated taxation, so as to direct new taxes specifically at large incomes, and the selective taxation of 'unearned' income, were others.

In seeking to isolate potentially safe and profitable targets for new forms of direct taxation, Liberals focused on what they deemed 'unearned' and 'surplus' income. By 'unearned' income, they normally understood rents and dividends, and the purpose behind isolating them as unearned was to subject them to differential taxation. The concept of 'surplus' income, as developed particularly by J. A. Hobson at the turn of the century, altered and extended the meaning of 'unearned', and in so doing provided a powerful theoretical case for the progressive graduated taxation of income.

For Hobson, income was divisible into two components, necessary and unnecessary or 'surplus'. The first, whether in the form of interest, rent, profits, salaries, or wages, represented those payments which were essential to secure the economic use of the factors of production; these were 'subsistence payments for the use of labour and capital'. The second comprised 'forced gains' or 'unearned income'; these were payments not earned by any effort of production, but instead constituted 'a gratuitous surplus' obtained by exploitation of a strong bargaining position, created by scarcity, monopoly, and other restraints on free competition. This unearned surplus was secured largely, although not entirely, by the owners of capital, land, and business capacity, and it constituted 'a fund upon which taxation must naturally settle'. As argued by Hobson, a graduated income tax represented the most effective means of ensuring that taxation would settle on the unearned surplus, assuming that the proportion of unearned income varied directly with the absolute size of incomes, and such taxation would not injure trade and production for the very reason that it fell on the unproductive portions of income.[35]

The implication of Hobson's theory of surplus value, later made explicit by him, was that income unearned by the individual was ultimately created by society, and that in taxing such income the state was simply recovering what belonged to society. This was already the position held by many Liberals in regard to income derived from the ownership of land, and in the Edwardian period landed income remained for Liberals the primary instance of unearned income.

In the Liberal search for new sources of revenue, land, and notably urban land, exercised a magnetic attraction, though the Liberal interest in land value taxation ran very much deeper than a simple concern for new revenue. For many Liberals the taxation of land values constituted not merely a fiscal expedient, but a major social and economic reform on its own account.

The agitation for the taxation of land values, which reached its peak between the Anglo-Boer War and World War I, derived from the 1880s. The specific case for taxing future unearned increment in land values went back even further, to J. S. Mill's *Principles of Political Economy*, first published in 1848, but it was in the 1880s that the relation of land to taxation became for the Radical section of the Liberal party a question of major concern.

Several factors operated in the 1880s to create a strong movement for the taxation of land values. One was the influence of the American land reformer, Henry George, and his proposals to shift all taxation on to the value of land. In the 1880s George exerted a massive influence on left-wing thought and politics in Britain, which he toured on five occasions to popularize his single tax proposals, first in association with Socialist groups and later, after clashing with the Socialists, in association with the Radical section of the Liberal party.[36] Two organizations, the English and Scottish Land Restoration Leagues, provided for the propagation of George's ideas on a regular basis.

For the single taxers, land values represented a gift from the community to the landowners in that land values were the creation of society. Land values were in no sense earned by the landowners, but were rather appropriated by them to the impoverishment of society. Consequently, by taxing land values the community would be reclaiming for its own uses what it had created, and the single tax, by eliminating all other taxes, would entirely free the resources of the society for productive use.

Few Liberals ever became outright single taxers, but the idea of taxing land values possessed an enormous attraction for Radicals in the Liberal party in the 1880s and afterwards. An important factor in promoting Radical interest in land value taxation was their reading of the future of British politics; another was their concern to tackle the problems of overcrowding and inadequate housing in urban Britain.

In the 1880s Radicals were defined virtually by their conviction that the politics of the future would be 'social politics' and their concern to ensure that this would not lead to the polarization of politics along class lines within the industrial community, between employers and workers. The landed interest had traditionally served as a target for middle-class

Radical antagonism, partly as a political device for uniting the middle and working classes by providing them with a common enemy. By mounting a campaign for the taxation of land values Radicals believed they might again rally 'the people' against the landed class. Radicals, impressed by the reaction of the working classes to Henry George, reckoned that on the land issue generally, and land value taxation particularly, they had a 'social' issue which would cut across class lines in its appeal to urban voters. All urban social groups, from entrepreneurs to slum-dwellers, who believed themselves the victims of exorbitant rents, could identify the urban landlord as an enemy of their own welfare.[37]

Radicals also genuinely believed that the question of land held the key to solving the urban problems of congestion, slum conditions, inadequate housing, unemployment, and low wages. By means of 'back to the land' policies they sought to relieve some of the overcrowding and competition for employment in the urban areas, and by the local taxation of land values they hoped to promote urban redevelopment and to provide more effectively for working-class housing. It was through the interest of municipal reform groups in securing the rating of land values that Radicals in the Liberal party established their first organizational links with the single taxers.[38]

The view held by the London Municipal Reform League, founded in 1881 and which included Radicals like Sir Charles Dilke and Sydney Buxton, was that one of the major obstacles to the healthy development of towns and cities, and to the provision of adequate housing for the working classes, was the existing rating system, which both restricted the land available for development and penalized improvements. Rates were assessed on the annual present use value of land and buildings taken together; unoccupied, non-income-bearing land, irrespective of its market value, paid no rates, and land used for agricultural purposes, irrespective of whether it could be developed for urban building purposes, paid rates assessed on its agricultural rent. Land used at its best paid the highest rates. Such a system, the London Radicals claimed, had two detrimental results. The one was to encourage landowners to keep land needed for building either unoccupied or used for agricultural purposes only until they could extort the highest possible rent or price for their land, with the upshot that landowners were inclined to throttle and blackmail the towns and cities. The other result was positively to discourage improvements. The remedy, as suggested by the London Municipal Reform League, was to charge rates on the capital value of land and to exempt improvements. In 1885 the Royal Commission on the Housing of the Working Classes accepted part of this thesis, and went so far as to recommend that undeveloped building land be rated at 4 per cent of its selling value so that 'the owners of building land would be forced to offer their land for sale'.[39] In 1887 the London Radicals and Georgeite single taxers linked forces to form the Joint Committee for the Taxation of Ground Rents and Values, with Lord Monkswell as president.

Another major factor that came into play in helping to create a strong movement for the taxation of land values was the reorganization of local government in 1888/9, notably the formation of the London County Council, and the steep rise in rates to finance local government. The escalation in local government expenditure and rates prompted, particularly at first in London, a growing interest in the separate rating of site values as a device for raising new revenues or for equalizing the burden of rates as between landowners and occupiers, the latter of whom were levied for rates in England and Wales. In the face of ever higher rates the sense developed among occupiers and leaseholders in London, which operated generally on a 99-year system of leasehold tenure, that landowners were paying little or nothing towards the rates. The simultaneous falling in by the 1890s of a large number of leases, both for business premises and houses, in London, and the sometimes massive increases in the ground rents under the new leases, intensified feelings of bitterness against landowners and the sense that the owners of sites which increased so enormously in value should be made to contribute directly to the rates through the separate rating of site values.[40]

Until the mid 1890s the Progressive party, which dominated the new London County Council, led the municipal campaign for the rating of site values. Thereafter Glasgow and the freehold towns of the North of England came to play an increasingly prominent role in that campaign, primarily it seems with a view to freeing improvements from the burden of rates.[41]

In the 1890s the campaign for the rating of urban site values was part of a much broader demand for the relief of existing rates, and for the equalization of rates, not only between occupiers and owners, but between poorer and richer districts. In 1896 the Unionist Government of Lord Salisbury secured the passage of the Agricultural Land Rating Act to de-rate agricultural land by half, supposedly with a view to relieving farmers suffering from the impact of agricultural depression. Lloyd George and other Radicals denounced it as a measure designed to benefit not the farmer but the landowner. In the same year a Royal Commission on Local Taxation was set up, and its final reports in 1901 provided the next major landmark in the campaign for site value taxation.

The simplest method of relieving rates, and of equalizing the burden of local taxation between poor and rich districts, was to increase imperial subventions for the provision by local authorities of 'national' services, notably education and poor relief, and to revise the antiquated system by which these subventions were distributed. This, with variations, was the line of action recommended in the Final Report of the Royal Commission on Local Taxation. In the main, the commission saw only the difficulties in any radical overhaul of the system of local taxation. However, in a Separate Report on Urban Rating and Site Values five of the commissioners, including Lord Balfour of Burleigh, the chairman, and Sir Edward Hamilton and Sir George Murray from the Treasury and Inland Revenue, recommended the introduction of a moderate rate on site values in urban areas to help meet local expenditure on urban improvements which increased the value of urban land. Such a rate, they contended, by enabling some of the burden of local taxation to be removed from improvements made on the site, would do 'something towards solving the difficult and urgent housing problem'. The Separate Report also made the point that such a rate would 'show that there is no large undeveloped source of taxation available for local purposes, and still less for national purposes'.[42]

Despite its lukewarmness, the separate Report marked the beginnings of a new stage in the forward development of the campaign for land value taxation. In 1902 C. P. Trevelyan, the Liberal MP for Elland, introduced in the Commons an Urban Site Value Rating Bill to carry out the recommendations of the minority report, and this was followed in the next year by a Separate Assessment and Rating of Land Values Bill introduced by Dr T. J. Macnamara, the Liberal member for Camberwell North. Even before Joseph Chamberlain launched his crusade for tariff reform, the land taxers had begun to mount a regular campaign in the Commons for land value taxation.

Chamberlain's drive for tariff reform none the less gave an entirely new impetus to the campaign for land value taxation. Sensing their opportunity, the land taxers urged that the Liberal leadership should respond to Chamberlain by making land value taxation the party's constructive alternative to tariff reform.

For the committed land taxers, land value taxation was a major social and economic reform, and not merely a fiscal expedient, and as such constituted Liberalism's effective answer to the 'quack' solution to Britain's problems offered by Chamberlain. In the contention of the land taxers, by placing a sufficiently high tax or rate on the capital value of all land, regardless of its present use or non-use, and by de-rating buildings and other improvements, more land would be diverted on to the market, prices would fall, building would boom, the housing shortage would be resolved, industry would be liberated, and unemployment would recede. 'The chief object of the proposed taxation', C. P. Trevelyan explained to Campbell-Bannerman in a letter of October 1903, 'is to relieve buildings from their present enormous burden, whether they are used for industry or habitation. The help afforded would not be to one particular kind of manufactures, but to all industries.' Trevelyan warned that 'The Liberal position will be rather pathetic if Mr. Chamberlain came forward with a great scheme for the relief of rates as a compensation for his food-taxation, instead of the Liberals introducing it as a substitute for his proposals.'[43]

Campbell-Bannerman himself was, and remained, sceptical of the claims made by the ardent land taxers, as he was also about the practicability of graduating the income tax, while others in the Liberal party stood opposed to the very principle of land value taxation. These included landowners and old Whigs who resented land being singled out for special taxation, agriculturalists who feared that agricultural land might fall within the scope of the new taxation, and some businessmen who saw investment in land as simply one form of capital investment, and suspected that a successful campaign against the property and 'unearned' increment of the landowner would ultimately lead to a wider campaign against all property and profit.[44]

None the less, by 1905 it was evident that no future Liberal government would easily be able to ignore the question of land value taxation. The land taxers comprised by then a formidable pressure group within the party, and they enjoyed a   considerable   general   support   among   party   colleagues who, while never regarding land value taxation as a panacea, saw it as a necessary fiscal expedient if free trade finance was to repel the challenge of tariff reform. Asquith was one of these. Instead of resorting to tariffs, he told a meeting at Stockport in January 1904, the country should recognize that it was weighted down by a large amount of unproductive and unnecessary expenditure, and that 'there was lying untaxed a large reservoir from which he believed a substantial contribution might be made to fertilize the country at large, and that was the taxation of land'.[45]

V

When the Liberals took office under Campbell-Bannerman at the end of 1905 the lines between them and the Unionists on questions of public finance were becoming firmer. The Liberals were committed to retrenchment on armaments expenditure, and had virtually accepted as policy that they would reduce the proportion of indirect to direct taxation, secure the differentiation and graduation of the income tax, and include land value taxation in any major overhaul of the system of local finance. On the Unionist side, the party generally favoured a 'broad base for taxation', whereby a range of taxes would rest lightly at different points, and stood opposed to a supertax or any other form of graduated income tax on the grounds that it would drive capital abroad, weaken the reserve function of the income tax, and allow and encourage the taxation of one class for the benefit of another.

Following the Liberal 'landslide' victory in the general election of January 1906, one of the first actions undertaken by Asquith, as Chancellor of the Exchequer, was to set up a Select Committee on Income Tax, chaired by Sir Charles Dilke, to inquire into the practicability of graduating the income tax and differentiating between 'permanent' and 'precarious' incomes. By the end of 1906 the committee had reported that while a complete system of graduation was administratively inexpedient, it was a practicable proposition to charge a supertax on larger incomes, and differentiation was likewise practicable. In his Budget for 1907/8, Asquith duly introduced differentiation in the income tax on earned and unearned incomes by reducing the tax on earned incomes under £2,000 from 1*s.* to 9*d.* in the £.

During his tenure as Chancellor of the Exchequer, until Campbell-Bannerman's resignation as Prime Minister in April 1908, Asquith was able to carry out a number of other reforms. Retrenchment on armament expenditure proved feasible, allowing Asquith to secure a significant reduction in the National Debt and to cut back on the levels of indirect taxation. Furthermore, in a highly significant move, he brought to an end the system of assigned revenues, whereby the proceeds of certain taxes had been paid directly into the local taxation accounts. As provided in the Finance Act of 1907/8 the proceeds from these taxes would in future be paid into the Exchequer, and the Consolidated Fund would be charged with payment to the local taxation accounts of a sum equivalent to the proceeds of those taxes at the rates then in force. In future, in other words, it would be possible to increase the rates of certain taxes, notably the licence duties, for the benefit of the Exchequer rather than of local government authorities. In the only increase in taxation for which Asquith was responsible, he increased the rates of the estate duty for estates over £150,000.

In carrying through his fiscal policies and changes, one of Asquith's main purposes, as he intimated to the Commons, was to prepare the way for free trade finance to provide for large measures of social reform. In introducing his Budget for 1907/8, Asquith told the Commons that what had killed tariff reform in the 1906 general election had been the food taxes, and he then added:

But, Sir, I can conceive the protectionist invitation being couched in much more insidious and much more alluring accents. I think, therefore, that it is wise for us who are ... not only the party of social reform, but the party also of free trade, to make it clear if we can — and I believe we can make it clear — that the attainment of the one is not incompatible with the maintenance of the other.[46]

The one area in which Asquith failed to take an initiative was land value taxation. According to the diary entry of Sir Edward Hamilton, Joint Permanent Secretary to the Treasury, Asquith did discuss the possibility of taxing land values in February and March 1906, but during his tenure as Chancellor of the Exchequer he made no positive move to provide for land value taxation in any of his Budgets.[47] The question was not, however, allowed to rest, and the initiative was taken up in the Commons by the land taxers themselves.

In the new House of Commons the land taxers formed the largest organized pressure group on the Government. When J. H. Whitley, the Liberal MP for Halifax, organized a Land Values Group to 'initiate and promote land value legislation in Parliament' it acquired 280 Liberal and Labour MPs as members before Easter 1906. It was the nearest thing to a comprehensive Radical caucus that existed in the new Parliament.

The Radical wing of the Liberal party was not in the nature of a highly organized, tightly knit, cohesive faction within the party. Rather those who were considered 'Radicals' encompassed a wide range of persons, opinions, and attitudes on a variety of issues, and they did not consistently act together to realize a clearly formulated programme. They included 'old-fashioned Radicals' who were radical primarily on the issues of temperance reform and the attainment of religious and political equality; 'Social Radicals' who deemed the 'social question' to be the primary concern of Radicalism, and who pressed for radical measures dealing with income distribution, unemployment, housing, and land; and 'pro-Boer Little Englanders' who were primarily opposed to foreign entanglements and bloated armament expenditures. Even Radicals who were 'extreme' on the land question were ideologically divided between land nationalizers, such as Chiozza Money, and fervent single taxers, such as Josiah Wedgwood. For all the diversity there was none the less a Radical consensus on certain fundamentals, notably the primacy of domestic reform, the central importance of the land question to domestic reform, retrenchment on armament expenditures, and, as events developed, the curbing of the powers of the House of Lords.[48] Radicals, in so far as their strength lay in the back-benches, were also distinguished by their attitude that government was not a matter of leadership from above but of responsiveness to the convictions of the rank and file of the governing party. The Liberal Governments of Campbell-Bannerman and Asquith were to find that in determining policy they could never ignore Radical back-bench pressures upon them. From the first, the most persistent pressure was that which came from the Land Values Group.

The Land Values Group comprised not only committed land taxers, but also land nationalizers, many of them Labour MPs, who required a land valuation for the purposes of nationalization and who advocated a site value rate to help finance compulsory purchase. The hard core of the Group were the MPs belonging to the English and Scottish Leagues for the Taxation of Land Values, as the Land Restoration Leagues had been rechristened; according to *Land Values,* the monthly journal of the movement for land value taxation, the English League had forty-five of its members returned to the Commons in January 1906. No list was given of the MPs who belonged to the Scottish League, but of the forty-eight Liberal MPs returned for Scotland, some thirty-five were pledged to land value taxation.[49]

In the first year of the new Parliament a steady pressure

was kept on the Government to take up land value taxation. On 26 February a large deputation presented to the Government a petition on behalf of 518 municipal and rating authorities for land value taxation so as to provide local governments with an 'additional reservoir' to meet their growing responsibilities and expenses; in the Commons J. E. Sutherland introduced a Land Values Taxation (Scotland) Bill, which was referred on the Government's advice to a select committee after receiving a second reading; and in July C. P. Trevelyan presented to Campbell-Bannerman a memorial signed by 300 MPs for legislation next session on land value taxation. At the end of the year a full deputation from the Land Values Group waited on the Prime Minister and John Burns, the President of the Local Government Board, to press the case for legislation in the new year.[50]

For the 1907 session the Government produced a Land Values (Scotland) Bill designed to ascertain land values in Scotland; it provided for the insertion on the valuation roll of each county and burgh in Scotland of an additional column for 'Capital Land Value'. In August the bill was rejected by the Lords. Nothing at all was forthcoming in 1907 from the Government to secure land value legislation for England and Wales, though the King's Speech for 1908 did hold out the prospect of a valuation measure. After a meeting of back-benchers, Trevelyan wrote to Campbell-Bannerman on 4 February that he had been asked to urge the Prime Minister 'to have the Valuation Bill which is promised in the King's Speech introduced at the earliest possible moment'.[51]

In 1908 questions of public finance and taxation became urgent. Local elections in 1907 had provided evidence, notably in London, of a mass ratepayers revolt against the continual increases in rates, thereby underlining the need for the Government to tackle the question of local government finance.[52] In the field of imperial finance the stable situation of the previous two years was suddenly transformed by three developments — the recognition that the Government would have to provide for an increased programme of naval construction to meet the growing German naval challenge; the introduction of non-contributory old age pensions, which proved very much more costly than Asquith had estimated;

and the deepening of a trade recession, which had begun late in 1907, which reduced markedly the revenue from existing indirect taxes. The recession, and the fact that substantial new taxation became unavoidable, gave a new urgency to the issue between free trade and tariff reform. The recession helped to make unemployment, which rose to 8.65 per cent among registered trade unionists, and the whole 'condition of the people' question a matter of pressing concern for the Government, and gave a new lease to the Tariff Reformers, with their claim that tariffs would help protect the jobs of British workmen. On the question of new taxation, the lines between the Liberals, in their opposition to any new tariffs or food taxes and their commitment to progressive direct taxation, and the Unionists, who warned of the dangers of 'confiscatory' class taxation, came to look more and more like battle lines.

In April 1908, when Asquith became Prime Minister and Lloyd George Chancellor of the Exchequer, the financial difficulties that were to confront the Government were not yet fully evident. Indeed, Asquith was still sufficiently confident to take what afterwards seemed the rash step of remitting part of the sugar duty in the Budget for 1908/9, introduced in the Commons in May. Thereafter the financial situation worsened dramatically, and at the same time the political pressures on the Government greatly intensified. The Labour party, which by its very existence posed a threat on the left to the Liberals, became increasingly assertive; by-elections went badly for the Liberals; and the Government's relations with the Unionist-dominated House of Lords approached crisis point, especially when the peers rejected the Licensing Bill, the Government's main legislative measure for the year.

When Asquith replaced Campbell-Bannerman as Prime Minister, it already seemed evident to many Liberals that financial policy held the key to the future of the Liberal Government. Through finance the Government might regain the political initiative it otherwise seemed to be losing. By means of financial policy, the *Nation* emphasized, the Government might furnish the revenue for the work of social reform, and it might even by-pass the veto of the House of

Lords on certain issues, such as land valuation.[53] In short, finance, over which the Lords supposedly had no control, appeared the one major instrument of reform the Government might rely on. As it became increasingly evident during the year that the Government would in fact have to raise substantial new revenue in 1909/10, so it became recognized on all sides that the new taxation to be proposed by Lloyd George was likely to prove of vital consequence for the future of the Government, and perhaps even for the long-term future of the Liberal party and of free trade.

III. Asquith's Inheritance

I

When Herbert Henry Asquith succeeded the dying Campbell-Bannerman as Prime Minister on 8 April 1908 it was recognized on all sides that he had taken over the Liberal Government and party at a critical juncture in their fortunes. As the Liberal press and backbenchers saw it, it was a 'time of trial'. The wave of enthusiasm that had swept the Liberal party following the great 'landslide' victory in the general election of January 1906 had distinctly begun to ebb, cracks were beginning to show up in the Liberal coalition, much of the Liberal programme had already been thwarted or blocked by the House of Lords, trade had turned downwards, and by-elections had started to go against the Government. The question was whether Asquith could succeed in warding off the threatened major decline in Liberal fortunes and in giving his party a sense that the great promise of 1906 would yet be fulfilled.

Campbell-Bannerman's Government, while not without its achievements, had simply not succeeded in becoming the power-house of reform that many, including a large proportion of its own supporters in the Commons, had anticipated after the 'landslide' election victory of January 1906. In dealing with the 'condition of the people' question, Campbell-Bannerman had never sought to provide his Government with a strategy of social reform. Too much of an old Gladstonian for that, he was furthermore fearful lest his Government expose itself too openly to Unionist charges of socialism. His ideal was a 'balanced' programme. As he had written to Asquith on 21 January 1906: 'If you have two sops for Labour, we ought to have some other Bill besides Educn. of general interest, to balance them. Otherwise will not the enemy blaspheme, & will not colour be given to the assertion which seems to me to be their main weapon now, that we are in the hands & at the mercy of Labour (which =

51

Socialism).'[1] Apart from a general concern to cater for the major sections in the Liberal coalition, and to ensure that the middle classes were not frightened off, it had not been part of Campbell-Bannerman's style to provide for the systematic direction of his Government; rather he had been content to allow individual ministers and their departments much of the initiative in policy. The over-all result, as *The Times* justly commented on Campbell-Bannerman's resignation, was that 'If we ask what it was that the late Government essentially lacked, the answer must be that it lacked a policy. Under it many policies were pursued, but the Government as a whole had none.'[2]

If Campbell-Bannerman's legacy was not an easy one, and if he had failed to provide his Government with an over-all policy or strategy of reform, it was still true that he had given his Government very much the sort of leadership it had required. What he had appreciated was that his Government stood at the head of a broad coalition of diverse, and sometimes even conflicting, sections and interests, and that his Government always possessed the potential to tear itself apart should old ideological and personal differences be allowed to reassert themselves. He had consequently put a premium on satisfying important sections within the Liberal coalition, particularly those who had powerful grievances arising out of the past decade of Unionist government, and otherwise he sought to offer flexibility rather than positive leadership, and to act as a broker rather than provide inspiration. 'Campbell-Bannerman', Goldwin Smith commented to John X. Merriman in June 1906, 'is the right man to hold a motley Government together. But a very motley Government it is: Home Rulers and anti-Home Rulers; Imperialists and anti-Imperialists; Capitalists and Labour men; Feminists and anti-Feminists; moderate Liberals and extreme Radicals; looking with anything but favour on each other.'[3] What Campbell-Bannerman's methods and manner helped achieve was to make his Cabinet, in the judgement of Morley, 'the most harmonious that ever was'.[4]

The very breadth and diversity of the Liberal coalition stemmed directly from Campbell-Bannerman's strategy in the period of Liberal revival from 1902 to 1905 for reunifying his party and constructing a truly broad-based alliance against the Unionists. Towards these ends he had been greatly assisted not only by Chamberlain's 'reckless criminal escapade', which Campbell-Bannerman saw as 'playing old Harry with all party relations', but also by Balfour's own policies as Prime Minister, particularly in so far as rallying Nonconformist support was concerned.[5] Balfour's Education Act of 1902, which provided among other things for the maintenance of Church schools, overwhelmingly Anglican and Catholic, out of the rates without infringing their particular religious identities, had infuriated Nonconformists. Temperance-minded Nonconformity had likewise been thoroughly annoyed by Balfour's Licensing Act of 1904, because of the provision it made for paying compensation, from a special fund levied on 'the trade', to licensees who were deprived of their licences in the interests of temperance. The effect of this, the temperance reformers charged, and the Liberal party upheld, was to convert an annual holding into a form of property and to erect a barrier to the speedy reduction of licences.

Apart from the effect Unionist policies had in reviving Liberal strength and spirit, Campbell-Bannerman also succeeded in winning the active co-operation of the Labour Representation Committee and the Irish Nationalists in a broad alliance to destroy the Unionist hegemony in the constituencies.

It was the Liberal Chief Whip, Herbert Gladstone, working with Campbell-Bannerman's blessing, who negotiated and supervised the secret constituency arrangement with the recently formed Labour Representation Committee. The electoral deal between Gladstone and James Ramsay Mac-Donald, the first secretary of the L.R.C., was effectively reached in September 1903, amid rumours of Chamberlain's impending resignation and the possibility of a general election. Negotiations for such a deal predated Chamberlain's attack on free trade, and would probably have reached fruition without it; none the less the defence of free trade and cheap food provided the Liberals and Labour with more of a common platform than they would otherwise have shared.

Essentially the Gladstone—MacDonald pact allowed the L.R.C. an 'open field' in thirty seats in England and Wales, in return for which the L.R.C. would 'demonstrate friendliness' to the Liberals in those constituencies where it had influence. The pact was of obvious advantage to both sides: it eased the strain on Liberal funds, guaranteed the L.R.C. a solid core of representatives in the next House of Commons, and guarded against mutual destruction at the polls. To Gladstone the pact promised 'solidarity of voting' against the Unionists.[6]

Campbell-Bannerman's single greatest personal contribution to building up an extensive anti-Unionist alliance was in working out a compromise formula for Ireland that was accepted alike by the Liberal Imperialists (apart from Rosebery), the Gladstonian Home Rulers, and the Irish Nationalists, thereby bringing the Irish Nationalists into the anti-Unionist alliance without at the same time wrecking the fragile unity of the Liberal party. On 14 November 1905 Campbell-Bannerman breakfasted with John Redmond and T. P. O'Connor, the Irish Nationalist leaders, and informed them that while it was impossible for him to pledge his party to full Home Rule in the next Parliament, he intended to pass 'some serious measure which would be consistent with and lead up to the other'. He also promised to ensure as much moderation on education as was possible. The Nationalist leaders accepted his explanations and under-takings, and Redmond gave his promise that the Irish Nationalists would seek to ensure that their numerous 'friends' in England would vote for the Liberals in the coming elections and that they themselves would support the Liberals in the next parliament.[7] This compromise formula over Home Rule, announced by Campbell-Bannerman in a speech at Stirling on 23 November, was accepted by all Liberals, except Rosebery, who completed his isolation from the party he had once led by proclaiming two days later that he could never serve under Campbell-Bannerman's Home Rule banner.

In early December 1905, when Balfour resigned and the King asked Campbell-Bannerman to form a new government, what had threatened to upset the new-won unity of the Liberal party, and with it the whole anti-Unionist alliance so carefully constructed by Campbell-Bannerman and Gladstone, was the 'backstairs' attempt by the Liberal Imperialists to implement schemes for excluding Campbell-Bannerman from effective leadership. In the so-called 'Relugas Compact' of September 1905 Asquith, Sir Edward Grey, and Haldane had agreed not to serve in a government headed by Campbell-Bannerman unless he went to the Lords, leaving Asquith as leader in the Commons. It was an arrangement that the Radicals in the Liberal party would not willingly have accepted, and by successfully standing firm in December against the suggestions and demands that he go to the Lords Campbell-Bannerman preserved not only his own leadership but also his party's unity. In the event, Asquith, Grey, and Haldane all accepted office in the new Government even though Campbell-Bannerman refused to budge from the Commons, and the Cabinet consequently conprehended all groups and sections of the Liberal party. 'For the sake of Free Trade', Haldane had finally reckoned, according to his own account, 'it was ... highly expedient that the Government should be as strongly as possible permeated with the spirit of Liberal Imperialism.'[8]

The Liberal 'landslide' in the general election of 1906 had followed. The swing against the Unionists in votes was an unprecedented 10.6 per cent, but the real landslide was in seats, with the Unionist representation being cut by over half. The Liberals returned 401 members, the L.R.C. 29, the Irish Nationalists 83, and the Unionists 157, giving the new Government a massive working majority in the Commons on most issues and a secure absolute majority over all possible combinations on the Opposition benches.

The problem by 1908 was that, while Campbell-Bannerman's leadership might have kept the Cabinet together as a harmonious unit, no coherent programme of social reform had as yet been devised by the Government, and alarmingly little had been achieved to satisfy the hard core of the Liberal party's traditional middle-class support. In this latter respect it was not so much Campbell-Bannerman's style of leadership that was to blame, as it was the obstructionism of the House of Lords.

The House of Lords, with its massive Unionist majority, was never the blind and indiscriminate opponent of all reform that some of its Liberal critics pretended or wished it was. On the contrary, for the duration of Campbell-Bannerman's premiership it was careful not to obstruct Government proposals that catered specifically for working-class needs and interests, as instanced by the passage of the Trades Disputes Bill of 1906. None the less, the Lords was an undisguisedly partisan body, and Balfour together with Lord Lansdowne, the Unionist leader in the Upper House, had no hesitation in employing it for partisan purposes. It was during the last period of Liberal government, from 1892 to 1895, that the Lords had first been effectively and consistently used as a major instrument of party warfare, when the Unionist peers had destroyed Gladstone's second Home Rule Bill and wreaked havoc with much of the remainder of the Liberal programme, and it was to the Lords that Balfour and Lansdowne again turned in 1906 in their effort to combat and undermine the Liberal Government and its huge majority in the Commons.

What convinced the Unionist leaders that it would again be safe and profitable partially to frustrate the Liberal Government through the Lords was their fundamental assumption that the Liberal party remained a fragile and vulnerable coalition of divergent groups and sections, and that it was in no sense genuinely representative of 'the nation'. Indeed, Balfour reckoned that the 'moderate' members of the Cabinet would positively welcome some of the checks imposed by the Lords. 'I conjecture', he put it to Lansdowne on 13 April 1906, 'that the Government methods of carrying on their business will be this: they will bring in Bills in a much more extreme form than the moderate members of their Cabinet probably approve: the moderate members will trust to the House of Lords cutting out or modifying the most outrageous provisions. . . '[9] Beyond the more obvious division between 'moderates' and 'extremists' or 'radicals', the Unionist leaders and their followers saw the Liberal party to be, at bottom, little more than a collection of disruptive log-rolling minority groups, with no natural cohesion and no real identity with 'the nation', and ultimately they believed, or trusted, that in any confrontation between the Lords and the Liberal minorities 'the nation' would decide in favour of the Lords. George Wyndham, Chief

Secretary for Ireland in Balfour's Government from 1902 to early 1905, gave clear statement to this belief when he wrote privately on 6 December 1909:

The root of the matter is that no Second Chamber, however composed, would pass the kind of Bill that a modern Liberal Government brings in, i.e. a Bill to please one relatively small minority — e.g. Licensing Bill, which is passed through the H. of C. by other log-rolling minorities expectant of their turn. If the Liberal Party cannot exist without that, then either there can be no Liberal Party, or no Second Chamber; and if the Liberal Party drive the country into that choice, the country will — I think — prefer a Second Chamber to the Liberal Party. That is a matter of opinion. I am not certain and no one can be. But that — for what it is worth — is my view; and the view of some Liberals.[10]

The policy Balfour and Lansdowne had agreed upon in early 1906 was to use the Lords not so much as a bludgeon but as a fine operating scalpel for excising or modifying the 'extreme' provisions in Liberal bills. In practice they employed the Lords rather more ruthlessly than Balfour had initially suggested. In April 1906 Balfour had put it to Lansdowne that tenacious resistance in the Commons would facilitate compromise in the Lords, but in the event it encouraged the opposite effect. Having fought a Liberal proposal all along the line in the Commons, Balfour found himself either unwilling or politically unable to concede ground and arrange a compromise in the Lords. More than that, the very ineffectiveness of the Liberal Government in the face of the Lords encouraged Balfour to become ever bolder in his use of the Upper House.

By 1908 the pattern had established itself that Liberal legislative proposals that catered for 'minorities' could expect hostile reception and treatment in the Lords. The more or less *ad hoc* Liberal measures to provide for the needs of the working classes were not being obstructed, but the Government was making little progress in the more traditional areas of Liberal concern. In 1906 the House of Lords, at Balfour's instigation, had so amended the Government's Education Bill, designed to redress the grievances of the Nonconformists at the Balfour Act of 1902, that Campbell-Bannerman had been obliged to withdraw it, and the peers had also totally rejected the Government's Plural

Voting Bill, intended to eliminate the practice of privileged electors voting in more than one constituency. In 1907, again, the Unionist peers had attacked a series of Liberal land bills: they had amended a Small Holdings and Allotments Bill for England and an Evicted Tenants Bill for Ireland, and rejected outright the Small Landholders (Scotland) Bill as well as the Land Values (Scotland) Bill.

The upshot was that by 1908 the Liberal Government had achieved very little to satisfy the demands of the 'minority' sections and interests allied to it. The Nonconformists had not been satisfied on the education issue; the Government had not yet dared to proceed with temperance reform; and virtually nothing had been achieved for the 'Celtic fringe'. The Government's land bills for Scotland had been rejected by the Lords, and Lloyd George was having to explain to the Welsh National Liberal Council that in the prevailing circumstances it was pointless putting up a bill for Welsh Disestablishment. The Irish Nationalists, who had renewed the 'Liberal alliance' for the 1906 general election, found they had nothing to show for it apart from an Irish Universities Act and an Evicted Tenants Act that had gone through the mangle of the Lords.

Where the Government had been rather more successful was in securing the passage of its labour and social welfare measures; in 1906 and 1907 Balfour and Lansdowne had not allowed the peers to refuse legislation that might have a genuinely popular appeal, no matter how distasteful they themselves might have found it. The principle that Lansdowne asserted when he advised the peers to pass the Trades Disputes Bill was that they should only join issue with the Government 'upon ground which is as favourable as possible to ourselves'.[11] They could safely wreck the Government's Education Bill, for in Unionist eyes it fitted the expected formula of destructive legislation designed to cater for a disruptive minority, but it was wiser not to sabotage legislation that provided for a major working-class interest and that could conceivably give the Liberals their opportunity to whip up a broad popular agitation against the hereditary chamber.

Like a guerilla force, in short, their lordships were summoned by Balfour and Lansdowne to swoop down on the

Liberal army whenever they could do the maximum of damage at the minimum of cost to themselves; when any possibility of a Liberal counter-attack suggested itself, the peers quietly retired to their mountain fastness leaving the Liberals to fulminate helplessly below.

The challenge of the Lords was one that Campbell-Bannerman had taken no effective steps to overcome. The Lords was regularly denounced in ministerial speeches, and in June 1907 Campbell-Bannerman even secured in the Commons the passage of a resolution affirming that the power of 'the other House' to alter or reject bills 'should be so restricted by law as to secure that within the limits of a single Parliament the decision of the Commons must prevail'. But as a warning to the Lords the resolution had no obvious practical effect in 1907: it certainly did not deter the Lords from mangling the Government's land bills. There is no evidence, moreover, that Campbell-Bannerman had developed any strategy for dealing with the Lords in 1908. He and his colleagues appear simply to have clung to the hope that in the year ahead the Lords might be encouraged to play the politics of compromise rather than confrontation on the questions of licensing and education.[12]

Instead of a strategy for tackling the Lords, what Campbell-Bannerman left to Asquith in April 1908 was a legislative log-jam that followed inevitably from the peers' deliberate attempts to disrupt what they saw as Liberal log-rolling and the Liberal failure to retaliate effectively. The King's Speech for 1908 promised a Licensing Bill, held over from the previous year; another Education Bill; land valuation for England and Wales as well as Scotland; and also a national scheme of old-age pensions. 'Now they have all the dragons on their hands at once,' the Liberal journalist, J. A. Spender, commented to James Bryce shortly before Campbell-Bannerman's resignation, 'Church, Land and Liquor.'[13] The year 1908 was clearly going to prove at once difficult and crucial in determining whether the Liberal Government could meet its legislative commitments and satisfy its own supporters.

Liberal difficulties by 1908 ran very much deeper than the obstructionism of the House of Lords. In the country at large the Liberals had to contend with the beginnings of a substantial revival in the tariff reform movement, and also they sensed a new challenge on the left from Labour, and the prospect that Labour might break loose from its alliance with the Liberals.

What served to bring new life to the campaign for tariff reform, and new discontent with the Government, was the economic recession which developed from late 1907 onwards. Popular support began to ebb away from the Government, as was dramatically brought home in early 1908 by Unionist by-election victories at Mid-Devon on 17 January and at Camberwell (Peckham) on 24 March, both of which were claimed as triumphs for tariff reform. In the Mid-Devon contest a Liberal majority of 1,283 was converted into a Unionist majority of 559, and at Camberwell a Liberal majority of 2,339 was turned into a Unionist majority of 2,494. After the Mid-Devon setback, John Burns noted in his diary that it was 'a portent' and that he was 'prepared for worse'.[14] Camberwell suggested that he was right in expecting the situation to worsen.

At the same time that the Unionists and tariff reform were gaining ground, the Liberals sensed a new challenge from Labour on the left. In July 1907 Liberals were startled by the loss of two seats to Labour in by-elections. On 4 July the Labour party candidate, Pete Curran, won a four-cornered contest at Jarrow, and two weeks later Victor Grayson, an independent Socialist who had failed to get official Labour party backing, captured Colne Valley in a three-cornered fight. These Labour advances at Liberal expense caused both resentment and alarm in Liberal circles, though Jesse Herbert, the Liberal Chief Whip's secretary, warned against an openly aggressive response by Liberals. In a letter to Arthur Ponsonby, Campbell-Bannerman's private secretary, on 16 October 1907, he advised that while 'a few violent anti-Liberal Socialists' had managed to seize control of the Labour party machine, he was successfully co-operating with 'the Liberal-Labourmen to capture the machine and drive the extremists into a cave of their own'. The pending link-up between the Miners' Federation and the 'Lib-Labs' with the Labour party, he explained, meant that 'the Liberal party are about to capture the L.R.C.'[15]

What seemed evident to many Liberals by early 1908 was that positive steps needed to be taken to ensure the party's continued hold over working-class voters in the face of Labour assertiveness and, in immediate terms, the more serious challenge being mounted by the Tariff Reformers. At the beginning of 1908 the Radical press detected a new thrust by the 'vigorous' Tariff Reformers, who were alive to the necessity of 'buying' the support of the working classes by measures of social reform, to exploit the opportunities offered by the recession to capture the working classes for tariff reform, and this gave an altogether new urgency to the need for the Liberal Government to devise and implement constructive schemes of social reform. The 'social question', C. F. G. Masterman declared in his article on 'Politics in Transition' in the *Nineteenth Century* for January 1908, had at last 'arrived' in England, and henceforth 'it must dominate the situation'.

These were developments welcomed by advanced Liberals; they gave social reform a new priority. But they also added enormously to the pressure of business crowding in on the Liberal Government, and made it imperative that the Government carry a series of substantial measures in 1908.

In all, when Asquith took over from Campbell-Bannerman in April 1908, Liberal morale was low but far from defeatist. There was a sense that a political mistake might have been committed when the Government failed to dissolve against the Lords following the effective rejection of the Education Bill in 1906, and frustration among Welsh Nonconformists at the lack of any action to secure disestablishment for Wales had produced a 'revolt' during 1907.[16] But in other ways the obstructionism of the Lords had served to promote a greater sense of solidarity among Liberals in the face of a common enemy, so much so that Morley complacently observed at the end of 1906 that the Lords had 'done us a service by giving us something to swear at and swear by'.[17] Those Nonconformist leaders who had not been altogether happy with the provisions of the Government's Education Bill had found their loyalty to the Government rekindled by the opposition of the Lords.[18]

The general sense among Liberals in early 1908 was that

the year ahead would be critical in determining whether the Liberal Government would go down as a failure or whether it would become one of the greatest reforming ministries of all time. As the *Nation* declared in its leader of 4 January 1908, entitled 'A Critical Year': 'The situation is not a gloomy one. It is rather the testing of great capacities: the occasion for which previous energies have provided a training and a preparation.' The enforced change in Prime Ministers in April 1908 added to the sense of challenge.

II

The ministerial team Asquith inherited from Campbell-Bannerman was maintained by him with some reshuffling, but without fundamental reconstruction. He left thirteen of Campbell-Bannerman's Cabinet at their posts, transferred four others, dismissed one, and promoted two junior ministers to Cabinet office. Neither in personnel nor in policy did the formation of Asquith's Government mark a radical break from its predecessor.

In his methods of leadership Asquith sought quite clearly to operate in Campbell-Bannerman's tradition. He was more a mediator than an initiator; he continued to permit individual ministers considerable freedom from direction by the Prime Minister in running their departments and in preparing policy proposals; and perhaps even more than Campbell-Bannerman, he delayed coming to grips with particularly difficult problems, in the hope that time might help resolve them. Certainly, he was not prepared to force the pace in tackling issues and problems if that entailed forcing open Liberal divisions. He was essentially a practitioner of 'consensus' politics.

Aged fifty-five when he became Prime Minister, Asquith was at the height of his powers. Those powers were formidable. He was generally recognized as possessing the most powerful and effective intellect in the House of Commons; his mind was described by Lord Esher as a 'perfect instrument', and to A. G. Gardiner it was 'a faultless mechanism'.[19] In debate and on the public platform he drove home his points with devastating logic and force, and was particularly effective in the tariff controversy.[20] In the Commons, when Campbell-Bannerman sent for 'the Sledgehammer' to demolish the arguments of the other side, he sent for Asquith.[21] In administration, again, Asquith was virtually unrivalled among Liberals as an executant of policy, having proved his workmanship and ability to get things done, first as Home Secretary in the Gladstone and Rosebery Governments between 1892 and 1895, and then as Chancellor of the Exchequer in Campbell-Bannerman's Government, when he had quietly but efficiently proceeded to prepare government finance to meet the costs for a new programme of social reform.

Asquith's accession to the premiership following Campbell-Bannerman's resignation was unquestioned and unchallenged, but this did not mean he was at all a popular successor, and nor did it entirely obscure questions as to whether he was suited for leadership. He was certainly not very popular among Radicals, who had resented his championship of the Anglo-Boer War and who generally found him a remote and unsympathetic person. In 1906, according to Arthur Ponsonby's diary, Asquith went through a period of 'extreme unpopularity' in which his 'want of sympathy, his tendency to ride roughshod over the party & his lack of humanity' were noticeable.[22] By early 1908 Courtenay P. Ilbert, the clerk of the House of Commons, found Asquith to be distinctly 'less unpopular' than he had been. His obvious loyalty to Campbell-Bannerman during the latter's premiership had gradually restored his standing in the party as a whole, though according to Ilbert 'the man below the gangway' would always find it difficult entirely to trust Asquith, given the social career and connections he had developed since his marriage in 1894 to 'a society woman', Margot Tennant, following the death of his first wife.[23]

As a party leader, one of the chief concerns about Asquith, particularly among party zealots on the left, was whether he had the ability to provide the inspiration they believed the party required at a time when the political pendulum was beginning to swing against the Liberals. 'Asquith', according to J. A. Spender in his memoirs, 'was thought to be the last man to check it or give it the reverse impulse.'[24]

Together with an inability either to arouse or respond to enthusiasm, what Asquith most conspicuously lacked was imaginative vision. 'He is the constructive engineer of politics', A. G. Gardiner wrote of him in 1908, 'not the seer of visions. He leaves the pioneering work to others and follows after with his levels and compasses to lay out the new estate.'[25] Lloyd George was rather more harsh in his estimate. In April 1908 he told Morley that the new Prime Minister was 'a man of no initiative, and requires to be briefed'.[26]

The suspicion that Asquith lacked initiative, and not simply vision, and the feeling that he was without any real fervour, underlay the reservations about his capacity to lead the Liberal Government into a new era of reform and to revive the party's fortunes. What gave reformers and party zealots encouragement about Asquith were his growing intellectual commitment to the New Liberalism, his proven ability and tenacity of purpose, and some of the changes he made in the personnel and distribution of offices in the Cabinet, notably the appointments he gave to David Lloyd George and Winston Churchill.

As Cabinet colleagues Lloyd George and Churchill were rapidly to form a close political partnership — at times they became so close that John Burns dubbed them 'the two Dromios' — and from the outset their names were invariably linked in the press comments on Asquith's reconstruction of the Cabinet. Their appointments were seen as reflecting Asquith's concern to preserve the balance of forces and opinion in the Cabinet, which might otherwise have been upset by his replacement of Campbell-Bannerman, and together they were expected to serve as the standard bearers of advanced Radicalism in the Cabinet, and the best guarantees of its reformist direction and political resourcefulness.

The promotion of Lloyd George, who was quite without any previous experience in matters of public finance, to the Exchequer was not quite as inevitable as Asquith's elevation to the premiership. At first Asquith contemplated retaining the Exchequer along with the premiership, at least until the end of the current parliamentary session, or else installing Haldane there, and 'half-offered' the post to him in mid-

March.[27] Asquith finally gave the post to Lloyd George after making a token offer of it to Morley in recognition of his seniority. According to what Morley told Lord Esher, Lloyd George in fact 'put a pistol' to Asquith's head 'and *asked* for the Ch. of the Ex. with a threat of resignation'.[28]

There is no corroborating evidence to indicate that Lloyd George was ever driven to the length of putting 'a pistol' to Asquith's head, though he might well have threatened to do so in conversation with Morley. What Lloyd George certainly did do was to help inspire a campaign in the *Manchester Guardian,* beginning in early March, for the acceptance by 'sound' Liberals of Asquith's leadership 'only with adequate guarantees for the fullest representation in the councils of the party of the sounder and more decided Liberal traditions', and to see to it that it was made clear to Asquith that if he was to secure the confidence of the Radical wing of his party he would need to install Lloyd George at the Exchequer.[29]

Aged forty-five when he moved into No. 11 Downing Street, Lloyd George was generally recognized as the leading Radical in the Government. His Radicalism was rooted in a deep hostility to 'special privilege', and the injustices that followed inevitably from entrenched privilege, as well as in a quick sympathy for human suffering. It was a Radicalism that had as its targets the social and economic privileges of the landowning classes, the political privileges of the peers, and the religious privileges of the Established Church, and it was a Radicalism that was becoming increasingly advanced in its notions of how to cure social evils and promote the welfare of society. On becoming Chancellor of the Exchequer, Lloyd George's ideas on social reform were still very much in the process of formation, but there seemed no question about his commitment to tackling 'the condition of the people' question.

Before taking office as President of the Board of Trade in Campbell-Bannerman's Government at the end of 1905, the basic cast of Lloyd George's political career had been as a critic and rebel, and as a champion of minority interests, especially those of his native Wales and of Nonconformity. First elected to Parliament in 1890 as the member for

Caernarvon Boroughs, Lloyd George had emerged from the back benches in 1896 in opposing the Agricultural Rating Bill of that year, which he denounced as an endowment of the landlords at the expense of the tax-payer, and he had become a politician of truly national stature by virtue of his determined and courageous opposition to the Anglo-Boer War, which had established him among the leaders of the Radical wing of the Liberal party. His role in fighting Balfour's Education Bill of 1902 had further added to his reputation. Though, as John Grigg has shown, he acted more out of a sense of political necessity than of conviction, he virtually took control of the Liberal opposition to the Bill in the Commons, fighting it with considerable skill. At the end of the session even Balfour singled him out to compliment him on establishing a position for himself as 'an eminent Parliamentarian'.[30]

In the tariff controversy, when for the first time Lloyd George was called upon to undertake a sustained defence of an established policy, he maintained his political prominence by some scathing attacks on Joseph Chamberlain and the proposed 'stomach taxes', but his actual defence of free trade was not among his conspicuous achievements. 'His nimble wit', a friendly critic put it in late 1903, 'is less at ease with the fiscal question than with the Education Act.' Nor did Chamberlain's 'squalid argument' lead Lloyd George to develop any new ideas on social reform. He certainly appreciated the need to 'propose something better than Mr. Chamberlain', but could only suggest that the Liberals display 'more boldness' in dealing with the education, temperance, and land questions.[31]

Inspired, it seems from the evidence of his speeches, by the publication of Seebohm Rowntree's *Poverty: A Study of Town Life,* Lloyd George had been giving some thought to the whole question of poverty in Britain before the launching of Chamberlain's campaign, and had reinforced his prejudices by coming to the conclusion that landlords, rural as well as urban were primarily to blame for urban poverty and slum conditions. Rural landlordism and the miserable wages paid to agricultural labourers in vast areas of rural England, Lloyd George explained in a speech at Newcastle in

April 1903, was not simply a rural problem; it was a town problem, for owing to the operation of the rural land system thousands were being driven each year from the countryside to the towns to compete with the workmen there, depress wages, and swell the slums. Urban congestion and slums likewise derived directly from the operation of the 'great land trust' of the town landlords, whose land gained enormously in value from the community's growth and who nevertheless, so Lloyd George charged, contrived to avoid contributing a penny towards municipal development. 'As long', Lloyd George predicted, 'as the landlords are allowed to charge prohibitive prices for a bit of land, even waste land, without contributing anything to local resources, so long will this terrible congestion remain in our towns.'[32]

This speech, which marked the beginning of Lloyd George's systematic attack on the 'land monopoly', contained all the positive proposals he was to urge over the next few years as a counter to Chamberlain's 'squalid argument' for tariff reform. At Newcastle, and in his speeches thereafter, Lloyd George consistently argued that the keys to fighting poverty lay in a fundamental reform of the land system, so as to cultivate a strong independent peasantry and attract people back to the land, coupled with an overhaul of the system of local taxation, designed to release land and funds for urban developments; in the containment of the drink traffic, which he held responsible for 60 per cent of the poverty in the country; and in the creation of a strong system of national education under popular control.

To the dismay of advanced social reformers Lloyd George, during his remaining years in opposition, provided little indication that he was willing to advance beyond the ideas and proposals that he had set forward in his Newcastle speech. The Webbs, indeed, concluded that he was really 'apathetic' on the issue of social reform, and the Labour leader, Keir Hardie, thought him 'a politician with no settled convictions on social questions'.[33] Lloyd George, still very much involved in the education issue and engaged in the fight against Balfour's Licensing Bill, did not in fact give any fresh thought to social reform, and took no part in the agitation over unemployment in 1904/5. When Campbell-Bannerman formed his Government, W. T. Stead classed Lloyd George among the 'educationists' in the new Cabinet but not among the 'social reformers'.[34]

What Lloyd George had grasped from the tariff controversy was that the capacity of government to embark on 'constructive' schemes of social reform was severely restricted by its financial resources, and that any Liberal government would have to give careful thought to finance before it could ever seriously seek to provide for a radical new programme of social reform. In his election campaign of January 1906 Lloyd George, with a cautious eye to his own role in 'exposing' Chamberlain's willingness to trade promises of old-age pensions for votes, deliberately refrained from making a definite pledge of pensions, and stressed rather the need for the new Government to put the national finances in 'spick and span order', by cutting down on wasteful expenditure and by devising a more just and efficient system of taxation, before it could contemplate pensions to save the aged 'from the humiliation of the workhouse or parish relief'. At Croydon on 5 January 1906 he put the whole relationship of reform and finance in a nutshell when he asserted: 'They had to carry great measures of social reform and introduce a just system of taxation, because social reform had to do with taxation.' What he envisaged was the enlargement of the sphere of direct taxation, and this was to include the taxation of ground values and mining royalties.[35]

With his appointment in December 1905 as President of the Board of Trade Lloyd George began an altogether new phase of his career, and won for himself in the public eye a new reputation as an efficient administrator, energetic legislator, and remarkable conciliator. What he also demonstrated was that business had nothing to fear from his brand of Radicalism; his purpose throughout at the Board of Trade was to promote the interests of British industry and commerce, and it was from 'men of business' that Lloyd George reaped the main harvest of his praise.

The extent to which Lloyd George was personally responsible for initiating the major legislative measures of his tenure at the Board of Trade, the Merchant Shipping Bill of 1906, the Patents and Designs Bill of 1907, and the Port of

London Authority Bill of 1908, is not altogether clear. According to William Beveridge, who joined the Board of Trade as a civil servant in 1908, Lloyd George simply took up the 'string of measures' waiting for him when he assumed office.[36] But there was no doubting his tact and negotiating skill in reconciling the conflicting interests of the various parties concerned.

There was also no doubting Lloyd George's refusal to be restricted by any narrow interpretation of free trade. Indeed, both his Merchant Shipping and Patents Bills were hailed by the Chamberlainites as sound protective measures, and some of his colleagues were obviously disturbed by his free-and-easy attitude to the dogmas of free trade. 'Of course you disagree with us,' Reginald McKenna told Balfour in May 1907, 'but you *can* understand our principles. Lloyd George doesn't understand them and we can't make him!'[37] Never a man to be bound by dogma, Lloyd George's attitude to free trade from his Board of Trade days onwards was that it remained 'defensible' but was by no means 'sacred'. 'Some of you chaps have got Free Trade consciences', he told Master-man in 1910. 'Now, I have not!'[38]

Conspicuously missing from Lloyd George's list of legislative achievements at the Board of Trade was any major measure of social reform or important new provision for labour. None the less, in terms of his own development, Lloyd George's period at the Board of Trade brought him into closer contact with the world of labour than he had ever been before − he was remarkably successful in conciliating labour disputes, winning praise all round for averting a national railway strike in October 1907 − and he enhanced his reputation as a Radical by publicly exhorting the Liberals to 'cope seriously with the social condition of the people', by intensifying his attack on the 'land monopoly', and by lashing out against the obstructionism of the Lords.

For long convinced that the powers of the Lords needed to be curtailed, Lloyd George believed it a mistake for the Government not to have appealed to the country against the Lords following the mutilation of the Education Bill of 1906, and in his public speeches, in between furiously denouncing the peers, he sought both to warn against a policy of inaction and to reassure impatient Liberals that the Government 'knew how to deal' with the obstacle of the Lords. It was his denunciations of the Lords that caught the public attention, and also the attention of King Edward VII, who regularly found himself compelled to complain to Campbell-Bannerman about Lloyd George's 'indecent' attacks on the Lords. In practical terms, what Lloyd George's verbal fusillades meant was that he established himself in the forefront of the agitation against the Lords, and encouraged the notion that he was 'the best fighting general' in the Liberal army.

By the end of his tenure at the Board of Trade Lloyd George had successfully built up and sustained two public reputations for himself. As the *Sheffield Independent* put it, he presented 'the curious dual phenomenon as a fiery Hotspur on the platform and a shrewd go-ahead administrator in the office and the legislative chamber'.[39] Later, after the experience of Lloyd George the coalitionist, some observers wondered whether he did in fact possess a dual personality. 'As time went on', J. A. Spender commented in his memoirs, 'one always had to remember that this adroit smoother and negotiator was living in the same tenement of flesh with the Limehouse orator and robber of hen-roosts. They were at times uneasily yoked, and the alternation of the two figures was always a puzzle to those who saw both.'[40] But during his term at the Board of Trade, and in his handling of the 'People's Budget', the 'two figures' of Lloyd George were skilfully controlled by him, and effectively deployed to secure his ends. There was, to be sure, an impulsive streak in him, especially in the use of his tongue, whether on the public platform or in cabinet. To his friends he freely admitted that 'he says things on the spur of the moment which he ought not to say', but added 'he is made that way and you must take him or leave him'.[41] Otherwise, in his studied actions and assertions, and in his alternations between 'sweet reasonableness' in Parliament and fiery demagoguery on the public platform, Lloyd George was a master of political calculation; he knew precisely when and how to charm and persuade, and when and how to rally popular support in the country and unnerve his opponents. He possessed, A. G. Gardiner wrote of him in 1908, both passion and calculation, and the latter mastered the former.[42]

To Gardiner the secret of Lloyd George's achievement lay in his audacity. 'He sweeps down on opportunity', Gardiner remarked, 'like a hawk on its prey.' It was his almost uncanny ability to get advantage out of virtually any political situation, and more especially to turn adversity into gain, that seems to have impressed contemporary observers most about Lloyd George. 'He profits by every attack made upon him', W. T. Stead wrote admiringly in 1904, 'and rides to victory on the wave which seemed as if it were destined to overwhelm him.' For Stead, indeed, Lloyd George's distinctive feature was his 'faculty of turning to advantage the efforts made by his enemies to crush him'. He was 'never so fortunate as when in extremity'.[43]

It was precisely Lloyd George's resourcefulness and his proven fighting abilities that made his installation at the Exchequer so hopeful to Radicals. By a more or less common consent he was regarded as being placed in command of the Government's key instrument, finance, in its struggle against its enemies and in its search for positive achievement. 'Finance', the *Nation* commented, 'is not only the key to the fight with the Lords, but it opens up the centre of the warfare with Protection and the struggle to provide a fund for social reform.'[44] Given his new position, and given the political situation, Lloyd George now occupied a position of real power in the Cabinet.

In the new Cabinet Lloyd George had as his closest ally Winston Churchill, promoted from Under-Secretary for the Colonies to take over from Lloyd George as President of the Board of Trade.

A renegade from the Unionist party on the tariff issue, Churchill was regarded by Radicals as a valuable addition to the Cabinet as much for his inherent combativeness and his fighting qualities as for his emerging interest in social reform. With a view to the struggle against both the Lords and the Tariff Reformers, the *Nation* could but welcome the inclusion in the Cabinet of 'the best fighting man that Liberalism has gained since Mr. Chamberlain changed the face of politics'.[45] Within the Cabinet circle, however, Churchill's combativeness and tireless energy were not always appreciated, particularly when he began to delve into the affairs of other departments. As perceived from the outside by Charles Hobhouse, who became Financial Secretary to the Treasury, Churchill added an 'electricity' to the Cabinet atmosphere which had previously been entirely missing.[46]

To the Board of Trade Churchill brought with him the broad outlines of a large programme of social reform, which he had put forward in an article on 'The Untrodden Field of Politics' in the *Nation* of 7 March 1908, and in a letter to Asquith on 14 March. 'Dimly across the fields of ignorance', he had written to Asquith, 'I can see the outline of a policy which I call the National Minimum.'[47] At the Board of Trade, which had major responsibilities concerning labour as well as commerce, Churchill was ideally situated to develop and put into practice some of his ideas on social reform, beginning with sweated labour and the creation of labour exchanges. The more he delved into the possibilities for social reform, the more he became convinced that the salvation of the Liberal Government lay in the promotion of constructive measures of social reform.

The only other newcomer in the Cabinet was Walter Runciman, promoted from Financial Secretary to the Treasury to President of the Board of Education. He had apparently told Asquith that if Lloyd George was made Chancellor he would refuse to continue as Financial Secretary because 'he does not consider Lloyd George's personal probity above suspicion, while he knows that Lloyd George would sacrifice anyone & allow any amount of suspicion to fall on anyone to save himself, if a scandal occurred'.[48] Runciman was essentially a businessman's Liberal, the son of a shipowner and an expert on finance and commerce, and he was to prove a regular thorn in Lloyd George's side.

In other shuffles in the Cabinet, Lord Crewe replaced Lord Elgin, who was sacked, as Colonial Secretary; Lord Tweedmouth, who was 'patently potty', was moved from the Admiralty to become Lord President of the Council; and Reginald McKenna was switched from the Board of Education to the Admiralty. The latter shift was to prove of the greatest significance for Lloyd George and the financial policies of the Asquith Government.

McKenna, who had some reputation as a Radical, had shown himself intensely conservative on taxation reform when he had served Asquith as Financial Secretary to the Treasury from December 1905 to January 1907. Highly regarded as an administrator, his main public image was that of a strict 'economist', and he was consequently expected to keep the navy estimates down. A former associate of Lloyd George, he and the new Chancellor had fallen out personally, and, after McKenna became a convert to the naval programme of the Sea Lords, war between the two men was virtually constant. 'The inner history of these times', J. A. Spender accurately pin-pointed in his memoirs, 'was in no small degree the record of their battles.'[49]

The thirteen Cabinet ministers who remained at their posts had all clearly established their respective roles, thereby giving Asquith the assurance of continuity and predictability. Sir Edward Grey (Foreign Secretary), Richard Burdon Haldane (Secretary for War), Sydney Buxton (Postmaster General), and Sir Henry Fowler (Chancellor of the Duchy of Lancaster), who was made Lord Wolverhampton, were Liberal Imperialist followers of Asquith; Lord Ripon (Lord Privy Seal), John Morley (Secretary of State for India), who went to the Lords, Lord Loreburn (Lord Chancellor), John Sinclair (Secretary for Scotland), Augustine Birrell (Irish Secretary), and Herbert Gladstone (Home Secretary), represented the Gladstonian followers of Campbell-Bannerman; Lord Carrington (President of the Board of Agriculture) along with Lord Crewe represented the Whig tradition; and John Burns (President of the Local Government Board), and Lewis Harcourt (First Commissioner of Works) were Radicals by reputation, though Burns had shown himself a bastion of social conservatism in office.

At the junior ministerial level Asquith made several positional changes and new appointments. For Lloyd George, the most important of these was the transfer of Charles Hobhouse from Undersecretary for India to Financial Secretary to the Treasury, and the appointment of C. F. G. Masterman as Secretary to the Local Government Board.

Lloyd George would have far preferred Hudson Kearley, his second-in-command at the Board of Trade, as Financial

Secretary, but instead Hobhouse was installed as a sort of 'watchdog' over the new Chancellor's policies and actions. The two men were destined never to hit it off. Lloyd George quickly dismissed Hobhouse as a third-rater, and Hobhouse equally rapidly came to the conclusion that Lloyd George was idle, ignorant, and totally impossible as an administrative chief. As a Gladstonian in his ideas, Hobhouse simply could not approve Lloyd George's methods of finance.[50]

Masterman's appointment, by contrast, gave new weight to the social reform element in the Government, and he was to be of far more valued assistance to Lloyd George in the preparation of the 'People's Budget' than Hobhouse. As a former social worker in south London, and as MP for the working-class constituency of North West Ham, Masterman belonged to the small but committed group of Social Radicals in the Commons who had been pressing the Government for radical measures dealing with unemployment, housing, and land ownership and use. Masterman relished his appointment to the Local Government Board as little as did Burns, and had stipulated as a condition of his taking up the appointment that the Government would introduce housing and valuation legislation in 1908.[51] In the event, the proposals of the Local Government Board for valuation never reached the Commons, but the expertise Masterman acquired in the matter was to prove of considerable value to Lloyd George in the preparation of the land value clauses of the 'People's Budget'.

Finally, in the changes he made, Asquith asked Jack Pease to take over as Chief Whip in succession to George Whiteley, who was soon to retire, and with instructions to pursue a different course of fund-raising than Whiteley, who 'had been skating on too thin ice in selling honours'.[52]

III

In April 1908 there was an almost universal consensus in the press that Asquith had succeeded in producing a Cabinet that was stronger and better balanced than its predecessor. What reservations there were came from the Radical press, which believed that the Radical groups in the party were still under-represented in the Cabinet. 'The Cabinet as a whole', the *Manchester Guardian* complained on 13 April, 'is still not fully representative of the party either in the country or in the House of Commons', and it looked for further changes 'at no very distant date'.

Essentially, Roy Jenkins is correct when he asserts that Asquith's formation of a government marked no new point of political departure.[53] On the domestic front the Liberals continued to focus on the attempt to clear the backlog of their legislative commitments in land, licensing, and education; Asquith offered no radical innovations in the content and methods of prime-ministerial leadership; and no group within the Cabinet had been granted the means of establishing its ascendancy over the others. None the less, the formation of Asquith's Government served to give new sharpness to trends and pressures that had been building up during Campbell-Bannerman's premiership and it did open up the possibility for new developments. Irish Nationalist pressure on the Liberal Government was intensified in response to the change in Prime Ministers; the Cabinet changes coincided with and gave new encouragement to what the Webbs saw as a 'scramble for new constructive ideas' in the ministerial ranks; and the new positions of power occupied by Lloyd George and Churchill, together with the freedom Asquith allowed to their assertiveness, helped to bring to a head disputes within the Cabinet over army and naval expenditure.

It was the very tenacity with which Lloyd George opposed the army and navy estimates for 1909, together with the cul-de-sac the Government had reached in its conventional politics by the end of 1908, and the quiet support of Asquith, that enabled him, a year after the formation of Asquith's Government, to carry through an otherwise largely unsympathetic Cabinet his 'People's Budget' and to lead the Government into radical new paths.

IV. Lloyd George at the Treasury

I

Lloyd George did not owe his appointment to the Treasury to any particular expertise in matters of public finance; he was what was known as a 'non-financial' Chancellor of the Exchequer. As he readily confessed to a banker friend, he needed to be given 'the a,b,c' of finance.[1] What he did bring with him to the Treasury was an attitude to spending, a willingness to experiment, and an approach to office work and administration all of which jarred with the traditions of the Treasury. 'At the Treasury', Charles Mallet bluntly stated in his biography of Lloyd George in 1930, 'he was in the wrong place.' His mind seethed with plans for spending public money, whereas the Treasury had traditionally looked upon itself as 'the watchdog of finance'; he did not master very thoroughly the economic or financial problems with which he had to deal and was forever making proposals the consequences and complexities of which he did not understand; and he refused to read papers, tossing them aside, no matter how important, and inviting his officials to talk to him instead.[2]

As an administrator there was, for the times, little that was conventional about Lloyd George. His inclination was to avoid office work and paper work; whenever he could abandon the office desk for the golf course he did so, to the fury of those who had to deal with him. 'He even refused to go to the Bank to negotiate a loan,' Charles Hobhouse complained very early in his tenure as Financial Secretary to the Treasury under Lloyd George, 'but went off golfing, leaving Murray and myself to deal with the matter.'[3] To Jack Pease, who somehow always seemed to find Lloyd George 'away as usual — playing golf at Walton Heath!', he was simply an 'idle dog'.[4] Lloyd George, however, regarded his breaks from the office desk as essential to his creativity. 'I could never do good work by slaving away day in and day out', he explained to George Riddell. 'I believe in giving one's brain and one's body a chance.'[5]

Paper work was Lloyd George's main aversion. He found reading papers quite as tedious as their preparation, preferring, as A. G. Gardiner put it, to 'pick up a subject as he runs, through the living voice, never through books'. 'He does not learn,' Gardiner grasped about him more readily than the Treasury officials, 'he absorbs, and by a sort of instantaneous chemistry his mind condenses the gases to concrete.'[6] There was an essential lack of system in his approach; as C. F. G. Masterman discovered when assisting him with the land clauses of the 'People's Budget', he was 'very erratic and unmethodical as a colleague'.[7] 'I am like a hawk', Lloyd George told George Riddell, the proprietor of the *News of the World*. 'I always swoop down on a thing. Sometimes I miss it, and then I have to go up and strike again.'[8] According to Du Parcq, it was Lloyd George's unmethodical, darting style that won for him from the Treasury and Revenue officials the nickname of 'the Goat'; he was always leaping from point to point.[9] Less kind souls have suggested that it was his agility in leaping from bed to bed that earned him the epithet.

The Treasury in 1908 was still an exceptionally small establishment. Its upper establishment consisted of one permanent secretary (Sir George Murray), two assistant secretaries (William Blain and Thomas Heath), four principal clerks, eight first-class clerks, one acting first-class clerk, and ten second-class clerks, a total of twenty-six.[10] The Treasury was also, as Asquith had discovered on his appointment as Chancellor of the Exchequer, 'steeped in the Gladstonian tradition'.[11] To a remarkable extent, indeed, the heads of the Treasury were active partisans of Gladstonian finance, by which they understood strict economy and free trade. In 1902/3 Sir Francis Mowatt and Sir Edward Hamilton, then Joint Permanent Secretaries, played a positive role in helping to frustrate Chamberlain's plans to employ the corn registration duty to establish the principle of imperial preference, and Mowatt, who even disapproved strongly of Balfour's 'anaemic policy', so transgressed 'the normal limits of official impartiality' in his defence of free trade that he found himself obliged to resign.[12] When the Liberals came to office Hamilton and Sir George Murray, who was appointed Joint Permanent (Administrative) Secretary in Mowatt's stead, sought both to encourage 'economy' and to curb Asquith's zeal for taxation reform, including the differentiation of the income tax and the introduction of land value taxation. Asquith found that when he first proposed differentiation 'he was at once met with the objection, which was considered fatal, that Gladstone had always declared that any such scheme was impracticable'. Following Hamilton's retirement in 1907, Murray became sole Permanent Secretary, remaining in that position until 1911. Described by Hobhouse as 'hard-working, cynical and devil-may-care, very fond of gossip', Murray was never to hide his dislike of Lloyd George's methods and proposals as Chancellor, and transgressed propriety, and even the requirements of impartiality, by gossiping endlessly about Lloyd George's supposed incompetence and advising Lord Rosebery of his disapproval of the 'People's Budget'.[13]

A relative of the Duke of Atholl, a product of Harrow and Oxford, and a former private secretary to Gladstone and Rosebery, Murray looked upon Lloyd George as an untutored outsider, and, unlike Sir Francis Hopwood at the Board of Trade, refused to make any concessions to Lloyd George's style and methods. At the Board of Trade, as Churchill found out, the officials had at first regarded Lloyd George as 'impossible', but after adapting to his style 'came to regard him as having done more for their Department at the finish than any other Minister'. When Hopwood, the Permanent Secretary during Lloyd George's first year at the Board of Trade, discovered that Lloyd George would not read anything, he promptly fitted in to Lloyd George's style and methods and 'put before him in a personal interview the salient points of a case, which he absorbed with a quickness and power of assimilation wholly remarkable'.[14] At the Treasury even Hobhouse conceded that: 'Lloyd George has an extraordinary power of picking up the details of a question by conversation.'[15] Murray, however, who thought Lloyd George was lazy, refused to operate by interviews, and depart from the time-honoured practice whereby ministers were informed and enlightened by written minutes, and many of his subordinates were in fact temperamentally unsuited to Lloyd George's style. Heath, as a major case in point, was 'always more at ease on paper than in debate', and disliked giving 'oral advice' and participating in committee discussion as much as Lloyd George disliked reading papers.[16]

The outcome was that Lloyd George, who had taken with him to the Treasury his private secretary from the Board of Trade, William Clark, instead of recruiting a Treasury official, worked little with most of the leading figures in the Treasury. Murray, whom Lloyd George seems to have regarded as a mediocrity, was largely ignored by him, and Heath, who was no innovator, had nothing to offer the new Chancellor. Blain was advanced in his ideas on taxation reform, but his sudden death in December 1908 meant that Lloyd George had to rely mainly on John Bradbury, the principal clerk at the head of the crucial first or finance division of the Treasury, for his main official support from within the Treasury for his schemes of taxation reform.

Lloyd George had also to deal with the officials of the Revenue departments; the Inland Revenue, Customs and Excise. With the Chairman of the Board of Inland Revenue, Sir Robert Chalmers, he developed excellent relations, but not so with the Chairman of the Board of Customs, Laurence N. Guillemard. In 1908 Excise was still attached to Somerset House, but under the provisions of the 1908 Finance Act it was transferred in early 1909 to Thames Street, thus separating direct and indirect taxation. The change, inspired by Chalmers, was designed to free the Inland Revenue to concentrate on the work of reforming direct taxation.

At Customs, Guillemard was entirely disconcerted by Lloyd George's apparent hit-and-miss approach. 'Hardly a day passed', he complained bitterly to Sir Almeric Fitzroy, the gossipy clerk of the Privy Council, in April 1910, 'without some crude idea which had fermented in his fertile but parochial brain being flung to the Board for serious examination: schemes for a duty in this direction or that, taken up, put sometimes into legislative form, and then rejected as impracticable, or perhaps exchanged for something more impracticable still; and yet the minister's self-confidence suffers no check, but from every fresh exposure seems to draw a more daring hardihood'.[17]

It was in Chalmers at the Inland Revenue that Lloyd George found his chief official support. A product of the system of open competitive examination for the upper division of the civil service, Chalmers had risen to the position of assistant secretary in the Treasury by 1903, and in 1907 was appointed Chairman of the Board of Inland Revenue. Like most successful Treasury and Revenue officials he was a Liberal, but he was a highly partisan one and was not cramped by the Gladstonian traditions of finance or by the traditions of the Treasury itself. According to one Treasury official 'Chalmers found it difficult to restrain his strong, almost passionate, Liberal convictions.'[18] He was also strongly committed to the reform of direct taxation along progressive lines, though still mindful of its departmental implications, and consequently less eager than Lloyd George for a complete overhaul of the income tax.

Chalmers was none the less the key official in helping to produce the 'People's Budget'; when it was rejected by the Lords he was heard to shout 'I would like to festoon this room with their entrails.'[19] Somewhat hot-tempered, but with a whimsical sense of humour, and a flair for nicknames — it was apparently he who christened Lloyd George 'the Goat' — Chalmers possessed the ideas and the attitudes that enabled him to co-operate effectively with the new Chancellor. He was an innovator; he conveyed his own judgements in 'a devastating economy of words' and urged his juniors to do likewise in their memoranda; and he was willing to cut corners.[20] According to W. J. Braithwaite, one of the Inland Revenue officials who assisted with the preparation of the land value taxes of the 'People's Budget', Chalmers suited Lloyd George precisely because he went in for 'a good deal of short-circuiting of Murray':

Traditionally the commissioners of Inland Revenue used to report to the Chancellor of the Exchequer through the Treasury, but Chalmers, having direct access to L.G., dispensed with this formality and L.G., not getting very much help from Murray, turned to Chalmers on other than Revenue matters, and also used Bradbury in the Treasury rather than Murray . . . Thus Chalmers was obtaining the reputation with L.G. for getting things done . . .[21]

From almost all accounts the permanent officials at the Treasury began by regarding Lloyd George as entirely 'illiterate' in financial matters. In July 1908 Sir Francis Mowatt informed St. Loe Strachey, the editor of the Unionist free trade *Spectator,* that 'he heard from the Treasury people that Lloyd George was absolutely without any arithmetical sense and found it quite impossible to understand the explanations of officials on financial matters'.[22] Arithmetic, in fact, was never one of Lloyd George's strong points, and his use of figures in a political argument was always suspect. 'The trouble with our Lloyd George', Harcourt told Austen Chamberlain after some debates in the Commons relating to the 'People's Budget', 'is . . . that he uses figures *exactly as if they were adjectives.*'[23] Deprecatory comments, emanating from Treasury sources, about Lloyd George's lack of knowledge of finance and his inability to master the technical details of Treasury work continued to circulate until about mid-way through the passage of the 'People's Budget' in the Commons, when 'the Treasury people' began to drop the word that Lloyd George had taken a commanding grip of the details of his Budget. On 11 August Ilbert, the clerk of the House of Commons, wrote to Bryce that 'The Treasury people tell me that Lloyd George, who began with knowing nothing about the Bill, now knows it better than anyone else.'[24]

To Lloyd George's own undisguised relief he was not called upon to introduce the Budget for 1908/9, which had already been prepared by Asquith and which the new Prime Minister proceeded to introduce in the Commons on 7 May. But Lloyd George was certainly not idle in his first months at the Treasury. As one of the leading 'economists' in the Cabinet, determined to press the Liberal election pledges to cut down on military and naval expenditure, he immediately sensed the opportunity his wide-ranging new brief as Chancellor of the Exchequer gave him to carry through to a more satisfactory conclusion the attack he had launched on Haldane's army estimates earlier in the year. In February Haldane, whom Lloyd George referred to as the 'Minister for Slaughter', had managed to rebuff Lloyd George on the estimates for 1908/9, but Lloyd George was now in a position to mount a more effective onslaught with a view to reducing army expenditure for the next financial year. On 18 May he prepared for his Cabinet colleagues a memorandum on 'The Financial Situation — This Year and Next', in which he indicated that he faced a prospective deficit of about £8,000,000 for 1909/10. Old-age pensions would have to be paid for, and they had been estimated to cost about £6,000,000, and the increase in the navy estimates was likely to be in the order of £2,000,000. Part of this deficit could be offset by a reduction of £3,000,000 in the National Debt charge, but that still left £5,000,000 to be accounted for, and the case he argued was that it was an 'absolute necessity' for the Government to avoid the imposition of new taxation to provide for those £5,000,000, particularly in the light of Asquith's reduction of the sugar duty in the Budget for the current year. 'On no other hypothesis', he contended, 'could we hope to   defend the remission of £3½ millions of taxation at a time when we are introducing an Old Age Pension scheme which is calculated to impose a permanent charge of at least 6 millions a year on the Exchequer.' That meant, he submitted to his colleagues, 'we have nothing to fall back upon, except a reduction of expenditure upon the Army and the Civil Service'.[25]

This was Lloyd George's strategy until it was defeated in late June: he sought to secure a substantial reduction in army expenditure before he would admit the necessity for new taxation in the first Budget he would be responsible for. 'I am not going to increase taxation to pay Old Age Pensions', he wrote to his brother on 12 May, 'until I have exhausted all means of reducing expenditure.'[26] A Cabinet Committee on Estimates, including Lloyd George, Churchill, and Harcourt, was set up, and Churchill temporarily installed himself at the War Office to prepare a brief for the reduction of the army.

In the previous year, Haldane had succeeded in reducing the army estimates by some £2,000,000, but it came as no surprise to him that he should be singled out for further cut-backs in expenditure. He none the less told Lloyd George that he refused 'point blank' to undertake reductions in the army.[27]

The actual work preparing the case for reductions and economies in the army was carried out by Churchill rather than Lloyd George. In his memorandum of 18 June for the Cabinet Committee Churchill contended that Haldane's expeditionary force was far larger than the 'legitimate' needs of British policy would ever require or justify, and he claimed also that on the administrative side the army was grossly overstaffed and overpaid.[28] When Haldane rebuffed these arguments in a memorandum of 26 June, pointing out among other things that Churchill seemed to assume that India was the only area that might require the expeditionary force in accordance with British policy needs and that he had ignored 'the possibility of our being called upon to operate on the Continent of Europe or in other parts of the world, as the nearer East', Churchill resorted to ridicule.[29] He refused to be frightened by the 'nightmares' that had been conjured up for his benefit: 'We are to encounter Russia in Afghanistan, to stamp out the flames of "a religious war" in India (and I gather simultaneously in Egypt too), and at the same time to be prepared with sufficient forces either to resist the German invader at home, or (perhaps even *and*) to co-operate effectively with some other great Power upon the continent.' Whether doubled or halved, the army would be equally incompetent to cope with any such formidable conjunction of dangers.[30]

Having raised, to an extent he did not seem fully to have appreciated, vital questions of policy concerning the expeditionary force, including its possible use on the continent, Churchill was finally warned off policy matters at the Cabinet Committee of Monday 29 June. Churchill was restricted to the 'test question' of reinforcing the Anglo-Indian army in the event of a Russian attack on the North-West Frontier, and obliged to confine his recommendations within the 'rigid data' prescribed by the India and War Offices and the Committee on Imperial Defence. The data required an expeditionary force of sixty-seven infantry battalions available for dispatch to India. 'It is a very lucky thing that this number, upon which all depends,' Churchill commented in disgust, 'should almost exactly correspond with the number of battalions we have been accustomed to maintain in the United Kingdom for so many years.'[31] The Treasury official sent by the Cabinet Committee to check on the War Office's costing for the expeditionary force could find no significant loopholes. 'I am glad to say that I am near the top of the great mountain which has been in my way', Haldane wrote in relief to his mother at the end of June. 'I have come to a preliminary agreement with the Chancellor of the Exchequer which frees my hands for the present and relieves me of immediate anxiety. I took the bull by the horns and acted firmly.'[32]

Churchill was not, however, completely through. In a memorandum of 4 July he still managed to calculate a 'surplusage' of 12 battalions even upon 'the arbitrary bases' prescribed for him, and altogether presented a case for reductions and economies in the army amounting to £1,000,000. But Lloyd George and Churchill had lost the battle for large-scale savings on the army estimates for 1909/10; in the event, the decrease on 1908/9 amounted to a mere £24,000. What Lloyd George suggested was that the navy might ultimately have to bear the brunt of the defeat he and Churchill had suffered. Although the discussion by the Cabinet Committee on the prospective navy vote for 1909/10 was purely perfunctory, as provisions for ordnance works and shipbuilding were excluded, Lloyd George plainly warned Esher, a member of the Committee of Imperial Defence and confidant of King Edward VII, on 26 June: 'No reduction in Army Estimates next year means no Dreadnoughts.'[33] Esher rightly dismissed this as 'bounce'; nevertheless it was clear that Lloyd George would make a fight of it before he would allow the navy any more than the £2,000,000 increase he had virtually already accepted, and that he was becoming seriously worried about the financial situation that he would have to face for 1909/10. When Churchill met Balfour at a house party on Sunday 21 June he 'did not attempt to conceal that they were in an awful mess about next year's finances and at their wits' end how to provide for their expenditure'.[34]

By late June Government expenditure, so far from offering any real prospect of economies, was threatening from Lloyd George's standpoint to get out of hand. The main culprit was old-age pensions. What concerned Lloyd George was that Asquith might have under-estimated the cost of his pensions proposals, putting it at £6,000,000 in a full year when it could run to over £7,500,000, depending on how many claimed their pensions, and on top of that Lloyd George found himself politically obliged to make concessions in the Commons that substantially increased the cost of the scheme.[35]

The Liberal Government's plans for old age pensions had first been announced in the Commons by Asquith in his Budget speech of 7 May, representing the culmination of two years planning and preparation. While Campbell-Bannerman's Cabinet had lacked any real strategy of social reform, most ministers, with the notable exception of Morley, had from the beginning accepted old-age pensions as 'inevitable', and much of Asquith's Budget strategy had been directed towards providing for them. On 7 May he had at last been able to declare that the financial situation 'admits of a substantial first step being now taken', and the proposal he had then outlined for a scheme of non-contributory pensions provided for pensions of £13 per annum for individuals over seventy with annual incomes less than £26, and of £9 15s. per head for married couples living together with joint annual incomes less than £39. Excluded from the operation of the scheme were aliens, lunatics, paupers, criminals, loafers, and wastrels, helping to limit its application to an estimated 572,000 out of the 1,262,232 persons over seventy.[36] Apart from being non-contributory, the scheme bore all the hallmarks of an attempt severely to restrict its initial cost.

After seeming 'almost apologetic' when introducing the second reading of the Old Age Pensions Bill in the Commons on 15 June in his capacity as Chancellor of the Exchequer, Lloyd George rapidly found himself obliged to give way on two of the general criticisms levied against the parsimony and unfairness of the Government's scheme. On 23 June he abandoned the flat cut-off rate of £26 per annum for eligibility for pensions in favour of a sliding scale, a move which he estimated would cost the Exchequer an additional £100,000, and on the next day he withdrew the Govern-

ment's 'penalization' of married couples, but on the understanding that the Liberals in the Commons would thereafter
help him ward off all further demands on the Government
purse. He estimated that the concession on married couples
would add another £334,000 to the cost of pensions.[37]

It was against this background of the escalating costs of
old-age pensions and the defeat of his attempt to cut down
on army expenditure that Lloyd George, at the end of June,
finally conceded the principle that he would need to resort
to fresh taxation for 1909/10. 'I have no nest eggs', he
confessed to the House of Commons on 29 June 1908, and
added in a phrase that gained instant notoriety and made
the Treasury 'wince': 'I have got to rob somebody's hen
roost next year. I am on the look-out which will be the
easiest to get and where I shall be least punished, and where
I shall get the most eggs, and, not only that, but where they
can be most easily spared, which is another important quali-
fication.'[38]

That, by the end of June, Lloyd George had come to
regard the Government's financial position as extremely
difficult was something he made no attempt to hide. On
3 July, in marked contrast to the public assurances given by
Asquith and other leading Liberals about the resources of
free trade finance, Lloyd George bluntly told the Lord
Mayor's annual Mansion House dinner for City bankers and
merchants that he was in a tight spot, confronted not only
by 'a stunning deficit' but by 'a falling revenue and a depression of trade'.[39] From that point onwards, as J. A. Spender
later complained, Lloyd George consistently painted the
financial situation for 1909/10 in 'the worst colours'.[40]

II

Lloyd George was by no means alone in painting the financial
situation in lurid colours; Unionists did so even more luridly.
By mid-1908 Chamberlainite 'Whole Hoggers', Balfourites,
and Unionist Free Fooders were all alike unanimous in
declaring that in the space of a single Budget Asquith's
Government had succeeded in bringing free trade to its
crisis point. As Leverton Harris, a leading Tariff Reformer,

put it on 25 May, during the debate on the Budget resolutions, the Government had 'crossed the boundary of safe and sane free trade finance and had arrived within the danger zone'. For Leverton Harris, and for Unionists generally, the meaning of Asquith's simultaneous reduction of the sugar duty and introduction of old-age pensions at a time of declining trade and diminishing revenue was that free trade finance now had no recourse but to heavy direct taxes which would 'cripple trade and industry and stretch to the breaking point the elastic sources of revenue which should only be stretched in time of great national emergency or peril'. Leverton Harris could consequently welcome, and the Unionist Free Fooders consequently deplored, Asquith's Budget for 1908/9; both declared 'there was never a greater step taken towards tariff reform'.[41] 'From the moment when I heard Mr. Asquith make his Budget statement in the House of Commons last April', Lord Cromer, who became president of the Unionist Free Trade Club in 1908, recalled in a confidential memorandum at the end of the year, 'I felt that a heavy blow had been given to the Free Trade cause.' In his opinion if Asquith 'had wished to facilitate the work of the Tariff Reformers, he could not have done so more effectively'.[42]

Even before Asquith had brought in his Budget for 1908/9, the Chamberlainites had gone far to put the revenue argument for tariffs at the front of their case for a general tariff. They had done so essentially for three reasons. The first was with a view to establishing their credentials as social reformers; they could hold out the prospect that the revenue from tariffs would, as Chamberlain had first suggested in May 1903, provide the necessary means for government to help finance old-age pensions and other advanced schemes of social reform. Chamberlain, certainly, had always valued his reputation as a social reformer, and immediately after the massive Unionist defeat in the general election of January 1906 he had sensed that the crucial moment had arrived for the Tariff Reformers to assert themselves as constructive reformers in the social sphere. Impressed by the scope given to questions of social reform by many Liberals in the election campaign and by the 'scientific' organization of the Labour vote, he believed it politically necessary for the Tariff

Reformers to prevent the Liberals from establishing proprietary rights over social reform and for them to devise new strategies for attracting working-class voters away from the Liberal—Labour alliance, perhaps even weaning Labour itself away from the Liberals.[43] Moreover, he held it politically opportune for the Tariff Reformers to advocate social reform, for he claimed that the general election had effectively rendered 'defunct' the 'whiggish' elements in the Unionist ranks who had been as much opposed to social as to fiscal reform.[44]

Second, following from the assumption that the issue for the future would be not so much the desirability or necessity of social reform but rather questions of method and finance, Chamberlain believed tariff reform finance would prove positively attractive to those groups apprehensive about increases in direct taxation to provide for social reform. As he put it to the Commons on 16 May 1906, the only alternative to revenue from tariffs was the Radical policy of 'confiscation'.[45] Only tariff reform, Austen Chamberlain reiterated in an *Outlook* article of January 1907, could provide without 'robbery or jobbery' the necessary financial basis for further social reform. It was precisely this aspect of tariff reform that concerned Cromer in 1908; he regarded it 'as almost certain that a very large number of shaky, even perhaps some rather strong Free Traders will practically combine with the Tariff Reformers rather than bear any very heavy fresh burthens in the shape of direct taxation'.[46]

Third, as everyone realized, tariffs imposed in the first instance ostensibly for revenue purposes, offered a potential 'backdoor' to protection and imperial preference. It was precisely such a 'backdoor' Chamberlain had sought to exploit in 1902/3, until thwarted by Ritchie.

The revenue argument for tariffs certainly played an important role in drawing Balfour closer to the position of the Whole Hoggers. A number of factors help to explain his move towards them in the course of 1907. Joseph Chamberlain's stroke in July 1906, and consequent withdrawal from the active political scene, encouraged Balfour to assert his mastery over the party by making himself the recognized leader of tariff reform; he said he was impressed by the demand of the majority of the premiers at the Colonial Conference in London in the summer for a system of imperial preference, and by the progress made by tariff reform in the party; and he was greatly influenced by his 'tutoring' by Professor W. A. S. Hewins, the secretary of the Tariff Reform League and a 'Tariff Reformer who really knows something about his case', who had forcibly presented the arguments for both imperial preference and revenue from tariffs. Hewins had given particular emphasis to the revenue argument, pointing out that ever since 1840 the country had been transferring the burden of taxation to direct taxes and contending that only through tariff reform could the trend be reversed or the existing balance maintained.[47]

In a long discussion with Balfour on Asquith's Budget for 1907/8, and in a follow-up memorandum, Hewins developed the special theme that free trade finance had almost reached the limits of its resources, and that any substantial increases in existing taxes would prove politically unacceptable. As perceived by Hewins, the key problem facing free-trade finance, and threatening it with breakdown, was that normal expenditure was growing more rapidly than the population, and that revenue from existing resources was becoming increasingly inelastic. It was his contention that significant increases in the existing indirect taxes were impossible either because, as was the case with the tea and sugar duties, the public would not tolerate them or, as in the case of beer, wines, spirits, and tobacco, they would so diminish consumption as to leave the revenue unaffected or even reduced. As for the most important items of direct taxation, the income tax and estate duties, Hewins argued that higher rates for either were bound to react on one another and lead to a partial realization of the estimated increase. 'Speaking generally,' he put it to Balfour, 'the continued high rate of income tax must tend to depress the average rate of death duties, and vice versa.' More specifically on the income tax, he held that the existing rate was already burdensome, and that the point had been reached where any future legislation would have to allow further reductions at the lower end of the scale, which represented the larger proportion of incomes subject to taxation. He calculated that any system for the graduation of the income tax that it was 'expedient to introduce' would not yield very much.

Hewins was equally dismissive of the possible new sources of revenue which he thought had the approval of the Liberal party. Any tax on motor cars would not benefit the national government as local authorities would demand the revenues from it for the maintenance and renewal of highways; it was becoming generally agreed that the taxation of site values belonged to the domain of municipal rather than national finance; and the movement for the overhauling of the taxation of liquor licences was directed mainly to the restriction of liquor consumption and also the number of licensed houses. From these sources, Hewins confidently concluded, no considerable further sum could be raised.

What all this added up to, for Hewins, was that the Government would soon be in acute difficulties over finance. The Government was already pledged to a number of schemes involving massive new expenditure, notably old-age pensions, the feeding of schoolchildren, the establishment of small holdings, and the payment of election expenses for MPs, and had made no provision even for the nucleus of old-age pensions.[48]

The idea that the existing system of taxation was verging on 'breakdown' thereafter remained with Balfour, and served as one of his main bridges across to the Whole Hoggers. In his speech before the annual conference of the National Union in Birmingham on 14 November 1907, in which he signalled his 'conversion' to the idea of a general tariff, Balfour gave pride of place to the case for 'broadening the basis of taxation'.

In accepting a general tariff, Balfour also accepted that it was politically necessary to link the revenue from tariffs to the financing of social reform, and duly sought to make it clear in his Birmingham speech that 'social reform has long been the work of the Unionist party'.[49]

Balfour's assertions at Birmingham gave a real satisfaction to the Tariff Reformers. 'Balfour', Bonar Law wrote to Deakin in Australia, 'is now definitely fighting on the right side and I think he is going to carry his party almost solidly with him and his leadership on the right side has always seemed to me the only thing necessary to make success assured.'[50] The policy of the Birmingham speech was thereafter held up by Balfour, the Central Office, and the Tariff Reformers as the 'official' policy of the party; only those Unionist MPs and candidates who accepted Balfour's Birmingham speech on fiscal matters would be given the assistance of the Central Office.[51] The Tariff Reformers were now in a position to embark on a final purge of the Free Fooders in the party.

The response of a good many of the Unionist Free Fooders to Balfour's Birmingham speech, and the Central Office policy of applying it as the party orthodoxy in assisting candidates, was one of defeatism. Lord Hugh Cecil, Balfour's cousin and perhaps the most talented as well as tenacious of the Free Fooders, sought to assure his friends 'that the game of Free Trade within the Unionist Party is by no means up', but others, like Strachey, the editor of the *Spectator,* were overcome by a terrible sense of impotence.[52] By their own failure to make themselves formidable, Strachey complained to Arthur Elliot, the Unionist Free Fooders had rendered themselves 'men of no importance to either side, with the result that we have been ignored by Balfour and that we have no influence with the Liberals'.[53] Free trade itself, he now convinced himself, was approaching its demise, and both in his private correspondence and in the columns of the *Spectator* he predicted that the introduction of old-age pensions was likely to prove its grave.

The almost hysterical response of some of the Unionist Free Fooders to Asquith's Budget for 1908/9, including the introduction of old-age pensions, derived directly from a sense of their own political plight and their conviction that large new expenditure on 'improvident' schemes of social reform would play immediately into the hands of the Tariff Reformers. In the *Spectator* during May 1908 Strachey contended that the Government had now put itself in a position where it would have to raise some £13,000,000 by fresh taxation in the next year, and that this could well prove disastrous for the maintenance of free trade in that it would encourage electors to try the 'quack remedy' for raising money offered by the Tariff Reformers.[54]

So loud was Strachey's wail that Asquith himself felt obliged to write privately to rebuke the *Spectator* for 'losing its way — I might add its head — in the whole domain of finance' and to explain the strategy he had pursued as Chancellor of the Exchequer to provide for the financing of social reform along free trade lines. He put it to Strachey that:

I have realised from the first that if it could not be proved that social reform (not Socialism) can be financed on Free Trade lines, a return to Protection is a moral certainty. This has been one of the mainsprings of my policy at the Exchequer. I prepared the way by steadily reducing the principal of the debt — at the cost of the taxpayer and by means of the war taxes — till I shall have brought it at the end of this year to the level of 20 years ago . . . Old Age Pensions were inevitable. I have secured an ample fund to meet them without any extra taxation.[55]

Asquith's claim that old-age pensions could be paid for without any extra taxation was sanguine; as was to become evident by the time of the next Budget, he had been wrong by over £2,000,000 in his estimate of how much old age pensions would cost in a full year. Even his provision of £1,200,000 for the start of old age pensions payments in the last quarter of the 1908/9 fiscal year proved badly off the mark, and in February 1909 a supplementary vote of £910,000 had to be provided.

By late 1908 it was clear to everyone that Lloyd George would have to raise large sums in new taxation. The refrain by then of both the Whole Hoggers and the Balfourites was that he would find the resources of free trade finance virtually exhausted, and they loudly proclaimed that the question of finance had now reached the point where it would ensure the triumph of tariff reform. As Lord Lansdowne told the annual meeting of the Liberal Unionist Council on 20 November 1908: 'We shall be driven to it [tariff reform] by the exigencies of the financial situation.'[56] Lloyd George was determined to prove him wrong. Asquith, moreover, had already mapped out some of the ways by which Lloyd George could establish that the resources of free trade finance were by no means exhausted.

III

If Campbell-Bannerman's Government had lacked an over-all strategy of social reform, Asquith as Chancellor of the Exchequer had none the less devised and followed a definite strategy for financing and implementing old-age pensions, and for reordering the fiscal system along progressive free trade lines. As Haldane put it to him in August 1909: 'We have not *stumbled* into the introduction of an Old Age Pension system, nor into the increase of the proportion which direct bears to indirect taxation. These two changes are Reforms which the True Spirit has called us for as definitely as it called for Electoral Reform in 1832.'[57] As Chancellor of the Exchequer Asquith had sought to prepare the financial ground for old-age pensions by securing a considerable reduction in the principal of the National Debt and by retrenchments on expenditure for the army and navy so as to free existing funds for new areas of expenditure. He had also cut back on the levels of indirect taxation and cleared some of the ground for the imposition of new forms of direct taxation.

According to Treasury classification, in 1905/6 roughly equal amounts were raised by direct and indirect taxes. The direct taxes, the property and income tax, the house duty, the land tax, estate duties, stamps, and excise licences and railway passenger duty, accounted for 50.3 per cent of the revenue raised by taxation, and the indirect taxes, which were all the customs and excise duties excepting licences and railway passenger duty, accounted for 49.7 per cent.[58] Unionist strategy for 'broadening the basis of taxation' was designed at least to hold the balance between direct and indirect taxes; Asquith's strategy as Chancellor of the Exchequer was directed towards making it possible to raise a larger proportion from direct taxes, but without at the same time threatening and thereby antagonizing the large majority of income tax payers and voters. It was a strategy directed mainly against those persons Lloyd George liked to refer to as 'the rich'.

The main engine of direct taxation was the property and income tax, which Asquith blandly asserted in his Budget speech of 1907 was now to be 'regarded as an integral and permanent part of our financial system'. Levied under five schedules, income tax was charged on the profits or salaries received or earned by those persons whose incomes exceeded £160 per annum. Abatements, benefiting about 75 per cent of all income tax payers, were granted to incomes ranging between £160 and £700 per annum. Some two-thirds of the income tax was collected 'at source', an administrative practice Somerset House was strongly attached to as a means of preventing evasion and avoidance. The most lucrative of all schedules, and the one with the most loopholes for evasion and avoidance, was Schedule D, which applied to the profits from commercial and industrial undertakings, and incomes from professional and vocational practices. The amount raised by the income tax in 1905/6, charged at the rate of 1s. in the £, was £31,350,000. The number of income tax payers was generally estimated at about 1,000,000, with a growth rate of at least 10,000 per annum.

The death duties provided the second major instrument of direct taxation; in 1905/6 they raised £17,330,000, constituting with the income tax 39 per cent of the total tax revenue for the year. In his fundamental revision of the death duties in 1894, Sir William Harcourt had provided for a single estate duty on all forms of property, personal and real, settled and unsettled, charged on the pooled value for the entire estate of a deceased person, regardless of its future destination, and graduated according to the size of the aggregate estate. The duty ranged from 1 per cent on estates between £100 and £500 to 8 per cent on estates over £1,000,000. Settled property was to pay the duty only once in the course of a settlement, but was further liable to a 1 per cent settlement estate duty. Legacy duty on personalty, and succession duty on realty, were levied at rates graduated according to relationship to the deceased; the range was from 1 per cent for parents or children to 10 per cent for strangers in blood. In the memorandum Bernard Mallet drew up for the Inland Revenue on the 'Incidence of Public Burdens' in 1902, he reckoned that the death duties fell 'almost exclusively on the Income Tax paying class'.[59]

The most lucrative of the indirect taxes were the duties

on liquor, which yielded £35,840,000 in 1905/6, constituting 29 per cent of total tax revenue. This none the less represented a significant decline from the high of £40,560,000 in 1900/1, when the prevailing charges of 11s. per gallon on spirits and 7s. 9d. per barrel on beer had been imposed. The duties on wine averaged about 2s. a gallon. From the standpoint of 'the trade', alarmed at the slump in business from 1903 onwards, liquor was in fact grievously overtaxed, and on 10 March 1906 a deputation from the National Trade Defence Association urged Asquith to remit the increases imposed during the Anglo-Boer War.[60] In addition to the liquor duties, 'the trade' also paid licence duties, amounting to £2,200,000 in 1905/6, although this benefited the Exchequer only marginally as, apart from the proceeds of the manufacturers' licences, the monies received were allocated in relief of local taxation.

Tobacco, generally classified by Liberals along with drink as a 'luxury' item in working-class consumption, produced £13,400,000 in 1905/6 as against £14,100,000 for the remaining indirect taxes, the 'food taxes', customs duties on tea, sugar, and lesser items of consumption.

How the burden of taxation was distributed among classes in proportion to income was a matter of considerable analysis by the early twentieth century, and the conclusions reached varied fairly substantially according to how the sums were done, though it was generally accepted that the direct taxes fell almost entirely on the class of income tax payers.

In his 1902 memorandum for the Inland Revenue, Bernard Mallet estimated the number of income tax payers at 900,000, representing 4,200,000 people in the income tax paying class, as against 8,030,000 families, or 37,300,000 persons, in the non-income-tax-paying classes. He put the income of the former class at £750,000,000, and that of the other classes at £905,000,000. In his calculations, the income tax paying class carried 63 per cent of the total burden of imperial taxation, and on average paid 11.4 per cent of their income in imperial taxation, as against an average of 5.7 per cent by the non-income-tax-paying classes. The average for the income tax paying class, Mallet commented, was higher than might have been anticipated, and this he attributed primarily to the operation of the death duties on large estates, which inflated the average percentage for the income tax paying class as a whole.

As Mallet conceded, attempts to calculate the burden of taxation in the United Kingdom were still very rudimentary, and were particularly hampered by a lack of sufficient data; not even the number of income tax payers was known with any certainty in the absence of required returns from all income tax payers. Calculations as to the burden of rates were even more imprecise, so much so that Mallet claimed that 'no conclusions arrived at can be of any real value'. He nevertheless ventured that 70.5 pcr cent of the burden of rates fell on the income tax paying class, taking 4.4 per cent of their income, as against the 1.5 per cent of income paid by the non-income-tax-paying classes. In all, according to Mallet's calculations, the income tax paying class carried 64.9 per cent of the total burden of taxation, representing 15.8 per cent of their income, and the non-income-tax-paying classes 35.1 per cent of the burden, representing 7.2 per cent of their income.[61]

The figures drawn up by Herbert Samuel in 1902 and Chiozza Money in 1907 gave a rather different picture. Samuel, in his study of *Liberalism,* excluded from his estimates the death duties on the ground that they were special imposts on unearned income that stood apart from the general system of taxation, and according to his calculations for 1900/1 the average working-class income was taxed at 6.9 per cent, an income of £200 at 4.6 per cent, an income of £500 at 7 per cent, and an income of £5,000 at 8.4 per cent. In other words: 'Working-class incomes are taxed at a considerably higher rate than incomes of £200 a year and thereabouts, they are taxed at about the same rate as incomes of £500, and at a rate only slightly lower than incomes of £5,000 or over.'[62]

In 1907 L. G. Chiozza Money, the Radical MP for Paddington North and author of *Riches and Poverty,* largely confirmed Samuel's picture in the statistics he prepared for the Cabinet, at Asquith's request, on the distribution of taxation. In *Riches and Poverty*, an examination of the maldistribution of wealth in the United Kingdom published in 1905, Money had calculated the national income at £1,710,000,000, £830,000,000 of which went to the income tax paying class. For 1905/6 he estimated the total number of income tax payers at 1,050,000, representing 5,250,000 people out of a total population of 44,000,000. In his calculation the income tax paying class was, in 1905/6, taxed for imperial purposes at the average rate of 8 per cent on their incomes, and the non-income-tax-paying classes at the average rate of 6.2 per cent. The main point Money made to the Cabinet was that 'the question of ability to pay is practically disregarded by our present taxation'. According to his estimates, the lower classes paid an 'income' tax of nearly 1*s.* 3*d.* in the £, while the very rich paid only 1*s.* 7*d.* in the £. Indeed, what Money's figures suggested was that even within the income tax paying class, the very rich escaped relatively lightly. According to his figures, the average total tax for the income tax-paying class was 1*s.* 7.2*d.* in the £; incomes between £160 and £700 paid 1*s.* 6.5*d.* in the £, between £700 and £5,000 1*s.* 9.4*d.* in the £, and over £5,000 only 1*s.* 6.9*d.* in the £.[63]

Apart from their distinct divergences on the question of the distribution of the national income, perhaps the main point of difference between Samuel and Money on the one hand and Mallet on the other was in their estimates as to the distribution of the indirect taxes among the various classes of the community. Samuel and Money worked on the assumption that the average working-class family consumed as much in dutiable articles as the average family in any other class, and consequently divided indirect taxation per head of population, whereas Malett sought to probe more carefully into the spread of particular taxes among various groups.

Information on the distribution of indirect taxes was particularly scanty, though a collection of nearly 2,000 household budgets compiled by the Board of Trade in 1904 did provide a basis for framing estimates. In 1908, after Asquith's Budget for that year had reduced the sugar duty from 4*s.*2*d.* to 1*s.*10*d* per cwt, the Inland Revenue used the Board of Trade inquiry to produce figures on the amount of taxation falling on 'typical' working-class families with weekly incomes between 35*s.* and 40*s.* According to the Inland Revenue figures the teetotal, non-smoking family in this category paid a mere 1.1 per cent of total income in imperial taxes, and a drinking and smoking family 6.1 per cent of income.[64] Apart from this limited study, hard data on the distribution of taxation among the working classes was sadly lacking even within official quarters, and Mallet's memorandum of 1902 remained the best official attempt to gauge the distribution of indirect taxes among all classes of the community. Neither Asquith nor Lloyd George saw fit to order a thorough investigation of the burden of taxation among the working classes.

Although without full and accurate data on the distribution of the burden of taxation, Asquith as Chancellor of the Exchequer none the less had clear targets in mind in readjusting the basis of taxation, and in preparing the way for new forms of direct taxation. By reducing the tea and sugar duties he reduced the burden of indirect taxation on the 'necessaries of life', largely for the benefit of the working classes, and by introducing differentiation in the rates of income tax on earned and unearned incomes, he both eased the burden of direct taxation on the large mass of middle-class income tax payers and isolated a particular category of income for later increases in taxation. According to the figures Asquith gave the Commons in April 1908, 750,000 out of roughly 1,000,000 income tax payers benefited from the relief given to earned incomes under £2,000 in the previous year, when the rate of such incomes had been reduced to 9*d*. in the £, as against the standard rate of 1*s*.[65]

With regard to the financing of social reform and other new expenditure, Asquith was convinced that should fresh taxation be required it should include some new forms of direct taxation, notably a supertax and possibly land value taxation as well. He had proposed both to the Treasury officials in 1906, and by 1908 had gone far to prepare the Treasury for the introduction of a supertax; indeed, he had intended making provision for a supertax in his Budget for 1907/8, finally abandoning his plans for its introduction in 1907 in the face of opposition to it from Sir Edward Hamilton, Joint Permanent Secretary of the Treasury, Sir Henry Primrose, Chairman of the Board of Inland Revenue, and Reginald McKenna, Financial Secretary to the Treasury, and on the ground that 'differentiation was enough to proceed with during one session'.[66]

In short, Asquith took the opportunity provided by three years of virtually static expenditure and general prosperity marginally to reduce and redistribute the burden of taxation and at the same time to prepare the way for raising fresh revenue from the income tax by means of heavier rates on large and unearned incomes. Implicit in differentiation, and explicit in the proposals for a supertax, was a concern to expose certain groups of income tax payers to heavier rates than the large majority subject to income tax. When differentiation was introduced, Sir Edward Hamilton advised King Edward VII that some of the propertied classes might indeed detect in it 'the commencement of an era when the rich will have to pay for the poor', and the King confessed himself 'nervous' on this score.[67] If it was not Asquith's intention to proceed to 'soak the rich', it was certainly part of his purpose to make it possible through differentiation and a supertax to raise more revenue from the income tax without having to resort to an increase in the general rate, and thereby without having to arouse the ire and opposition of all income tax payers. As McKenna noted in a private memorandum for Asquith in December 1906: 'In its present incidence the income tax falls hardest on persons earning incomes between £700 and £2,000 or £3,000 a year, and it is the resistance of these persons which stands most in the way of raising it when the Exchequer has to be replenished.' This class of income tax payers, he added, was 'formidable as a body by their influence on public opinion'.[68] It was precisely this class, marked off for protection by Asquith, that Lloyd George's 'People's Budget' exempted from increases in the income tax.

When Lloyd George took over as Chancellor of the Exchequer, the Liberal strategy with regard to the income tax, including the introduction of a supertax, had been clearly marked out for him. The Select Committee of the House of Commons which Asquith had set up in May 1906 to inquire into the practicability of graduating the income tax had reported at the end of the year that a supertax upon larger incomes was indeed practicable. The contention of Sir

Henry Primrose that a supertax, by requiring direct personal assessment of the individual taxpayer, would destroy the existing system of assessment at the source was set aside by the committee, which recommended that the general rates of the income tax should continue to be collected at the source, but that persons with incomes over £5,000 would be required to make a separate return for supertax purposes.[69] Within the Treasury, moreover, William Blain had prepared what came to be accepted as the 'definitive' memorandum on the case for imposing a supertax. The memorandum, written in February 1907 when Asquith was contemplating introducing a supertax in his forthcoming Budget, was a perfect statement of the Liberal free trade argument for the supertax. Blain stated outright that the Liberals could finance social reform only by increasing direct taxation; as it was, the indirect taxes formed 'so large a proportion of the whole that the poorest classes contribute an excessive share' and, anyhow, increased indirect taxes on beer and spirits were no longer certain of raising substantial new sums. 'The country', Blain observed, 'refuses any longer to drink itself out of its financial straits.' The political argument for raising more money from direct taxes was equally strong. 'While the present position continues,' Blain asserted, 'it puts a powerful weapon in the hands of the advocates of Tariff Reform.' Tariff Reformers were able to point out that the desire of the Government to effect social changes was thwarted by the absence of elasticity in the present revenue. 'No better answer to the most specious argument on their side', he contended, 'could be found than a fiscal change which would enable additional revenue to be raised at need without an increase – indeed, with a diminution – of the proportion of burden falling upon the most numerous classes.' Increased revenue from direct taxation would have to come from the estate duty or the income tax; as increased revenue from the former would be severely limited and unreliable in any one year, that left the income tax as the main engine for raising large new sums, and before the income tax could justifiably be used to add substantially and permanently to the revenue some means would have to be devised to mitigate or remove the inequalities in the existing tax. Differentiation would mitigate some of the inequalities but would not remove the obstacles to an increased income tax, for it would still leave incomes of the same class, whether large or comparatively small, subject to the same rate of tax; the only feasible remedy, Blain concluded, was the introduction of a supertax on large incomes. As a start, he recommended the imposition of a modest new tax on incomes over £5,000; such a tax would not be worth levying for the sake of its immediate yield, but it would provide the opportunity for setting up the machinery of an effective supertax, and would throw much-needed light on the number and amount of large incomes.[70] It was precisely such a tax that the 'People's Budget' was to impose.

There is no evidence to suggest that Lloyd George ever had to wage a major battle over the principle and practicability of a supertax with the officials of the Treasury and the Board of Inland Revenue. Asquith had waged such a battle, and when Lloyd George succeeded him as Chancellor of the Exchequer the battle had already been won. Two of the major opponents of the introduction of a supertax, Sir Edward Hamilton and Sir Henry Primrose, had retired, leaving Sir George Murray as the last of the old Gladstonians opposed to a fundamental reform of the income tax, while Chalmers, Blain, and Bradbury supported the principle of a supertax. The way, in short, was open to Lloyd George to proceed with the introduction of a supertax.

If Liberal strategy on the income tax had been clearly marked out for Lloyd George, and the way already prepared by Asquith for the introduction of a supertax, the same could not be said of the other major innovation in direct taxation that Asquith had contemplated when becoming Chancellor of the Exchequer. He had made no positive moves to provide for the imperial taxation of land values. Rather, the policy of Campbell-Bannerman's Government had been to treat the question of land value taxation as entirely a matter of local rather than imperial finance, and pledges were given to introduce valuation bills for Scotland, and England and Wales, that would make it possible for local authorities to impose rates upon site values. Although the Government managed to produce a Land Values (Scotland) Bill in 1907, no equivalent for England and Wales appeared, despite the fact that the King's Speech for 1908 had put valuation on the agenda for the year. Part of the explanation for the non-appearance of a valuation bill for England and Wales was the hostile reception given in the Lords to the Scottish bill; in 1907 it was thrown out by the Lords, and in July 1908 it was so modified by the Lords that the Government dropped the measure. In these circumstances, the Government clearly could not hope to carry through the Lords a bill providing for the ascertainment of land values in England and Wales. But more important, the Government simply could not agree on a draft bill that it could present to the Commons. John Burns, at the Local Government Board, had been given the task of preparing the Government's valuation proposals for England and Wales, and the draft Valuation Bill that he produced in May 1908, while it provided for a uniform system of valuation for both imperial and local purposes, did not include any provision for the separate ascertainment of land values, a matter which Burns thought should be reserved for a separate and later measure.[71] In June 1908 a committee of the Cabinet was appointed to settle the draft of the Valuation Bill, so that it might at least be introduced in the Commons before the end of the session, and while clauses for the ascertainment of land values were submitted to the committee by W. S. Robson, the Attorney-General, profound disagreements between Robson and Burns helped to prevent any further progress.[72] As the ardent land taxers had for long perceived the matter, Burns was 'simply a Tory' on the question of land valuation.[73] The upshot was that on 14 October 1908 Asquith announced in the Commons, in reply to a question by Josiah Wedgwood, that valuation for England and Wales would be held over until the next year.[74]

It was at this juncture that Lloyd George became determined to include land value taxation in his Budget for the next year, and this was a course that the land taxers themselves urged. In November Wedgwood presented to Asquith a petition for the taxation of land values in the next Budget. It was signed by 241 Liberal and Labour MPs.

Until this point there had been no real pressure on the Liberal Government to provide for the imperial taxation of land values. It had always been intended by the land taxers that local authorities should be the primary beneficiaries of land value taxation, partly on the grounds that it was the improvements provided by local authorities that helped to increase land values, but largely because they wanted to relieve the burden of rates on buildings and other improvements undertaken by private individuals. Consequently the main agitation had been for the Government to make it possible for local authorities to rate site values. There had none the less always been advocates within the movement for land value taxation for an imperial tax on land values, the main proceeds of which should go in relief of rates. C. L. Davies, the secretary of the United Committee for the Taxation of Land Values, for instance, wrote to Wedgwood in January 1907:

My own idea would be that a national tax shld be raised on L.V.s & applied in relief of such part of rates, — educn., main roads lunacy etc. which are held to be national rather than local in character (i.e. a sort of equalisation fund to meet those charges); & that the local authorities shld be left to raise the rest of their requirements — for local services & local improvements which directly maintain & increase local land values, by rates on land values.[75]

When, in late 1908, the land taxers urged the Government to incorporate land value clauses in the next Budget, they did so primarily as an expedient to get round the veto of the Lords on the question of securing a national valuation of land, and on the assumption that any imperial tax on land values would not poach on municipal preserves but would become part of a larger scheme for the reorganization of the financial relation between the central government and local authorities.

Whether imposed as an imperial tax or a local rate or both, the key questions in land value taxation were which land values were to be taxed, the extent to which they were to be taxed, and who was in practice to pay the taxes, and on these questions even those in the Government who positively favoured land value taxation were at odds with one another. The answers given to these questions depended in part on what was understood to be the primary purposes of land value taxation.

In the agitation for the local taxation of land values, four main arguments had commonly been put forward in support of the separate rating of site values. First, it would provide local authorities with a desperately required new source of revenue, and one to which they were fully entitled in so far as their expenditure contributed very largely to the increase in site values. Second, by making owners responsible for a separate site value rate, a fairer distribution of the incidence of local taxation might be secured as between owners and occupiers, the former of whom benefited directly from the increase in site values created by the growth of the community and the latter of whom were alone levied for rates in England and Wales. Third, by rating site values and by de-rating improvements, positive encouragement would be given to building and other forms of improvement. Fourth, by rating the capital value of vacant, undeveloped, and underdeveloped land, the better use of land would be encouraged, and more land would come on to the market at a cheaper price. By 1908 the ardent land taxers in the Commons were less concerned with the campaign to secure the fiscal benefits of a site value rate, including relief to occupiers in leasehold towns and cities, notably London, and had come to focus far more on the supposed development benefits of site value rating.[76]

Basically, what was wanted by the ardent land taxers, particularly from the North and Scotland, was a new standard of rating based on the capital value of land apart from the buildings and improvements upon it (i.e. site value), and that this should become the sole standard of rating. In the Government Alexander Ure, the Solicitor-General for Scotland, who chaired the Select Committee on the Land Values Taxation (Scotland) Bill, was the only advocate of putting the rates entirely on site value. The alternative of an additional rate on site value had much wider support within the Government, so long as it was accepted that such a rate would not interfere with existing contacts which provided for the payment of rates by the occupier. In other words, the Government would not assist in shifting the incidence of local rates between occupiers and owners, but it was prepared to contemplate a shift in the distribution of the burden of rates between different districts and different properties. The effect of placing a reasonable rate on site values, and of correspondingly de-rating buildings and other improvements, would be to transfer more of the burden of rates from the suburbs to the city centres and from valuable buildings to valuable sites.

The ardent land taxers claimed that these shifts in the burden of rates would constitute a major social and economic reform. Land for development purposes would become freely available at cheaper prices in so far as the owners of vacant, undeveloped and underdeveloped land, including land ripe for building on the outskirts of towns, would be encouraged to sell or develop rather than hold back their land because they would now be paying rates on its capital rather than present-use value. Again, the de-rating of buildings and other improvements would give an enormous encouragement to industry, commerce, and building. As argued by the land taxers, perhaps the major social benefit that would flow from cheaper land and the de-rating of buildings would be better and cheaper houses for the working classes. Indeed, they argued that these conditions were essential to make it profitable for builders to provide adequate new housing for the working classes. The criticism the land taxers made of John Burns's Housing and Town Planning Bill, when it was first introduced in the Commons in 1908, was that so long as it avoided the question of the rating of land and houses it could only remain 'a somewhat dangerous piece of tinkering with a much wider question'.[77]

Even to some of the supporters of the principle of land value taxation it seemed evident that, unless carefully managed, site value rating itself might have disastrous consequences for the housing of the working classes. The point made by W. S. Robson, the Attorney-General, in a confidential memorandum for the committee on the Government's valuation proposals for England and Wales, was that in London and the great towns of Yorkshire and Lancashire it was the common case for working-class houses to occupy valuable land in the central districts, and the inhabitants of these houses would simply be driven out if the land was rated on its capital value. 'It would be necessary', he claimed, 'for the landowner to evict the population as quickly as possible in order that he might devote the land to some purpose capable of producing the building rent at which it is assessed.' To help meet this problem Robson proposed a scheme for the deferment of any site value rate on such property 'until the building value from being prospective becomes immediate'.[78] Burns thought the proposal counter-productive, in that one of the main objects of site value rating was supposedly to force land on to the market, and Lloyd George's attitude became simply that Robson was intent on protecting the slum landlords.[79]

The positive contribution to working-class housing from the rating of the capital value of land lay in the anticipated encouragement to suburban housing development. What this raised was the question of whether the rating of site values should be extended beyond urban boundaries so as to apply to building land in neighbouring rural areas. Robson in his memorandum strongly advised such an extension, and what he recommended particularly was a tax on the future unearned increment of such land. The case commonly urged against an unearned increment tax, he pointed out, was that the measure came too late for the towns, but it certainly would not come too late for the rural districts. The tax, Robson suggested, should be levied not only at intervals but whenever land was sold to ensure that 'the local authority gets its share whenever the landowner gets his'.

What Robson did not seem to appreciate was that an unearned increment tax would prove far less effective than a straight capital value tax in forcing land on to the market and, in so far as it was levied when land was sold, its effect in fact would be to make land more expensive to buy. The primary purposes to be served by an unearned increment tax were rather the raising of revenue and the recovery by government of the land value increments created by the growth of the community. For these very reasons, indeed, Lloyd George rather favoured the idea of an unearned increment tax when he turned his mind to providing for land value taxation in his Budget for 1909/10. During his visit to Germany in August he investigated the operation of the unearned increment tax pioneered in 1904 by Frankfurt-am-Main, consequently known as the Frankfurt tax, and on his return he got Bernard Mallet to prepare him a special memorandum on the taxation of increment value in Frankfurt and other German cities.[80] His idea was to couple such a tax with a straight capital value tax, a move not altogether welcome to the ardent land taxers in the Commons and the country. 'Lloyd George will try to tackle Land Values & ruin the whole business', Ralph Wedgwood predicted to his brother Josiah. 'He is an unprincipled speculator in want of funds, and it is the worst thing that can happen to Land Values that it shd be brought in as a means of raising the wind and not as a *transference* of a burden.'[81]

In practice, of course, Lloyd George could expect very little by way of new revenue in 1909/10 from either land value taxes or a supertax; land value taxes in particular, which necessitated an altogether new valuation, would require several years before they could ever produce much revenue. A far more promising potential source of new revenue for 1909/10 which Asquith had helped to open up was the licence duties. As a consequence of the alterations Asquith made in 1907/8 in the system for central government funding of local taxation accounts, it was now possible for Lloyd George to benefit the Exchequer itself by increasing licence duties. On licensing, again, as on land valuation, taxation in the next Budget offered the Government a potential means for attaining some of its political objectives against the wishes of the Lords.

In February Asquith had introduced the Government's Licensing Bill in the Commons. The Bill provided for the reduction in the number of on-licences to a scheduled minimum, based on the ratio between licences and population, in a period of fourteen years; at the end of the period the number of existing licences would have been reduced by about a third, representing at least twice as many reductions likely to be secured under the provisions of the 1904 Licensing Act. During the period compensation for licences abolished for redundancy would continue to be paid out of the compensation levy on 'the trade' provided for in the Licensing Act of 1904, but thereafter compensation would cease to be payable, all licences being treated as new, with the 'monopoly value' created by the grant of a licence being recovered by the state. The chief features of the Bill, in short, were the speeding up of the process of licence reduction and the imposition of a time-limit for the payment of compensation.

Time and again, while the Licensing Bill was progressing through the Commons in the face of a furious opposition from the Unionists and 'the trade', Government spokesmen warned that if the Bill was thrown out when it reached the Lords this would inevitably mean 'high licensing' in the next Budget. Some temperance reformers, indeed, held that a system of high licensing would in fact prove more effective than the Licensing Bill in reducing the number of licensed houses; the less profitable houses would simply be taxed out of existence. The contention urged by Joseph Rowntree and Arthur Sherwell in *The Taxation of the Liquor Trade,* the second edition of which appeared in 1908, was that 'While we are spending time and effort and money, and incurring great risks, in our endeavour to secure the reduction of licences, we could easily effect a greater reduction than the most ardent temperance reformer anticipates by a simple but just revision of the licence duties.' The United Kingdom Alliance itself, however, did not regard high licensing as an adequate substitute for temperance legislation. It warned the Government: 'It cannot be assumed that any financial rehandling of duties on the Liquor Trader can act or be accepted as a substitute for the legislative measures which are indispensable for temperance reform.'[82]

On 27 November the Lords went ahead and rejected the Licensing Bill, a move which Lloyd George positively welcomed from the standpoint of his finances for the next year. He soon let the word out that he had organized a 'thanksgiving service' in the Treasury. As he told George Riddell, 'he was looking foward to taxing the trade'.[83] Churchill's response to the rejection of the Licensing Bill was more belligerent in tone. At dinner with the Mastermans and the Buxtons he announced: 'We shall send them up such a Budget in June as shall terrify them, they have started the class war, they had better be careful.'[84]

What the rejection of the Licensing Bill made unmistakably clear was that the Government had reached the end of the road in its attempts to carry the traditional aspects of the Liberal programme by conventional means.

IV

Lloyd George began active preparation of his first Budget in October. By the end of the month the Inland Revenue prepared proposals and estimates for increasing the income tax on unearned incomes and for a supertax on incomes over £4,000, and for increases in the estate duties and stamps. The Board of Customs was simultaneously preparing proposals for 'any increase of Licence duties'.[85] The taxation of land values in the next Budget was being considered by the Cabinet committee set up in June to review Burns's valuation proposals.

Before starting work on his Budget, Lloyd George had visited Germany in the company of Harold Spender and Charles Henry, the millionaire Liberal MP. Lloyd George's German visit to study the Bismarckian system of social insurances has sometimes been seen as marking his transformation into an advanced social reformer, but the experience of managing the Government's old-age pensions scheme in the Commons had more to do with this transformation than the visit to Germany itself. The constant references in the Commons debates to the German system of contributory old-age and sickness insurance inspired Lloyd George, quite typically, to take a firsthand look at the German system for himself, and on his return he closeted himself with Churchill to work out a grand design for adding a system of national health and unemployment insurance to the provisions already sanctioned by Parliament for old age pensions. Hitherto the Liberal Government had lacked a strategy of social reform; Lloyd George and Churchill were now devising such a strategy, and Lloyd George intended that his forthcoming Budget should provide the fiscal underpinning for a comprehensive programme of social reform. If he had his way, the next Budget would not simply be a makeshift attempt to meet an immediate deficit.

From the standpoint of Liberal thinking on matters of finance and taxation, the novelty of the Budget Lloyd George had in mind lay not in any of its individual proposals, for much of the groundwork had already been laid for each of the proposals, but in the fact that they were all to be included within the framework of a single Budget. The demands of politics and finance alike encouraged Lloyd George to produce a Budget that would at one and the same time prove the resources of free trade finance, provide a fund for advanced social reform, and offer a way round the veto of the Lords on the issues of land valuation and licensing. As Hobhouse detected, Lloyd George became determined in the autumn of 1908 that his Budget should include a wide range of new taxes, even if they were not absolutely essential to help him meet his real deficit for 1909/10. 'Ll.G.', Hobhouse remarked in his diary on 17 November, 'is now on a new tack, he encourages ministers to spend, so that he may have justification for the extra millions he proposes to ask for next year.'[86]

One of the question marks in the autumn of 1908 was whether Lloyd George would carry sufficient weight with his ministerial colleagues to get their sanction for the far-reaching and radical Budget he had in mind. His stocks were then lower than they had ever been since he became a Cabinet minister. The Prime Minister, to begin with, thought Lloyd George had made himself 'ridiculous' in his attempts to play the 'Peace promoter' during his visit to Germany, and that he had only been stopped from 'making an ass of himself' by the 'really strong' telegram Grey and Asquith had found themselves obliged to send to him in Berlin.[87] In the Cabinet, again, the Lloyd George–Churchill combination had made itself so disliked and distrusted that their colleagues were inclined to 'distrust everything they advance'.[88] John Burns, who in October suffered through their interventions on the unemployment question, even suspected them of 'intriguing for a dissolution in the Spring'.[89] Some Treasury officials, moreover, led by Murray, were disseminating fairly indiscriminately stories of Lloyd George's incompetence and laziness; according to the Unionist peer, Lord Midleton, the Treasury were *'openly* mutinous' about Lloyd George, and Walter Long found Murray 'very amusing about his Chancellor'.[90] Treasury officials seem also to have had a hand in spreading scandals about Lloyd George's friendship with Charles Henry's attractive American-born wife, Julia. The *Bystander* had already suggested that Lloyd George might be named as co-respondent in a divorce case, and the further scandal-mongering about his friendship with Julia Henry was sufficient to occasion a long talk on the matter between Asquith and Jack Pease at the end of October. Pease assured the Prime Minister that he thought the relationship was purely 'platonic' and that it was 'due to a pushy American heiress' desire to get on socially'.[91]

The Westminster cliques hostile to Lloyd George sensed in the second half of 1908 that the Chancellor might in fact be riding for a fall. Margot Asquith reckoned Lloyd George's failure at the Treasury as 'inevitable', and Haldane even felt encouraged to suggest to Asquith that the Budget for 1909/10 be taken out of the Chancellor's hands.[92]

In the event, when in March 1909 Lloyd George came to present his Budget proposals to the Cabinet, he possessed more leverage with his colleagues than most of them cared for. The majority in the Cabinet did not particularly like much of the 'People's Budget', but the political plight the Government found itself in more or less obliged them to accept the over-all design of Lloyd George's proposed Budget. With by-elections continuing to go against the Government, unemployment deepening, the Tariff Reformers becoming increasingly assertive, and the Government's own following increasingly restive, a bold new initiative was required. As the *Manchester Guardian* made clear after the rejection of the Licensing Bill by the Lords, the Liberal rank and file were not inclined to accept another round of 'mere disorganized demonstration in verbal force' from the Government in response to the defiance of the Lords.[93]

The Budget proposals Lloyd George was to produce represented a bold initiative along a wide front, and one that was likely to rally the rank and file. No alternative initiatives were forthcoming.

V. Preparation of the Budget

I

The question of whether Lloyd George designed his 'People's Budget' so as to invite its rejection by the House of Lords is one that has long intrigued scholars and political commentators. The view that he did so prevailed until the early 1950s, and then went largely out of favour following the publication in 1954 of Roy Jenkins's *Mr. Balfour's Poodle;* thereafter it became generally accepted that Lloyd George devised his Budget as an alternative to rather than as a means to a confrontation with the Lords. As argued by Jenkins, and others since, Lloyd George assumed that the peers would not dare tamper with a finance bill, and he consequently looked to his Budget as a way around the veto of the Lords; by means of it he hoped to attain some radical objectives against the wishes of the Lords.[1]

Lloyd George's design in preparing the 'People's Budget' was far more complex and politically astute than is generally recognized. He set out to achieve a number of goals and to cater for several contingencies, including the possibility that the Lords might reject the Budget. He intended that his Budget should prove the resources of free trade finance, that it should provide the fiscal foundations for a comprehensive programme of social reform, and that it should attempt to circumvent the veto of the Lords on the issues of land valuation and licensing. Contrary to what is sometimes held, both he and Asquith were aware that the Lords might go so far as to reject or amend such a Budget, and what the evidence indicates is that Lloyd George regarded such a possibility as a contingency which had to be guarded against before he ever looked upon it as an objective worth realizing.

Lloyd George's over-all political goal in the Budget was to restore the Government's credibility and, as he had put it to his brother when he took over as Chancellor, to 'stop the electoral rot'.[2] In the winter of 1908–9 rejection or amendment by the Lords seemed more likely to follow from a Budget that failed to improve the standing of the Government, than from one that succeeded. 'He agrees with me', Courtenay Ilbert, the clerk of the House of Commons, entered in his diary on 29 March 1909 after having discussed the prospects of the forthcoming Budget with Lloyd George, 'that if the Gov: is weak & the budget unpopular, the Lords would not hesitate to throw out the Finance Bill in the autumn.'[3]

Two key elements in the political situation in which the Budget was prepared were, first, that Asquith's Cabinet was intensely pessimistic as to the immediate electoral prospects of the Liberal party, and, second, that Unionists were already threatening to force a general election by securing the Budget's rejection in the Lords.

Following the rejection of the Licensing Bill, the Cabinet anxiously debated the question of a dissolution. On 9 December it reached the unanimous decision that an immediate dissolution was to be avoided.[4] The reason for the unanimity was not hard to seek; resignation, as Burns noted in his diary, meant 'defeat inevitable and crushing'.[5] This remained the accepted verdict among Cabinet ministers up to the introduction of the Budget in the Commons. At the end of March 1909 Lloyd George told Ilbert that 'if there were a general election now the forecast would be a minority'. Trade, he explained, was bad, and the South of England was scared.[6]

The Cabinet's rejection of the idea of an immediate dissolution did not mean an automatic decision in favour of 'holding on' for another two years. According to what Riddell heard from J. M. Fuller, a Junior Whip, at the Cabinet meeting of 9 December three ministers, supposedly including Lloyd George and Churchill, argued in favour of preparing the ground for an early dissolution, perhaps to follow the Budget.[7] The information Lloyd George gave to his brother was that there was to be 'no dissolution — at least not before the Budget is over'.[8] The Government's own options, clearly, would depend heavily on the Budget and the reception it received.

In looking to their prospects for 1909, Asquith and his

colleagues had to take into consideration that the decision
for a dissolution might not rest with them but with the
Unionists, acting through the Lords. They could not ignore
the fact that the idea that the Lords should reject the next
Budget was being actively canvassed in Unionist circles, but
they were never certain as to how seriously they should take
such a threat.

The possibility that the Lords might reject the Budget for
1909/10 was first seriously mooted in November 1908, and
by Budget Day on 29 April 1909 there already existed the
nucleus of a movement for the peers to take drastic action
against the Budget with a view to forcing a general election.
In November 1908 the Liberal threat that the rejection of the
Licensing Bill by the Lords would inevitably mean high
licensing duties in the next Budget, together with the pressure of the Land Values Group for a land valuation scheme
to be incorporated in the next Budget, raised the question of
whether the peers would allow the Government to get away
with any resort to a finance bill as a means of getting round
the veto of the Lords. Sections of the Unionist press strenuously urged the peers to prevent the success of any such
tactics by throwing the Budget out.[9] By April 1908, moreover, the more ardent Tariff Reformers, convinced that
circumstances now strongly favoured them, were anxious
to force a general election by getting the Lords to reject the
forthcoming Budget. At the beginning of April Henry Chaplin
wrote to Balfour from Cairo advising the rejection of the
Budget; he had no doubt that the moment to strike had
come.[10] On 23 April Lord Ridley, the chairman of the
Tariff Reform League, publicly proclaimed that the time had
come for the House of Lords to 'take its share' in the financial
legislation for the country.[11]

Lloyd George's own initial reaction to the suggestions and
threats that the Lords might reject his Budget was to dismiss
the idea. On 24 November, at breakfast with Riddell, he
'ridiculed the rumour that the Peers would or could interfere
with or reject the Budget'.[12] This did not stop him, in some
of his speeches, from daring the Lords to carry out any such
threat, but he does not seem to have been able to convince
himself that matters would come to such a pass. On 29

March he agreed with Ilbert that if the Government was weak, and the Budget unpopular, the Lords would not hesitate to throw the Finance Bill out, but he added that he somehow doubted whether 'the Opposition are really playing for a general election in the autumn'.[13]

Asquith, for his part, took the threat that the Lords might reject the Budget seriously enough to advise Pease to keep such a contingency in mind. On 8 December Asquith discussed the over-all political situation with Pease, and was told by Pease that the party was against an immediate dissolution, but 'wanted something said to show we were not taking the Lords rebuff to the Commons lying down'. Then, according to Pease: 'We discussed what would happen if the Lords threw out the budget. He said keep it at the back of your mind that we may have a dissolution in July if they do.'[14]

Three days later, in a speech at the National Liberal Club, Asquith made his first public allusion to the possibility that the Lords might force a general election by rejecting the Budget. What he suggested in his speech was that finance was 'an instrument of great potency and also of great flexibility' that might provide 'a partial solvent' to the problem of the Lords, but in discussing the question of a dissolution he also indicated his awareness that any seeming attempt at 'tacking' in the next Budget would provoke a furious outcry in the Lords, perhaps leading to the Budget's rejection by the peers. The comment his remarks drew from *The Times* was that the Prime Minister had inferred that 'the Budget will contain applications of the power of finance of such a character that the House of Lords may be driven to reject the Budget Bill itself'.[15]

Ten days after Asquith's speech, Lloyd George made his first public reference to the question of the Lords and the next Budget. In a speech at Liverpool he suggested that, when the time came for the Budget to go to the Lords, the Tariff Reformers might seek to force a showdown on finance by getting the peers to throw his Budget out, and he sought to make it clear that he was fully prepared for any such contingency, and that he and his colleagues were preparing their strategy to do decisive battle with the enemies of Liberalism. 'The Budget', he declared, 'has got to go on some time next year, and if they want to put the alternative of taxing bread, by all means let them do it.'[16]

After these speeches, Churchill got 'inside' word that Lansdowne would have nothing to do with the idea that the Lords should reject the next Budget. On Boxing Day he wrote to Asquith: 'I learn that Lansdowne in private utterly scouts the suggestion that the Lords will reject the Budget Bill . . . On this assumption you will I presume be making your plans for two more complete sessions.' Thereafter Churchill bombarded Asquith with plans for a comprehensive programme of social reform to carry the Liberal Government over the next two years. His advice to the Prime Minister in his letters of late December was that it would be politically more advisable, and intrinsically far more important, for the Government to unfold and carry through 'an impressive social policy' than it would be for it to focus on the Lords issue and work towards an early general election.[17]

This remained Churchill's theme until the eve of the introduction of the Budget in the Commons. On 22 January he wrote to H. W. Massingham, the editor of the *Nation*, that he did not think the Lords would interfere with the Government's plans to produce and to finance during the next two sessions a comprehensive programme of social reform. 'I am sure', he observed, 'they cannot do so without coming near to creating that conjunction of forces which is most dangerous to them.'[18] But as Budget Day approached, and as threats that the Lords might reject the Budget revived, Churchill became more ready to concede that the Budget might be thrown out by the peers. 'Tomorrow', he wrote to his wife on the eve of Budget Day, 'is the day of wrath! I feel this Budget will be kill or cure! Either we shall secure ample funds for great reforms next year, or the Lords will force a Dissolution in September.'[19]

From the foregoing exchanges and speeches, it is impossible to conclude that Lloyd George, or any of his major colleagues, intended that the Budget should provoke a final crisis between the Liberal Government and the Lords. He and they recognized that the Lords might be tempted to throw out the forthcoming Budget, but such a prospect seemed remote, and there is no indication that Lloyd George was encouraged by it to devise a Budget designed to force rejection upon the Lords. Rather, Lloyd George and the Cabinet showed themselves more anxious to deny the Lords positive reason or justification for tampering with the Budget. It was so as to deny the Lords any constitutional justification for interfering with the Budget that Lloyd George persuaded the Cabinet that the land valuation clauses had to include provision for raising some money in 1909/10; without such a provision the land valuation might justifiably be regarded as a 'tack'.[20] For the rest, it is probably true to say that the contents of the 'People's Budget' would have been no different even if there had been no prospect that the Lords might reject or amend the Budget. The decision to include land valuation clauses in the Budget in the first place, and the remainder of Lloyd George's proposals, were inspired by considerations independent of any prospect that the Lords might reject the Budget.

II

From the moment Lloyd George began the active preparation of his Budget in October 1908 he was determined that its yields should be as much political as financial, and it was his frankly political approach that gave rise to much of the Treasury murmurings about his work methods in the latter part of 1908. According to what Lord Midleton heard from his Treasury sources in late November, Lloyd George could hardly bring himself to 'understand the commonest figures, his whole mind being set on bargains and party catchwords'.[21]

Among Lloyd George's first concerns was his determination to break what he saw as the Government's pattern of abandoning its declared objective whenever it was faced by obstruction by the Lords, and to use his Budget to restore confidence in the Government's ability to respond effectively to the challenge of the Lords. Once the Cabinet decided it would not proceed with a valuation bill for England and Wales in 1908, Lloyd George became determined to include valuation clauses in his Budget. On 21 October he called in C. F. G. Masterman, the Parliamentary Secretary to the Local Government Board, who was to lend considerable assistance in preparing the land value taxes, and 'went off' about the Budget, land taxation, and the Government's behaviour in dealing with the Lords. In between urging Masterman to convert Churchill, who hardly qualified as a fiscal radical, to the cause of land taxation — 'he is not with us on that' — and suggesting that he was about to take the field for 'a real democratic policy', Lloyd George fulminated about the Government's readiness to drop its proposals and turn its attention to something else once the Lords obstructed the way:

First we said, "We'll have the parson out of the schools". The House of Lords said "No you shan't". We said "What, you say we shan't. Then we will have a go at the Scotch Landlords". Then the House of Lords said "Hands off the Scotch Landlords", and we said "What, you won't let us touch the Scotch Landlords, then we'll go for the brewers". Then the House of Lords will say "Hands off the brewers" and we shall say "You won't let us touch the brewers. Then we shall go for the Welsh Church". I tell you, Masterman, when the Lords rejected Birrell's bill, there were only two of us in the Cabinet in favour of a dissolution; I was one and Edward Grey was the other.[22]

By making provision in his Budget for land valuation Lloyd George intended that on that issue at least the Government should not abandon its declared objectives in the face of the opposition of the Lords.

Once it became clear that the Lords would reject the Licensing Bill, Lloyd George was equally determined to use the Budget to realize, so far as was practicable, the objectives of the Licensing Bill. On 25 November, the day after Unionist peers had met at Lansdowne House to determine the fate of the Licensing Bill in the Lords, Lloyd George wrote to his brother: 'I am thinking out some exquisite plans for out-witting the Lords on Licensing.'[23] He welcomed the opportunity to hit back at the Lords, as well as needed the money from taxing licences. The problem he was to face was that of devising licence duties that would at one and the same time promote a reduction in the number of licensed houses and guarantee him the revenue he wanted.

Another of Lloyd George's primary concerns in his Budget preparation was to establish, once and for all, the resources of free trade finance and give free trade a new popularity as against tariff reform. In the opinion of *The Economist,* Lord Cromer put the challenge before Lloyd George 'very fairly' when he said at Leeds on 18 January 1909 that: 'What Mr. Lloyd George has to show is how he can meet the very heavy liabilities he has incurred and yet preserve intact the system of Free-trade.'[24] Lloyd George's response to the challenge was to seek to prove that he could provide the funds to meet, not only his liabilities for 1909/10, but all foreseeable future liabilities, without infringing the canons of free trade finance; his Budget was to be a conclusive demonstration of the ability of free trade finance to cater for a vast programme of social reform and the growing defence requirements of the nation. More than that, his Budget was to be an example of 'democratic' finance. It would be a 'People's Budget', not only in the sense that it would raise the money for old-age pensions and other social welfare schemes, but also in the sense that it would tap the required new sources of revenue in a democratic way. Rather than resort to a 'stomach-tax', he would provide the basis for land value taxation and a supertax. The whole controversy between free trade and tariff reform, he hoped, could then be reduced to the beautifully simple issue of taxing the land of parasitic landlords and the incomes of the rich as against taxing the food of the people.

In short, Lloyd George intended that his Budget should be an effective rejoinder to the Tariff Reformers as well as to the obstructionism of the Lords on the issues of land valuation and licensing. By means of providing a sound financial basis for further social reforms, moreover, he intended that his Budget should open up new possibilities of constructive achievement in a field where the Lords had shown itself reluctant to obstruct the Government's work.

At the end of 1908 Lloyd George found himself obliged, both by the pressure of his budget work and the complications surrounding his invalidity scheme, to abandon all thought of introducing a scheme for national health insurance in 1909. He and Churchill consequently agreed to postpone both health and unemployment insurance until 1910.[25] Nevertheless, Lloyd George intended that his Budget should provide the financial underpinnings for national insurance, as well as the funds required for old-age pensions, Churchill's labour exchanges, and the various development schemes he and Churchill were thinking of for 1909. As Lloyd George was constantly to impress upon his Cabinet colleagues, and later the Commons, he designed his Budget not simply as a short-term solution to an immediate financial emergency, but as a 'War Budget' for raising the money to wage 'implacable warfare against poverty and squalidness'.

In terms of the Government's planning for the future, this meant that Lloyd George, in his Budget preparation, was taking direction of all planning, and encompassing in his Budget the Government's entire programme for the future. What was certainly made evident to him in early December was that the Government had no programme other than what he was to provide in his Budget.

All the evidence suggests that at the meeting of 9 December the Cabinet was quite at a loss on how to plan for the future. It was agreed that a dissolution in response to the rejection of the Licensing Bill was out of the question, and that the next Budget would be vital, but nothing more was settled. As Crewe informed Morley, who had missed the meeting: 'The feeling seemed to be that the Budget must be our next landmark, and that it was not much use to think of particular measures at present.'[26]

Uncomfortably aware that the Government had reached the end of the road in the attempt to realize the traditional Liberal programme by conventional means, and wondering how much of a future was left to it, several members of the Cabinet were overcome by feelings of helplessness. Balfour and the Lords, Carrington confessed in his diary entry for 5 December, were 'masters of the situation' and he added: 'It is difficult to know what to do.' A week later he gloomily recorded: 'We are in a very tight place: if not actually on the rocks.'[27] What the Government had throughout been lacking, Morley suggested to Crewe on 10 December, was any real leadership or sense of direction: 'The truth is we have never had chart, course, or compass.'[28] A large part of Lloyd George's purpose in his Budget, and the whole purpose of Churchill's post-Christmas letters to Asquith, was to provide the Government with a chart that could carry it through the the next two years.

Where Churchill diverged from Lloyd George was in the single-minded commitment he developed for devising and carrying through an 'impressive social policy', thereby providing a perfect example of what Lloyd George complained about, namely the readiness of his colleagues to abandon earlier objectives once they had been obstructed by the Lords and to turn to action on other matters. In his letter of 29 December to Asquith, urging the case for a 'tremendous policy of Social Organization', Churchill contended that all the items he had in mind could be 'carried triumphantly', and even if it proved they could not, he argued that it was 'much better to fail in such noble efforts, than to perish by slow paralysis or windy agitation'.[29] What Churchill seems to have lost sight of was the pressure from the rank and file of the party, not for a 'windy agitation', but for a real plan of action for dealing with the Lords to be unfolded in the new year.

The beauty of the Budget Lloyd George had in mind was that it would cater effectively for all the major options and possibilities before the Government and at the same time it would restore credibility in the ability of the Government to respond effectively to the challenges of the Lords and the Tariff Reformers. The Budget he was devising was intended as a political 'catchall' — it would provide the financial foundations for the 'impressive social policy' Churchill envisaged for the next two years and it would simultaneously seek to meet the electioneering requirements of the party in the event of an early general election becoming desirable or necessary; it would attempt to 'circumnavigate' the veto of the Lords on the issues of land valuation and licensing, and it would seek to undermine the revenue argument for tariffs and give a new popularity to free trade. In all its aspects, Lloyd George's handiwork was inspired by his conviction that 'the fate of the Government depends on the Budget entirely'.[30]

III

The preparation of the 'People's Budget' proved a long and complicated undertaking that strained the resources and the tempers of the officials involved. Lloyd George had begun active preparation of the Budget in October, a good six months before it was due to be presented to the Commons, and by early December the main outlines of the Budget had taken shape after he had spent November 'working hard and systematically (for a wonder)' at it. By 9 December he was able to report to his brother: 'The Prime Minister has approved my plans as they now are. I was with him now. Budget sensational.'[31] According to Hobhouse's diary, Lloyd George was then planning to raise an additional £12 million 'by lowering the range of the income tax so as to fully tax people with incomes of £500, by a surtax on incomes over £5,000; by a 2/- capital tax on non agricultural land: and by high licences and increase on tea'.[32] All but the proposals with regard to the income tax and tea, if ever seriously entertained, formed the core of the Budget Lloyd George presented to the Cabinet in March and April of the next year.

An outstanding feature of the administrative preparation of the Budget was the hostility that Lloyd George's proposals and methods of work engendered among senior officials. To an extraordinary extent Lloyd George had either to bully or short-circuit certain senior officials, and he had also to bully members of the Cabinet Committee assigned to assist with the preparation of the land value duties. With Guillemard at Customs and Excise, who resented Lloyd George's directives and his erratic methods, the Chancellor had to adopt a very firm attitude, and Murray at the Treasury he largely ignored, along with Hobhouse. As Hobhouse sensed, he regarded 'Murray and myself as mere marplots'.[33]

Part of the explanation for the irritation and hostility that Lloyd George aroused in officials was his style and method, or apparent lack of method. He knew basically what he wanted to tax, but his ideas as to how those taxes should be levied were often very fluid, and his grasp of detail was, from all accounts, shaky at best. The result was a plethora of projected schemes for taxing land, estates, stamps, incomes, and licences. According to Hobhouse, Lloyd George badly strained his relations with heads of departments by demanding 'the preparation by Depts. and Draftsmen of successive schemes of licences, land taxation, and death duties each more impossible than the other'. By mid-April, if Hobhouse is to be believed, the heads of departments were 'in a state of revolt and insubordination' which was 'quite indescribable'.[34] This was certainly true of Murray and Guillemard, and even Chalmers at the Inland Revenue had sometimes lost patience at Lloyd George's darting proposals and demands for estimates, as is evident from the stiff tone of the memorandum he sent Lloyd George on 6 March on income tax abatements.[35] Another source of irritation with officials was that papers simply ceased to circulate once they reached Lloyd George's desk. 'It is impossible to get papers out of the C. of E.', an exasperated Bradbury wrote to Chalmers in early March. 'So please both for my convenience and to save yourself trouble in future send me duplicates of everything.'[36]

The main source of hostility among certain senior officials was, however, the nature of Lloyd George's proposals. Guillemard strongly objected to using licence duties for any purposes other than raising revenue, and Murray disliked the whole design of the projected Budget. At the end of December, in an extraordinary breach of official confidence, Murray wrote to Lord Rosebery: ' . . . I cannot believe that your House will swallow the Budget if the mature infant turns out to be anything like the embryo which I now contemplate daily with horror.'[37] Hobhouse shared Murray's opinion of the Budget proposals, if not his indiscretions. 'Such proposals,' he commented in his diary on 8 December, 'if propounded to the country, ought to insure the rejection of the budget by the Lords, enforce a dissolution, and ensure our irretrievable defeat.'

What is evident from Hobhouse's diary and Treasury gossip is that Lloyd George, rather than his officials, was responsible for the basic design of the 'People's Budget'. Lloyd George, to be sure, relied to a considerable extent on the advice of Chalmers at the Inland Revenue, whom Margot Asquith regarded as the real author of the Budget.[38] Chalmers was certainly fully armed with proposals for direct taxes, notably for the income tax and supertax, but the main design of the 'People's Budget' derived from Lloyd George's understanding of the strategy Asquith had developed for Liberal finance, his own perception of the political requirements of the

Liberal Government, and his own commitment to social reform.

What Margot Asquith attributed directly to Chalmers was the Budget's 'somewhat oriental method of asking for more than it intended to take'. The whole tendency, encouraged by Chalmers, in devising the estimates for the Budget was in fact to accentuate rather than to minimize the prospective deficit for 1909/10.

The question of the estimates, and the deficit to be catered for, was central. Whatever the juggling of figures, Lloyd George was confronted by an exceptionally large prospective deficit, but he seems to have been intent on making his deficit appear rather larger than it really was so as to provide fiscal justification for all his new taxes and so as to ensure a surplus at the end of the year, thereby underlining the capabilities of free trade finance. The estimates arrived at in early March 1909 for the returns for 1909/10 from existing taxes were consistently conservative, and the estimates for certain items of expenditure made liberal allowances for contingencies. At the same time Lloyd George was determined to contain his real deficit, and strenuously resisted the demands of the Admiralty to escalate the planned shipbuilding programme for 1909/10.

As set out on 26 February by A. Stair, the figures for the Inland Revenue for existing taxes were as follows:[39]

	Budget Estimate 1908/9 £	Anticipated Revenue 1908/9 £	Budget Estimate 1909/10 £
Excise	34,230,000	33,215,000	32,800,000
Estate Duties	19,500,000	18,269,000	18,500,000
Stamps	8,080,000	7,680,000	7,650,000
Land Taxes etc.	2,600,000	2,610,000	2,650,000
Income Tax	33,000,000	33,500,000	33,000,000
Total	97,410,000	95,274,000	94,600,000

As it proved at the close of the fiscal year, Stair had underestimated the yields for 1908/9 by a little over £1,000,000. Excise yielded £435,000 more than his estimate, estate duties £101,000, the land tax and house duty £20,000,

and income tax £430,000.[40] His figures none the less provided
the basis for the estimates adopted in early March, which
were to be presented to the Cabinet in early April, except
for the income tax, which was revised substantially upwards.
On 2 March Chalmers reckoned the estimate of £33,000,000
too low, and claimed there was no reason to put it below
£33,500,000.[41] The estimate given the Cabinet on 7 April
provided for £33,900,000 from the income tax. At the
behest of Guillemard at Customs, which was to be amalgamated with Excise on 1 April, Stair's estimate for excise was
reduced to £32,560,000.[42]

The estimates presented to the Cabinet on 7 April were:

	£
Excise	32,560,000
Estate Duties	18,600,000
Stamps	7,600,000
Land Tax etc.	2,650,000
Income Tax	33,900,000
Total	95,310,000

The figure for customs, as for excise, anticipated a marked
decline in consumption, and the estimated returns for 1909/10
were substantially lower than receipts for 1908/9. The
estimate for customs given to the Cabinet was £28,100,000,
as against receipts of £29,200,000 in 1908/9.[43]

With regard to expenditure Lloyd George's two major
new items were old-age pensions and increased naval construction. On the first, Lloyd George was anxious to make
generous allowances for contingencies; on the second he was
determined to resist the Admiralty's demands for six or even
eight new Dreadnoughts in 1909/10 instead of the previously
anticipated total of four. He had allocated £2,000,000 for
additional naval expenditure in 1909/10, and was anxious to
keep to something like that figure. To give in to Admiralty
demands might add substantially to his real deficit, and
perhaps even sabotage his design to make his Budget a show-
piece of free trade finance. As he told his brother after the
Cabinet meetings of December 1908 on the naval estimates,
McKenna, as First Lord of the Admiralty, threatened to
'ruin my financial plans by his extravagant demands'.[44]

On old-age pensions, the Government had been badly caught out on its original estimates; their cost, in practice, proved far higher than ever anticipated. Asquith had put the cost of his old-age pension proposals at about £6,000,000 in a full year, whereas by March 1909 it was evident that over £8,000,000 would be required to meet the bill for 1909/10. In Asquith's estimate, some 572,000 persons over seventy were likely to qualify for pensions; by 31 March 1909 as many as 668,201 persons had already been granted pensions, and 54,421 claims were still outstanding. A total of 102,100 claims had been rejected. The average weekly pension for the entire United Kingdom was 4s. 9d.[45]

Ireland provided the chief explanation for the 'startling' underestimate of the total number of likely pensioners. As Lloyd George told the Commons in February 1909, the estimate for Great Britain had proved 'surprisingly' accurate, but Ireland was another matter. According to a report of A. J. Tedder, Chief Inspector of Excise, which was responsible for the administration of pensions, it had always been accepted that the greatest problems would be experienced in Ireland, but 'no one had the faintest idea that the claims would be anything like the number actually received'. The main difficulty in Ireland, Tedder intimated, arose from the absence in many districts of documentary proof of age, and this had resulted in many fraudulent claims being made. In 1908 more than 5 per cent of the claims received in Ireland had been rejected on the score of age, against only 1¼ per cent in England.[46] None the less, the number of pensions actually awarded in Ireland greatly exceeded all estimates; of the 596,076 pensions paid from 1 January 1909, Ireland accounted for 170,382. In 1911 the census for Ireland showed a staggering 84 per cent increase in the population aged between 70 and 80 years over the 1901 census.[47]

In Lloyd George's opinion the successful 'avoidance' of the pauper disqualification was a key factor in explaining the burgeoning number of pensions awards, and he reckoned 'avoidance' would result in rather more grants during 1909/10 than his officials calculated. The memoranda he received from his officials in early March 1909 all suggested that the genuine initial claims were by then nearly exhausted, with the remaining outstanding claims being largely 'try-ons'. New septuagenarians, not disqualified by poor relief and not offset by deaths among existing pensioners, were calculated by R. G. Hawtrey to add 2 per cent to the number of pensioners during the course of 1909/10. In memoranda of 5 and 6 March, he put the total charge of pensions for 1909/10 at £8,516,820.[48] Bradbury, Hawtrey's chief at the finance division of the Treasury, thought a total estimate of £8,500,000 would be quite safe, but given that the Chancellor held that 'avoidance' of the pauper disqualification would have a greater financial effect than his officials anticipated, and given that the Chancellor had made it clear that he was 'very anxious to avoid an under-estimate', Bradbury reckoned on 6 March that the estimate had better be in the order of £8,750,000.[49] This was the figure finally adopted. The actual charge for old age pensions in 1909/10 proved to be £8,496,395.

With regard to expenditure on the navy, Lloyd George had by December 1908 reconciled himself to having to provide an additional £2,000,000 in 1909/10 for various projects, including the laying down of four new Dreadnoughts. Whatever fuss Lloyd George had in June threatened to create over the £2,000,000 was no longer politically feasible by the end of the year, given reports of an acceleration in German naval construction. What dismayed Lloyd George in December was that McKenna's navy estimates called for an additional £3,000,000, not £2,000,000, and included provision for six rather than four new Dreadnoughts. According to Asquith's report to the King on the Cabinet's deliberations of 18 and 19 December, the navy estimates were in substance approved after much discussion, but with the reservation that consideration of the extra two Dreadnoughts would be held over until the New Year.[50]

In the new year Lloyd George found that he had to fight furiously to keep the provision for the navy down to McKenna's original estimate. In January the Sea Lords urged that German acceleration in shipbuilding now required that Britain lay down eight new Dreadnoughts in 1909/10, the last two at the end of March 1910, for completion by the spring of 1912.

In conjunction with Churchill, and supported by Burns, Harcourt, and Morley, Lloyd George responded by challenging head-on 'the very crude and ill-considered Admiralty demands'. Controversy raged in the Cabinet until late in February. At the Cabinet meeting of 24 February the issue of new construction was finally resolved when Asquith took 'immediate advantage' of a 'sudden curve' in the argument and secured agreement to lay down four new Dreadnoughts in 1909, and another four no later than 1 April 1910 if the necessity for them was proven.[51] In that event, Treasury bills to meet expenditure for gathering materials for the extra four ships would be issued in 1909/10, but the actual cost would be a liability on the subsequent financial year.[52] 'And so', Austen Chamberlain snorted in disgust after this compromise arrangement had been outlined in the Commons, 'Lloyd George's Budget was to be eased, the Little Navy men were to be told it was a programme of only four ships and the Big Navy men were to be assured that it was really eight.'[53]

When the navy estimates were published on 12 March, they provided for a total of £35,142,700 in 1909/10, an increase of £2,823,200 on the previous year. New construction for the year would cost £8,885,194, as against £7,545,202 in 1908/9. Two battleships would be laid down in July and two in November, much earlier in the financial year than usual. As provided in a footnote to the estimates, the Government was also empowered to make preparations in 1909/10 for the rapid construction of four more ships, starting on 1 April 1910 for completion by March 1912. When, in July, the Government decided to go ahead with the preparation of the four contingent Dreadnoughts, McKenna intimated in the Commons that if any payment was required before April 1910 there would be a supplementary estimate.[54]

In the press it was generally reckoned that the outcome of the battle over the naval estimates would have a crucial bearing on the Budget for the next year and on its fate. Both the Unionist press, which had been agitating since the turn of the year for a large shipbuilding programme, and the Liberal press accepted that the question of the extent of the over-all deficit to be met in 1909/10 underlay the whole contest over the naval estimates. For the *Daily Telegraph,* the Government decided in the end to 'imperil the whole priceless heritage of centuries' simply so as 'to balance a party budget'.[55] For sections of the Liberal press, led by *The Economist,* already alarmed at the potential size of Lloyd George's deficit, the whole naval 'scare' smacked very much of a plot engineered by the Tariff Reformers to embarrass free trade finance in the next Budget.[56]

In the Commons and in the press, the Unionists clamoured in March for a firm commitment from the Government to proceed with the four extra Dreadnoughts. 'We want eight', they demanded, 'and we won't wait.' In the *Observer,* Garvin even suggested that should no commitment be given to the eight Dreadnoughts in 1909/10 the Lords must force a dissolution by rejecting the Budget.[57] It was a suggestion that appealed to Unionists who believed that in the navy they possessed a 'patriotic' issue which, together with tariff reform, would sweep the country for them. In his letter to Balfour from Cairo on 5 April, Henry Chaplin firmly advised that unless Asquith unequivocally accepted the Opposition demand for eight Dreadnoughts he hoped 'the Lords will seize the opportunity; make Dreadnoughts the issue — & throw out his Budget'. The Unionists would be in the position to fight the election on the navy, fiscal reform, and Home Rule, and it was simply not possible to wish for better than that.[58] The furore over the navy estimates, culminating in Balfour moving a vote of censure on the Government at the end of March, served, in short, to revive the stirrings within the Unionist ranks to secure the rejection by the Lords of the as yet unseen Budget for 1909/10.

Within the Cabinet, the prolonged battle over the navy estimates, and the concession of the four contingent Dreadnoughts, worked on balance to strengthen Lloyd George's hand in getting his Budget proposals approved. To be sure, he and Churchill antagonized some of their colleagues by their combativeness, and succeeded for a while in so irritating Asquith that he was sorely tempted to 'cashier' them. But otherwise, the concessions made to the 'Big Navy' men, the highlighting of the fact of the deficit confronting Lloyd

George, and the warnings he made about the growing disaf-
fection of the Radicals in the party, all helped further to
underline the political and financial need for a radical Budget.
It was, indeed, the opinion of Sir Almeric Fitzroy, the clerk
of the privy council, that the row over the navy estimates
was virtually staged by Lloyd George and Churchill with a
view to softening up the Cabinet for Lloyd George's controversial Budget proposals. 'The battle over the Budget', he was
to comment in his diary on 1 May, 'really began before the
onslaught upon the Admiralty programme, which was in fact
the outcome of it.' The main object for Lloyd George,
according to Fitzroy, was to discredit McKenna and at least
neutralize his criticisms of the projected land taxes:
'McKenna, who, whatever his defects as an administrator, is
an accomplished financier, was one of the most strenuous in
exposing the hollowness of Lloyd George's views on the taxation of land values and the predatory tendencies they
barely concealed, and it was as a counter-move to his opposition, with the hope of bringing about his removal from the
Cabinet, that Winston Churchill and Lloyd George set themselves to thwart his plans for providing the country with
sufficient ships.'[59] This was rather far-fetched, but Fitzroy
was basically right in suggesting that the battle over the navy
estimates was to assist Lloyd George in getting his Budget
through the Cabinet.

Unlike the navy estimates, those for the army passed
smoothly through the Cabinet. The real battle over the army
had been fought, and won by Haldane, in June of the previous
year, and since then Haldane had taken out additional
insurance by promising to assist Lloyd George with his
land value taxes.[60] On 24 February 1909 Haldane's army
estimates, showing a trifling reduction of £24,000 on 1908/9,
were duly approved by the Cabinet.

In February and March estimates by officials as to Lloyd
George's total prospective deficit for 1909/10 on the existing
basis of taxation ran as high as £18,000,000.[61] Estimated
expenditure showed an over-all increase of about £10,000,000
on the estimates for the previous year; existing taxes were
estimated to bring in some £5,000,000 or 6,000,000 less than
the estimate for 1908/9; and, as Stair's calculations at the end

of February indicated, a substantial realized deficit for 1908/9 was thought likely to materialize. At the end of March Lloyd George gave the Cabinet the figure of £17,000,000 as his likely deficit for 1909/10.[62] In the event, the realized deficit for 1908/9 proved to be only £714,000, and in early April Lloyd George's projected deficit for 1909/10 was consequently revised downwards to £15,652,000.[63] This did not, however, lead Lloyd George to abandon any of the major proposals for new taxes he had prepared for the Cabinet's consideration.

IV

In preparing his proposals for the Cabinet, Lloyd George worked primarily with three groups — the officials of the Inland Revenue, the officials of the Customs and Excise, amalgamated under a single board chaired by Guillemard on 1 April 1909, and the Finance Committee of the Cabinet, consisting of Crewe, Loreburn, McKenna, Haldane, and Buxton, as well as the Chancellor, and assisted by Hobhouse (Financial Secretary), Robson (Attorney-General), and Alexander Ure (Solicitor-General, Scotland).[64] The chief task of the Finance Committee was to assist with the preparation of the land value duties, which were the first of Lloyd George's proposals to go before the full Cabinet in mid-March.

Lloyd George's proposals for land value taxation were two in number. He wanted a 1*d.* in the £ tax on the capital value of all land worth over £50 an acre, and a duty on increment value to be charged on any conveyance or transfer on sale or lease of any land subject to the capital value tax. To support his proposals he had circulated in December and January to members of the Finance Committee a memorandum by Edgar Harper, the statistical officer of the London County Council who was regarded by the land taxers as a 'master' on the question of valuation, putting the case for a national tax on the capital value of land, and also memoranda on American and Australian methods of land taxation.[65] Towards the end of January Asquith passed on to the committee letters from three interested but anonymous

Liberal MPs criticising the idea of a tax on the capital value of land — one was described as an MP from a mixed urban and rural constituency in the Midlands, another as a 'West country agriculturalist' (E. J. Soares, MP for the Barnstaple division of Devon), and the third as 'a landowner on a considerable scale' (Sir John Dickson-Poynder, MP for the Chippenham division of Wiltshire).[66]

The letters from the Liberal MPs made two main points about the taxation of capital land value. The first was that under no circumstances should agricultural land be subject to such a tax. All three letters stressed that it would be politically fatal for the Government to tax agricultural land. The second was that land value taxation should not interfere with existing contracts between tenants and landlords for the payment of rates and taxes. 'But the greatest difficulty of all', Dickson-Poynder observed in regard to a tax on site value, 'is occasioned by the question of existing contracts.'

The concern not to antagonize rural voters, who had made a major contribution to the Liberal 'landslide' in 1906, was to dog Lloyd George's land value taxation proposals in both the Cabinet and the Commons, until purely agricultural land was entirely exempted from the new taxes. This never particularly worried Lloyd George. As he conceded in a memorandum for the Finance Committee on 30 January, the inclusion of agricultural land was not an essential part of his scheme, and he had already drafted an alternative clause which would have the effect of altogether exempting agricultural land from both valuation and taxation. He none the less added: 'Before the Committee, however, decide to adopt this clause, I should like them to bear in mind that large sums must be raised by this Budget for the financing of proposals which must inevitably relieve agricultural land of a large share of the burden now imposed upon it for the maintenance of the poor.'[67] Lloyd George was later to show himself quite willing to exempt agricultural land from new taxation, but not from the valuation.

On contracts Lloyd George's problem was very real in that his clear intention was that his proposed tax on the capital value of land should be paid, at least in large part, by landowners. His attempted solution was to integrate the proposed new tax very closely with Schedule A of the income tax, in other words, with the tax on the gross rental value of real property. Any person who paid income tax under Schedule A in respect of land subject to the new tax would be entitled to deduct from his share of the land tax which represented realized value the sum actually payable by him under Schedule A. The realized capital value of the land was taken as twenty-five times the annual rental value of the site.[68]

As argued by Lloyd George in his memorandum of 30 January, his proposal for a national tax on site value, unlike schemes for site value rating, did not involve any shifting of an existing burden in spite of contracts but rather an extension of the existing property tax to the whole of a site value, part of which presently often escaped taxation altogether. Since Peel's Act of 1842, he pointed out, the property tax was levied upon the landlord without regard to existing contracts. 'I fail therefore to see', he contended, 'why the balance of this tax, which may only represent one-fifth of the whole, should not be borne by the landlord on the same conditions.'

The crucial question giving rise to the problem of contracts was the incidence of the proposed tax. Lloyd George's object was to tax those who actually enjoyed the capital value of land, unrealized even more so than realized, for it was the former that had previously remained untaxed, and it was also a large part of his purpose to encourage owners to realize the full value of their land, particularly land ripe for building.

In a memorandum of 4 February, Arthur Thring, the Government draftsman, suggested that the best method of dealing with the incidence of the burden of the tax was to distribute it according to the rent received by each person in a premises, which was the method used for Schedule A of the income tax, with the proviso that for any part of the land value that was unrealized the tax would be distributed according to the time period for which each person in the premises was entitled to the enjoyment of the premises.[69] In the draft clauses that were sent to the Cabinet it was provided that the tax would be paid in the first instance by the occupier, and that its burden would then be distributed among the various interests in the land by a process of rent deductions. For that part of the tax on capital value that did not represent ground rent it was provided that the deductions were to be determined either by agreement among the parties concerned, and approved by the Inland Revenue, or by the Inland Revenue in accordance with the principle that 'the distribution shall, as far as practicable, be in proportion to the present market value of the share which each person interested in the land, either in possession or expectancy, has in respect of that part of the capital value which does not represent ground rent'. It was also specifically provided that contracts for payment of rent that did not allow for the prescribed deductions 'shall be void'.[70]

The purpose of these provisions was to ensure that the senior interests in a hereditament would in practice pay the new levy, and that in the vast majority of cases this would mean the ground landlord only. As Lloyd George pointed out in his accompanying memorandum to the Cabinet, as a consequence of the deduction allowed for payments under Schedule A, 'the only owners of house property who would be liable to pay the land tax would be those whose buildings are of less value than their interest in the site'. He claimed that these would prove very exceptional cases.[71]

Within the Finance Committee, Lloyd George's plans for a tax on capital land value met with powerful criticism, not least from McKenna and Hobhouse, and in response to a request from Asquith Hobhouse spelled out the major reservations about the clauses submitted to the Cabinet.[72] He pointed particularly to the difficulties and costs of administration, to the infringement of existing contracts, the burden on reversioners who were willing to develop but who had leaseholders standing in the way, and to anomalies in the incidence of the proposed tax as it affected realized values. Builders, he claimed, would in certain instances bear an 'unfair burden', whereas lessees of land built upon who sub-let would get off 'scot free' when in fact they enjoyed a substantial profit-rent on pure land value. What he concluded was that if the desire to make land value taxation yield an immediate return were to be abandoned, it would prove comparatively simple to secure both land valuation and an annually increasing revenue from taxation imposed first on the transfer of all land, and second on increment accruing on any such transfer.[73]

On 10 March Lloyd George did in fact consult Ilbert on whether land value clauses might be included in the Budget for 1909/10 without making provision for bringing in substantial revenue during the year. Ilbert's opinion then, and later, was that something at least would have to be raised in the current year from such clauses.[74]

Lloyd George's proposed increment duty, which could not possibly produce anything significant in 1909/10, received a far more positive reception from the members of the Finance Committee than did the capital value tax. 'This can be worked simply', Hobhouse commented approvingly of the proposed 20 per cent tax on future unearned increment in land value, to be levied whenever land was sold or leased.[75]

For securing the valuation for the purposes of the land taxes, the draft clauses that went from the Finance Committee to the Cabinet put the onus on owners themselves to determine the value of their land. They were required to declare both the total value and the capital value of each piece of land owned by them which was under separate occupation. Total value was defined as the amount which the fee simple of the land would be expected to realize if sold in the open market by a willing seller, and capital value as that part of the total value that belonged to the site itself, divested of any buildings or other structures, and if the land was sold free from any burden or charge arising by operation of law. Allowance was made for deductions for certain improvements, such as draining, levelling, and fencing, completed within ten years of the valuation.[76]

Hobhouse was clearly irked by Lloyd George's handling of the land taxes in the Finance Committee. 'The Chancellor of the Exchequer', he complained in his diary on 7 March, 'won't read and can only pick up ideas by talking.' Haldane was not even certain that Lloyd George had acquired much understanding by listening to the others on the committee.[77] For his own part, Lloyd George was convinced that his performance in the committee constituted something of a political triumph. 'I had to fight and bully and badger my way against everybody', he told Herbert Lewis. 'I drove the

Lord Chancellor out of the Cabinet Committee by taunting him: "You are concerned for your friends the Dukes," and the Attorney-General with: "You are concerned for the slum-owners." '[78]

Lloyd George's estimate for the land taxes for 1909/10 was consistently kept at £500,000 although it was highly problematic whether he would get even that. For the taxes that came within the portfolio of the Inland Revenue, Lloyd George looked to income tax, death duties, and stamps as his effective instruments for raising new revenue in 1909/10.

On the income tax, Chalmers was well prepared with proposals when Lloyd George began work on the Budget in October 1908. In a memorandum of that month he mapped out for the Chancellor the main proposals the Cabinet was ultimately to accept for the income tax and supertax.

In the memorandum, Chalmers rejected as 'administratively impracticable' the scheme that Lloyd George favoured for graduating the income tax by extending the system of abatements. Lloyd George's inclination was to increase the general rate of the income tax from 1s. to 1s. 6d. in the £, subject to abatements of 3d. for incomes between £3,000 and £5,000 and of 6d. for all incomes falling short of £3,000. Such a scheme, Chalmers pointed out, would involve either the collection of a large amount in excess and refund by 'sheer repayment' at the end of the year, or an adjustment on assessment to minimize 'the repayment evil'. The latter, however, could increase the work of the surveyors of taxes to the point of breakdown, and could not be entertained.

Instead, Chalmers argued the case for increasing the general rate of the income tax to 1s. 2d. in the £, which would affect unearned income and earned income where the total exceeded £2,000, and for introducing a supertax of 4d. in the £ for income over £5,000. When differentiation was introduced, he asserted, it had been recognized that, with a tax of 9d. in the £ on earned income, 'a not improper figure for unearned income would have been 1/2d. in the £, and I know that this opinion is still held by some ministers'. On the assumption that the 9d. rate was to be maintained for earned income under £2,000, he held that it was 'entirely practicable' to raise the rate on unearned income and earned income over £2,000 to 1*s*. 2*d*. The financial result of such a step he calculated as an increased yield of £3,750,000 in the first year, and £4,700,000 for each succeeding year. He also held that it was 'entirely feasible, both on administrative and other grounds' to blend the introduction of a supertax scheme with an increase in the general rate of the income tax. He estimated that an ungraduated supertax of 4*d*. in the £ on all income over £5,000 would bring in £2,000,000 a year, though he added that 'administrative policy *per se* suggests that the proceeds of the super-tax should not be available until the second year, i.e. in 1910/11, if super-tax be imposed in the Budget of 1909'.[79]

Despite Chalmer's administrative objections to Lloyd George's proposal for graduating the higher reaches of the income tax, the Chancellor persisted with this line of approach, and prepared a scheme whereby the general rate of the income tax would be increased to 1*s*. 2*d*. in the £, another 2*d*. would be charged on all income over £3,000, and 2*d*. more on all income over £5,000.[80] He was to present this scheme to the Cabinet, along with a supertax scheme based on Chalmer's proposals. The Cabinet opted for the latter.

What was agreed upon throughout was that the general rate of the income tax should go up to 1*s*. 2*d*. in the £, and it was also agreed that this would necessitate certain concessions. For Chalmers and the officials of the Inland Revenue it was taken for granted that a 'necessary consequence of a normal 14*d*.' would be an extension of abatements to all incomes up to £1,000. But on this matter Lloyd George was to override the advice of Chalmers, as well as Bradbury and Murray, and insist on his own proposals for concessions in the income tax. To begin with, Lloyd George had been 'strong' on extending abatements to all incomes up to £1,000, as against the existing limit of £700, impressing upon Chalmers that he was anxious 'to lighten the burthen somewhat at the bottom while increasing it at the top', and desirous to assist 'the professional classes like Solicitors and Doctors'. But in March Lloyd George irked Chalmers by setting aside the scheme he had prepared for extending abatements to £1,000 in favour of reviving the allowance for children that Pitt's Income Tax Act of 1799 had given. Lloyd

George's proposal in this regard was to extend an abatement of £20 per child under sixteen, up to a maximum of three children, to persons with incomes under £500. Chalmers, 'with little to go on in data', reckoned £1,000,000 would cover the cost of the proposal.[81]

The sum of £1,000,000 represented the accepted target for any new concessions in the income tax. As the increase in the general rate of the income tax to 1s. 2d. was calculated to bring in £3,750,000 in the first year, this meant that a total of £2,750,000 was to be forthcoming in 1909/10 from the overall changes in the income tax.

For death duties, the Inland Revenue prepared a number of alternative scales for increasing the estate duty, a scheme to abolish the settlement estate duty and to charge settled property with estate duty on cession of every life interest, and another scheme for doubling the legacy and succession duties. As estimated on 4 March, the estate duty scale to be adopted would give £3,950,000 in the first year, the new charge on settled property £1,000,000, and nothing would be forthcoming from the legacy and succession duties until the second year. With a minor deduction, the estimated total from the alterations in the death duties for 1909/10 was £4,865,000, and ultimately £10,915,000.[82]

On stamps, Lloyd George took a particularly active role in putting forward proposals for new rates, and in February called for estimates for a wide range of possible increases. The estimate on 4 March for increased stamps was £1,250,000, possibly reaching £1,500,000, for the first year, and £2,000,000, in the second year. By 24 March, when Lloyd George finalized his stamp proposals for presentation to the Cabinet, his proposed increases had been whittled down from eighteen to twelve, and the estimate for 1909/10 had been lowered to £750,000, partly in anticipation of a late date for the passage of the Budget.[83]

The preparation of increases for indirect taxes and for revamping the licence duties was the responsibility of the Customs and Excise officials. Technically Excise remained attached to Somerset House until 1 April 1909, when Excise was formally amalgamated with Customs under the chairmanship of Guillemard. To ensure continuity, Guillemard

Was involved throughout in the preparation of the excise licence duties, which were to cause him and the Excise officials many a headache.

The preparation of new duties for spirits and tobacco seems to have been relatively straight-forward; by the end of February plans were firmly in hand to raise the duty on spirits by 3s. 9d. a gallon and to increase the duty on tobacco from 3s. to 3s. 8d. a pound.[84] But the saga of formulating the licence duties was to last virtually until the Finance Bill itself was introduced in the Commons in late May.

By mid-February, some three schemes for licences had been drafted. From Lloyd George's standpoint their purpose was dual: to raise more revenue, and to encourage a reduction in the number of licensed premises. A large part of the problem in drafting the licence duties was to strike a balance between these two objectives. As Lloyd George was consistently warned by Guillemard, some of the increases he was contemplating for licensed houses would 'certainly lead to enormous opposition, and possibly to such a diminution in the number of licences as practically to fail altogether as a real source of increased revenue'.[85] Guillemard repeated the warning to the Cabinet for the rates Lloyd George submitted to it.

As finalized by Lloyd George for presentation to the Cabinet, the licence duty proposals possessed two outstanding features among a host of contemplated changes. One was the proposal to abolish the fixed duties for manufacturers' licences for beer and spirits, and to charge the duties in proportion to production, with a maximum duty of £500 for both brewers and distillers. Before 1880 a graduated scale, according to production, had existed for brewers, but this had been abandoned by Gladstone in that year as a trade-off for his new tax on beer and general rearrangement of all licence duties. In 1880 the duty for a manufacturers' licence for beer had been fixed at a nominal £1 per annum. The existing duty for distillers was 10 guineas. The other outstanding feature of the licence duty proposals was a major restructuring of the duties for 'on' licences, particularly full licences and beerhouses, which incorporated the recommendation made by Joseph Rowntree and Arthur Sherwell in *The Taxation of*

the Liquor Trade for the creation of a scale of minimum
duties graded according to population.[86] The final effect of
Lloyd George's proposals was to more than double the
anticipated revenue from licences.

For public houses and beerhouses Lloyd George proposed
to steepen and graduate at shorter steps the existing scale of
licence duties, to increase very considerably the rates on highly
valued premises, to impose minimum annual values in proportion to the population of the localities in which they were
situated, and to secure for the purposes of licence duty a new
valuation based on full market value.[87] The new valuation,
to be completed later in the year, would be undertaken in
terms of the Kennedy judgement of 1906 for establishing
compensation value for the purposes of the Licensing Act of
1904; it would include not only the shop value of the
premises as unlicensed and the annual value added by the
licence, which together provided the existing basis for taxation,
but also goodwill. Lloyd George's point in wanting a new
valuation was that for small houses the existing annual
value often amounted to only half the real market value.

The proposals Lloyd George presented to the Cabinet for
public houses and beerhouses constituted at least the fourth
scheme drawn up for him by the Excise officials since early
February. The basic principles behind his proposals had been
set forward in Scheme A, except for the idea of securing a
new valuation, which eliminated the need for the complicated scales, based on population, advanced in Schemes
B and C for ensuring that licensed premises were taxed on
something like their real value.

The new graduated scales Lloyd George proposed to the
Cabinet represented a considerable steepening of existing
charges, which ranged from a minimum of £4.10s. for public
houses to a maximum of £60 for premises with an annual
value of £700 or over. The selection given opposite from the
proposed new scale for public houses indicates the nature
of the changes recommended. For premises of an annual
value of £700 and above, another £5 was to be charged
for every additional £50 or part thereof of annual value.
Beerhouses were to be charged at rates of roughly two-
thirds of those levied on public houses. For *bona fide*

Annual Value £	Proposed Duty £	Existing Duty £
minimum rate	6	4½
10–15	8	6
15–20	10	8
20–25	15	11
40–50	30	20
80–90	50	25
100–150	75	30
400–450	205	45
650–700	230	55

hotels and restaurants required to take out full licences, but whose receipts from liquor were less than one-third of total receipts, concessions on the new rates were given.

In percentage terms, the increases over existing charges were highest for premises with high annual values. The real thrust against small houses was in the proposed minima in proportion to population, and in the proposed new valuation. The idea was to tax the less profitable small houses in urban areas out of existence, to reduce the value of premises for compensation purposes, and to raise substantial new revenue from the more profitable small houses. The principle of imposing minimum annual values in proportion to population was not a new one, in so far as it already applied to new licences except for Scotland, and its further extension reflected the concern of Liberals, as evidenced in the Licensing Bill of 1908, to cut down on the number of licensed premises in crowded areas particularly.

The detailed proposals for minimum duties Lloyd George presented to the Cabinet were based largely on Schemes B and C, with the difference that the increased minima in proportion to population began to apply to urban communities of 2,000 or more, whereas Scheme B, following Scheme A, had taken urban population areas of 10,000 as its starting point for the additional duties, and Scheme C urban areas of 5,000.

For public houses, the minimum duties in accordance with size of population proposed to the Cabinet, as compared to the proposals in Schemes A, B, and C, were as follows (overleaf):

Population	Scheme A	Scheme B	Scheme C	Cabinet
	£	£	£	£
Below 2,000	8	8	8	6
2 to 5,000	8	8	8	15
5 to 10,000	8	8	13	20
10 to 25,000	18	21	22½	25
25 to 50,000	18	21	30	25
50 to 100,000	22	30	38½	40
100 to 300,000	26	41	48	50
Over 300,000	26	46	58½	50

In the preparation of the licence duties, in other words, the over-all tendency was to increase the proposed new minima except for the minimum for population areas under 2,000, which was set at £6 for public houses in the proposals put before the Cabinet, as against £8 in the prior schemes.

The latter move was intended as a concession to Ireland. In an explanatory memorandum of 16 February on Schemes A to C, Lloyd George had been advised that the imposition of a minimum duty of £8 for the entire United Kingdom would not seriously affect Scotland, but might have a devastating impact in Ireland. Out of a total number of 17,151 public houses in Ireland, no less than 10,517 occupied premises of an annual value under £15, and Lloyd George was warned that it was possible that 'the increase of duty for those licences from 4*l*. 10*s*. (under 10*l*.) and 6*l*. (under 15*l*.) to 8*l*. may result in the closing of many of them'.[88] Irish public houses none the less still stood to suffer considerably from the minima Lloyd George proposed to the Cabinet.

The effect of the minima proposed to the Cabinet was both to heighten the projected charges on the smallest houses in population areas over 2,000, and to extend the range of the scheme as originally formulated. Under Scheme A the minimum duty for public houses in urban areas of 100,000 or more had been based on a minimum annual value of £50; in the proposals presented to the Cabinet the minimum duty represented a minimum annual value of £80. Of the 14,254 public houses in the metropolis and county boroughs in England with populations over 100,000, only 1,128 were of existing annual values under £50; another 3,083 possessed existing annual values between £50 and £100.[89]

As a consequence of these and other changes in the proposals advanced in February, the estimate for the proposed new licence duties for 1909/10 was increased from £2,250,000 to £2,500,000, which was the figure given to the Cabinet.[90]

What was to strike Runciman about all the proposals for new taxes that reached the Cabinet was that the estimates for them appeared inordinately conservative. This impressed him as being particularly true of the new direct taxes.[91] These estimates were in fact deliberately made conservative. The instruction given out by Chalmers was that all estimates for new taxes 'should be pruned for Budget purposes, so as to be certain of realising the Estimate in the first year, during which experience will be gained for the more important second year, 1910/11'.[92] On 4 March, the over-all estimates for new taxes were as follows:[93]

	£
Estate Duties	4,865,000
Stamps	1,250,000
Income Tax (minus £1 million for abatements)	2,750,000
Super Tax (if levied in 1909/10)	1,600,000
Land (Chancellor's estimate)	500,000
Licences	2,250,000
3/9 Spirits	1,800,000
8d. Tobacco	2,000,000
Gross possible total 1909/10	17,015,000

For presentation to the Cabinet the estate duties were rounded off at £4,500,000; stamps were reduced to £750,000; the income tax, without provision for concessions, was rounded off at £3,500,000; the supertax was reduced to £1,000,000 to allow for administrative difficulties and uncertainties in the first year; and £400,000 was knocked off the indirect taxes to meet forestalling. In the opposite direction, the estimate for licences was raised by £250,000. In all, these alterations reduced the total estimate for the new taxes for 1909/10 by £865,000 to £16,150,000, without any allowance being made in this figure for income tax concessions, should any be allowed by the Cabinet in the face of the prospective deficit confronting the Government.

In compressing his estimated yields for the new taxes, Lloyd George possessed considerable justification. No one knew exactly what impact many of his projected increases would have; with a long parliamentary tussle over the Budget in prospect, even the most careful of estimates were likely to get disrupted; and it was highly problematic whether the entirely novel taxes, the land value duties and the supertax, would produce very much in 1909/10. Ideally, Lloyd George might have preferred not to collect any monies from these latter taxes in 1909/10, but regarded himself as bound by constitutional requirements to raise revenue from them during the year if they were included in the Budget for the year. The estimate of £500,000 from the land value duties was nothing much more than a token estimate designed to give the appearance that some revenue would be raised from them in 1909/10. The land valuation would take years to prepare, and it would be impossible to collect the full site value tax until it had been completed. None the less, as Lloyd George advised the Cabinet, it was 'quite essential from the constitutional point of view' to levy the tax, so far as was possible, on vacant land, mining royalties, and ground rents during 1909/10 'in order to justify the inclusion of land values in the Budget'.[94] Whether collection in 1909/10 would amount to anything was questionable. The Frankfurt tax, again, could not possibly come into operation in 1909/10 to any meaningful extent. As regards the supertax, Chalmers had advised that administrative considerations required that its collection should be deferred for a year after its imposition. Once it had been firmly decided that attempts should be made to collect the tax in its first year of imposition, the estimate for the first year was consistently revised downwards, first to £1,000,000 and then to £500,000.

In practice, the land value duties and the supertax were hardly intended by Lloyd George as a real contribution to the finances for 1909/10, and the estimates for them were essentially nominal. They were put in for political and constitutional reasons, and there was a good chance that they would not be realized. In that event, they would have to be 'carried' by his other proposed new impositions.

Even with regard to Lloyd George's proposed increases for existing taxes, the estimates for the increased yields were by no means certain. It was not easy to assess how the increases on tobacco and spirits would affect consumption of these articles, and in the event the estimate for spirits was to prove very much over the mark. On licences, again, Lloyd George was repeatedly warned that his proposals might lead to so extensive a 'slaughter' and 'watering down' of licensed premises as to nullify their ability to raise new revenue. As for the new stamp duties, the return would depend very largely on when the Budget was passed.

None the less, it is clear that in all the estimates Lloyd George gave the Cabinet he was anxious not to underestimate expenditure or to overestimate revenue. His concern was both to provide financial justification for the inclusion of all his new taxes in a single Budget and to ensure that he would have a realized surplus rather than deficit at the end of the year. As Lloyd George stressed all along, he was budgeting not for one year but for several. His fundamental purposes in so doing were twofold. He was determined to provide the financial basis for a far-reaching programme of social reform, and he was equally determined to establish that free trade finance was perfectly capable of meeting the financial challenge of the times.

V

In the preparation of the Budget Lloyd George was regarded as too 'theoretical' and 'impractical' as well as excessively 'political' by many of his officials. Several of his proposals, notably for graduating the income tax and for imposing land value duties, were accepted as possibly excellent in theory, but administratively they were looked upon as a bureaucrat's nightmare, in an age when bureaucratic expansion was still regarded as an evil even by the bureaucrats themselves. Several of his proposals, including the land value duties and the licensing duties, were also regarded as being inspired as much, and perhaps even more, by political rather than strictly financial considerations.

What is evident over-all, is that in the preparation of the Budget Lloyd George saw himself as taking over the responsibility of guaranteeing the immediate future of the Liberal Government and party. He was fashioning policy, so as to satisfy important pressure groups within the party, to put the enemy on the defensive, and to give the Government itself a sense of direction and purpose.

In a final thrust at policy-making in the preparation of his Budget, Lloyd George proposed to establish two central funds and authorities to promote public investment in national development. A special fund, to be raised by a new graduated scale for motor car licences and by a duty of 3*d.* per gallon on all petrol used for motor vehicles, was to be put at the disposal of a Road Board, which would make grants to local authorities for the improvement of roads, including diversions round villages, and help finance the construction of entirely new roads. The 'motorists', Lloyd George told his brother, were 'startled and delighted' when he outlined to them his 'great scheme for developing national routes'.[95] A second fund, a Development Grant to be put at the disposal of a Development Commission, was to be created out of existing monies spent 'in a spasmodic kind of way' on 'work of national development', an additional grant of £200,000, and any realized surplus available at the end of each fiscal year. The proposed Commission would devote these funds to schemes for promoting 'the development of the resources of the country', through schools for forestry, the purchase and preparation of land for afforestation, scientific research in the interests of agriculture, the organization of transport for agricultural produce, the promotion of co-operative marketing, and through assistance given to land reclamation and the creation of small holdings. The emphasis was very definitely on promoting the country's rural and agricultural development, and on encouraging labourers to return from towns to the land. The proposals would require separate legislation.[96]

Lloyd George's foray into national development, and the related questions of unemployment and urban congestion, was indicative of the far-reaching brief he had undertaken in the preparation of his first Budget. There was hardly a question, which could in any way come under the purview of his Budget, that he did not tackle. Although ultimately repulsed, he probed deeply into the affairs of the army and the navy; he sought both to prepare for the Government a strategy of social reform and to provide the financial base for the reforms he had in mind; he struck out against both 'the trade' and 'the landlords' and reckoned to 'dish' the Lords on the issues of licensing and land valuation; and perhaps above all he sought to establish that free trade finance could provide for immediate and all foreseen demands on terms that would prove politically acceptable, and even advantageous to the Liberals in their efforts to ward off the mounting challenge of the Tariff Reformers.

VI. The Budget in the Cabinet

I

Lloyd George always maintained afterwards that it was only with the greatest difficulty that he secured the sanction of the Cabinet for the 'People's Budget'. By far the most difficult fight he had, he told Frances Stevenson in May 1936, was in the Cabinet, not in the country. 'Harcourt', he elaborated, 'was the most inveterate in obstructing his proposals, while posing all the time as an ardent Radical. Crewe, while not liking them said very little. Grey said nothing. But at heart they were all against him.'[1] The story he consistently gave out was that it was only Asquith's support that enabled him to carry his more controversial proposals through the Cabinet. Asquith rarely spoke out in positive support of his proposals, but settled contested points by ruling in Lloyd George's favour. According to what Lloyd George told his son, Richard, Asquith would lean back in his chair and say: 'Well, there seems to be substantial agreement with Mr. Chancellor's proposal. Next item . . . ?'[2]

The Budget was indeed very closely scrutinized by the Cabinet – it was examined and discussed virtually clause by clause, and line by line – and there is no question that a good many in the Cabinet thoroughly disliked and distrusted Lloyd George's proposals. At least a third of the Cabinet objected to the fundamental design of the Budget, and feared that the scale and nature of its direct taxes would frighten away middle-class support from the Liberals. Morley, for one, was 'frightened' by the likely political effects of the Budget. As he had explained to Crewe in December, he did not overmuch like the prospect of a 'Henroost Budget' for the effect of such a 'fascinating operation' would be to 'still further estrange the sober, sensible, middle class, and the battle will be not against H. of L. but against Property – a very different thing'.[3] Lord Wolverhampton, for another, 'hate[d] the whole scheme as heartily as any Tory', though

he was too much of a lightweight to pose any serious threat
to Lloyd George.[4] Of more importance were the objections
of the younger members of the Cabinet who possessed
Treasury experience. Lewis Harcourt, who had assisted his
father with the preparation of the famous Death Duties
Budget of 1894, consistently challenged Lloyd George on
points of both principle and detail. 'His criticisms', Asquith
informed Jack Pease, 'are points of substance & he knows
a good deal about it.'[5] In a note he passed to Runciman early
in the Cabinet discussions on the Budget, Harcourt confided
his fundamental political objection to Lloyd George's
proposals: 'This Budget will ensure the triumph of Tariff
Reform.'[6] Runciman, who had served under Asquith as
Financial Secretary to the Treasury, likewise had grave mis-
givings about the general content of the Budget, and suspected
that Lloyd George was attempting to get Cabinet approval
for more taxes than he really required.[7] McKenna, who had
also served as Financial Secretary to the Treasury under
Asquith, disliked the Budget, and played an important
role in frustrating Lloyd George's proposal for a straight
penny tax on the capital value of land.[8] John Burns, who was
without Treasury experience but who had initially been
responsible for the Government's valuation policies for
England, was another who questioned the whole enterprise;
he regarded Lloyd George's handiwork as 'the most kaleido-
scopic Budget ever planned, and but for revision and pruning
would have made us a laughing stock of Parliament'.[9] Crewe
and Grey, who, like Burns, had little to say in the Cabinet
discussions of the Budget, were regarded by Lloyd George
as basically opposed to his proposals, and Crewe was certainly
treated as an ally by Harcourt.[10]

   Other ministers with major reservations about the Budget
included Lords Fitzmaurice and Loreburn. Fitzmaurice
focused his scepticism on the land value duties, which he did
not think would prove practicable.[11] Loreburn, for his part,
while not necessarily disapproving in principle of any of
Lloyd George's proposals, believed that the Chancellor had
committed the political error of attempting too much in a
single measure and of attacking too many major interests at
once. He feared that 'the combined opposition and odium

will be *very* serious', and concluded it would be wiser to
reserve land valuation for 1910.[12]

Of all the members of the Cabinet, only Lord Carrington
is on record as having welcomed Lloyd George's proposals
with genuine enthusiasm. He opposed any taxation of agricultural land but generally thought the Budget 'bold, Liberal
and humane'.[13] Because of illness Carrington missed most the
Cabinet discussions of the Budget, and apart from Asquith's
support, Lloyd George received his most useful assistance in
the Cabinet from Haldane and Churchill. Haldane was in
principle essentially in agreement with the broad design of
the Budget; a great deal of money had to be raised and he
believed it should be raised mainly by direct taxation.[14]
Churchill, for his part, did not particularly care for many of
the Budget's imposts, notably the land value taxes, but his
concern for the financing of social reform made him a willing
worker on behalf of the Budget. He was later to take up the
cudgels for it in the country as chairman of the Budget
League.

That Asquith should have given a vital general support to
Lloyd George was put down by Hobhouse to the Prime
Minister's fear of Lloyd George's popularity and influence
with the press.[15] This was unfair to Asquith, who as
Chancellor had approved in principle, and helped prepare
the ground for, much of what Lloyd George was attempting,
and who sympathized with the new Chancellor in his
extremely difficult undertaking.

To an extent that historians have not appreciated, Lloyd
George's Budget was considerably modified during its progress
through the Cabinet. The straight penny tax on the capital
value of land was thrown out, his proposed changes in the
duty for settled property were discarded, and the Budget
was revised and pruned in matters of detail. Yet, for all the
changes and alterations made in the Cabinet, the basic design
of the Budget remained intact and, in one form or another,
the main principles for which Lloyd George contended were
incorporated in the version the Cabinet finally approved.
As Sir Almeric Fitzroy appreciated, the Budget that was
presented to the Commons at the end of April represented
a triumph in the Cabinet for Lloyd George. 'The impression

left on my mind', he entered in his diary on 1 May, 'by the net result of the consultations held upon the financial proposals of Mr. Lloyd George is that he and Winston Churchill have at last succeeded in wearing down the opposition of their more important colleagues. Certainly some of the proposals embodied in the scheme constitute an acceptance of principles which I have the best reason for knowing the Cabinet as a whole had no wish to endorse.'[16]

As Fitzroy suspected, the earlier fuss that Lloyd George and Churchill had created over military and naval expenditure facilitated the Chancellor's task of carrying through the Cabinet the taxes he claimed were necessary to meet the Government's expenditure. Asquith's support in settling a number of disputed points also greatly assisted Lloyd George in his task. But that the basic design of the Budget was not disrupted was due largely to Lloyd George's own deftness and argumentative ability, his willingness to accept revisions and make concessions in order to preserve the substance of his proposals, and the political predicament the Cabinet found itself in. Whether the members of the Cabinet liked Lloyd George's proposals or not, they were already committed to the Budget as the main measure for the year, and they had perforce to accept that a tame Budget was politically out of the question. As he reminded his colleagues when they began the consideration of his Budget, on education, temperance, and land valuation, they had to date been thwarted and checkmated by the Lords, and it was only by resorting to a finance bill that they could hope to attain some of their objectives against the wishes of the Lords; the alternative to accepting his more controversial proposals was the acceptance of political impotence, and the estrangement of their own supporters. In the final analysis, the Cabinet accepted the 'People's Budget' for the want of any effective political alternative.

II

The Cabinet began its consideration of the Budget proposals on 15 March, and between then and Budget Day (29 April) some fourteen Cabinet meetings were given over largely to the discussion of the Budget. The land taxes were taken first, and they occupied at least four meetings.

Lloyd George presented his proposals for a land value tax of 1*d*. in the £ on the capital value of all land assessed at over £50 an acre, and for a 20 per cent tax on the future 'unearned' increment in site values, as a means around the veto of the Lords on the matter of land valuation. In a memorandum he prepared for the Cabinet on 13 March, Lloyd George submitted to his colleagues that, owing to the opposition of the Lords, it would be impossible to secure the passage of a separate Valuation Bill during the existing Parliament, and that therefore the only possible chance the Government had of redeeming its pledges in this regard was by incorporating valuation proposals in a finance bill. It had however to be borne in mind, he continued, that land valuation proposals which did not provide for the raising of revenue would probably be regarded by the Speaker of the House of Commons as being outside the proper limits of a finance bill. 'I have consulted Sir Courtenay Ilbert on this subject,' he informed his colleagues, 'and he is distinctly of opinion that, unless it is contemplated to raise substantial revenue during the year, valuation clauses would be regarded by the authorities of the House as being a fit subject for a separate Bill, and not for a Finance Bill.' He therefore planned to raise £500,000 in the coming year on the basis of his proposed land value taxes.[17] In the outline notes of the case he urged at the Cabinet meeting of 15 March, he began by emphasizing that he did in fact need the £500,000 from his proposed land taxes, and he continued by stressing that the Government simply could not afford to neglect the opportunity offered by a finance bill to legislate against the wishes of the Lords on land valuation:

> = Want revenue
>   Want millions more next year
> = Just in that position where an extra £500,000 makes all difference between screwing estate duties or income tax to point where they will appear oppressive
> = Incidental advantage of the first magnitude — Enables us to legislate on one of the greatest questions sub-

mitted to the country despite the House of Lords. This is really what makes our supporters so keenly desirous for it

How do we stand in reference to the H. of Lords?
 = Education
 = Temperance
 = Land Valuation   Thwarted
                          Checkmated
Beginning to look silly
Menace followed by inaction or rather by action on something else
Country sees this — produces a sense of our ineptitude & impotence
Short of dissolution we can only walk round the Lords by means of our financial powers.
Licensing — but this imperfect remedy — even if it be a remedy
Valuation we can completely circumnavigate them.[18]

Lloyd George argued valiantly for his 1*d*. capital value tax, but the weight of the Cabinet was against him for legal and political reasons. The central problem was the incidence of the tax, and its infringement of existing contracts.

Lloyd George's clear intention was that, although the tax would have to be paid in the first instance by the occupier of the land, it should, in the case of tenancies, be transferred largely or entirely on to the ground landlords, regardless of any previous contracts they might have entered into with tenants on the payment of rates and taxes. For the first two years, until the administrative preliminaries, including the separate valuation of sites and buildings, had been completed, the tax would be confined to vacant land, mining royalties, and ground rents. As Asquith reported to the King on 19 March, the Cabinet refused to allow the taxation of ground rents of land built upon 'on the ground that it would involve an interference with existing contracts'.[19]

Instead of his 1*d*. capital value tax, regarded as the equivalent of a 2*s*. in the £ tax on annual value, Lloyd George had to settle for a tax of ½*d*. in the £ on the capital value of undeveloped land and minerals, excluding purely agricultural land, and a reversion duty of 10 per cent on the value of any benefit accruing to a lessor by reason of the termination of a lease. Lloyd George's initial provisions for the collection and incidence of the undeveloped land duty were jettisoned by the Cabinet, again on the ground that they interfered unduly with existing contracts. Lloyd George's initial proposal was similar to that for his capital value tax: the occupier should pay the tax in the first instance and recover it by means of rent deduction, regardless of any contract to the contrary.[20] What was at issue was whether the principle of state infringement of existing contracts should be given such direct expression in the Finance Bill, and the Cabinet refused to allow it to be so enshrined. The formula finally adopted provided that the tax should be 'recoverable from the owner of the land as a debt due to His Majesty'.[21]

Lloyd George's proposed 'Frankfort tax' of 20 per cent on the future unearned increment in land values, to be levied whenever land was sold, leased or passed on after death and, in the case of land held by bodies 'corporate or unincorporate', at certain periodical intervals, was retained basically intact, despite Harcourt's contention that its effect would be to encourage the 'holding up' of the marketing of land for building, whereas supposedly a large part of the purpose of land value taxation was to bring land onto the market.[22]

Despite its rejection of the straight capital value tax, the land duties the Cabinet approved still required the ascertainment of both the total and the site value of landed hereditaments, and for the valuation the Cabinet accepted Lloyd George's proposal to make owners responsible for declaring separately the total value and the site value of their land. Failure to submit a 'satisfactory' return would lead to the value of the land being fixed by the Commissioners of the Board of Inland Revenue, subject to appeal to a referee appointed by the Treasury, whose decision would be final.[23]

From the land value taxes the Cabinet turned next to a consideration of Lloyd George's licence duty proposals, estimated to bring in an additional £2,500,000. The Cabinet accepted the substance of all Lloyd George's recommendations with regard to licences, though some of the proposed rates were to be revised several times before Budget Day.

Lloyd George's proposals for a moderate increase in the rates for wholesale dealers' licences, and for establishing a new four-stage graduated scale for 'off' licences for spirits and beer, were approved by the Cabinet without alteration. Where important changes were made were in the proposals for manufacturers' licences and for 'on' licences.

In late March the Cabinet revised downwards the charges of the proposed new duties for manufacturers' licences for brewers and distillers in proportion to the quantity brewed or distilled, subject to a maximum charge of £500.[24] After Easter, on Lloyd George's initiative, the Cabinet agreed to abandon the maximum. Brewers would pay £1 for licence to brew 100 barrels, and thereafter 12s. for every 50 barrels or fraction thereof, which meant that Guinness and Company, on the basis of barrels brewed in 1907/8, would pay a total duty in the order of £25,600, as against £1 previously. Distillers would pay a duty of £10 on the first 50,000 gallons of spirits distilled, and an additional £10 thereafter for every 25,000 proof gallons or fraction thereof. As was pointed out in a note to Asquith, presumably from Guillemard, the new duties were in effect excise duties on beer and spirits, with beer paying another 3d. a barrel over the existing beer duty of 7s. 9d. a barrel.[25]

In late March, the Cabinet significantly revised Lloyd George's proposed new rates for 'on' licences so as to soften the blow against small houses and to increase further the charges on what Lloyd George called the 'prosperous liquor palaces of the great towns' which enjoyed high annual values. After Easter it was decided to simplify the rates for public-houses by charging them at a flat rate of 50 per cent of annual value, subject to minima in proportion to population. Until the new valuation had been completed, the duty was to be payable on existing annual value. The minima approved by the Cabinet were significantly lower than those first proposed by Lloyd George (see overleaf). Beerhouses were to be charged at one-third of annual value, subject to minima two-thirds the amount of those imposed for public-houses.[26] The question of the rates of duty for *bona fide* hotels and restaurants proved enormously complicated, and

Population	Proposed £	Approved £
below 2,000	6	5
2 to 5,000	15	10
5 to 10,000	20	15
10 to 50,000	25	20
50 to 100,000	40	30
over 100,000	50	35

in May much of the time of the Cabinet in finalizing the terms of the Finance Bill was devoted to working out an acceptable scheme at significantly lower rates than first proposed.[27]

One important duty proposed by Lloyd George and approved by the Cabinet under the head of licences, though it was not strictly speaking a licence duty, was a tax of 3*d.* in the £ on the liquor receipts of clubs. In large towns clubs had mushroomed in recent years in direct proportion to the closure of licensed premises, and while clubs were to remain unlicensed, they were no longer to continue untaxed.

As a consequence of the changes the Cabinet made in late March in Lloyd George's licence proposals, the estimate for the new licence duties was revised downwards to £2,250,000. The changes approved by the Cabinet after Easter brought the estimate up to £2,600,000.

In all, the licence duty proposals that emerged from the Cabinet constituted a major overhaul and streamlining of the system of licence duties. They comprised an integrated whole, not merely an *ad hoc* expedient, and brought a new degree of uniformity to duties throughout the United Kingdom. For all the neatness gained from the administrative standpoint, Lloyd George's insistence on uniformity did pose special difficulties for Ireland, and to a lesser degree, Scotland. As Guillemard made a point of emphasizing in his memoranda that went to the Cabinet, it was on Lloyd George's specific instructions that the new proposals for 'on' licences were prepared so as to include Ireland, and he consistently predicted that the new rates might lead to the non-renewal of a very considerable number of licences in Ireland. 'In Ireland', he advised in his memorandum of 20

May on the excise licences, 'it is reported that occupiers of many licensed houses find considerable difficulty at the present time in paying the existing rates of licence duties.' With regard to the proposals adopted in April by the Cabinet for 'on' licences he repeated his general warning that: 'Such an increase of the duties as is proposed in this scheme will certainly lead to enormous opposition and it is quite impossible to forecast what the actual effect of the scheme may be as a source of additional revenue.' It was to be assumed, he commented, that the scheme would 'meet the wishes of persons anxious to see a diminution in the number of licensed houses'.[28]

The Cabinet had first reviewed Lloyd George's licence duty proposals in late March; it turned next to stamps and approved without alteration Lloyd George's recommendations for increases in the stamp duties. The duty on conveyances of sale was to be doubled from 10*s*. to £1 per cent and the same rate was to apply in future to gifts *inter vivos* previously charged at a fixed rate of 10*s*. The duties upon leases and bonds to bearer, except for those of a colonial government, were likewise to be doubled, with the rate of £1 per cent applying in most cases. A graduated scale for the transfer duty on stocks and shares was to replace the existing fixed duties. Two of the stamp duties initially approved by the Cabinet — an increase in the loan capital duty and the introduction of a duty on the first issue of share certificates — were withdrawn at the last Cabinet before Budget Day, reducing from £750,000 to £650,000 Lloyd George's estimate of the amount the increased duties would bring in during 1909/10.[29]

Accompanying Lloyd George's recommendations for stamps was a proposal, supported by Sir George Murray, for doubling the existing duty on bills of exchange. Lloyd George had examined the case for and against such an increase in mid-March, and it was apparently at Murray's insistence that the proposal was brought before the Cabinet. In a memorandum submitted to the Cabinet, Murray claimed that a doubling of the duty on bills of exchange would produce another £800,000 in a full year, and he contended that it was 'hardly possible' to raise such an amount out of stamps 'in a way which is less likely to do damage to financial or commercial interests'. Sir Robert Chalmers took the contrary view, and asserted in his memorandum for the Cabinet that a major increase in the duty on bills of exchange would endanger 'the international pre-eminence of London in the matter of foreign bills (and of much else in consequence)'.[30] Lloyd George, who had been in touch with Lord Rothschild on the matter, sided with Chalmers, taking the line that he was most anxious not to threaten the position of London.[31] The proposal was finally killed at the meeting of 7 April, when the Cabinet reviewed the over-all content of the Budget before breaking up for the Easter recess. 'Bills of exchange stamp is gone', Harcourt reported to Crewe after the Cabinet meeting of that day.[32]

The Cabinet had carried out its main review of the stamp duties on 26 March, and at the meetings of 30 and 31 March, the last before the conclusion of the current fiscal year, it began its discussion of the over-all design of the Budget in the light of Lloyd George's preliminary estimates of the deficit that would have to be met in 1909/10. At these meetings he put his likely deficit on the basis of existing taxation at £17,000,000. The extraordinary size of the projected deficit, he explained, was due not only to new items of expenditure, but also to an anticipated shrinkage in the revenue from existing sources. The reaction of a good many in the Cabinet to the figure of £17,000,000 was one of amazed disbelief, and on 1 April, when the preliminary figures for the 1908/9 fiscal year became available, they proceeded to query Lloyd George's calculations. According to John Burns the Cabinet meeting of that day witnessed:

L. G. piano, deftly fighting for his view nearly all against him for good and sound reasons. His deficit [on 1908/9] only £700,000 as against his prediction of 5 or 6 millions. His estimate of Trade for year just as wrong. He is very much out of his depths, and but for his friends would have been submerged. His enemies and he has promoted them have corrected his vagaries and in so doing helped him and themselves.[33]

Most members of the Cabinet anticipated better trade during 1909/10 than did Lloyd George, and were consequently more sanguine about the revenue to be obtained from dutiable commodities. 'There is no doubt', Asquith wrote to the King in his report on the three Cabinet meetings between 1 and 6

April, 'that there is a distinct and growing improvement in the trade of the country which ought before long to show its effects in increased consumption of dutiable commodities, and a consequent rise in the normal revenue.' He informed the King that the Chancellor now put his estimated deficit for 1909/10 at 'not more than' £16,000,000, and that the Prime Minister himself was 'not without hope that before the Budget is introduced the latter figure may be substantially reduced'. He also informed the King that the Cabinet had been considering the Chancellor's proposals with regard to the income tax and the death duties and that all the Chancellor's proposals would come up for further consideration, on their own merits and in relation to one another, after Lloyd George had submitted his proposals for indirect taxation.[34]

For the income tax Lloyd George's proposal to the Cabinet was to increase the rate by 2*d*. in the £ on all unearned incomes over £700, and on all incomes, earned or unearned, over £2,000; he estimated the yield from this at £3,500,000 in 1909/10 and at £4,350,000 in the following year. For a supertax, which the Cabinet was in principle agreed to introduce, Lloyd George put forward two possible schemes. The first was to tax incomes over £5,000 at 1*s*. 6*d*. on the whole income, and to tax incomes between £3,000 and £5,000 at 1*s*. 4*d* on the whole income. The second, which Chalmers wanted, was to impose a supertax of 6*d*. in the £ on all incomes over £5,000 and to charge it on the amount by which they exceeded £3,000. Whichever formula was adopted, he estimated a yield of roughly £1,000,000 in 1909/10, bringing the combined estimate for income tax and supertax to £4,500,000.[35]

As Edwin Montagu, the Prime Minister's parliamentary private secretary, had advised Asquith on 25 March, Lloyd George's first scheme for the supertax differed from most others in that the heavier tax was to be levied on the entire income. He further advised Asquith that Harcourt objected most strongly to starting any supertax scheme under £5,000.[36]

Harcourt duly prepared for the Cabinet a memorandum in which he set forward his views and own proposals. Any system where the taxpayer found himself liable to supertax on the whole of his income the moment that income exceeded £5,000, he contended, 'would be so violently assailed by one of the largest classes of income taxpayers as to make the passage of such a proposal almost impossible'. What he recommended instead was the scheme contemplated in 1894 by his father, Sir William Harcourt, for a separate rate of supertax on each progressive block of £5,000 after the first £5,000 of income. If the supertax rate progressed by ½d. steps on each block of £5,000, Harcourt estimated a yield of £622,000 in 1909/10, and ultimately of £1,866,000.[37]

Harcourt's estimates were not taken too seriously by Somerset House; they were regarded as 'hyper-Chiozza in their extravagance'.[38] The main case against his scheme, as presented in a memorandum by Sir Robert Chalmers, was that by entirely exempting the first £5,000 about £50,000,000 of income would be removed from the scope of the new tax, and such a sacrifice of revenue could not really be contemplated. Chalmers proposed that by levying the supertax on incomes over £5,000 and exempting the first £2,000 or £3,000 the principle for which Harcourt contended could be recognized.[39] This formula, exempting the first £3,000, was the one Lloyd George advocated once it was made clear that he could not get his own graduated scheme. Harcourt, and some others in the Cabinet, remained opposed to taxing any part of the first £5,000 at the super-tax rate, but at the Cabinet meeting of 6 April Lloyd George finally got his way, with due assistance from Asquith. 'Budgeting all day', Lloyd George reported to his brother on 6 April. 'Got on extremely well on one point where Cabinet was very divided, but on which I was very keen. Prime Minister decided in my favour to my delight.'[40]

Lloyd George also got the Cabinet's approval for raising the general rate of the income tax from 1s. to 1s. 2d.. Two sets of concessions were decided upon by the Cabinet. The one was to extend the relief Asquith had granted to earned incomes by allowing earned incomes not in excess of £3,000 to pay 9d. on the first £2,000 and 1s. between £2,000 and £3,000. The other, along the lines of Lloyd George's own recommendation, was to grant an abatement of £10 for every child under 16 years for persons with incomes under £500.[41] After these concessions had been made the combined estimate for the increased income tax and the supertax was put at £3,500,000, £3,000,000 being allowed for income tax and £500,000 for supertax.[42]

On his proposals for the death duties Lloyd George again ran into major resistance, again led by Harcourt. Harcourt made a dead set against the proposal to abolish the settlement estate duty established by his father and to charge the cession of every life interest in a settled property with the regular estate duty, and he also protested the 'savagery' of the proposed new scale for the estate duty. At the Cabinet meeting of 7 April, Harcourt got his way on settled property and it was agreed to scrap Lloyd George's proposal in favour of a simple doubling of the existing one-per-cent settlement duty on the principal value of an estate.[43] This was not, however, the formula used in the draft of the Finance Bill prepared on 8 April. Clause 49 of the draft provided that the new settlement duty should be 30 per cent of the amount of estate duty payable and that, as Harcourt wrote in protest to Asquith, was 'a very different thing'.[44] When the Cabinet reconvened after the Easter recess, Harcourt finally won his case for a settlement duty of two per cent on the value of the estate. On the scale for the estate duty, Harcourt's success was rather more limited. Lloyd George's proposed new rates were eased for estates below £150,000, but the rates approved by the Cabinet still represented a heavy increase on the existing rates. In the scale approved by the Cabinet, which shortened the steps of graduation, the new rates began for estates valued at £5,000, which were to be charged at 4 instead of 3 per cent, and reached a maximum of 15 per cent on estates valued at £1,000,000 or over.[45] Previously estates of £1,000,000 had paid at the rate of 11 per cent, and the maximum of 15 per cent had only applied to estates over £3,000,000.

As a consequence of the decision to abandon Lloyd George's proposal for settled property, and the trimming of part of his new scale for estate duty, the estimate for the new death duties was revised downwards from £4,500,000 to £3,200,000 on 7 April.[46] The marginal changes made in

Lloyd George's proposals for increasing the rates for the legacy and succession duties did not affect the estimates for 1909/10 as these duties were not as a rule payable until the end of the executor's year, and no new revenue was expected from them until 1910/11.

At the crucial meeting of 7 April, the last before the Easter recess, the Cabinet approved increases in the duties on spirits and tobacco estimated to yield £3,400,000 in 1909/10, and then reviewed the over-all content of the Budget in the light of Lloyd George's revised estimates. The general result, Asquith reported to the King, was that of the £16,000,000 that had to be provided, £10,200,000 would fall on direct taxation, £3,400,000 on indirect taxation, and the balance would be taken from the Sinking Fund.[47] The over-all balance sheet, on the basis of existing taxation, as it stood on 7 April was:[48]

Expenditure	£164,552,000
Revenue	£148,900,000
Actual deficit	£ 15,652,000
Deficit to be provided for	£ 16,000,000

The detailed estimates for the existing taxes were:[49]

	Estimate 1909/10 £	Receipts 1908/9 £
Customs	28,100,000	29,200,000
Excise	32,560,000	33,650,000
Estate Duties	18,600,000	18,370,000
Stamps	7,600,000	7,770,000
Land Tax	750,000	730,000
House Duty	1,900,000	1,900,000
Income Tax	33,900,000	33,930,000
Post Office	22,400,000	22,300,000
Crown Lands	530,000	530,000
Suez Canal Shares etc.	1,166,000	1,171,466
Miscellaneous	1,394,000	2,026,829
Total	148,900,000	151,578,295

The estimates for the new taxes were:[50]

	£
Estate Duties	3,200,000
Income Tax	3,000,000
Super Tax	500,000
Stamps	750,000
Licences	2,250,000
Land	500,000
Indirect	3,400,000
	13,600,000
Sinking Fund	2,500,000
Total	16,100,000

From the Cabinet meeting of 7 April Harcourt came away highly pleased with the result. 'We had a hard fight', he wrote to Crewe, 'but an almost complete triumph at the Cabinet today.' Lloyd George's settlement duty proposal had been abandoned, the stamp duty on bills of exchange was gone, and he had been instructed to see Lloyd George and Thring, the Government draftsman, to arrange the rephrasing of the clauses for the reversion duty so as to make it clear that, in estimating the total value of a hereditament for the purposes of the duty, buildings were not to be estimated at their full value if the ground rent was originally a low one in consideration of a covenant for the erection of the buildings and their surrender in tenantable repair at the end of the lease.[51] But if Harcourt was well pleased with the changes made in the provisions of the Finance Bill on 7 April, Runciman was most unhappy about the balance sheet presented to the Cabinet that day, and after the Cabinet meeting he wrote to Asquith challenging the validity of Lloyd George's estimates and suggesting that the Chancellor had manipulated them in an effort to justify the full barrage of his new taxes:

Private   7 April, 1909.

My dear Prime Minister,

This morning's Balance Sheet leaves my mind in an uneasy state & I do hope that we have not finally said Goodbye to it. My grounds for uneasiness are these: first, it is clear to me that even the revised income tax figures are too low; second, the estimate of the yield of the Supertax seems to have £1,500,000 at least deducted for evasions, machinery & incomplete collection out of less than twice that amount of tax; third, the estate duties are based on this year's figures & I strongly suspect that Chalmers has been manipulating this year's takings; fourth, the new Stamps estimate seems to me to bear no exact relation to any Inland Revenue estimate — it is a mere personal shot.

Of course it is impossible to say accurately — unless one were at the Treasury — what "round figure" deductions have been made from the officials' estimates, or to what extent they were told to make the estimates conservative. But I feel sure that the yield of the *new* taxation (apart from the compression of existing yields) is put at least at £2,000,000 too low.

That is in itself serious enough to justify our dropping one or part of one of the Direct taxes. I fancy that George anticipates pressure of this kind & will want to drop the new *Indirect* taxes, when he is run to earth.

Further, the cutting down of the figures for the yield of the new taxes affects 1910—11, & if my guess be correct the natural increase of revenue from them will be quite enough to meet the additional foreseeable liabilities without calling on the Sinking Fund for a penny more then. The foreseeable liabilities calculated even on the haphazard method of last week don't amount to more than £7,000,000, if we exclude Winston's Unemployed £1,100,000 & the dole to local authorities of £2,000,000 neither of which is even outlined to the Cabinet.

I don't like having to challenge George's estimates or contest his claims to our consent to the whole of his new taxes without exception, but I feel that we have no justification for taking from the taxpayer more than is really necessary & if we allow the figures presented this morning to go out untested, we (or those of us who know Treasury methods) cannot support them without serious misgiving. None of us desire the House to be misled, or more money than necessary to be exacted.

My instinct may be at fault or I may have miscalculated the income & super tax items, but I think I am not wrong in saying that, apart from all other considerations, we are running the risk on this morning's figures of leaving a huge nest egg for our successors.

Please forgive me for pouring out my uneasiness to you, & believe me to be

Very sincerely yours,
Walter Runciman[52]

The immediate upshot of Runciman's attack on Lloyd George's revenue estimates was that Asquith, on the afternoon of 7 April, asked Sir George Murray to inquire into the matter. Murray reported back to Asquith in a letter from his home that evening.

There was no doubt, Murray stated at the outset, that the revenue estimates, both for the new and existing taxes, were very much on the safe side, and could perhaps be scaled up to the extent of £1,250,000. However, he could hardly criticize a Chancellor of the Exchequer who declined to do so, for, he submitted:

There never was a Budget in which the uncertain elements of calculation bulked so largely — e.g. Supertax, an entirely new system, brought into operation very late in the year, with all kinds of indirect effects; coupled with an enormous increase (33%) of one of the drink duties, and a murderous increase of licence duties. Then you have also to take into account (a) disturbance of this year's revenue owing to fore-stalling in last year, (b) a rather late Budget, giving opportunities for more tricks of the same kind, and (c) a still later date for the passing of the Finance Act — which affects Stamps more particularly.

Regarding the estimates for the existing taxes, Murray thought that 'an exuberant man' might add £200,000 or £300,000 to excise, and £100,000 to the income tax, but he did not believe that £18,600,000 was an underestimate for the estate duties. Chalmers assured him, he informed the Prime Minister, that there had been no 'hanky panky' over the estate duty figures. The £19,070,000 received in 1907/8, he explained, was about £350,000 more than it should have been. As for the new taxes, he was 'pretty sure' that the death duties were about right, though the estimate for the income tax was decidedly on the low side. He then added:

But the supertax is a leap in the dark; and so is the concession to "brats", and to the earned incomes between £2,000 and £3,000. It would be a very good thing to get rid of both of these: the first introduces a new principle into our fiscal system, and in a rather ridiculous way; the second is not wanted at all. But as regards *super tax*, it must be remembered that an entirely new machinery will have to be set up at very short notice, that there will be no time to correct people's returns, that for this year at any rate we shall have to trust entirely to their own admissions, that some very smart intellects are already hard at work devising methods of evasion or avoidance, that it will be some years before the "Intelligence Dept." of the I. R. will be able to make much impression on the assessments, and that the indirect effects of such a tax are quite incalculable at present. It may also be politic to put the estimated yield low, so as not to frighten people.

Still, after allowance had been made for all these considerations, he thought the Chancellor could increase his estimates by £400,000 or £500,000. The yield of the new licences, he continued, was 'quite an unknown quantity', and he could not say that £2,250,000 was too low. Stamps, he conceded, might be rather under the mark, but land at £500,000 was too high, and he doubted whether they could get half that. Spirits, he believed, ought to get more than £1,500,000. He concluded: 'But the whole thing is a leap in the dark, & we have absolutely no experience to guide us. Nevertheless I do not think that, on the whole, it would be rash to count on the new taxes yielding nearly 1 million more than the C. of Ex. expects.'[53]

Murray, in short, both supported Runciman's contention that the revenue estimates were very conservative, and partially justified Lloyd George in making them so. This was good enough to serve Lloyd George's purposes, and the challenge to his estimates, which went back to late March, seems to have petered out at this point. Certain ministers, including Harcourt, remained convinced that 'expenditure is over-estimated and revenue under-estimated', but there is no evidence that Lloyd George's estimates were seriously challenged at the Cabinet meetings of 26 and 28 April, after the Easter recess.[54] Indeed, he seems to have mesmerized his critics within the Cabinet by reducing substantially some of his revenue estimates over the Easter recess and then putting up a case for new taxes in addition to those already approved.

For the Easter recess Lloyd George, in a quite extraordinary move, took himself and his 'entourage' of officials off to Brighton where, virtually incommunicado to the outside world, they spent a week going over the Budget proposals and estimates. Only Harcourt, who sent off a strong memorandum on the settlement estate duty, seems to have elicited any response from the Chancellor at Brighton; on 16 April Lloyd George wrote back to 'The First Commissioner of Works' expressing 'surprise' at the fact that a copy of the latest draft of the Finance Bill should have reached him, and assuring the First Commissioner that he naturally intended to inform the Cabinet of the alteration he had made in the settlement estate duty and to give his reasons for proposing it.[55] Asquith, for his part, could get no reply to the letter he sent asking Lloyd George when he was likely to

be ready to meet the Cabinet again, though he does not seem to
have been either surprised or perturbed by this. 'Lloyd
George's methods of finance', he explained to Pease, who was
anxious to settle the date of Budget Day, '[were] astonishing,
and it was not unreasonable that he should shut himself up at
Brighton. . . .'[56]

On his return from Brighton Lloyd George discovered two
'errors' in his estimate, which suddenly left him badly short
of revenue for the year. In a rather garbled entry in his diary
for 20 April, Pease recounted that after first seeing Lloyd
George to discuss the date of the Budget, which was obviously
to be delayed as the Chancellor was not ready:

I had a subsequent talk with Asquith & then asked Ll. George to join
us – he explained how 2 errors had occurred creating deficit of
£500,000, had only been noticed that day – one item of £350,000
had been put in before item decided upon, & reappeared afterwards
again, when cabinet decided upon it. Chambers [*sic*] was to sit up,
& try how to arrange a graduated tax on ? House property [*sic*] to
meet it.[57]

The error of £350,000 referred to the estimate for the new
death duties, which was reduced by precisely that amount to
£2,850,000 for the Cabinet meeting of 26 April, the first
after the Easter recess.[58] Also revised downwards, by some
£510,000, was the estimate for existing excise duties, bringing the estimate from existing sources down to
£148,390,000.[59] The expenditure estimates remained fundamentally unaltered – the provision of £400,000 for 'services in
sight' in the balance sheet of 7 April was reduced slightly to
£350,000, which was to be the provision for the year for labour
exchanges and the development grant – with the result that,
instead of focusing on paring down Lloyd George's new taxes,
as Runciman and Harcourt wanted, the Cabinet after the
Easter recess had to consider ways and means of warding off
Lloyd George's proposal to introduce yet another new tax by
providing for graduated rates for the inhabited house duty.[60]
To make up part of the leeway between estimated revenue
and expenditure, Lloyd George recommended, and the
Cabinet accepted, adjustments in the licence duties that
raised the estimate by £350,000 to £2,600,000. Otherwise the effective choice before the Cabinet was between

the graduated house duty and a further raid on the Sinking
Fund, and the latter course was finally decided upon; another
£500,000 was diverted from the Sinking Fund, raising the
total diversion to £3,000,000. The Cabinet decision in
favour of Harcourt's formula for the settlement duty in
preference to Lloyd George's did not affect the estimates for
the year, and the decision to drop two of the stamp duties,
worth £100,000, was balanced by an increase in the estimate
for the tobacco duties, which became £1,600,000. Altogether,
after these changes, the balance sheet stood as follows:[61]

Existing basis of taxation

	£
Expenditure	164,502,000
Revenue	148,390,000
Actual Deficit	16,112,000
Deficit to be provided for	16,500,000
New taxes	
Estate Duties etc.	2,850,000
Income Tax	3,000,000
Super Tax	500,000
Stamps	650,000
Licences	2,600,000
Land	500,000
Spirits	1,600,000
Tobacco	1,900,000
	13,600,000
Sinking Fund	3,000,000
Total	16,600,000

This left Lloyd George with the rather substantial 'margin
for contingencies' of £488,000, but with the contingent Dreadnoughts in mind a large margin was deemed necessary. Should
no contingencies arise and the Budget produce a realized
surplus Lloyd George sought, in another of his novel moves,
to divert the surplus away from the Old Sinking Fund into
roads and development. One of the Budget resolutions
approved by the Cabinet on 28 April provided that any
surplus should 'be applied in such manner as the Treasury

direct for promoting transit facilities in the United Kingdom and the general economic development of the Kingdom, in accordance with any scheme which may be sanctioned by Parliament for the purpose'.[62] The petrol tax of 3*d.* a gallon, and the new graduated scale for motor car licences, approved by the Cabinet were treated apart from the regular finance for the year; the estimated yield of £600,000 from these taxes for 1909/10 was to go into a special fund for the improvement of roads.

III

In the main, the changes made to Lloyd George's proposals in the Cabinet served to accentuate rather than to mitigate the progressive features of the Budget as a measure for raising revenue. Where rates were altered, as for 'on' licences and the estate duty, they were generally lightened in their lower reaches, and, in the instance of the 'on' licences, heightened in their upper reaches. Again, the effect of the decision to maintain the existing rates of income tax on earned incomes up to £3,000 was to protect the vast majority of income tax-payers against the higher general rate, at least in so far as their incomes were earned. It meant that the burden of the increase in the general rate was to be carried by unearned income and the 25,000 or so tax-payers with incomes over £3,000. The scheme adopted by the Cabinet for the supertax meant that its burden was to be carried entirely by the 10,000 or so persons with incomes over £5,000.

In the case of the settlement estate duty, the Cabinet's decision in favour of Harcourt's proposal to increase the existing rate to 2 per cent of the value of the estate in preference to Lloyd George's proposal for a duty of 30 per cent of the estate duty payable, meant the abandonment of any graduation of the settlement estate duty, and in this instance the decision was to the detriment of the smaller estates and to the benefit of the larger. Whereas an estate of £6,000 would have paid £72 under Lloyd George's scheme, it paid £120 under Harcourt's scheme, and whereas an estate of £201,000 would have paid £6,633 under Lloyd George's scheme, it paid £4,020 under Harcourt's.[63]

In political terms, the changes made in the Cabinet in the proposed new taxes were designed to mitigate the opposition that the land value taxes would inevitably arouse, to narrow down the number of income tax payers who would be significantly affected by the increase in the general rate of the income tax, and to make the licence duties more effective as a means for raising revenue by seeking to avoid precipitating too great a 'slaughter' of public house and beerhouse licences.

The end product was a Budget which, as *The Times* commented, struck the wealthy and the fairly well-to-do in every sort of way — through the income tax, the death duties, the stamps upon their investments, their land, their royalties, their brewing dividends, and their motor cars.[64] The indirect taxes which affected the working classes, the spirit and tobacco duties, affected their 'luxuries' only, and the estimated yield of £3,500,000 was only marginally higher than the amount released in the previous year by Asquith's reduction of the sugar duty. In the circumstances, it was not surprising that *The Times* should conclude that the Budget prepared by Lloyd George, and sanctioned by the Cabinet, was 'a vindictive Budget, which strikes heavily and repeatedly at the classes which do not favour the party now in power'.[65] It was above all the persons who lived off 'unearned' income, by inheritance, the ownership of land, and investments, who were 'repeatedly' called upon by the 'People's Budget' to make the financial sacrifices necessary to preserve the system of free trade and avert large-scale taxation of the people's food.

As Lord Carrington noted with satisfaction in his diary, 'The chief burden is laid on the shoulders of people who have between 5 and 50 thousand a year . . . but the working classes are only taxed on their luxuries drink, & tobacco: while the middle classes earning under £2000 are not hit at all. Agricultural land escapes very easily and is hardly taxed at all.'[66]

IV

The final drama in the preparation of the Budget was the drafting of Lloyd George's Budget speech. According to the marvellous story told by Frank Owen, in *Tempestuous Journey,* the final draft of the speech was prepared by John Bradbury and 'Willie' Clark, Lloyd George's private secretary, who both hurried down to join Lloyd George in Brighton over the week-end before Budget Day. As Owen relates the story:

They got to bed at 6 a.m. on Monday morning, rushed back to London by the early train with many corrections, as well as several new ideas. Two confidential typists, a man and a woman, then went into action on the revised Budget Speech. At 2 a.m. on Tuesday, Budget morning, the woman broke down, and was sent home by taxi. The job was completed by dawn, and then faithful Willie Clark went off to bath, breakfast, and be back in the office by nine o'clock.[67]

Much of the story rings true, but the main problem with it is that Budget Day was on Thursday, 29 April, not the Tuesday.

For the week-end concerned, Lloyd George wrote to his brother, in an undated letter, that he had 'Got the whole thing well in hand now. Pretty well all written and if I distrust my memory I shall read it out from start to finish. The House won't mind. It will be too interested in the substance to concern itself with form and delivery.'[68]

There were too many critics around, among his Cabinet colleagues as well as among the Unionists, to let him off the latter point.

VII. The Budget in the Commons and the Country

I

Lloyd George introduced his historic Budget in the House of Commons on 29 April. As a parliamentary performance his Budget speech was not a success. He read it from manuscript, and read it badly. For four and a half hours he stumbled over his sentences while members complained they could not hear him. Afterwards Leverton Harris, the Unionist member for Stepney, commented to Haldane that the Chancellor read his speech like a man who did not understand what he was reading. 'Of course he doesn't', Haldane replied. 'Why, we have been trying for weeks to make him understand clause — of the Bill, and he *can't*!'[1]

From the outset of his speech Lloyd George made it clear that he was not interested in a mere 'temporary shift' to carry the country's finances over until the next year, and that he intended his Budget as a 'social reform' Budget. The Budget, Lloyd George told the House, had been framed with future needs clearly in mind and was designed to provide the wherewithal to meet inevitable expansion of expenditure for national defence and social reform. It was on the latter that he placed his emphasis. In a long survey of the 'urgent' social problems that confronted the nation he foreshadowed virtually the Government's entire social reform programme for the next two years: the removal of pauper disqualifications from old age pensions, the introduction of unemployment and sickness insurance, the creation of a national system of labour exchanges, and the establishment of a Development Grant for the work of national economic development. At the end of his speech he proclaimed: 'This, Mr. Emmott, is a War Budget. It is for raising money to wage implacable warfare against poverty and squalidness.'[2]

Three principles, Lloyd George informed the House, underlay his financial proposals. The first was that the new taxes should be expansive in character, designed to grow in

172

yield with the growing demands of the state. The second was that the taxes should not inflict any injury on the trade or commerce which constituted the sources of the nation's wealth. The third was that all classes in the community ought to be called upon to contribute in the current financial emergency, though he had kept it in mind that the industrial classes were already paying in taxation more than their share in proportion to their income.[3]

In short, Lloyd George declared in his Budget speech that he intended his handiwork as a 'People's Budget', in the sense that it would provide the finance required for an advanced programme of social reform, in that it would impose greater increases in direct than in indirect taxation, and in that it would seek at least to equalize the burden of taxation between classes in proportion to income. At the same time the Budget represented nothing less than the free trade solution to the 'financial emergency' brought on by the pressing demands of defence and social reform.

To the Unionists the proposals came as something of a shock. 'What a Budget it is!', Austen Chamberlain exclaimed in a letter to Mrs. Joseph Chamberlain. 'All the rumours were wrong, and there is the super-tax and land values tax and the unearned increment tax, besides countless other changes and increases.'[4]

What Lloyd George had done was to have caught the Unionists temporarily off guard. In December the Unionists had freely predicted a 'vindictive' Budget, but Lloyd George had since then sought to still their fears and lull them into the expectation of an essentially conventional Budget. After his provocative Liverpool speech of 21 December he had become the very image of sweet reasonableness and conciliation. When speaking before the Law Society on 29 January, he had disclaimed any intention of using the Budget for a punitive expedition against the tribes which had been molesting the Government, and had repudiated as a 'bad joke' his statement of the previous July that he was looking for 'someone's hen-roost to rob' in order to pay for old-age pensions.[5] His professions had had the desired effect. *The Times*, certainly, took them to mean that the responsible sections of the Liberal party had now gained control and that the Budget would not be of a vindictive nature.[6] On the very morning of Budget Day, *The Times* predicted 'in looking for his fifteen millions Mr. Lloyd George will keep very much to the old ways'.[7] The next day *The Times* could only conclude of the Budget that 'it would seem as if it were intended to be provocative'. It struck 'almost exclusively' at the wealthy and fairly well-to-do; it raised and attempted to prejudge several controversial issues; and the Budget speech had opened up a number of questions which went beyond the proposals in the Budget and seemed 'rather to invite controversy'.[8]

On the Liberal side of the House of Commons, Lloyd George's Budget was greeted with general enthusiasm and a real sense of excitement. As Herbert Samuel, the Home Undersecretary, reported to Herbert Gladstone, who had missed the Budget speech because of ear trouble: 'The general opinion is that it was not a great speech though — so think most of our men — it is a great Budget.' He added: 'Some think we could never have anything better to fight the Lords on.' The over-all reaction of Liberal MPs Samuel described as 'one of frightened satisfaction, the kind of feeling one has of being launched down an exhilarating, but steep and unknown toboggan run'. Some Liberal MPs, however, entirely disapproved of the Chancellor's proposals. Sir Thomas Whittaker, the member for Spen Valley and the leading spokesman of the temperance reformers in the Liberal party, thought the Budget 'absurd, preposterous and fantastic', and told Samuel that the Government ought to 'burn it to-morrow morning and introduce another Budget on business-like lines'.[9]

Lloyd George himself seemed well pleased with the initial reaction, and was impressed by the fact that Consols rose one-eighth per cent the day after the Budget statement. On 1 May he wrote to his brother: 'Budget going strong — overwhelmed with congratulations. Prime Minister delighted with its reception. The most extraordinary thing is the way the City have taken it. F. E. Smith told me the Lords are not such fools as to throw it out. "Do you think they are mad?" he said to me.'[10]

What greatly troubled Lloyd George even at this early

stage was the problem of finding the parliamentary time to get the Budget through the Commons, for he was under no illusions that his proposals would be tenaciously contested. From the first he recommended procedure by guillotine, even for the Budget resolutions, but neither his Cabinet colleagues nor Pease, the Chief Whip, would hear of it.[11] Any such procedure, Harcourt contended, would encourage and justify the Lords in rejecting or amending the Budget with the general concurrence of the country.[12] The conclusion that Lloyd George came to, perhaps unfairly, was that his Cabinet colleagues would like to see the Budget 'killed by time'. 'But they won't', he assured his brother, 'as the Party is behind me.'[13]

On 24 May, when the Budget resolutions reached the report stage, Lloyd George still claimed to be enormously pleased with the reaction to the Budget in the country. From what he had been told, he informed J. A. Spender, the Budget had 'put new heart' into the party, whereas he heard that the 'other side' could arouse no indignation except amongst the very wealthy, and that the Tariff Reformers were especially depressed, 'as they are convinced that if the Budget goes through their cause is lost'.[14] None the less, the feeling was by then growing among Liberals that Lloyd George had made the mistake of attacking too many powerful interests at once, and over the next two months Lloyd George was to come under substantial pressure to drop the land value taxes.

Until July the political tide appeared to be running against the Budget and the Government. The Finance Bill itself, which was read a first time on 26 May, did no more than inch its way through the Commons; in the country the interests affected by the Budget succeeded in working up a loud clamour against the proposed new taxes; and within the Liberal ranks a serious 'cave' against the land taxes, which were taken first, emerged. By August the tide was seen by all sides to have turned, and this turn was assisted by the formation of the Budget League, and by a series of decisions taken by the Cabinet.

On 10 June, after four days' debate, the Finance Bill passed its second reading. During the second reading debate, though the role that the Lords was to take was as yet left shadowy, the major battle lines that were to dominate the fight over the Budget were drawn.

In the course of the second reading debate, the Unionists made three points abundantly clear. The first was that the Tariff Reformers had no intention of running away from the 'challenge' that the Budget represented to the cause of tariff reform. As Austen Chamberlain, who had assumed the leadership of the Tariff Reformers following his father's stroke, declared, when moving the rejection of the Finance Bill: 'We are told that it is the final triumph of Free Trade and the death blow to the policy of Fiscal Reform. Sir, in the spirit in which it is offered, I accept the challenge, and I am ready to go to the country at any moment upon it.' The Budget, he asserted, was a weapon of oppression and confiscation, and if that represented the 'highest offer' of free trade finance confronted with a fiscal emergency, then the sooner they took their two alternatives to the country the better.[15]

The second point made clear in the second reading debate was that the Unionists planned to center much of their campaign against the Budget on the allegation that it represented the first step in a socialist war against property. Before the introduction of the Budget, Philip Snowden had suggested in an I.L.P. pamphlet, *A Few Hints to Lloyd George,* that the Chancellor should impose a supertax, increase the estate duties, tax land values, and place a special tax on industrial monopolies.[16] In the Budget, Lloyd George had seemingly followed Snowden's main suggestions, and in the Commons Snowden complimented him on proving an 'apt pupil'.[17] Too apt, was the Unionist charge. For the first time, Bonar Law told the Commons, they were face to face with a socialist Budget. In a point Unionist speakers were to make time and again, he insisted that there was no justification for treating land differently from other forms of property, and warned that the Government's supporters were living in a fool's paradise if they imagined the confiscatory proposals of the Budget were going to stop at land. The Socialists, he reminded them, had avowed over and over again that they intended to apply the same principles to all forms of property.[18] British Conservatism, as was to become apparent, had launched its first crusade against socialism.

A third point made evident in the second reading debate was that the Unionists were at least preparing their ground to challenge the constitutionality of the Budget. Several Unionist speakers, including Chamberlain and Balfour, queried Lloyd George's estimates, with Balfour stressing that the Chancellor had so far steadfastly refused to answer the criticisms that he had utterly miscalculated his revenue, and they said it was clear to them that a desire to get around the Lords, rather than a desire to produce revenue, underlay some of his proposals.[19] Possible action against the Budget by the Lords was not referred to directly, but Bonar Law stated outright: 'These proposals are admittedly revolutionary ... They come from a Government which has lost, and knows that it has lost, the confidence of the country ... Now I say deliberately that under these circumstances that such proposals coming from such a Government should actually be carried into law is utterly intolerable, and I think it is impossible.'

The Irish Nationalists, for their part, took particular exception to the new indirect taxes, notably the whiskey duty, and the licence duties as being unfair to Ireland. In the voting on the second reading, sixty-two Irish Nationalists sided with the Opposition. There was no cross voting by either Liberals or Unionists, but some thirty-eight members were absent unpaired on the Liberal and Labour side.

For directing the fight against the Budget in the Commons, the Unionists formed a general committee, with Austen Chamberlain as chairman, which was divided into four subcommittees. Subcommittee A, again chaired by Chamberlain, was deputed to deal with the Budget proposals for income tax and the death duties; B, chaired by Sir Frederick Banbury, a City financier, with customs and the stamp duties; C, chaired by George Faber, the MP for York, with licences; and D, chaired by E. G. Pretyman, a landowner, with the land taxes.[20] These subcommittees worked closely with the respective 'interests' affected by the Budget, gathering information as to the general distress and particular hardships and anomalies likely to be promoted by the Budget proposals, and preparing amendments. In the instance of subcommittee C, the secretary of the National Trade Defence Association, W. E. Montgomery, not only suggested amendments to Faber, but even put forward 'a sort of Chairman's Agenda' for the important meeting of 18 August before licences were taken in the Commons.[21]

What alarmed many Liberals as the Finance Bill passed its second reading and entered the committee stage was the massive anti-Budget campaign that the Unionists and the 'interests' allied to them had begun to mount in the country. At the organizational level, the Tariff Reform League, the Middle Classes Defence Organisation, the Liberty and Property Defence League, and the Anti-Socialist Union were all mobilized; the Brewers' Society, the National Trade Defence Association, the Licensed Victuallers' Central Protection Society, and the Licensed Victuallers' National Defence League all came out strongly against the new licence duties; the Land Taxes Protest Committee was organized by professional groups and corporate bodies directly and indirectly interested in real estate; and in a letter published in *The Times* on 14 June Walter Long announced the formation of a Budget Protest League to concert action on the part of the community against the Budget. Long himself was president of the new League, and Captain H. M. Jessel, the former Unionist MP for St. Pancras South, was the chairman.

The loudest complaints against the 'unfairness' of the Budget came from the City, 'the trade', and the 'interests' involved in land.

In May and June City bankers, merchants, and businessmen, organized two major protests against the Budget. On 14 May they submitted a protest to the Prime Minister, and on 24 June Lord Rothschild presided over a protest meeting attended by nearly a thousand 'merchants and traders'. What the City resented most was the sense that Lloyd George had deliberately picked on the wealthy to carry the main burden of the new taxation, so as to make his Budget politically acceptable to the electorate. As Sir Felix Schuster, chairman of the Union of London and Smiths Banks and a Liberal, complained at the City meeting, the Budget 'put nearly the whole of the extra expenditure on one and a numerically small class of electors, and the great majority of the voters were practically untouched by it'.[22] At the meeting the City spokesmen stressed their willingness to accept their fair share of taxation, and claimed that their ground for opposing the Budget was that it would seriously damage the nation's commerce and industry, but Lord Carrington could not escape the conclusion that 'it really was a meeting of the rich men who won't pay for the Dreadnoughts they were clamouring for'.[23]

The brewers were truly incensed by what they deemed the 'vindictive' nature of the licence duties. They were outraged by the manufacturers' licence duty, which breached the 'compact' of 1880, and resented the provision that in the case of tied-houses the landlord brewer and not the licence holder was to pay the licence duty. As it was, the brewing trade was experiencing a slump, and London brewers particularly predicted that the effect of Lloyd George's new duties would be to make it impossible for many brewing companies to continue to pay a dividend. [24] On the stock exchange, however, brewing shares proved remarkably resilient.

Landowners likewise resented the land value taxes as an unfair discrimination against a particular form of property, and were convinced that political hostility rather than fiscal necessity underlay the new imposts. Even more so than the brewing trade, the property market was in a depressed condition, and Lloyd George's taxes were seen as likely to depress the market further. As the *Estates Gazette* saw it, 'Enormous sums of money must necessarily be lost before the market gets over the shock produced by this wanton differentiation between one class of property and another.' As was also pointed out by the *Estates Gazette* the great bulk of those professionally concerned with land were opposed to the new land value taxes, including even the surveyors and valuers for whom the Budget promised plenty of work.[25] In a memorandum of June the Council of the Surveyors' Institution condemned the land taxes as likely to 'send up rents and prices and diminish employment'.[26] None of the major interests involved in land, including builders, who often relied on a speculator's profit on their site, welcomed any tampering with the property market.[27]

What Unionist politicians sought to stress was that it was 'property' itself, and not simply particular forms of property, that was ultimately under attack in the Budget. That this might indeed be the case was a point that troubled a good few Liberals, and this concern was one of the factors that gave rise to the 'cave' that appeared in the Liberal ranks during the debate on the land value taxes. These were taken first in the committee stage of the Finance Bill rather than at the end, when they would become vulnerable to the argument that they should be dropped on the ground that there was insufficient time left to discuss them properly and as they were not essential for the financial needs of the year.

Before the committee stage was reached it was apparent that the land taxes might cause the Government more trouble than they could possibly be worth, and Ilbert, the highly partisan clerk of the House of Commons, seriously doubted the Government's wisdom in 'burning their boats' by taking them first.[28] The Liberal whips were of like opinion. During the debate on the Budget resolutions they had been greatly alarmed at the prospect of a large-scale revolt against the land taxes. According to what Alick Murray told Asquith, the representations made at the Whips' Office were far more numerous on the subject of the land taxes than any other, and he estimated that nearly 100 Liberal MPs would be 'irreconcilably opposed' to the duty on undeveloped land.[29]

When the Liberal 'cave' was organized in a series of meetings chaired by Sir Edward Tennant, the member for Salisbury City, in the week before the beginning of the committee stage, about 30 MPs were directly involved, and as many again were mentioned in the press as being sympathetic.[30] The 'cave' included landowners, most prominently Sir John Dickson-Poynder, who had left the Unionists to join the Liberals over the tariff issue, and Sir Thomas Glen-Coats, who was also a director of J. & P. Coats, the sewing-cotton manufacturers, and several MPs from rural constituencies who were apprehensive about the taxation of agricultural land, but was by no means confined to these groups. It was indeed a rallying-point for Liberal

MPs who disliked the general drift of Liberal politics and who particularly disliked the Budget, detecting in it an attack not merely on land but on 'property'. The 'cave' included several manufacturers and company directors, such as F. W. Chance, the managing director of the Carlisle cotton manufacturers, Ferguson Brothers; the personal followers of Lord Rosebery, notably Lord Dalmeny, Rosebery's eldest son, Sir Robert Perks, Rosebery's chief aide, and other prominent members of the Liberal League, including J. M. Paulton, the joint secretary of the Liberal League; Harold Cox, the maverick MP for Preston; Sir Thomas Whittaker, the temperance reformer, and Samuel Whitbread, the brewer. H. H. Raphael, the MP for Derbyshire South, expressed the attitude of a good many of the 'cavemen' when he wrote to Sir Henry Norman that the Budget was 'dishonest withal and very dangerous', and that he would have no truck with Socialism.[31] That the Budget was 'Socialistic' was the public stance adopted by Rosebery, who, in a famous speech at Glasgow on 10 September, declared Socialism to be 'the end of all', the negation of faith, family, property, monarchy, and Empire.[32]

As a significant proportion of the 'cave', including Glen-Coats, Chance, and Raphael, were members of the Liberal League, Sir Robert Perks, the MP for the Louth division of Lincolnshire and treasurer of the League, thought for a while of using the League as a base for organizing Liberal opposition to the Budget, but soon abandoned the idea.[33] Perks, as with ten of the twenty-two 'cavemen' named by *The Times*, was not to stand for re-election in January 1910. Cox did stand again for Preston, but as an independent Liberal, after having been thrown over by the constituency association, and A. C. T. Beck transferred his candidacy from the Wisbech division of Cambridgeshire, where he quarrelled with the local association over the Budget, to the Chippenham division of Wiltshire, where Dickson-Poynder was the retiring member.[34]

As it turned out the 'cave' was by no means as extensive as had initially been feared by the party whips, and it failed to inspire a sustained organized revolt among back-benchers against the Budget.

The climax of the revolt against the land taxes, and particularly the proposal for a national valuation of all land, including agricultural land, was reached on 23 June at a meeting of Liberal MPs summoned by Pease to discuss the organization of a Budget campaign in the constituencies. Over 200 MPs attended the meeting in the Committee Room of Westminister Hall. Haldane, who presided in place of Asquith, had to direct much of his energy to heading off the threatened resignation of some of the dissidents, who had been outraged by the attempt of the land taxers to arouse feeling against them in the constituencies, including their own.[35] Haldane wrote afterwards to his mother that '6 M.P.s came with their resignations in their pockets. It was a real Elija business, but I managed to smooth things over & to make peace. Everyone — from Lloyd George onwards was grateful.'[36]

In the circumstances, what the members of the 'cave' feared was that Pease's proposed Budget League would be used to bring pressure on them in their own constituencies, and Haldane's primary task was to reassure them that it would be no part of the League's purpose to take any kind of hostile action against Liberals who had doubts about certain parts of the Budget. The request made by Thomas Lough (Islington West) and Ivor Guest (Cardiff District) was that no meetings should be held by the League in the constituency of any Liberal member except with the member's consent. No formal resolution was taken to this effect, but Haldane gave the assurance that the League would secure the permission of Liberal MPs before acting in their constituencies. Chiozza Money, the Liberal MP for Paddington North and a land nationalizer, then asked that the English League for the Taxation of Land Values should not be affiliated with the Budget League, and protested against the intolerance shown to Liberals by that body, which had the temerity to denounce him as a Tory. The meeting thereupon approved the formation of the Budget League, with Haldane as president, Churchill as chairman, and Sir Henry Norman, the MP for South Wolverhampton and a former assistant editor of the *Daily Chronicle*, as secretary. Sir John Dickson-Poynder was co-opted onto the executive committee, though he soon left it.[37]

After the meeting of 23 June pressure was maintained by concerned Liberals to secure concessions for agricultural land from the application of the increment duty, and a handful of Liberal MPs found it impossible to reconcile themselves to the undeveloped land tax, but nothing more was heard of an organized revolt against the land value taxes or the Budget as a whole.

In point of fact, Lloyd George and the Cabinet were highly anxious to appease the 'agriculturalists', and at the Cabinet meeting of 23 June discussed ways and means for doing so, and for generally rallying more support to the land taxes. The Cabinet decided that half the proceeds of the land taxes should be handed over to local authorities, a move which Carrington believed would 'bring in an immense amount of support from the municipalities', and it was agreed that it should be made clear in the Finance Bill that no increment duty would be charged on the increased value of agricultural land arising out of the exertions and expenditure of those interested in the land or improvements in the general condition of agriculture.[38]

It had all along been one of the Cabinet's concerns not to antagonize unduly the rural constituencies, and as Ilbert informed Bryce, they really did not want to tax ordinary agricultural land.[39] The problem was to exempt purely agricultural land from the increment duty without at the same time exempting it from the valuation, and to ensure that agricultural land which possessed a special value, because in the vicinity of a growing town, did not escape the duty. The 'solution' that Lloyd George announced in the Commons on 13 July was to exempt from the increment duty land which had a purely agricultural value, and he also exempted the land of small occupying owners, but the valuation remained. The result, the Political Notes of *The Times* commented on 14 July, was to reduce the possibility of revenue from the increment duty to a minimum and to give more prominence to the scheme for a national valuation of the land.

Though the direct challenge from within the party's parliamentary ranks had subsided, and though Lloyd George believed he had 'squared the Agriculturalists' by his concessions of 13 July, the place of the land taxes in the Budget was not yet entirely secure. It did not become so until after Lloyd George had successfully repelled Pease's agitated demands of 16 July to 'lighten' the Budget, primarily by getting rid of the undeveloped land tax.

By mid-July, two considerations more or less obliged the Cabinet to review the situation concerning the land taxes. First, the progress of the land taxes through the committee stage was proving painfully slow, and exhausting to all MPs. By 13 July, after a series of late-night sittings, only three of the 28 clauses devoted to the land taxes had been dealt with. Second, talk that the Lords might reject or amend the Budget was spreading like wildfire, and it was widely held that only the abandonment of the land taxes would save the Budget from hostile action by the Lords.

In this situation Lloyd George produced at the Cabinet meeting of 16 July plans for procedural changes to shorten unnecessary discussion and to accelerate the progress of the Budget through the Commons. He accepted that the adoption of the guillotine would represent a triumph for the Opposition's tactics, and recommended instead what became known as the 'kangaroo', whereby the Chairman or Deputy Chairman of the House in committee could select or reject, by leave of the House, amendments for debate. Jack Pease was called in to give his views and, after approving Lloyd George's procedural plans, he 'let fly' and 'told the cabinet they were asking the House to do more than was physically possible, prudent or wise in interest of party or for chances of the bill, & asked for land to be lightened by ½d. tax postponed'. Lloyd George responded by making 'the usual cabinet threat of resigning' if 'lightening' was insisted upon, and ended up by saying that he had compromises and concessions in hand.[40] Some of these he had already worked out with Asquith, and they included the substitution of a tax on mining royalties for the tax on undeveloped minerals.[41] But the undeveloped land tax remained, and the land taxes had survived their last major test in the Cabinet.

While Lloyd George had all along shown himself conciliatory in the Commons and prepared to grant concessions on the land taxes, his whole inclination was against any fundamental retreat that would involve the abandonment or distortion of the valuation. He could not abandon the undeveloped land tax, he explained to Ilbert, precisely because it would lead to a distortion of the valuation: 'If the duty on undeveloped land were dropped, landowners would overvalue that land for the purposes of increment duty. The two taxes cut like the two blades of a pair of scissors.'[42] For political reasons, he impressed on J. A. Spender in a long letter of 16 July, he was determined to press ahead with the land taxes despite threats that the Lords would throw the Budget out. Basically he made three political points. The first, repeating earlier refrains, was that if the Government was again seen to run away at the first hint of menace from the Lords it would lose all credibility with its Radical supporters; indeed, he claimed that if the Government did surrender 'there are hundreds of thousands of Liberals who will say that the Party in its present form is perfectly hopeless as an effective machine for progress, and that it is high time either to form, or to federate with, another'. The second was that the land proposals had in fact revived that fighting spirit of the Liberal forces. The third was that he was not at all convinced that the passage of the Budget would have been any easier without the land taxes, and he contended that the popularity of the land taxes in the country, more than anything else, would make the Lords hesitate over rejecting the Budget.[43]

In the Commons the progress of the Budget speeded up somewhat after the concessions of 13 July, though there were some stormy scenes and distinct signs of strain all round. Lord Winterton accused Will Thorne, the Labour MP for West Ham South, of being drunk, and Asquith himself, according to Hobhouse in his diary, was drinking 'pretty hard'.[44] Emmott, the Deputy Speaker and committee chairman, was also under strain, and clashed with Lloyd George over the proposed procedural changes. 'There is no love lost between him and Lloyd George', Ilbert commented in his diary after their meeting on 19 July to discuss procedure. 'He thinks that L.G. hustles & L.G. thinks Emmott ineffective.' On the administrative side, Thring, the Government draftsman, broke down, and was ordered off for some rest.[45]

At 7.13 a.m. on 21 July, after an all-night sitting, the Commons carried clause 9 of the Finance Bill, and thereby completed the committee stage of the increment and reversion duties. The House was then given a three-week break from the Finance Bill, though not other business. On 26 July McKenna made the crucial announcement in the House that the Government would proceed with the four contingent Dreadnoughts, thereby blunting the Unionist campaign on the naval issue. In the meantime, Lloyd George prepared concessions on the remainder of the Finance Bill, and in the country the Liberals mounted a massive campaign to promote the Budget. When the debate on the Finance Bill was resumed on 9 August it was accepted that the Budget had gained enormously in popularity in the country.

II

Up to the end of June, Liberal ministers and MPs sympathetic towards the Budget had been troubled by the apparent failure of the Budget to ignite popular enthusiasm. Most of the running in the country had been made by the opponents and critics of the Budget, Liberal as well as Unionist. As was no doubt anticipated, several wealthy Liberals in the country had taken strong exception to the Budget. Sir Felix Schuster, who had stood as a Liberal candidate for the City of London in 1906, played a prominent role in City protests against the Budget, and Sir Walter Runciman, the shipowner and father of the Cabinet minister, thought the Budget 'hadn't the merit of being more than a concoction of loot', and consequently wanted to resign the chairmanship of the Northern Liberal Federation.[46] What was disturbing was the apparent lack of compensating enthusiasm from the working and ordinary middle classes, for whom the Budget was designed to appeal. These classes were in fact feeling the pinch of the Budget first, in increased prices for spirits and tobacco, and in the announcement that from 1 July beer in London would go up 1*d.* a quart.

In the main, the Liberal press had received the Budget enthusiastically, though not without reservations. The *Manchester Guardian* welcomed it as 'one of the most evenly distributed schemes we have ever had'; the *Daily Chronicle* likewise acclaimed it as according alike 'with democratic principle and with the dictates of justice' and predicted it would revitalize Liberalism; the *Westminster Gazette* praised it for 'taking toll of superfluity' and for not placing an undue burden on the middle class, though was disconcerted by the Budget's 'complexity'; the *Nation* hailed it as 'The First Democratic Budget'; and the *Review of Reviews* thought Lloyd George had seized the right moment for a comprehensive and far-reaching Budget, but it did express concern as to whether the working classes would respond to Lloyd George's appeal or would turn against him in their short-sightedness for adding to the cost of their whisky and tobacco.[47] The main carping came from those parts of the Liberal press with special 'hobbies' and interests. *The Economist,* which consistently bewailed the disappearance of 'economy', stated that: 'In our judgment the new taxation is objectionable mainly because much of the expenditure which has caused it is mischievous and unnecessary.'[48] For its part, *Land Values,* the organ of the land taxers, welcomed the Budget's provision for a universal valuation of land but was highly critical of the failure to provide for a straight tax on site value. On the Labour side, many spokesmen in the Commons and the country had been fulsome in their praise of the Budget, except the tobacco duty, on the main ground that 'rich people will pay 75 per cent of the new taxes'.[49] The *Labour Leader,* however, was rather more muted in its praise. In its view the Budget operated mainly 'in the interest of the smaller middle class', but it nevertheless welcomed the 'beginning of a system of taxing the wealth of the rich rather than the poverty of the poor'.[50]

Like Lloyd George, the *Labour Leader* in May believed that the supertax, the increased estate duties, and the land taxes were 'very popular in the country'. None the less, in the face of the clamour against the Budget created by its opponents, and the popular resentment against the immediate increases in the price of tobacco and spirits, and in the absence of a concerted Liberal drive to popularize the Budget in the country, many Liberals at Westminster sensed that the Budget as a whole had failed to 'catch on' in the country. 'It is difficult to understand why the Country is not more with us', Carrington mused in his diary on 1 July:

We have no doubt attacked a good many interests: and the Brewers are very sore and very active, and refuse to meet or help Asquith or Lloyd George in any way. We are told we have tried to do too much: and no Ministry that has to raise 16 millions can have a chance. But still when the people begin to understand the Budget: when they see that Agricultural Land is untaxed: and when no man who earns under £2,000 a year has to bear any extra taxation: surely they will support us against the cruel alternative of taxation of the poor man's food.

It was for the purposes of propagandizing the Budget in the country that, largely on Churchill's initiative, the Budget League was formed in late June. It was thereafter to play an important role in rallying popular support to the Budget.

The first clear sign that the Budget possessed a greater popularity in the constituencies than at first seemed evident from Westminster was provided by the outcome of the four by-elections contested in July. All four seats, the High Peak division of Derbyshire, Dumfries Burghs, the Cleveland division of Yorkshire, and Mid-Derbyshire, had been won by the Liberals in 1906. The Liberals retained the three seats they contested, and in Mid-Derbyshire the Labour candidate defeated the Unionist. Most attention was focused on High Peak, a mixed urban and rural constituency which was marginal and which the Unionists had high hopes of winning. The victory there of Oswald Partington, who had been made a Junior Lord of the Treasury, was acclaimed as a great triumph for the Budget and the land taxes. 'High Peak', C. P. Trevelyan wrote, 'was unquestionably won on the Budget and especially the Land Taxes. I frankly did not expect the win and it is a great victory. For, if we can keep that sort of seat we can keep anything.'[51] In all, the by-election successes of July were taken by the Liberal press to signify that the Budget had reversed the trend against the Government in the constituencies.

Simultaneous with the by-elections, the Budget League launched its concerted campaign in the constituencies and the press. In its first few weeks of existence, the League experienced great difficulty in getting Cabinet ministers to agree to address its projected mass meetings in London and the major provincial cities. The foundation of the League had not been discussed in the Cabinet, and Sir Henry Norman's initial requests for Cabinet ministers to speak at its meetings received a decidedly chilly response. On 29 June Norman complained bitterly to Pease that he had approached personally almost all the leading members of the Cabinet and had met with an almost universal refusal to speak. He could consequently only appeal 'to you & to P.M. thru you' and urge that it was absolutely essential to 'show that Gov. is solidly and enthusiastically behind the propaganda'.[52] Pease responded immediately by sending a circular to all members of the Cabinet, and by 12 July the League was able to announce an imposing list of meetings to be addressed by Cabinet ministers.

The scheme approved by the League's executive on 21 July provided for three classes of meetings — Class A to be addressed by Cabinet ministers and other members of the Government; Class B by MPs, including the seventeen paid speakers of the party; and Class C by others, supplemented if required by gramophone recordings of appeals for support by Asquith, Lloyd George, and Churchill.[53] Ten gramophones with operators were provided by the League, and in this way, Sir Henry afterwards proudly claimed, 'hundreds and thousands of people in humble circumstances, who could never possibly have cherished the hope, except by means of the gramophone, of hearing the Prime Minister', were able to 'thrill' to his spoken words.[54]

In another 'new departure' which was to exert 'a most useful influence', Norman arranged a conference on 9 July between the League's executive committee and the editors of twenty-four Liberal newspapers to plan the publications and press campaign of the League. A Literature Sub-committee was established, under Masterman's chairmanship, to produce pamphlets and leaflets, suggest cartoons and posters, and distribute through the two Liberal news agencies special paragraphs and articles on the Budget. These latter were intended primarily for the evening and weekly papers, which could not rely on reporting speeches and required 'powder and shot' in the form of points.[55] By 21 July Norman was able to report that 140 weekly papers were taking the League's 'Weekly Column' and that arrangements were being made for a large number of dailies to receive each day 'Budget Points' prepared by Harold Spender.[56]

The first major meeting organized by the League and addressed by a Cabinet minister was almost of the nature of a disaster. This was Churchill's performance at Edinburgh on 17 July, when he threatened that if the peers tampered with the Budget the Government would dissolve and take the issue of the Lords to the country. Asquith was outraged by Churchill's presumption in taking 'upon himself to say things which in their very character are impossible to consider until the occasion arises'.[57] Churchill's defence was that the Cabinet had several times discussed the matter of the Lords and the Budget, and that he was 'certainly under the impression that the Cabinet contemplate a Dissolution in the event referred to & nothing else'.[58] But the fact was that the Cabinet had taken no decision, and Crewe, for one, wondered whether the cohesion of the Government would for long stand the kind of shock provided by Churchill's 'definite statement'.[59] For his sins, Churchill was formally rebuked in the Cabinet for 'purporting to speak on behalf of the Government' in a way that was 'quite indefensible and altogether inconsistent with Cabinet responsibility and Ministerial cohesion'.[60]

Norman put a high premium on mass meetings, though it was the various organizations interested in land reform, and not the League, which organized the monster demonstration in support of the land taxes staged in Hyde Park on Saturday 24 July. In late July Norman's drive for whipping up popular support for the land taxes focused on large meetings addressed by members of the Government, and it was at the end of the month, under the auspices of the League, that Lloyd George gave the speech that revealed the full demagogic potential of the land taxes, and sent the faint-hearted amongst the Unionists scurrying for shelter.

Since the introduction of the Budget Lloyd George had had very little to say outside of the Commons, where he had impressed even his opponents by his conciliatory tone. On 30 July, before a packed audience of 4,000 at the Edinburgh Castle, Limehouse, in the East End of London, Lloyd George proceeded, in the angry words of Sir Edward Carson, to take off 'the mask' and show himself again as the 'unscrupulous demagogue'.[61]

Aside from an opening sally against 'the rich' for their disinclination to pay for the Dreadnoughts they had demanded, and a brief statement that the Budget was designed to raise the money for social reform, Lloyd George's Limehouse speech consisted of a sustained attack on the landlords, their means of wealth, and their opposition to the land taxes. The landlord, Lloyd George declared, was a gentleman who did not earn his wealth: 'His sole function, his chief pride, is stately consumption of wealth produced by others.' So far from creating the value of their urban land, Lloyd George contended with the aid of a series of examples, landlords relied on the growth of the community and the enterprise of businessmen. Nor did they earn their mining royalties; they simply sat back while capitalists risked their money and miners their lives. The miners daily faced death, yet

...when the Prime Minister and I knock at the door of these great landlords and say to them: — 'Here, you know these poor fellows have been digging up royalties at the risk of their lives, some of them are old, they have survived the perils of their trade, they are broken, they can earn no more. Won't you give them something towards keeping them out of the workhouse?' they scowl at you and we say, 'Only a ha'penny, just a copper.' They say, 'You thieves!' And they turn their dogs onto us, and every day you can hear their bark. (Loud laughter and cheers). If this is an indication of the view taken by these great landlords of their responsibility to the people who, at the risk of their life, create their wealth, then I say their day of reckoning is at hand. (Loud and prolonged cheers).[62]

Limehouse, coming as it did after the July by-elections, had a quite extraordinary impact on the political atmosphere, and left the Unionists severely shaken. 'The cold fit will no doubt pass off,' Lansdowne reassured Sandars on 9 August, 'but the fall of temperature was extraordinary.'[63] Even Lord Northcliffe's mass-circulation *Daily Mail*, which had hitherto emphasized the Budget's unpopularity, was temporarily forced off course. On 5 August, after Northcliffe's first ever meeting with Lloyd George, the *Daily Mail* declared that the agitation against the Budget had fallen flat, a declaration that did nothing to help Unionist morale.[64] Nor was Unionist morale helped by a concerted ducal outburst against the Budget in response to Limehouse. In the circumstances, Joynson Hicks, the Unionist MP for North-West Manchester, could only wish that 'the Dukes had held their tongues, every one of them'.[65]

On the Government side, as the Political Notes of *The Times* observed on 4 August, an entirely new confidence was now evident. Those who were sensitive to impressions, the Political Notes commented, sensed a change comparable 'to the turn of the tide upon an estuary when the moored boats swing slowly round'. What was troubling, however, to Asquith was that Lloyd George, in his attempts to rouse popular enthusiasm for the Budget, was now running the risk of frightening off 'moderate & reasonable men'. As he put it to Lloyd George, in a letter communicating the King's annoyance at the Limehouse speech: 'There is a great & growing popular enthusiasm, but this will not carry us through — if we rouse the suspicions & fears of the middle class, & particularly if we give countenance to the notion that the Budget is conceived in any spirit of vindictiveness.'[66]

Contrary to the predictions in the Liberal press, the Unionists did not promptly hold up the white flag on the land taxes when the Commons resumed its consideration of the Finance Bill on Monday 9 August. It was rather in the next week that the Unionists gave the impression that they were anxious to see an end to the committee stage of the land taxes. On 17 August Ilbert commented in his diary: 'The landlords find that the debates on the Land Clauses of the Bill are damaging their party badly in the country, & they now want to get rid of them as soon as possible.' By midnight on 18 August the Commons had reached clause 27, when the Finance Bill was again put aside to dispose of the committee stage of the Irish Land Bill, and most Liberal MPs took a holiday.

What helped to speed up the progress of the land clauses was the implementation of the 'kangaroo' and the announcement of several major concessions. These had been approved by the Cabinet at its meetings on 30 July and 4 August, and included the substitution of a five-per-cent tax on mineral royalties, rents, and wayleaves for the tax on undeveloped minerals, the transfer from the owner to the state of the whole cost of the land valuation, and provision for the right to appeal to the High Court against decisions of the referees empowered to adjudicate disputed questions of land valuation.[67] Further, in an attempt to conciliate the building trades, land on which at least £100 per acre had been spent in the last ten years was exempted from the undeveloped land duty.

As the Unionists were only too well aware these 'concessions' served to underline the point that the duties based on the projected land valuation had nothing to do with providing for the year's deficit. On the contrary, Balfour stressed in response to the announcement that the state would assume the cost of the valuation, the land value duties were now adding to that deficit. Moreover, it was evident to the Unionists that the cumulative effect of Lloyd George's concessions was to make it appear that their continued opposition to the land taxes was motivated simply by their concern to protect the interests of the big urban landlords. As Balfour protested 'with vehemence' on 10 August, the undeveloped land tax as it then stood was a tax not for getting money but for getting votes. What emerged from Balfour's speeches in the Commons on 10 and 11 August was that the Government's 'concessions' had helped to sharpen his objections in principle to the land taxes and to the inclusion of a land valuation in the Budget. Because of their politically-motivated unfairness in taxing the few, Balfour contended, the land taxes represented the heaviest blow ever aimed at the nation's great traditions of finance, and the valuation simply had no place in a Finance Bill which ostensibly provided means to meet a deficit.[68]

On Wednesday 1 September, when the Commons again took up the Finace Bill, the remaining two clauses of Part I of the Bill were rapidly dealt with. In all, the committee stage of the land taxes had occupied twenty-two parliamentary days, pushing aside much other business and forcing the Government to abandon some ten bills, including the Welsh Disestablishment Bill, promised in the King's Speech.

As Asquith suspected by late August, the committee stage

of the land taxes had also decided the fate of the Budget in the Lords, and he consequently asked Pease to assemble reports on the prospects for a general election in January.[69] During August the *Morning Post, Standard,* and *Observer* all came out in favour of rejection by the Lords, and on 6 September *The Times* began to move in the same direction.

Rejection, however, was no longer a prospect that troubled Lloyd George; for him the developments during the committee stage of the land taxes had proved the political worth of his new imposts. 'Those fools,' he said of the dukes, 'won't realise that they have got the middle classes against them now. Every tradesman, every one who has had to build a house or wishes to enlarge his garden, has got a grievance against the town landlord.' Before Limehouse Lloyd George had always suggested in private that he was doing his best to avert rejection on the ground that rejection would be a consequence of Liberal weakness. After Limehouse his tone changed. 'I'm not sure we ought to pray for it to go through', he told the Mastermans at one of his breakfasts. 'I'm not sure we ought not to hope for its rejection. It would give us such a chance as we shall never have again.'[70] To his brother he wrote on 17 August: 'There is undoubtedly a popular rising such as has not been witnessed over a generation. What will happen if they throw it out I can conjecture and I rejoice at the prospect. Many a rotten institution, system and law will be submerged by the deluge. I wonder whether they will be such fools. I am almost wishing they should be stricken by blindness.'[71]

III

With the land taxes out of the way, the committee stage of the Finance Bill moved ahead more rapidly, though with the prospect of rejection by the Lords looming, the Government showed no desire to hasten proceedings unduly and bring about a general election on the old register. Time was given over in September for the consideration of Lloyd George's Development Bill and the passage of Birrell's Irish Land Bill, but the Finance Bill none the less made steady progress. On Wednesday 6 October the committee stage was finally completed. In all it had occupied forty-two parliamentary days, only six days short of the committee record established by Gladstone's second Home Rule Bill.

For each category of the direct taxes considered in September, major concessions were made. On the licensing clauses, which were taken by Asquith so as to give Lloyd George a rest, the Government announced modifications in the scale of duties for off-licences, a reduction in the minimum duty for small publicans in Ireland, and concessions for *bona fide* restaurants and hotels. The main concession in regard to the death duties was the reduction from five years to three of the period before demise during which gifts *inter vivos* would be subject to the estate duty, and with regard to stamps sales of land worth over £500 were exempted from the new rate of transfer duty. Finally, with regard to the income tax Lloyd George announced on 20 September provisions for increasing the deductible allowances to landlords for the money spent on their estates for repairs and maintenance, but he also declared that it had been found impracticable to transfer the taxation of land from Schedule A to Schedule D of the income tax, a move which would have enabled landlords to treat profits from land as trade profits. In June, with a view to mollifying the landlords over the land taxes, Lloyd George had agreed to investigate the possibilities of such a transfer, but came to the conclusion that it would only lead to 'interminable disputes and correspondence between land-owners and officials', and might even imperil 'the salutary system of taxation at the source'.[72]

The indirect taxes, the tobacco and spirit duties, passed the committee stage without major alteration. Lloyd George had shown himself 'a little nervous' about a combination of the Labour party and the Irish Nationalists on the tobacco duty, but in the event it was allowed to pass the committee stage undiscussed. On the spirit duty the Irish Nationalists voted with the Unionists for a reduction of the duty from 3s. 9d. a gallon to 1s. Altogether, from the standpoint of the Budget, September was a bad month for the Irish Nationalists and their relations with the Government, and the month ended with Redmond going direct to Asquith with the accusation that Lloyd George had broken faith with them on Budget concessions.

In Ireland the Budget had produced a deep hostility. The spirit duty dealt a heavy blow at the Irish distillers and wholesalers, while the minimum licence duties threatened the smaller publicans with ruin. The minimum duties hit Ireland exceptionally hard. In urban areas with a population between 5,000 and 10,000, for instance, the minimum duty of £15 affected 84 per cent of licences in Ireland, against 28 per cent in Scotland and 32 per cent in England and Wales. As was pointed out in a memorandum for Asquith: 'The severity of its effect is shown in the fact that no less than 18 per cent of all licences in towns from 5,000–10,000 inhabitants in Ireland will have their duty raised from £4 10s. to £15.' In towns between 10,000 and 50,000, again, the minimum duty of £20 affected 90 per cent of licences in Ireland, against 35 per cent in Scotland and 34 per cent in England and Wales.[73] The Irish were also perturbed by the likely impact of the land value duties on Irish land purchases, which Birrell's Irish Land Bill was supposed to facilitate.

Although the Irish Nationalists had voted against the second reading of the Finance Bill, they refrained from opposing the Government all along the line on the Budget, and by September even party loyalists were beginning to wonder whether it might not have been wiser to have embarked on a sustained and uninhibited opposition. 'You will understand', an exasperated T. P. O'Connor wrote to Lloyd George on 25 September, 'how far the feeling has gone when Joe Devlin — one of the most sanguine, ablest and truest men in our party — said to me on Friday night that Healy was right; and that we ought to have fought the budget from first to last.' Within the party, the Budget had given a new impetus to factionalism, with nearly a dozen Irish MPs, led by Tim Healy, breaking from the main body to focus on outright opposition to the Budget. Healy, O'Connor warned Lloyd George, 'thinks we are so discredited by the Budget that he can defy us and beat us.'

What O'Connor's letters to Lloyd George in September made evident was that the Irish Nationalist leaders were frantic about the prospects before them unless the Government made substantial concessions to Ireland. With a life-and-death struggle with the Lords apparently pending, they were desperately anxious not to have to carry out the threat to 'vote in force' against the third reading of the Budget. On the other hand, continued failure to offer outright opposition to a Budget virtually universally condemned by Irish opinion could threaten the credibility and the whole political position of the party in Ireland. The only way out for the Nationalists, O'Connor impressed upon Lloyd George, was for them to secure real concessions on the Budget, and he consequently urged the Chancellor to scrap the minimum duty for Irish publicans. 'If we could win on that', he assured Lloyd George, 'we could defy all our enemies; the Church, Healy etc.'[74]

After a meeting with Lloyd George on 26 August, Redmond believed that he had secured an undertaking that the Government would drop the minimum duties for Ireland, and supposedly on Lloyd George's instructions gave notice of an amendment to that effect in the Commons. Four days later, by his own account, he was 'astonished' to learn in an interview with the Chancellor that the Government refused to abolish the minimum duties for Ireland, and intended merely to reduce them. Redmond protested on the spot, and followed this up with a formal letter of protest. He later complained to Asquith that the letter was never acknowledged, and its contents had apparently never been communicated to the Prime Minister. According to the version Lloyd George gave to Asquith, which satisfied the Prime Minister that there was no ground for charging him with a breach of faith, what had happened was that on 26 August he had 'somewhat casually' used language from which Redmond might have inferred that the Government was prepared to exempt Ireland from the minimum duties, but when he found on reflection and after consultation with his colleagues that such a concession was impossible 'he at once — within twenty-four or forty-eight hours of his original statement' took steps to have Redmond informed of how the matter stood.

Lloyd George had clearly been caught out promising more than he could deliver, but equally clearly the Irish Nationalist leaders attempted to exploit the incident for more than it was worth in their frantic efforts to extract fundamental concessions from the Government. On 16 September Redmond again went to see Lloyd George and 'again protested against the violation of the undertaking given us', and at the end of the month he went direct to Asquith with the claim that 'we all consider we received a definite promise, and the Government is under an honourable obligation to carry it out'. It got him nowhere. The reductions allowed to Ireland were in fact very considerable and the Cabinet was not prepared to expose itself to allegations of a 'corrupt bargain' with the Nationalists by altogether excluding Ireland from the operation of the minimum licence duties.[75]

In the Commons, the Government's majority dropped to its lowest levels yet in the voting on the spirit duty. In an all-night sitting on 23/24 September, a Unionist amendment reducing the duty to 1s. was rejected by a majority of only eighteen (112 to 94), and a motion by J. J. Mooney, the Nationalist MP for Newry, for reporting progress was defeated by the even narrower margin of thirteen (110 to 97). In the absence of any far-reaching concessions from the Government, the prospect remained that the Nationalists might feel themselves driven to voting against the third reading of the Finance Bill.

By the end of the committee stage the dominant question was no longer the Budget itself, but its fate in the Lords. Speculation on whether the Lords would reject the Budget or not see-sawed rapidly from side to side, and it was clearly part of Balfour's tactic to keep the Government guessing to the very end. On the public platform the Liberals countered either by effectively daring the Lords to throw the Budget out, or else by professing to believe that not even the present peers could commit so great a constitutional outrage as to reject or amend the Budget. At Birmingham on 17 September Asquith adopted a forthright stance and declared that if the Lords was planning on revolution, the Liberal party was not only ready but eager and anxious to take up the challenge.[76] On 8 October both Churchill and Birrell took the opposite tack and proclaimed they could hardly believe the Lords would behave so unpatriotically as to throw the nation's finances into almost irremediable confusion by refusing to pass the Budget. The next day, in a speech at Newcastle in which he sought to out-Limehouse Limehouse, or as the

Unionist press preferred to put it, out-Slimehouse Slimehouse, Lloyd George taunted the peers with the consequences of rejection: 'The Lords may decree a revolution which the people will direct.'[77]

As was by now almost part of the routine after one of Lloyd George's provocative speeches, the King complained bitterly to Asquith about the Chancellor's inflammatory language, but this time his main complaint was that Lloyd George was making it extremely difficult for the Lords to avoid rejecting the Budget. 'The King', Asquith told Pease, 'was much annoyed at L. George's speech at Newcastle which makes things much more difficult for the Lords.'[78] To Emmott it was 'quite evident that if taunts & jeers will bring about the throwing out of the Finance Bill by the Lords, Lloyd-George will flout & jeer to his heart's content'.[79]

After a short recess from 8 to 18 October, the Commons embarked on the report stage of the Finance Bill, which lasted until 29 October. As reported, the Bill had expanded from the original 74 clauses to 97, and 250 fresh Government amendments, mainly on points of detail, made their appearance. Moreover, in an unprecedented step, Lloyd George submitted a revised estimate. Concessions and changes during the committee stage had on balance cost the Government an estimated £725,000 in revenue, the delay in collecting the land value duties an estimated £25,000, and the decline in consumption in spirits in response to the increased duty an estimated £800,000, making a total of £1,550,000. On the expenditure side additional liabilities amounted to £867,000. The over-all addition of £2,417,000 to the deficit was largely offset by the £488,000 reserved for contingencies, the increased yields from the death duties and stamps over the original estimates, worth £1,300,000 and £300,000 respectively, and an additional £200,000 from the Post Office, making £2,288,000 in all. To cover the deficit, and keep a margin in hand, Lloyd George took another £500,000 from the Sinking Fund, bringing the reduction to £3,500,000.

On the order of the third reading, taken on 2 November, the rejection of the Finance Bill was moved by Austen Chamberlain. In the ensuing three days' debate the main arguments for and against the Budget were recapitulated, and a furious clash took place between Alexander Ure, the Lord Advocate for Scotland and a fervent land taxer, and Balfour, in response to the Unionist leader's allegation that Ure had perpetrated a 'frigid and calculated lie' in supposedly claiming in his speeches in the country that the payment of old-age pensions would be discontinued if the Unionists returned to office, as tariff reform was unable to raise the finance required.[80] On Thursday 4 November the third reading was carried by 379 votes to 149.

Only two Liberals voted against the Finance Bill on its third reading — Samuel Whitbread and Julius Bertram, both with brewing interests and both members of the land values 'cave'. Four others, F. W. Chance, Sir Robert Perks, E. A. Ridsdale, the MP for Brighton, and A. E. W. Mason, the novelist and MP for Coventry, abstained, and three were absent unpaired. One Liberal, Carlyon Bellairs, the member for King's Lynn, had crossed the floor during 1909, primarily on the defence issue, though he had also delared himself alarmed by the 'Socialistic' policies of Lloyd George and Churchill.[81] In all, overt opposition to the Budget among Liberal MPs proved remarkably limited. Concern at the content of the Budget undoubtedly contributed to the large number of seventy Liberal MPs retiring at the end of the session, including all those who either voted with the Opposition or abstained in the vote on the third reading, and some of them no doubt shared Morley's sense that the Liberal party was young and strong, and had simply 'marched on with seven league boots', leaving them straggling behind 'in the mud'.[82]

The Irish Nationalists, with the exception of one negative vote, abstained rather than vote against the Government. Bad as many of the proposed taxes were from Ireland's point of view, Redmond explained, the party thought it of far greater importance to be free to take sides against the Lords should the peers decide to reject the Budget.[83]

Altogether, the passage of the Budget through the Commons had occupied seventy parliamentary days, with frequent recourse to late-night and all-night sittings. Of the 895 divisions during the year, 554 related to the Budget.

Lloyd George voted in 462 of these, a record surpassed among members of the Government only by Jack Pease (518) and Sir Samuel Evans, the Solicitor General (505).

For Lloyd George the guiding of the Budget through the Commons had turned into something of a personal parliamentary triumph. Early in the committee stage he had thrown off the first impression he had given of not seeming to understand his own proposals, and developed a real mastery of the numerous and complicated provisions of the Budget. Moreover, his courtesy, reasonableness, and humour throughout the Budget debates, and in receiving a stream of deputations, won for him the approval and admiration of both sides of the House. 'On the whole,' Lucy Masterman commented in her diary, 'the Opposition are very fond of George. He amuses Arthur Balfour by his quickness and acuteness, and he has a kind of magnetism over the whole House possessed by very few others.'[84]

What did not escape notice was that Lloyd George turned to few of his Cabinet colleagues for assistance and relief. Apart from taking control of the licence duties, Asquith played little part in the daily discussion of the Bill, and of the other members of the Cabinet only Haldane and Herbert Samuel, promoted to Chancellor of the Duchy of Lancaster in June, provided any real assistance. For the rest, Lloyd George relied for help primarily on Robson, Evans, Masterman, and Hobhouse.

Despite the heavy demands made by the Budget on the time of the Commons, and the consequent postponement of a large part of the Government's legislative programme, the 1909 session was not without some notable legislative achievements in other areas. In the imperial sphere two measures of fundamental importance were enacted – the South Africa Bill, establishing the Union of South Africa, and the India Councils Bill. For Ireland, the Land Bill, designed to accelerate land purchase, was passed by the Commons, and finally enacted with modifications introduced by the Lords. 'Social' measures included the passage of Churchill's Labour Exchanges Bill, Burns's Housing and Town Planning Bill, and Lloyd George's Development and Road Improvement Funds Bill. As provided in the latter, the Development Fund was to be financed by an annual parliamentary grant and by a charge on the Consolidated Fund but not, as Lloyd George had originally proposed in his Budget speech, by the diversion of any surplus revenue that accrued to the Exchequer. The Road Fund was to be financed mainly by the proposed motor car licences and petrol duties in the Budget. After first attempting to amend the Bill, the Lords finally passed it intact on 1 December.

IV

Following the transfer of the Finance Bill from the Commons to the Lords, which gave the Budget its first reading on 8 November, the Budget League and the Budget Protest League staged their last meetings in the country. Early in December Walter Long and his committee wound up the affairs of the Budget Protest League, claiming to have achieved their purpose of making it possible for the Lords to refer the Budget to the people.[85] The Budget League, for its part, continued its publications and posters campaign until after the January 1910 general election, finally closing down office on 29 April 1910, the day the Finance Bill became law.

What was universally accepted was that the Budget League proved eminently more successful as a propaganda agency than the Budget Protest League. Its first major asset was Sir Henry Norman, who showed himself an organizational genius, and whose management of the press was the envy of the Unionists. As a former journalist, with a keen eye for news value, he provided the Budget League's press campaign with the expert direction the Budget Protest League lacked, despite its possession of its own news agency. Norman also managed to establish excellent working relations with the Liberal editors, though his suggestion that the Liberal papers should appear black-edged the day after the Lords rejected the Budget did not find favour with the editors. Rejection, he was told, was a matter for rejoicing not mourning.[86]

The second major asset enjoyed by the Budget League was that it possessed a larger pool of effective campaign orators to call upon than its rival, and in Churchill, who was more active outside the Commons than inside, and in Lloyd George, it had two platform speakers the Unionists simply could not match. From the first, Norman sought to build his campaign in the country round great demonstrations addressed by 'star' speakers and, despite initial difficulties, the League managed to stage some 40 meetings addressed by Cabinet ministers, and 115 by other members of the Government, including 45 by Ure. Altogether, between its first public meeting on 9 July and its last on 10 November, the League staged 3,564 meetings, with a total registered attendance of 1,436,827, representing about one in five of the total registered electorate in Great Britain.[87]

The statistics for the Budget League's literature campaign likewise make impressive reading. Altogether the League printed and distributed 17,000,000 leaflets and pamphlets, gave away or sold 600,000 picture postcards, and displayed over 500,000 posters. It also produced and sold 30,000 copies of a sixpenny booklet, *The Budget, The Land, and The People.*[88] This literature was directed mainly at explaining and justifying the land taxes and at advertising the notion that the Budget was, in the title of leaflet No. 3, 'The People's Budget', which provided the money for social reform, and taxed luxuries but left food untaxed. Compared to the 'red-hot, brief, pungent style' of the Liberal literature, much of the Unionist literature was, in the opinion of J. L. Garvin, the editor of the *Observer,* 'largely dead stuff'.[89]

In its relations with the regular Liberal organizations, the Budget League got on remarkably well, working throughout in close partnership with the National Liberal Federation. He was astonished, Pease told Norman, by the lack of complaint and criticism in connection with the work of the League, though Pease himself was not happy about the continued existence of the League after the Budget had left the Commons, partly because he suspected that Lloyd George and Churchill wanted to control an organization of their own which had some money, and partly because, he told Churchill, he 'badly' needed to get back the money he had advanced to the League. Churchill retorted 'I think it is not extravagant to say that the £1,500 you have advanced us is far & away the best investment of any party funds in political agitation which any human being has ever been fortunate enough to make.'[90]

The League was never short of funds. By late November it had succeeded in raising almost £20,000; £2,000 had been provided by Pease and £15,000 by J. C. Horsfall, who received a baronetcy in return for his 'munificent contribution'. In December the League received another such contribution; £10,000 donated by James K. Caird, a jute manufacturer in Churchill's constituency of Dundee. At the end the League's total expenditure amounted to nearly £33,000, and it still had over £2,000 in hand. £19,000 was spent on printing and posters, nearly £11,000 on meetings and speakers, and £1,200 on by-elections.[91]

What outraged Pease about some of the Budget League's fund-raising was that it involved the blatant trading of honours, and the men he held responsible for this were Lloyd George and Churchill. His 'slippery friends' did not share his own scruples in fund-raising, and at a meeting of the Budget League's executive committee on Thursday 2 December Pease provoked an 'incident' over the sale of honours. He recorded in his diary: 'I denounced Lloyd George for buying funds for budget league by selling honours — I said it was scandalous, he took it lying down & Churchill who was in the chair, rebuked me & said what I felt should be reserved for another occasion — we agreed to distribute the funds in assisting the spread of budget literature & posters.'

By contrast with the smooth and efficient operation of the Budget League, the Budget Protest League was beset for much of its short career by friction and difficulties. Whereas the Budget League enjoyed the advantage of being recognized by most Liberals as essential to rally popular support to the Budget, the Budget Protest League found its operation hampered and restricted by the competing efforts of individual groups opposed to particular taxes and of the established propaganda organizations on the Unionist side. In commanding the attention of the country it was outshone by the Tariff Reform League. Even the anti-Socialist emphasis of the B.P.L.'s campaign had to be curtailed in consequence of the protests of the Anti-Socialist Union; in the compromise arrangement worked out in mid-July, the League agreed to confine its specifically anti-Socialist activities to London, leaving the Union free to exploit the rest of Great Britain.[92]

The B.P.L.'s campaign of meetings in the country got off to an appallingly bad start, from which it never really recovered. During the crucial month of July its meetings were badly attended, or else attended mainly by pro-Budget hecklers, and the B.P.L. offered nothing to rival Norman's imaginative opening gambit of 'half a dozen mass meetings on largest scale' to 'strike the right drum note'.[93] After Limehouse, Long himself admitted that the agitation against the Budget had fallen flat largely because it had lacked a grand campaign of meetings addressed by 'star' speakers. 'This is evident from the tactics of our opponents,' he submitted, 'for notwithstanding the fact that Asquith, Lloyd George and Winston Churchill have their hands fairly full in their Offices and in Parliament they are able to find time to address whole series of meetings in the country. We must I think take a leaf out of their book.'[94] Even after Limehouse, however, Balfour declined to appear on the B.P.L. platforms. Always a difficult man to persuade to appear on the public platform, Balfour reinforced his natural disinclination to speak in the country by reckoning that it would be tactically wiser to avoid doing so 'till I know what the Budget is *really* going to be'.[95] Balfour's tactical considerations apart, the heavy commitments in the Commons of the numerically weak Unionist MPs made it virtually impossible for the B.P.L. ever to rival the Budget League in the provision of 'star' speakers, though in September it began to make a much improved showing.

As seen by the Tariff Reformers and the regular party organizers, the B. P. L. 's initial ineffectiveness stemmed from its own policy decisions, and in the post-Limehouse reappraisal of the Unionist campaign in the country its strategy was violently assailed. In an attempt to attract Liberal and Free Trade voters, Long had instructed the League's speakers to refrain from advocating tariff reform as an alternative to the Budget, but this had given a rather negative quality to the League's campaign. It tended to focus on the defence of the landlords, and in Acland-Hood's opinion this was largely responsible for 'the temporary eclipse of Tariff Reform by the Budget' in July. Acland-Hood consequently insisted that for the remainder of the Budget campaign 'every speech, whether by the Budget Protest League, Tariff Reform or any other association, our speeches should be $\frac{1}{3}$ Budget $\frac{2}{3}$ Tariff Reform and unemployment'.[96] Thereafter the League's speakers gave increasing prominence to tariff reform, but they continued to have to battle with often hostile audiences.

The main contest between the rival party organizations in the autumn of 1909, as it became increasingly evident that the Lords would reject the Budget, was for the support of the working-class voters in England. Unionists emphasized that tariff reform would mean more work; Liberals that the Budget would raise the money for social reform by taxing monopoly values and the superfluities of the rich.

There is no question that the aggressive Liberal drive to rally working-class support to the Budget, and Lloyd George's demagogic speeches at Limehouse and Newcastle, troubled some traditional Liberals. The Budget itself had disturbed the Whiggish elements in the party, and Lloyd George's platform speeches had the effect of encouraging a number of prominent Liberals in the country to break publicly from the Government. In September Sir Alfred Pease, the mine and colliery owner and the Chief Whip's brother, withdrew his support from the Government because of local political considerations, the Budget, and the language and methods of the Chancellor of the Exchequer.[97] So-called 'moderate' Liberals were often far more alarmed by Lloyd George's demagogic style in the second half of the year than by the actual contents of the Budget. On 20 October Alfred Emmott put in his diary: 'The Budget is really becoming a decent Budget if advocated on Asquith's grounds, but on the Chancellor's grounds gives one furiously to think.'

Lloyd George's own reading of the situation, particularly once it became clear to him that the Lords would reject the Budget, was that the main concern of Liberals was to ensure that the working classes in England would be mobilized in support of the Budget, and that for him required not only fiery oratory but practical arrangements with the 'Labour men'. His interest was less in employing the Budget as an instrument to 'contain' Labour than in ensuring a majority for the Budget in the new House of Commons. As he explained to Ilbert, it was of vital importance that in a general election caused by the rejection of the Budget there should be a majority for the Government in England, 'the predominant partner apart from Scotland, Ireland & Wales'. He said he was consequently prepared to go to 'great lengths' in allowing seats to the Labour party, 'for the greatest danger to the Liberals will arise from a split between Liberalism and Labour, such as destroyed Liberalism in Germany & elsewhere'. As with many Liberals, Lloyd George had given up the South of England, not including London, as lost, and for him this meant the working-class voters in London and the North of England had to be co-ordinated to a fine degree if the pro-Budget forces were to gain a sufficient majority in England. What troubled him, he told Ilbert on 13 November, was that 'the Whips' office have a strong personal feeling against the Labour men, & are very reluctant to make a deal with them'.[98]

The feeling had rankled since the by-elections of 1907, and in October 1909 had been given a powerful new boost by the Labour party's insistence on running its own candidate in the Bermondsey by-election, thereby enabling the Unionist candidate to capture the seat from the Liberals with a minority vote. In November Pease's attitude to Labour was consequently rather threatening, and he was certainly more intent on containing Labour than on reaching a bargain that would allow more seats to it.

From Lloyd George's standpoint, the rigid attitude of the Liberal whips to Labour in November threatened to undo his own work in trying to make possible a Liberal and Labour understanding for a general election caused by the rejection of the Budget. In July he had dined with Keir Hardie to sound out the Labour attitude in the event of a dissolution, and on 17 September he had been assured by Ramsay Mac-Donald that: 'As the result of three or four days' steady negotiations, I think I have straightened out everything, and if an election should come, the anti-Budgetists will not get much comfort out of our relationship.'[99] In the event, MacDonald's influence in late November and December, following his return from a trip to India, and the general realization in the Labour ranks that they could not in the circumstances afford to challenge the Liberals, prevented the sort of split Lloyd George had dreaded.

From election forecasts, and from what Liberals said, it is evident that most Liberals believed a general election brought on by the rejection of the Budget would prove more favourable to them than any other. In November Loreburn told Ilbert that as an Englishman he hoped the peers would pass the Budget, but as a Liberal he hoped they would not 'for we should never have a better issue to go to the country upon'. Rejection would virtually ensure that the Liberals would be able to make the Lords the main issue of the general election, and provide them with the means for effectively rallying both the 'masses' and the 'sections' against the Unionists and the hereditary Upper Chamber. It would give them their best opportunity to maintain largely intact the broad anti-Unionist coalition that had produced the 'landslide' victory of 1906.

The Unionist leaders were fully aware that their party had little hope of winning a general election provoked by the rejection of the Budget by the Lords, but this did not hold them back from securing rejection.

VIII. Rejection

I

The decision of the Unionist leaders that the Budget should be rejected by the House of Lords was reached in August and September 1909. Balfour, who had begun to steel himself for rejection following Lloyd George's Limehouse performance, firmly decided by the end of August that the Budget would have to be thrown out. By mid-September he was letting it be known that 'if the Lords did not reject the Bill, he could not continue to lead the Party'.[1] Lansdowne, in August, favoured amendment of the Budget rather than outright rejection, but in early September he, too, reluctantly came to accept that if any action was to be taken against the Budget, it could be nothing less than rejection. By the end of September it was generally accepted in Unionist circles that the party leadership was committed to rejection. On 1 October *The Times* commented: 'There can no longer ... be much doubt as to the fate of the Finance Bill when it leaves the House of Commons.'

The decision of Balfour and Lansdowne in favour of rejection requires a good deal of explaining. Soon after Lloyd George had made his Budget proposals known in the Commons, Balfour and Lansdowne had intimated privately that they were 'not in favour of the Peers throwing out the Budget, unless there is a greater national movement against it than seems likely'.[2] Yet it was precisely when the Budget reached the height of its popularity in the country that Balfour became convinced that the Budget would have to be destroyed. At no stage did either he or Lansdowne show any real conviction that the Unionists would win a general election forced by the rejection of the Budget.

The main evidence that Balfour made up his mind in August in favour of rejection is provided by an autobiographical fragment J. L. Garvin, the editor of the *Observer*, wrote during World War I, and by the correspondence of

209

Jack Sandars, Balfour's private secretary, with his chief. Garvin, who had a long discussion on Unionist policy with Balfour and Northcliffe on 6 August 1909, and who was in constant contact with Sandars, categorically asserts in his autobiographical fragment that: 'From the beginning of August, Mr. Balfour's mind was made up. That was the master-fact of the whole situation long before the majority of the Cabinet thought it possible that the Budget would or could be rejected.'[3] That Balfour decided in August for rejection is confirmed by a letter of Sandars to him on 26 August, reporting the progress of Lansdowne's ideas on the fate of the Budget. Sandars wrote: 'I think that Lansdowne still hankers after *amendment,* despite the obvious handle it will give to the Government's supporters.'[4] It was not until September that Lansdowne accepted the case for outright rejection rather than amendment. Once he had done so, the task of justifying rejection to hesitant or recalcitrant peers fell to him, and his correspondence provides some major clues as to the calculations of the Unionist leaders in deciding to have the Budget thrown out by the Lords.

What is clear from the evidence is that Balfour and Lansdowne were not, as was once supposed, dragged into rejection by reckless and uncontrollable peers, provoked beyond endurance by Lloyd George, or even put into the position of being forced into it by any group in the party. As both Roy Jenkins and Neal Blewett have stressed, the rejection of the Budget in November was the result of an overwhelming consensus which developed within the Unionist party in the autumn of 1909 in favour of such action. What Balfour did was to anticipate this development and to help foster it.[5]

John Ramsden has severely criticized Balfour as a leader of the Opposition for his inability to provide his party with an effective lead, but in deciding in August 1909 to have the Budget rejected in the Lords Balfour made a definite attempt to put himself in the position of giving his party the lead, and to avoid any possibility of his seeming to have to give way to pressure for rejection.[6] His overt reasoning in deciding for rejection was that the Government had given him no option but to fight the Budget in the Lords, and that public opinion required it, but underlying his decision was a realization that he would find it extremely difficult, if not impossible, to control party militants, particularly the ardent Tariff Reformers, should he seek to allow the Budget through the Lords. After years of badgering from the Tariff Reformers, Balfour possibly had no stomach for again resisting their urgent demands, and he positively welcomed the opportunity to bind them to himself and to put himself firmly at the head of the party. Already by the summer of 1909 Joseph Chamberlain and the party militants were known to be inclining towards a fight, and F. E. Smith has intimated, on a claim to inside knowledge, that Balfour was greatly influenced by Chamberlain's attitude.[7] In later years Balfour was to attribute the 'false step' of rejection to Chamberlain's influence on the party.[8]

It was in direct response to Limehouse that Balfour began to move in the direction of rejection. In its immediate impact, Limehouse had two contradictory effects on Unionists; the faint-hearted advocated immediate surrender, and the more resolute became convinced that the battle would have to be joined, and consequently began to prepare themselves for rejection. Indeed, it was precisely the near panic which gripped the Unionist ranks after Limehouse that helped to convince men like Acland-Hood, Sandars, and Garvin that retreat was unthinkable, and that what Unionist strategy required was a more positive offensive, which would highlight tariff reform as an alternative to the Budget and would include even rejection of the Budget by the Lords. In early August it was these men who caught Balfour's ear.

Two considerations were impressed most strongly upon Balfour. The first, emphasized by Garvin in a long letter to Northcliffe on 4 August, which was handed on to Balfour, was that a Unionist capitulation on the Budget would ensure a disastrous defeat for the Unionists at the next general election. The second, stressed by Acland-Hood, was that the Unionist party could only recover lost ground in the country by playing tariff reform off against the Budget.

His sixth sense, Garvin explained in his letter of 4 August, warned him that a Unionist surrender on the Budget was distinctly probable, and his own view was that such a surrender would be disastrous for both the short and long term prospects of the Unionist party. The immediate effect of the passage of the Budget as it stood would be to give the Government a parliamentary triumph as brilliant as any in his recollection: 'They will be more popular and powerful than at any single moment since the General Election. They will have given us a knock-out blow. The Unionist Party will appear, by contrast, beaten, impotent and ridiculous.' Worse still, Garvin predicted, a Unionist surrender now would leave the Liberals free to resort to the methods of the Budget over and over again, giving them a permanent fighting advantage and ensuring another sweeping victory for them at the next general election, with disastrous consequences for everything Unionists cared for. 'If there is to be no General Election before 1912, and we are beaten then,' he warned, 'there will not be much of a chance after that for anything we care about.'

In what amounted to a confession that the Unionists had been completely outmanœuvred for the immediate future, Garvin admitted that the Unionists could not realistically hope to win a general election forced by the rejection of the Budget. But he was convinced that they stood a good chance of coming back from 280 to 300 strong and he believed such a result would put them in a position to win everything. 'The others', he submitted, 'would be dependent on the Irish vote, and that would transform the whole situation to their disadvantage and our gain. Then we might hope to win out and out in 1912 or before. Between now and then we should have two strong fighting chances, whereas if we submitted on this Budget as it stands . . . we should not have a fighting chance again for many years to come.'[9]

Acland-Hood, for his part, interpreted the reports he received from the Unionist constituency agents in late July to mean that if tariff reform could be pushed to the forefront of the Unionist campaign, the party would soon reverse the check it had sustained in July. In a letter to Sandars on 8 August he attributed this check to:

(1) Disappointment at High Peak
(2) The idea that in the House we have been fighting the battle of the big landlords (especially urban) only.

(3) The temporary eclipse of Tariff Reform by the Budget.
(4) The loss of nerve by Northcliffe, which has re-acted on our own
people, and given them a notion that the Budget is enthusiastically
supported in the Country.
(5) The Eight Dreadnoughts.[10]

What is evident from this last reference is that the Unionist campaign for eight new Dreadnoughts had backfired badly as a political issue, and that the timing of the campaign had proved extremely maladroit. The Government's decision in late July to proceed with the construction of the four contingent Dreadnoughts had taken the wind out of the sails of the Unionist clamour over the navy, and at the same time their furious opposition to the Budget opened them up to Lloyd George's charge that they and the 'interests' they represented were refusing to pay for the Dreadnoughts they had demanded, and which had been given to them. As some Liberals had seen it, the Unionists had engineered the naval 'scare' in order to embarrass Lloyd George in the preparation of his Budget. At Limehouse, Lloyd George had turned the tables. The rich, he declared, would not pay for the Dreadnoughts they had clamoured for. When the Government sent the hat round to workmen to pay for the Dreadnoughts, they all dropped in their coppers, but then: 'We went round Belgravia, and there has been such a howl ever since that it has well-nigh deafened us.'

By focusing the Unionist campaign in the country more on tariff reform and less on the Budget itself, Acland-Hood hoped to restore lost momentum to the Unionists, and he believed from his agents' reports that this would be possible. As Gerald Arbuthnot, recently installed as vice chairman of the Budget Protest League, reported from Lancashire after the High Peak by-election, it was imperative that the Unionists make tariff reform and bad trade, rather than the merits or demerits of the Budget, the issue of the early general election he anticipated. He contended: 'On a T.R. issue I believe we could carry the Lords on our backs, but not on land taxes, whisky and tobacco.'[11]

Acland-Hood's memorandum on the reports he received from his agents in late July has not been found, but in his letter to Sandars on 8 August he wrote: 'Since my memorandum of August 2nd on our agents reports I have had many letters, all of them in the same strain. "The universal experience of all speakers is that the Budget excites little attention one way or the other, Tariff Reform wakes up the audience at once." ' He consequently urged that if 'our Press and Party will only kindly not give way to panic', and that if the Unionist campaigners would consistently advance tariff reform as the alternative to the Budget, driving it home that the Budget as a whole meant less employment while tariff reform would protect and promote employment, then 'we shall be all right'.[12] In a general election caused by the rejection of the Budget, he believed the Unionists might still come back at least 320-strong.[13]

The arguments and considerations put forward by Garvin and Acland-Hood did not clinch Balfour's decision for rejection. When Balfour saw Garvin and Northcliffe on 6 August, he stressed that no firm decision could be taken until the final shape of the Budget was more apparent, and that for the moment the Unionists should continue to concentrate on fighting the Budget in the Commons. After the meeting Balfour reported to Sandars: 'Northcliffe was quite ready to admit the wisdom of fighting the measure in the Commons to the last: & Garvin quite recognised the difficulty in which the enormous concessions made & to be made by the Governmt. were likely to place us.'[14]

What seems to have finally clinched Balfour's decision for rejection were the 'concessions' the Government announced when the Commons took up the Finance Bill again on 9 August, after a three-week break. For Balfour the Government's 'concessions' on the land value duties literally paraded the fact that the real purpose of the land clauses of the Budget was to get round the Lords on the question of land valuation, and his opposition to the Finance Bill consequently hardened.[15] The Liberals had now taken their 'politicking' in the Budget to lengths that Balfour found quite unacceptable, and it was at this juncture that he seems to have moved decisively in favour of outright rejection. On 13 August Garvin learned from Balfour that the Budget was doomed, that the general election was expected to come in January, and that the policy of the party was to be 'Tariff Reform — full speed ahead!'[16]

Balfour's decision for rejection meant setting aside the advice of Lansdowne, who in early August strongly advocated amendment rather than rejection. Rejection, Lansdowne conceded in a letter to Sandars on 11 August, might become inevitable, but he wondered whether the new concessions made by the Government had not rendered this more difficult, and he was concerned that so drastic a course might lead to serious defections from the Unionist ranks.[17] At the end of the month Lansdowne was still 'hankering' after amendment, but in the early part of September he finally accepted the policy of outright rejection. On 14 September Austen Chamberlain wrote to his wife: 'I hear that Lansdowne has quite made up his mind in the right sense'.[18]

As a landowner and as the Unionist leader in the Lords, Lansdowne's primary objections to the Finance Bill concerned the land clauses. For him, they constituted a clear-cut case of tacking, and he feared that if the Lords allowed them through it would be regarded as an 'ignominious capitulation' on the part of the Opposition and the Upper House. In such an event, the position of the House of Lords would be gravely and permanently impaired. The Lords could never in future claim the right to stand in the way of the financial policy of a radical government, however outrageous that policy might be.[19] As he took his stance in August, what he wanted to see was for the Lords to throw out the land clauses, with some other portions of the Finance Bill as a counterpoise. Such a move, he explained to Sandars, would be a sufficient reply to the challenge of those who said the Budget must not be 'minced' by the Lords, and if, as seemed to him likely, the counter-challenge of the Lords was not taken up by the Government, then 'the laughter will be on our side'.[20]

In August two major fears made Lansdowne stop short of outright rejection. The first was that rejection would lead to major defections among the Unionist Free Traders. As the Unionist Free Traders were more numerous and prominent in the Lords than in the Commons, Lansdowne was more alive to this factor than was Balfour; he was worried lest rejection, with all the imprints it would bear of playing

Birmingham's game, might finally split the party on a permanent basis. It was Sandars who tried to still his fears on this account. When the two men lunched together at Brooks's in early August, Sandars impressed on Lansdowne that there could be no permanent split. In a remark indicative of the tremendous personal antagonism Joseph Chamberlain had aroused, Sandars assured Lansdowne that 'so soon as Joe leaves us' the two wings of the party were bound to come together again. For the immediate future, Sandars insisted that: 'When the issue is Socialism — as it will be — the division of our forces will be without meaning.'[21]

Lansdowne's second major worry about rejection was that it might lead to financial chaos. What he dreaded was that the Government might deliberately allow financial chaos to develop from rejection, saddling the Lords with responsibility for it and thereby ensuring the defeat of the Unionists at the polls. On this score, his doubts were never really stilled, and were in fact accentuated when on 12 October he was presented via the King with a Treasury memorandum prepared by Sir George Murray calculating the financial loss rejection would entail. By the end of the month his apprehensions drove him to consult Lord Milner, a former chairman of the Board of Inland Revenue, on the question of the financial repercussions of rejection. In so doing he pointedly reminded Sandars that he had 'always treated this aspect of the case respectfully — more respectfully, I think, than you have'.[22] Sandars well knew it, and in early November sought to pacify Lansdowne and assuage his fears by informing him that he had reliable information that the Government was preparing a stop-gap Budget.[23] Lord Milner likewise sought to quieten Lansdowne's fears by ridiculing Murray's estimates as to financial loss.[24]

In September, Lansdowne was made to see the objections to amendment as against outright rejection. For one, he came to recognize that the Lords possessed a much clearer right to refuse than to amend a money bill; amendment, as he later explained to Lord Balfour of Burleigh, would simply lead to controversies about the technical right of the Lords to revise money bills which would obscure 'the real issue'. For another, he came to accept the argument that if the peers acted only against the land and licensing clauses, they would open themselves to the charge of 'thinking of their own skins only'. By September Lansdowne was also aware that the groundswell developing in the Unionist party was in favour of rejection, and that amendment was being recommended only by 'rather crotchety people', led by the *Spectator*.[25] But the two factors that really seemed to have clinched Lansdowne's reluctant acceptance of rejection were the stance of Balfour and Sandars, and the reports from the Conservative agents that Acland-Hood collected at the beginning of September.

The agents, from all accounts, showed themselves strongly in favour of rejection. They reported that the Budget was losing popularity every week, that Limehouse had proved a ten-day wonder, and that the party workers were eager for a fight. As Acland-Hood informed Austen Chamberlain on 4 September:

All our people are spoiling for a fight and will be disappointed if they don't get it. If there is no fight we can't keep them at boiling point. All my reports say that there have been no defections on account of this Budget but that if we allow them time to bring in a *bribing* Budget next year, my agents won't answer for the result.[26]

It does not seem that the agents' reports gave Acland-Hood reason to expect a Unionist victory in the general election that would inevitably follow rejection, and he did not predict one. What he predicted was that the Unionists would return with 300 seats at the lowest in a House of 670, and most Unionist estimates in the autumn of 1909 revolved around that figure, which meant that the Liberals would be reduced to dependence on the Irish Nationalists for their retention of office.[27] The whole idea, Sandars explained to Lord Esher on 26 September, was not that the Government would be defeated outright, but that its majority would be 'practically' destroyed.[28]

Several historians have asserted that only an outright victory for the Unionists in the general election would have provided justification for the destruction of the Budget by the Lords.[29] That was not how Balfour and Lansdowne saw the matter when they decided on rejection. The line Balfour adopted was that the Unionists had no choice but to fight, whether they liked it or not.[30] Lansdowne adopted a similar stance, and argued that a great reduction in the Radical majority 'would be to some extent a justification of our conduct'.[31]

On the surface, it is perhaps strange that Balfour and Lansdowne, as leaders of an Opposition, should have decided to force a general election they knew they were likely to lose. However, they were desperate at least to restore the Unionists to a formidable minority in the Commons, even if they recognized they could not count on gaining a majority, and they believed that the Unionists would go down badly at the next general election if they allowed the Budget to pass the Lords. The initiative would then lie entirely with the Government, which might capitalize on the Unionist show of weakness and dissolve immediately or wait for a year and introduce a 'bribing' Budget, which reduced indirect taxation, as the prelude to a general election.[32] One way or the other, a disheartened Unionist party might again be routed, whereas rejection would encourage the party's fighting spirit and enable the Unionists greatly to reduce the Liberal majority in the Commons.

Given that the Unionists were in such a small minority in the Commons, it made a certain amount of sense for the Unionist leaders to force a general election that would at least give them a large minority in the House. But a general election forced by a peers' rejection of a finance bill would be no ordinary election, and Balfour and Lansdowne could not escape the fact that some of the possible consequences of rejection were even more appalling than the set-backs that the party and the Lords might suffer if the Budget was allowed to pass. Rejection entailed gambling on everything that Unionists supposedly held dear — the composition and formal powers of the House of Lords; the preservation of the full Union with Ireland (a Union which provided their party with its very name); the place of the Church in education, and perhaps even the established position of the Church; and, what was dearest of all to some, tariff reform. As Lord St. Aldwyn put it to Balfour on 20 September, the stakes would be so high, and the risk of losing so great, as to make rejection 'the worse gamble' he had ever known in politics.

What made rejection so appalling a gamble for St. Aldwyn was the near certainty that the Unionists would be beaten at the consequent general election. The political history of the last fifty years, he submitted to Balfour, showed that the Unionist (or Conservative) party could not win a general election without some special aid, such as Home Rule or the South African War. So far from offering them any aid, the rejection of the Budget promised to prove a liability. The 'interference of the Lords with taxation' would provide the Liberals with the very cry they wanted. He was thus convinced 'that we *shall* be beaten on the issue that would now be presented', and he warned Balfour that 'a defeat means that the Lords will lose all real power over legislation of any kind — a result inconceivably worse than the passing of the present Budget . . .'[33]

While Balfour and Lansdowne accepted that the Unionists might well be defeated at the polls, they anticipated that the margin of defeat would probably be fairly narrow, and they did not believe that the return of the Liberal Government would automatically result in the destruction of the powers of the Lords that St. Aldwyn feared. On the contrary they hoped and believed that the general election, by reducing the Liberals to dependence on the Irish Nationalists for their retention of office, would prepare the way for the return of the Unionists to office in the near future. It was conceivable that the Liberal Government might break up after such a result, particularly if the Irish Nationalists tried to drive too hard a bargain, but it was almost a certainty that the Government would then find itself obliged to contest a second general election before it could settle the future of the Lords. The first general election, they calculated, would deal with the Budget and tariff reform; it would require a second general election to settle the issue of the Lords. As Lansdowne assured Balfour of Burleigh on 2 October:

The radicals will no doubt do their best to confuse the issue and to make out that a verdict in favour of the Finance Bill carries with it a *carte blanche* to deal with the House of Lords. But the destruction or reform of the House of Lords is not to be accomplished in a few weeks or months; and when the heat and fury of the general election has spent itself, the country will, I believe, be quite able to discriminate between the two issues — and I do not believe the country desires a Single

Chamber system. By the time the House of Lords issue is ripe for treatment, the popularity of the Budget will, unless I am mistaken, have greatly diminished. We shall not, in my opinion, get through the present crisis without two general elections.[34]

In the second general election the Unionists could hope to win out and out, especially if they were given, in the revival of the Home Rule issue, the special aid St. Aldwyn thought so necessary for a Unionist victory at the polls.

Given that there were two general elections in 1910, historians have been rather slow to ask whether the Unionist leaders might not have calculated on two. Yet it seems to have been an essential part of their calculation that there would be two general elections. As Sir William Anson, one of the Unionist experts on the Constitution, argued, as the Lords was a 'co-ordinate branch of the Legislature' with the Commons, legislation and a second appeal to the country were necessary 'before its powers could be reduced to a nullity'.[35] That the Unionist leaders were counting on two general elections was recognized on the Liberal side. 'Your opponents', Edwin Montagu, Asquith's parliamentary private secretary, advised the Prime Minister, 'are concentrating their efforts and even determining the action of the House of Lords on a conviction that they can force you to two General Elections on this issue, and it is their victory in the second upon which they are calculating.'[36]

One consideration which haunted the Unionist leaders was that the King might not prove strong enough to insist on a second general election before he would ever agree to grant the Liberals 'guarantees' against the Lords. After speaking to the King's advisers, Lord Knollys, Lord Esher, and Sir Arthur Davidson, on 3 November, Sandars complained to Lansdowne that the political atmosphere the King breathed was 'Free Trade and political timidity combined'.[37] Lansdowne reiterated this concern when he wrote Sandars while the January 1910 general election was in progress: 'I wish the King had stronger men about him. He will be in a position to snuff out peremptorily any demands for guarantees against the interference of the H. of L.'[38] Ultimately, as the Unionist leaders and the Liberals recognized, a good deal would depend on the extent of the Liberal victory in the general election following the rejection of the Budget. As Lloyd George told Robertson Nicoll on 9 September: 'It is not enough to secure a majority: we must have such a majority as will convince the House of Lords, the Tory Party and the Sovereign that there is nothing to hope for by manœuvring for a further appeal to the people.'[39]

Thus in August and September 1909 Balfour and Lansdowne came to see the rejection of the Budget by the Lords as both necessary and expedient. It was necessary in order to avert humiliation and to maintain the fighting spirit of the party, and it was expedient in that they believed they would stand more of a fighting chance in the long run than if the Budget was allowed to pass the Lords unscathed. A. V. Dicey, another of the Unionist experts on the Constitution, provided perhaps the best summing up of the situation the Unionist leaders believed themselves to be in when he wrote to Strachey on 1 October: 'We seem to be in for a battle over the Budget. I go into it without high hopes of immediate success . . . We have been outmanœuvred, but we are not in for a battle but for a campaign. If all the Unionists will act on this conviction we may win through.'[40]

For Balfour, though not perhaps for Lansdowne, rejection was not without strong positive attractions. Temperamentally, Balfour's whole inclination was for a strategy of counter-attack. For all his outward charm and languid air, Balfour was a man of shrewd power, who revelled in opportunities to demonstrate this. 'I always feel he is a dangerous pilot in extremity,' Strachey complained of Balfour when it was known that the Lords would reject the Budget, 'as he is not only pleased to see the waves run high but also taking delight in just shaving the rocks.'[41] Politically, moreover, he welcomed the opportunity rejection gave him to unite his party effectively again under his leadership. By embarking on rejection he could be sure of binding the Tariff Reformers solidly to himself, and could confidently expect the support of the vast majority of Unionists. By September it was clear that it was on rejection, as on no other course, that the Unionist party could stand united.

As Blewett has amply demonstrated, Balfour was never required to assert strong pressure to secure acceptance of rejection by the peers and the party.[42] By the end of September there was, apart from the Unionist Free Traders, an overwhelming consensus in favour of rejection. The panic that had seemed to grip the Unionists in early August proved only momentary, and during September virtually every interest and group in the Unionist party that felt itself a special target of Lloyd George's Budget, clamoured for its rejection in the Lords. In the City several leading financial houses, including Messrs Rothschild, Gibbs, Schröder and Stern, organized a petition calling on the Lords to throw out the Budget; Liberal gossip abounded with stories of how the brewers threatened never to support the Unionist party again if the Budget was allowed to pass; the landed interest was strongly in favour of rejection; and the ardent Tariff Reformers had all along inclined towards rejection.

From all accounts, the Chamberlainites and the Liberal Unionist organization were more sanguine about the prospects of the Unionists in a general election forced by the rejection of the Budget than were Balfour and the Conservative party organization.[43] They believed that in tariff reform the Unionists possessed a card that might snatch them victory. 'Joe', Mrs Mary Chamberlain wrote to her mother on 17 November, 'is more optimistic of the result than most people but whatever happens we stand to win — for even if the Govet. are returned their majority cannot be a large one & we should be in a very different position in the House.'[44]

What made it impossible for the Tariff Reformers to accept the passage of the Budget was the fact that it had been presented as a challenge to them, and also their fear that its enactment would greatly weaken their position in the next Unionist government by removing the financial imperative for tariffs. Rejection, by contrast, would give the Tariff Reformers an enormous hold over the party for they alone had a positive programme to offer as an alternative to the Budget. In the event, the Unionist consensus that emerged in favour of rejecting the Budget entailed also a consensus in support of tariff reform as an alternative to the Budget. When Balfour made up his mind for rejection, he simultaneously gave the order for 'full speed ahead' on tariff reform.

The only group in the Unionist party which persisted in advising against rejection were the Free Fooders. In common with all Unionists they detested Lloyd George's Budget, which they saw as a socialist perversion of free trade finance, and several of them, led by Strachey in the *Spectator,* toyed for a while with the notion of amendment in the Lords. But outright rejection was a course they could never recommend for, from their standpoint, it meant playing into the hands of the Tariff Reformers. By temperament, moreover, they were disinclined to gamble, and they certainly resented the idea of gambling on the future of both the Lords and the Union for the sake of tariff reform. However, once the Budget had been rejected by the Lords, most of the Unionist Free Traders closed ranks with the majority in the party in the common fight against Socialism, Single Chamber Government, and Home Rule.

II

Once Balfour had made his decision for rejection, part of his tactic was to conceal that decision from his opponents, and to keep them guessing as to what would happen to the Budget in the Lords. In a speech at Birmingham on 22 September, in which he asserted that the real choice before the country was between taking the uphill road to tariff reform or the downhill slope to Socialism, Balfour studiously avoided any direct indication or prediction as to the likely fate of the Budget in the Lords, although he did allow Austen Chamberlain to read a letter from his father calling on the Lords to throw the Budget out. The Budget, Joseph Chamberlain declared, represented the last effort of free trade finance to find a substitute for tariff reform and imperial preference, and it was avowedly intended to destroy the tariff reform movement. He hoped the House of Lords would 'see their way' to refer the choice between the Budget and tariff reform to the people by forcing a general election.[45]

The Birmingham statements of Balfour and Joseph Chamberlain that the people themselves must settle the issue between tariff reform and the socialist principles of the Budget, together with Chamberlain's open summons to the Lords, were enough to convince several in the Cabinet that the Budget would most probably be thrown out by the Lords, but at the end of September Asquith himself still believed that the odds were in favour of the Budget passing.[46] Throughout October the Cabinet operated without any certainty as to what would happen to the Budget when it reached the Lords. On 26 October Haldane informed his mother: 'We do not know at all yet what the Lords are going to do to the Bill. My feeling is that they have not even yet decided, but it is a fair chance that they will throw it out.'[47] Thereafter Cabinet ministers became rather more convinced that the Budget was going to be rejected by the Lords. On 3 November Carrington noted in his diary: 'The impression is gaining ground that the Lords mean to throw out the Budget.' Even so, some of the peers in the Cabinet continued to believe, or hope, that rejection would in the end be averted.[48]

Uncertainty about the fate of the Budget in the Lords meant that in the autumn of 1909 the Cabinet had to prepare to meet the eventualities of both the rejection and the passage of the Budget. If the Budget was rejected, it was clear that the Government would have no option but to dissolve. But if the Budget was allowed through, it was not at all clear whether it would still pay political dividends for the Government to dissolve, or whether Liberal interests would be better served if the Government continued to hold on.

On 20 September, when Asquith first raised with Jack Pease the question of staging a general election if the Budget passed, he conceded that the pros and cons for such a move 'seemed pretty evenly balanced'. As Asquith presented it, the main advantages of a general election in January 1910, even if the Budget carried, consisted mainly of the opportunities it provided the Government for postponing action on a number of 'awkward questions' until the next Parliament and of avoiding 'the anti-climax of Welsh Disestablishment'.[49] The main disadvantage of an early general election, as Pease saw it, was that it would be extremely difficult to arouse the country against the Lords in the wake of the passage of the Budget.[50] By October this latter consideration weighed

most with Asquith, and he used it to reject the King's proposal that the Government agree to a dissolution and general
election in January in return for the Lords allowing the
Budget to pass.

In early October the King, on his own initiative, sought
to avert a major constitutional crisis by personally persuading
Balfour and Lansdowne to let the Budget through the Lords.
He believed they might prove amenable if they were guaranteed an appeal to the country immediately following the
passage of the Budget. Haldane, who was sounded out by
the King one week-end on the idea, initially thought 'there
was something in it'. Asquith, however, dismissed it as
absurd. As he told Pease on 5 October, when travelling by
train to Scotland to see the King at Balmoral: 'When the
Lords have climbed down, & we win a victory, there would
be nothing to appeal to the country on.'[51] When Asquith
saw the King the next day, he gave the go ahead for the
King to see Balfour and Lansdowne, but made it clear that
he would not arrange an election if and after the Lords passed
the Budget. The result of a general election fought under
such conditions, Asquith warned the King, 'was not unlikely
to be a very small majority either way between the British
parties, with the decisive vote in critical matters left to the
Irish; a very undesirable state of things'. But while Asquith
ruled out a general election in January if the Budget passed,
he granted to the King that he did not think that a dissolution could be 'very long delayed'.[52]

When the King saw Balfour and Lansdowne at Buckingham
Palace on Monday 12 October, he did not offer a general
election in return for the passage of the Budget. They, in
turn, did not offer any hard information on the fate of the
Budget, knowing that whatever they said would be relayed
to Asquith. The King and the Cabinet consequently remained
in the dark as to what would happen to the Budget in the
Lords, and Asquith and his colleagues were obliged to consider their responses both to the rejection and the passage of
the Budget. In the Cabinet, Churchill and Runciman advocated
a dissolution in any event, but Lloyd George was not so
certain, and most of the rest of the Cabinet were against a
general election if the Lords passed the Budget.[53] From early

in November the problem of what to do if the Budget was enacted effectively ceased to trouble members of the Cabinet as they became increasingly convinced that the peers intended to throw the Budget out. After the Cabinet meeting of Wednesday 3 November, Asquith reported to the King that rejection was now generally regarded as probable, and that the Cabinet had consequently begun taking steps to avoid financial and administrative chaos following from the action of the Lords.[54]

The Cabinet's handling of the two major practical problems posed by rejection, namely the timing of a dissolution and the provisions to be made for the nation's finances, has already been extensively investigated by Blewett.[55] The Cabinet had been anxious to avoid both a general election on the register for 1909, as an old register was generally deemed unfavourable to the Liberals, and a long delay between rejection and polling. Its dilemma was ultimately resolved by the decision of the Unionists to play for a January election in the anticipation that the popular appeal of the Budget would have started to wane by then, and in the belief that, on this occasion, the new register would be more favourable to them than the old as they had succeeded in getting large numbers of lodger voters on to the new register. With regard to finance, as rejection would immediately nullify the Budget resolutions of the Commons which gave authority for the collection of the income tax and tea duty as well as the new taxes, the Cabinet contemplated in early November legislation to authorize the collection of non-contentious taxes, but in mid-November abandoned such a course on the ground that any such legislation would tacitly concede the principle that the Commons did not have an absolute control over financial legislation.

A remarkable feature of the Cabinet's considerations of how to negotiate the question of the collection of taxes was the unashamedly partisan assistance it was given by Courtenay Ilbert, the clerk of the House of Commons and, as a former parliamentary draftsman, a recognized expert on constitutional law. Together with Robson, the Attorney-General, and John Simon, the Liberal MP for Walthamstow and a leading advocate, Ilbert was brought in to advise the Cabinet on the legal consequences of the Budget's rejection, and all three recommended against legislation for the collection of non-contentious taxes and advised instead procedure by House of Commons resolution.

The idea of collecting taxes on the basis of a House of Commons resolution seems to have been Simon's brainchild. He accepted that the Budget resolutions of the Commons provided no authority for the collection of taxes after the session had ended, but he none the less held that the Government, justified by a resolution of the Commons, should continue to collect taxes. 'Such action', he explained to Ilbert, 'would of course be extra-legal, & would have, like a proclamation of martial law, to be followed — after a general election — by a confirming & indemnifying act. The Government would be treating the action of the Lords as revolutionary, to be met with revolutionary methods.'[56] The notion of meeting revolution by revolution, and of standing uncompromisingly behind the rights of the Commons over finance, appealed to Ilbert, and also to Lloyd George, who had consulted Simon.

In discussion with Churchill, Sir George Murray, Chalmers, and Ilbert at the Board of Trade on Friday 12 November, Lloyd George said he was against any legislation to authorize the collection of taxes, and strongly in favour of proceeding by Commons resolution. He would chance the risk of conflict with the courts. Murray, as cautious as ever, wanted the legal protection that could only be given by legislation, but Chalmers said he was willing to risk trouble and serious leakage of revenue 'rather than sacrifice an important constitutional principle'. On the next day Lloyd George requested Ilbert to prepare a memorandum for the Cabinet which would advocate proceeding by resolution without submitting any finance bill, saying that such a memorandum from him would carry 'great weight'.[57] Ilbert duly submitted a memorandum to the Cabinet for its meeting on 16 November.

The main thrust of Ilbert's memorandum was that, while it was the responsibility of the Cabinet to minimize financial loss arising out of the rejection of the Budget, it was also the duty of ministers to maintain unimpaired the rights of the Commons over finance. This would not be achieved if the Cabinet resorted to a second finance bill, dropping taxes from the first. He consequently urged the Government 'to continue to collect, by executive and extra-legal action, the taxes which have been granted by the Commons'. He concluded: 'There are occasions when respect for the constitution must override respect for the law. This may be one of them.'[58]

The Cabinet, stimulated by the news that the peers definitely intended to reject the Budget, responded positively to Ilbert's arguments against temporary legislation, but the suggestion of extra-legal collection of taxes was too bold for many. Instead, the Cabinet was now willing to contemplate the non-collection of taxes, or their collection on a voluntary basis, for the period between the prorogation of Parliament and the assembly of a new Commons, probably in the second week of February. In this the Cabinet was encouraged by the Inland Revenue and Customs estimate that the shortage in the actual collection of taxes up to 31 March would probably amount to only £20,000,000, as against Murray's original estimate of £49,000,000, and that the irrevocable loss of revenue would not exceed £1,000,000. The consensus that emerged was that the Lords should be left to bear the responsibility for this loss. The general opinion in the Cabinet, Asquith afterwards reported to the King, was that there would be no necessity to introduce and pass a new bill. When the new Commons assembled in early February, it could at once pass the necessary resolutions imposing taxes which would date back retrospectively to the end of November.[59] At the next week's meeting of the Cabinet the firm decision was reached not to produce 'immediate legislation' to validate the collection of taxes.[60] What Ilbert learned after the meeting of the Cabinet's assumptions and intentions was that:

It is practically certain that, whatever the result of the general election, income tax & tea duty will, at the beginning of the next session, be renewed as from the dates when they expired. Account is kept of all tea delivered out of bond so importers will be told that if they take tea out of bond they will still have to pay their duty, possibly with interest.[61]

In the event, what happened after the Budget was rejected

was that, with regard to the indirect taxes, the traders concerned accepted, sometimes under pressure, the official suggestion that in taking delivery of dutiable goods they would deposit the full duties payable under the Budget resolutions, subject to refund if the new Parliament failed to legalize the duties; with regard to the direct taxes, the death duties were collected at the old rates, subject to a supplementary collection, with the option of paying at the new, subject to a refund, and the collection of the income tax was virtually abandoned. Income tax at the rate of 1*s*. 2*d*. in the £ continued to be deducted from dividends, but otherwise its collection was generally postponed.[62]

Before rejecting the Budget, the peers had no clear knowledge of whether the Government intended to collect the taxes or not, but they had been publicly warned by Churchill, in a speech at Bristol on 14 November, that they could not count on the Government and the Commons going out of their way to rescue them from the 'natural consequences' of their 'malevolent' action. 'I say', Churchill had roundly declared, 'we hold the House of Lords responsible for all the consequences.'[63] It was this note of defiance that distinguished all ministerial speeches in the middle of November, and which rapidly put an end to all speculation, mainly in the Unionist press, that the Government might negotiate a compromise with the Lords on the Budget.

III

On Monday 22 November, when the Finance Bill came up for its second reading in the Lords, Lansdowne moved: 'That this House is not justified in giving its assent to the Bill until it has been submitted to the judgement of the country.' In speaking to the motion, Lansdowne did not dwell particularly on the constitutional question. He asserted, with reference to the statement of the Commons of 1689, and more recent statements by former Liberal leaders, that the Lords possessed the undoubted right to reject money bills, and went on to contend that the comparatively recent innovation of grouping together all the measures dealing with different taxes in a single omnibus Finance Bill represented an obvious attempt to embarrass the peers in the exercise of their undoubted rights. The question before the House, Lansdowne urged, was not whether the Lords could reject the Budget, but whether it ought to. In a long review and critique of the Budget's provisions, in which he traversed much of the ground the Commons had gone over in the previous seven months, Lansdowne contended that the Budget was no ordinary Budget, but represented an attempt to pass licensing and valuation bills under the cover of a Finance Bill, and that it ought consequently to be referred to the electors. In the end, he justified rejection on the principles of plebiscitary democracy. The Lords, he held, were the guardians of the people's greatest constitutional right, the right to be consulted when fundamental political changes were demanded by the government of the day. By rejecting the Budget, the Lords would be insisting that this right should be respected.[64]

In response, Lord Loreburn, the Lord Chancellor, immediately pointed out that, except for 'one or two' sentences at the beginning of his speech, Lansdowne had largely ignored the grave constitutional questions raised by rejection. There was certainly no question, Loreburn said, that it was lawful for the Lords to reject the Finance Bill, but it was not constitutional. There was no 'tacking' in the Budget, and it in no way violated the long-established doctrine of the House of Lords that it was destructive of the constitution to annex foreign measures to privileged bills of supply. But by the rejection of the Budget, he asserted, the Lords would be invading the prerogative of the Crown and the privileges of the House of Commons. Rejection was intended to force a dissolution and would deprive the Commons of its power of the purse, thereby upsetting the balance of power in the constitution and permitting the House of Lords to 'hold the Government of the country in the hollow of its hand'. After defending the provisions and purposes of the Budget, Loreburn warned that in any appeal to the country, the voters would be considering other and graver issues than whether the Finance Bill ought to pass into law. 'It is, in my opinion', he declared, 'impossible that any Liberal Government should ever again bear the heavy burden of office unless it is secured against a repetition of treatment such as our measures have had to undergo for the last four years'.[65]

The debate in the Lords continued until nearly midnight on Tuesday 30 November. It occupied six parliamentary days and lasted rather longer than the Unionist managers had wanted. They had originally planned to limit the debate to four days, but so many peers were determined to speak that it proved impossible to prevent the discussion of the Budget from spilling over into a second week. Indeed, a feature of the debate in the Lords was the exceptionally large attendance of peers, including numerous 'backwoodsmen' rarely before seen at Westminister. Such was the anger of the 'backwoodsmen' against the provisions of the Budget that Liberals were convinced that even had Balfour and Lansdowne wanted to let the Budget through, they would have had an almost impossible task restraining their own peers from destroying the Budget in the Lords.

At several points during the course of the Lords' debate, the peers bent on rejection were warned by their 'friends' that they were jeopardizing the real interests of the Unionist party, the House of Lords, and the country itself, by proceeding with the destruction of the Budget. On the second day of the debate Lord Cromer, in declaring his intention to abstain, predicted that rejection would produce acute and prolonged dissension in the country, and he feared that such dissension would weaken the national defence at a critical juncture by diverting attention away from it.[66] On the next day Lord Rosebery aroused considerable Unionist anger by questioning whether the peers had chosen the best battleground on which to risk the attributes and perhaps even the existence of the House of Lords. In a speech at Glasgow on 11 September, Rosebery had given considerable encouragement to the Budget's opponents by denouncing it as 'a revolution without a popular mandate'. He now stated outright that from the national standpoint it was better for the peers to leave the Budget alone and to preserve the powers of the Lords intact for more vital matters, notably for restricting Home Rule. Rosebery's counsel, *The Times* lamented, might have been effective had it not been left to the eleventh hour. As it was, his Glasgow speech had possibly done more than any other single circumstance to persuade the Unionist peers not to pass the Budget.[67]

Prominent Unionist peers who joined in warning against rejection and its consequences were Balfour of Burleigh, Lytton, and James of Hereford. St. Aldwyn's absence eloquently expressed his views on the wisdom of rejection.

On the last day of the debate, the case for rejection was strongly put by Curzon and Cawdor, who stressed that if their lordships passed the Finance Bill they would have destroyed for ever the power and authority of their House. Crewe, the leader of the House, wound up the debate with a detailed defence of the Budget and a warning that the Lords was about to make a tragic blunder. He concluded by pledging that if the Liberals came back from the country with a majority they would at once set themselves to obtain statutory guarantees which would prevent that indiscriminate destruction of their legislation by the Lords which the work that night represented 'the climax and the crown'.[68]

When the House divided shortly after 11.30, so great was the crush in the Opposition lobby that it took close on half an hour for the Unionist peers to file through. The final result, announced as Big Ben tolled midnight, was 350 for rejection, and 75 against. A slight cheer and counter-cheer from the opposing sides greeted the announcement. Outside the House, hundreds of police shepherded the small crowd of spectators away from Parliament Square, and when the news of the result came it caused barely a ripple of excitement. In and out of the House a strange air of anti-climax prevailed. 'Yet', Ilbert sensed as he left the Lords, 'the carrying of this amendment may turn out to be the most momentous historical occurrence that I have ever witnessed, & to mark the opening of a new chapter in the constitutional history of England'.[69]

If the actual rejection of the Budget by the Lords was accepted quietly by the country, as something of a foregone conclusion, there was nothing reticent about the response of the Government and the Commons. The day after the rejection the Commons reassembled, and Asquith, loudly cheered by his supporters, tabled the Cabinet resolution: 'That the action of the House of Lords in refusing to pass into law the financial provision made by the House for the Service of the year is a breach of the Constitution and a usurpation of the rights of the Commons.' The next day, Thursday 2 December, in a crowded House, Asquith moved the resolution.

Asquith, at the top of his form, was earnest, eloquent, forceful, and sometimes humorous — 'cheap platform satire upon the House of Lords', was how *The Times* described it[70] — in a speech which brought the Liberal MPs to their feet, waving their hats and order papers in enthusiasm. In moving the resolution and simultaneously announcing that the Government had asked the Crown to dissolve Parliament at the earliest possible date, he denounced the action of the Lords as a constitutional outrage, ridiculed the idea that the Government should produce before the session ended 'an amended Budget, pruned and trimmed and refurbished' to meet the scruples and tastes of the Lords, derided the pretensions of the peers and the 'new-fangled Caesarism which converts the House of Lords into a kind of plebiscitary organ', and launched a general attack on the partisan behaviour of the partisan Upper Chamber. He concluded, raising his voice:

The House of Lords has deliberately chosen their ground. They have elected to set at nought in regard to finance the unwritten but time-honoured conventions of our Constitution. In so doing, whether they foresaw it or not, they have opened out a wider and more far-reaching issue. We have not provoked the challenge, but we welcome it. We believe that the first principles of representative government . . . are at stake, and we ask the House of Commons by this Resolution to-day, as, at the earliest possible moment we shall ask the constituencies of the country, to declare that the organ, the voice of the free people of this country is to be found in the elected representatives of the nation.[71]

Balfour, who was heard muttering 'I hate this damned dramatic occasion' as he entered the House, was not at the top of his form in making the reply.[72] He was unwell, and there had even been some question whether he would speak that day. He had been laid up, Ilbert remarked uncharitably in his diary, by his 'usual & useful attack of influenza', and was going to have Austen Chamberlain represent him until he 'thought better of it'. Ilbert found his speech 'thin & poor', but added 'I am prejudiced'.[73]

Balfour gave the first half of his speech over to sniping

at Asquith's remarks and the resolution before the House, taunting the Government for its passion for abstract resolutions and for the gross misrepresentation of English constitutional history contained in its latest resolution. 'The English Constitution', he snorted, 'did not begin in 1860. It is quite true that before the Budget embodying the taxes of the year was never rejected, because there never was a Budget Bill embodying them.' The second half of his speech he gave over to a defence of the action of the Lords. The Lords, he declared, had been doing its duty, and doing it fearlessly, and he somehow wondered how the Liberals hoped to 'persuade the people of this country that they are suffering some great wrong, some terrible indignity, by having their opinion asked about the Budget'.[74]

Once Balfour had finished, the House virtually cleared, and few remained to listen to Arthur Henderson announce Labour's whole-hearted support for the resolution. The division, taken somewhat earlier than members had expected, resulted in a vote of 349 for the resolution, and 134 against. The Irish Nationalists, who had taken no part in the debate, abstained.

On the next day, Friday 3 December, Parliament was prorogued.

Some Unionist peers left Parliament wondering whether they had not in fact walked into a trap deliberately set by their opponents. As Lord Newton had told the House of Lords, he sensed they had been 'driven, cornered, and jockeyed into a fight'.[75] In so far as a deliberate attempt had been made to provoke the Lords into rejection, that provocation lay not in the actual content of the Budget as it did in Lloyd George's public presentation of that content, at least from Limehouse onwards. Otherwise, if Unionists and the Lords found themselves in a trap by November 1909, they had done much to help fashion the trap themselves. By their use of the Lords and their agitation of the tariff issue, the Unionists had driven Lloyd George and the Liberal Government into producing a Budget that went well beyond providing for the immediate financial needs of the year; and by the very tenacity with which they contested the Budget in the Commons, and as a consequence of the refusal of the Tariff Reformers to allow the Liberals to entrench a free trade solution to the problem of raising large new revenues, Unionists had created their own sense that they had little option but to secure the rejection of the Budget in the Lords.

At the hour Parliament was prorogued, Lloyd George suggested to a luncheon meeting at the National Liberal Club that he had indeed manœuvred to trap the Lords into rejection, and proclaimed: 'We have got them at last, and we do not mean to let them go until all the accounts in the ledger have been settled.'[76] What worried thoughtful Liberals was that the Government might have no definite scheme of action for dealing with the Lords, and that the peers might yet succeed in evading retribution. The election campaigning, and the immediate post-election situation, did much to confirm such fears.

IX. The Budget Election

I

The campaigning for the Budget general election of January 1910 began the day Parliament was prorogued. At midday on 3 December Lloyd George gave the peers 'hell' in a 'fine fighting speech' to a large group of party workers at the National Liberal Club, and later the same day Austen Chamberlain and Lansdowne addressed an enthusiastic audience at the annual meeting of the Liberal Unionist Council in Plymouth. Polling began six weeks later, on Saturday 15 January 1910, and continued until 8 February, when Orkney and Shetland completed their voting.

The general election of January 1910 has already been extensively examined by Blewett.[1] What requires particular attention in this chapter is the place of the Budget in the general election. From the Liberal standpoint there were two main dimensions to this. The one was to ensure that in the new House of Commons there would again be a majority available to approve the Budget, and this was a task greatly complicated by Irish hostility to the Budget, particularly as there was a strong possibility that the Irish MPs would hold the balance in the new House. The other was the part to be given the Budget in the Liberal campaign to rally support to themselves, and how far it might fulfil its initial strategy of mobilizing working-class support for the Liberals without provoking large-scale desertions among the party's middle-class supporters.

After the election the complaint was made by *Land Values* that the Budget had been largely ignored or otherwise coldly treated by the party's leading spokesmen in their campaigning. In its view, the 'abandonment' of the Budget in the campaign represented 'the most humiliating spectacle that has been witnessed for many years in politics', and that this signified the 'stubborn conservatism' of the Liberal party, and its unwillingness to give primacy to social and economic reform.

Land Values was particularly harsh on Asquith for his Albert
Hall speech of 10 December, and his 'utter abandonment'
of the Budget in favour of Home Rule, Welsh Disestablishment 'and, most fatal of all, his emphatic yet careless and
loose treatment of the constitutional question in all its
emptiness'. The fundamental complaint of *Land Values* was
that, after its rejection by the Lords, the Budget had ceased
to be regarded by 'its nominal sponsors' as an end in itself,
but that it had become a mere means to an end, namely
constitutional reform.[2]

In his post-election analysis J. A. Hobson accepted that
Liberal candidates and leading party spokesmen all over the
country had placed the issue of the Lords rather than the
Budget itself at the front of their appeal, but he did not
believe that the Lords played so considerable a part off the
platform, and reached the conclusion that the voting cleavages in the election strongly reflected the 'growing pressure
of economic issues'. As with most contemporary commentators, Hobson was particularly struck by the geographic
cleavage that the election showed up between the North of
Great Britain, which was overwhelmingly Liberal and Labour
in its representation, and the South of England, which was
almost equally overwhelmingly Unionist in its representation,
and he gave a class explanation for this cleavage. The strength
of Liberalism and Labour in the North derived from organized
artisans and skilled workers, whereas Unionism found its
support among 'the great majority of the employing, the
professional, the shopkeeping, the leisured classes upon
the one hand, and a large proportion, usually a majority, of
the casual or semi-employed manual labour, and of clerks and
shop-assistants, upon the other'. As he summed up the
cleavage: 'It is organised labour against the possessing and
educated classes, on the one hand, against the public house
and unorganised labour, on the other.' For Hobson, in short,
the policy of land, industrial and social reform, with its
accompanying fiscal policy as embodied in the Budget, had
gone far to ensure the solidarity of the skilled and organized
working classes for Liberalism and Labour, with certain
special exceptions, notably the Birmingham area, but that it
had driven the possessing classes, and their intellectual and

economic dependants, into forming a 'new front of Conservatism' which had shown itself 'aggressively reactionary'
in the election campaign.[3]

What is evident from Liberal campaign speeches and
election addresses is that the Liberals sought to make the
Lords the 'dominant issue' of the election, and that they
were intent on attempting to reconstruct the anti-Unionist
coalition which had produced the 'landslide' of January
1906, which led them to return to more traditional 'sectional'
issues, education, temperance reform, Scottish land reform,
Welsh Disestablishment and Irish Home Rule, in conjunction
with the Lords. It was in direct response to Redmond's
demand for a firm Liberal commitment to Home Rule,
without which the Irish Nationalists would have to advise
their friends in England to vote against the Liberal candidates,
that Asquith gave his assurance at the Albert Hall that in the
new House of Commons a Liberal Government and a Liberal
majority would be free to pursue a policy of Home Rule for
Ireland.[4] It was on Nonconformist issues, again, that Lloyd
George had come to place his main faith for rallying middle-
class support to the Liberals and against the Lords. 'I believe',
he had written to Robertson Nicoll, the editor of the inter-
denominational *British Weekly,* in September, 'the Budget
has secured the enthusiasm of the vast majority of the
working men of the Kingdom; but it is Nonconformity
alone that can bring the middle class to our aid . . . '[5]

None the less, *Land Values* was very wide of the mark in
claiming that the Budget was not much emphasized in the
Liberal campaign, and that the Liberals returned primarily
to old issues in relation to the immediate issue of the Lords.
The Budget was central to the whole Liberal campaign, and
particularly the Liberal onslaught against the Lords and the
Tariff Reformers. As Churchill phrased the essential Liberal
thrust in his election address, the rejection of the Budget by
the Lords represented a dual 'conspiracy of protection and
veto' against democracy: 'The forces of reaction are out for
a double event . . . They are running a terrible risk to win a
tremendous prize. That prize is no less than the complete
tying up of democracy both through its politics and its
industry.' As he presented it, the first issue of the election

was the future of the Lords, and the repulsion of its attack on the rights of the Commons, an attack that had 'a deep social cause' in that workmen were 'beginning to use the electoral machinery for their own purposes' and were consequently causing 'profound disquiet' among 'powerful classes'. Not a 'whit less grave' than the constitutional issue was the choice before the country whether it was to have protection or free trade, the taxation of food or the taxation of luxuries, monopolies, and superfluities.[6]

The main functions performed by the Budget itself in the Liberal campaign were as a rallying point for working-class support and as a counterpoise to tariff reform, but a determined effort was also made to convince the middle classes of the Budget's essential fairness, especially towards themselves. 'Moderate' members of the Cabinet, and notably Grey, whose reputation stood high in the country as a man of fairness, did not shirk the duty of attempting to reassure the middle classes. Grey's own campaigning was confined largely to his own constituency of Berwick-on-Tweed, which was heavily agricultural, and Northumberland, with a brief visit to Scotland, but his speeches were widely reported. He consistently defended the Budget's fairness and reasonableness, even though he had not previously been recognized as a strong supporter of the Budget, as well as advocated his own proposals for a reformed Second Chamber. For the benefit of the middle classes he pointed out that the 'professional man' with an earned income under £2,000 paid less in income tax under the Budget than he had paid under the Unionists, that the rich rather than the general mass of the middle classes would be the actual beneficiaries of Unionist tariff policies, and that: 'The Budget was something which staved off Socialism, while tariff reform would bring Socialism nearer.' He regularly made a point of repudiating the notion that the Budget was revolutionary, emphasizing that it was based on sound Liberal principles, and that where it introduced a new principle of taxation in the land value duties, that principle was entirely fair. He declared he could not 'conceive a fairer subject for taxation' than the unearned increment in land values.[7]

The Liberals said that they were presenting to the electorate two clear issues in the Lords and the Budget but, as was to become evident after the election, there was a considerable lack of clarity among members of the Cabinet as to exactly what would happen to the Lords and the Budget if the Liberals were returned to office. There was some confusion as to whether the issue of the Lords would be given precedence over the Budget and, more than that, the Cabinet was quite without a clearly formulated procedure and policy for dealing with the Lords.

In the Commons on 2 December Asquith had stated that the Government would pass the Budget as its first act after the election, but at the Albert Hall on 10 December he asserted that: 'We shall not assume office, and we shall not hold office, unless we can secure the safeguards which experience tells to be necessary for the legislative utility and honour of the party of progress.'[8] In the opinion of the *Manchester Guardian* the 'generally accepted' interpretation which was placed on these words was that the Prime Minister had pledged 'that he would not take office or hold office without an undertaking from the Sovereign to force through a Bill restricting the Lords' legislative veto, if needful, by a great creation of peers'.[9] Similar pledges were given by Lloyd George at the National Liberal Club on 3 December, and by Churchill at Stockport on 4 December and at Manchester on 6 December.[10]

In fact, although in late November and early December the Cabinet had discussed the possibility of securing 'guarantees' from the King to overcome opposition in the Lords, the 'pledges' made by Asquith, Lloyd George and Churchill rested on their understanding of the general sense of the Cabinet rather than any formal Cabinet decision.[11] On 15 December the King informed Asquith, via Lord Knollys, the royal private secretary, that he would not consider himself justified in creating, or threatening to create, new peers until after a second general election.[12] Thereafter talk of 'guarantees' disappeared from ministerial speeches. The impression had none the less been given that the Government was committed to securing guarantees against the Lords if it was returned, and after the election, when Asquith and his colleagues were still to be found 'holding office' without 'guarantees', the Prime Minister was harshly criticized in the Liberal press for having misled the country in his Albert Hall speech.

Aside from the question of guarantees, the Government had no clearly formulated policy for the Lords. According to Carrington's diary entry for 10 December, the final decision of the Cabinet before the general election was that 'the absolute veto which the house of Lords possesses must go', but the Cabinet had reached no agreement on what scheme to implement to limit the Lords' veto, or whether action against the Lords was to include or exclude the reform of its composition. To be sure, the impression among Liberals in the country was that the Government did possess a definite plan ready for implementation — namely the Campbell-Bannerman plan of 1907 for a suspensory veto. But in fact since October 1909 the Cabinet had been reconsidering the virtues of the so-called Ripon plan of joint sittings to resolve deadlocks between the two Houses, and in early November Churchill prepared a note on House of Lords reform which he showed to Asquith, Morley, and Haldane.[13] No consensus existed in favour of Campbell-Bannerman's plan, and the upshot was that for the election the Cabinet fell back on Churchill's tactical recommendation that they should 'avoid if possible any showing of one hand in detail before the election & fight on the general phrase of "smash the veto" or any more sober variant of that'.[14]

Altogether, it is clear that before the election Asquith and his Cabinet had laid the minimum of plans for action after it, and that they deliberately deferred real planning until the polling was over, when they would know how large a majority they would have at their disposal in the new House of Commons, and whether it was an independent majority. 'Policy', John Burns commented in his diary on 21 January 1910, 'depends upon majority almost entirely.'

Several members of the Cabinet had clearly counted on the Liberals not losing more than about eighty seats, and therefore on maintaining their independence of the Irish Nationalists.[15] In the event, the result of the general election, which gave the balance of power in the Commons to the Irish Nationalists, made it virtually impossible for the Cabinet to attempt to require guarantees of the King as a condition of office, and greatly strengthened Edward VII's hand in asking for a second general election. From an 'informant' Sandars learned that Lloyd George conceded that: 'As the elections have turned out, it is obviously impossible for us to press the King over guarantees. If the results had been different, no doubt we should have.'[16] But in the absence of guarantees the question was whether the Liberals could ensure the enactment of the Budget, given Irish hostility to its provisions. The general election of January 1910 had produced a majority against the Lords, but not an automatic majority in the new Commons for the Budget.

II

The rejection of the Budget occasioned no concrete ministerial plan of action for dealing with the Lords, but a cry against the peers and an appeal that they should be put in their place. The cry did not stop with the peers, but extended to the 'interests' behind them and their 'revolutionary action' in throwing the Budget out. Much of the Liberal campaigning was directed at exposing these interests, and above all the interests clamouring for tariff reform.

The Liberal campaign had been officially opened by Asquith with his address before a capacity, all-male audience of 10,000 at the Albert Hall on Friday 10 December. In the effort to involve all the interests linked with the Liberal party in the fate of the Budget, he promised to set right the 'anomalies and injustices' of the 1902 Education Act for Nonconformists, to secure licensing reduction for temperance reformers, franchise reform for Radicals, Disestablishment for Wales, land reform for Scotland, and Home Rule for Ireland, in the event of the Liberals being able to curb the powers of the Lords. The obstacle to all these reforms, he emphasized, had been the Lords, which was now also impeding Liberal social reforms by throwing out the Budget designed to pay for them. It was primarily because the House of Lords had gone so far as to shatter the whole fabric of the year's taxation that they were all gathered together at the Albert Hall that night.

In the new Parliament, Asquith intimated, the first duty of the Government would be to make impossible a recurrence of the revolutionary action of the Lords by means of a statute giving explicit recognition to the 'settled doctrine' of the Constitution that it was beyond the province of the House of Lords to meddle in any way with national finance. But the rejection of the Budget had hurried on an even larger issue than the control of finance, and Asquith stated 'quite plainly' that no Liberal Government would again 'submit to the rebuffs and humiliations of the last four years'. Liberal ministers would not assume or hold office without the safeguards necessary for the legislative utility and honour of their party. It was not that they wanted the abolition of the Lords, but that the absolute veto would have to go. 'The will of the people,' Asquith demanded, 'as deliberately expressed by their elected representatives, must, within the limits of the lifetime of a single Parliament, be made effective.'

In his Albert Hall address Asquith set the points for the Liberal election campaign in three ways. First, he appealed directly to all the groups in the anti-Unionist coalition that had produced the 'landslide' of 1906 and held out to them the prospect that in the new Parliament their objectives would all be realized. Second, he quite clearly put forward the role of the House of Lords in the Constitution as the 'dominant issue' of the general election, and identified the Lords as the common obstacle to the goals of all the elements in the anti-Unionist coalition. In the subsequent election campaign Asquith was constantly to repeat, using always the same terminology, that the principle of representative government was at stake and that on the curtailment of the powers of the Lords depended all the great causes on which Liberal hearts were set. At the Albert Hall Asquith also specifically pointed to the link between tariff reform and the rejection of the Budget. The revolutionary interference of the Lords with finance, he insisted, was made all the more sinister by the fact that it had been brought about at the practical instigation and through the ceaseless pressure of those who for years past had been trying to effect a revolution in the nation's fiscal system. The Budget, Asquith declared, had been ordered destroyed not because it was a Budget of socialism and spoliation but because it constituted an effective substitute — 'I will go further and say a destructive substitute' — for what was called tariff 'reform'. Whereas the Tariff Reformers planned to tax the necessities of life, the Budget proposed to provide for the nation's finances by taxing the accumulations of the rich, the luxuries of the less well-to-do and monopoly values created by the community as a whole, and it was the fear of the Tariff Reformers that if this Budget took its place on the statute book their cause would become 'a forlorn hope'. 'It is that fear which has provoked and engineered this crisis.'[17]

Throughout the electioneering Asquith conducted an extensive campaign to 'expose' the connection between the Tariff Reformers and the rejection of the Budget. In his campaigning Lloyd George likewise stressed the relation between tariff reform and the rejection of the Budget. Behind the decision of the Lords to reject the Budget he detected the pressure of the Tariff Reformers, the machinations of the ground landlord, and the compelling fist of the brewer: these were the people, he claimed, who wanted to see the Budget destroyed and who would offer instead the taxation of the people's food. What they were after ultimately, Lloyd George alleged, was to escape paying their fair share of taxation. The Lords, he told an audience at Reading on 1 January, said the Budget was not fair as it placed burdens too heavy to bear on the rich men of the country. The Lords said: 'Tax bread, tax meat.' The Government's opponents, he reminded his listeners, had demanded the construction of eight new Dreadnoughts and the Government had agreed to give them eight, but when the bill was sent it was thrown out by the House of Lords, who said: 'If you want payment you pawn the workman's loaf.'[18]

The 'dear bread' argument against tariff reform, and the contention that the only alternative to the Budget was the taxation of the people's food, were staples of Liberal campaigning. By stressing the link between tariff reform and the rejection of the Budget, and by playing on the theme that through the tariff reform movement and the refusal of the Lords to pass the Budget the rich and certain great interests were seeking to transfer their tax burden to the people's food, the Liberals found perhaps their most effective means of arousing democratic anger against both the Lords and the Tariff Reformers. Those inveterate 'enemies' of the people, the peers and the food-taxers, now stood exposed as being in a 'sinister' alliance against the people. The contention of Sir Ivor Jennings that the Tariff Reformers did not get a fair run in the general elections of 1910 because the Lords' rejection of the Budget enabled the Liberals to go to the country on the issue of 'Peers v. People' really misses the point.[19] By pressing for the rejection of the Budget the Tariff Reformers had sentenced themselves to being trampled underfoot along with the peers in the final Liberal charge against the Lords, and the relation between the 'food-taxers' and the destruction of the 'People's Budget' served to give a new urgency to the old Radical cry of 'Peers v. People'.

The brunt of the campaigning by ministers was borne by Lloyd George, Churchill, and Asquith. Lloyd George undertook two major regional campaigns — Wales and London — in December and early January, and supplemented these with visits to the West Country and the Midlands in the week before polling began. Despite later claims that he 'won' the North of England for the Liberals, Lloyd George did not in fact undertake a major tour of the North, which was largely entrusted to Churchill, who in the period before Christmas captured the Liberal imagination and a good deal of press space with a masterful campaign in Lancashire and Cheshire. Thereafter Churchill was largely confined to Scotland, and particularly his own constituency of Dundee, venturing south for a short tour of the Midlands in the week before polling. After he had safely recaptured Dundee on 18 January he was rushed to the West Country, where his intervention helped to check the Unionist advance in the region. Asquith, for his part, ranged more widely. The Prime Minister spoke at Liverpool and Birkenhead just before Christmas, and at Haddington soon after the New Year on behalf of a sick Haldane. For ten days thereafter he toured a selection of English constituencies, speaking at Brighton on 4 January, Bath on the seventh, Ipswich on the eleventh, Salisbury on the twelfth, and Bradford on the thirteenth, before returning to Scotland, and contesting his own seat at East Fife on the twenty-sixth.

Lloyd George's special tasks in the campaign were to help retain Wales, London, and Nonconformity for the Liberals, and to bolster the spirit of party workers. Two of his major addresses in London, at the National Liberal Club on 3 December and at the Queen's Hall on 31 December, were attended primarily by party workers, and another address at the Queen's Hall on 16 December was at a Free Church demonstration, on which occasion Lloyd George dwelt on the Nonconformist case against the Lords. Apart from such direct appeals to the Nonconformists, Lloyd George in effect abandoned his own attempts to rally the English middle classes, and gave priority in his electioneering in England to the task of arousing the labouring classes.

Lloyd George's critics among his Cabinet colleagues afterwards blamed him for frightening away the middle-class vote and consequently causing more losses for the party than they had expected. Runciman, for one, claimed in a letter to Emmott that Lloyd George's speeches had lost the Liberals many middle-class votes, but Emmott, aware of the other side, responded by wondering 'how many votes . . . the unscrupulous little dodger won by his courage and back-bone'.[20] In Rendel's opinion, Lloyd George had probably won the party more seats than he had lost.[21]

Perhaps the most balanced view was provided by J. A. Spender in a letter to Bryce after the election. He ascribed to the Budget and the land taxes the near solidarity of Wales and the better than anticipated Liberal performance in London, and contended that Lloyd George's qualities had won the North of England for the Liberals but that his defects, including 'Limehouse' speeches and the mistrust he aroused, had done much to alienate the South.[22] What this adds up to is that in the election campaign Lloyd George effectively carried out the tasks of keeping Wales intact for the Liberals and of holding the London working classes, but that his polemical speeches served to scare the middle classes of the South, whom Lloyd George had anyhow given up as lost.

Churchill's Lancashire campaign in December won him

plaudits from all sections of the Liberal party, with the *Manchester Guardian* ranking it with 'the one or two other great political pilgrimages in English Parliamentary history'.[23] He began his campaign at Preston on 3 December by presenting the Budget as the means to an extensive programme of social reform; he continued at Southport the next day with a critical examination of the record of the House of Lords over the previous hundred years; and at Manchester on 6 December he stated the 'unanswered and unanswerable case of Lancashire against any form of protective tariff'. For the remainder of his Lancashire campaign he developed the three 'great issues' he had outlined in his first three speeches, and linked them together by way of the Lords' rejection of the Budget.[24]

Apart from the Home Rule and education questions, which he did his best to leave alone, Churchill's Lancashire speeches virtually governed the terms of the election debate in Lancashire, and he had his return in the firm showing of the Liberals in the Lancashire polls. Asquith's return on his tour of the English constituencies in early January was to be rather less satisfying. Ipswich and Bradford held firm for the Liberals and Labour, but the 'genteel' cities and boroughs he visited — Brighton, Bath, and Salisbury — all abandoned their Liberal representatives and returned to the Unionist fold. In his special task of reassuring the English middle classes, Asquith met with little success.

It seems, indeed, that the Unionists were highly effective in undercutting Asquith's attempts to balance Lloyd George and his reassuring the nervous that he had full control over the Government's policy and the 'hot-heads' in his Cabinet. Certainly, the Unionists made a point of representing Asquith as a mere front for the forces led by Lloyd George. Lord Curzon, who followed Asquith to Brighton, declared outright that the country would never learn from the Prime Minister the true character and purpose of the Budget; for that they would have to listen to Lloyd George. Asquith had appeared in Brighton 'in the garb . . . of the safe man, the sound, cautious statesman who was merely carrying on the traditions of the Liberalism of the past', but the truth was that he and the other supposed moderates in the Cabinet had capitulated to the extremists. 'If they wanted to discover the true views of the Government,' Curzon insisted, 'they would not read them in the speeches of the Prime Minister; they had to go to Limehouse and Newcastle and Cardiff and Reading, and all the numerous places where the shriek of the Celtic trumpet was heard.'[25]

Asquith, it is evident from some accounts, was by no means at the top of his form after his initial success at the Albert Hall.[26] He was loaded down by his family's 'great grief' over the death of Violet Asquith's fiancé, and he seems to have been thrown off his stride by the King's firmness on the creation of new peers. His platform appearances in January lacked zest and conviction, and he certainly could not claim to have succeeded in imposing his authority on the general election. As was to be evident from the pollings, the Budget had greatly facilitated the task of Lloyd George and the Radicals in arousing the enthusiasm of the working classes, but in England Asquith and the 'moderates' found it impossible to reassure the bulk of the middle classes.

III

The opportunities which Liberals enjoyed and exploited in the election campaign for attacking the Unionists as fiscal reactionaries were precisely those which Balfour had wished to deny them when, after the general election of 1906, he had sought to resist the demands of the Chamberlainites for a clear and constructive programme of tariff reform. Balfour had not only failed to hold the Chamberlainites back, but had given the go-ahead for the Lords' rejection of the Budget, which meant that when the election campaign opened in December 1909 the Government rather than the Opposition appeared the better positioned for an attack at the hustings.

The task before Balfour and his generals was consequently to attempt to outflank the Liberals and draw them on to ground more suited to Unionist attack. Before Christmas the Liberals still seemed to hold the initiative, but thereafter the flanking movements of the Unionists began to tell, and by the first polling day they were opening up major holes in the exposed Liberal defences. 'A bolder attitude in the earlier days', Austen Chamberlain was afterwards convinced, 'would have led to much greater success in the elections.'[27]

As seen through Liberal eyes, Unionist strategy and tactics in the campaign consisted of a series of cynical diversions made up of a German scare, a Home Rule scare, a Socialism scare, and an unemployment scare. Their whole purpose in raising stale old issues and bogeys, Lloyd George charged, was to divert the electorate away from the real issue, namely the case between the people and the peers.[28]

In the campaign Unionists certainly sought to raise a number of issues on which they believed the Liberals were particularly vulnerable, including the navy and Asquith's apparent pledge of Home Rule to Ireland, but these were essentially diversions and it was in tariff reform, and the related issues of Socialism and unemployment, that the Unionists found their primary electioneering weapons. As put forward by Unionists the basic issue of the election was between the Budget and tariff reform, which was the only alternative to the Budget. The plain issue before the country, as Acland-Hood stated the Unionist position, was whether they could meet increased expenditure and deal with the great question of unemployment better by the Budget or by tariff reform.[29]

Unionists were perforce required to justify the action of the Lords in rejecting the Budget, and they attempted to do so by emphasizing that the Budget was revolutionary, socialistic, and unjust, and that it would have been passed over the heads of the people had it not been for the Lords. Throughout, in the campaigning, Unionists sought to avoid falling into the trap of seeming to be intent on protecting the interests of the rich, and argued that the Budget was unjust to members of all classes. It was unjust because of its inequitable treatment of selected portions of the community. It placed the burden of new indirect taxation on those who happened to smoke and drink, it penalized the members of the middle classes who saved, and it discriminated unfairly against the holders of landed property.[30] In its principles, moreover, the Budget was pure Socialism, and on that ground alone the Lords was justified in referring it to the people. What Unionists warned was that if the Liberals were allowed to destroy the Lords as a genuine check on the Commons they would be removing one of the country's fundamental guarantees against the possibility of a Socialist dictatorship. As F. E. Smith presented the issue, the country could have either a Socialist party and one-chamber government, or a tariff reform party and two chambers.[31]

For rallying working-class support to tariff reform and against the Budget, Unionists contended that the effect of tariff reform would be to shift a significant proportion of the tax burden under the so-called 'People's Budget' from the working classes to 'the foreigner', who would supposedly pay a substantial portion of new import duties on manufactured goods, and they urged that tariff reform would help protect and promote jobs, whereas the Budget would accentuate the problem of unemployment by frightening capital away. The effect of tariff reform, Bonar Law insisted along with most Unionists, would be to secure markets for Britain's own manufacturers and workmen, and to give a feeling of security to the home producer which would attract energy and capital to home industries, stimulate production, and do much to remove unemployment.[32]

In unemployment, a good many Unionists believed that they possessed the key to the election. It was as a remedy for unemployment, Austen Chamberlain was convinced, that tariff reform could capture the working-class vote for the Unionists.[33] The *Observer* was of like opinion, and urged that: 'The master-word of this struggle in its appeal to industrial democracy must be this — Unemployment.'[34]

In accordance with his strategy, Austen Chamberlain gave considerable prominence to tariff reform as a means of tackling unemployment in his campaign speeches, beginning at Plymouth on 3 December and thereafter mainly in the Birmingham area, as did Bonar Law among the other prominent Unionist campaigners. In his election address, and in his tour of North-East England, a region of heavy unemployment, Bonar Law declared that the removal of the evil of unemployment, by way of tariff reform, would constitute the greatest of all social reforms.[35] Balfour, however, was at great pains to warn that while tariff reform would undoubtedly ease the problem of unemployment, it was no panacea. As he put it very carefully at Haddington on 30 December, he would 'neither now nor on any other occasion, in private or in public, tell any of my countrymen that the whole difficulty in unemployment is going to be solved by Tariff Reform'.[36] In the manifesto Balfour issued jointly with Joseph Chamberlain on the eve of the first polls, it was stated that tariff reform would 'lessen unemployment'.[37]

The muting of Unionist claims that tariff reform would resolve unemployment owed much to the attitude of Balfour, who would have no truck with 'crude promises', and what probably helped to detract from the unemployment issue was the fact that unemployment continued to fall, despite the onset of winter conditions.[38]

In his post-mortem on the election, Austen Chamberlain claimed the greatest difficulties Unionist campaigners had to contend with were the food taxes and, in certain key areas, notably London and Yorkshire, antagonism against the Lords, and above all the landlords.[39]

On the whole, Austen Chamberlain was convinced that those who had faced the difficulty of the food taxes most boldly came off best, and in his own speeches he certainly sought to grapple directly with the question of the food taxes, contending that even if, as was by no means necessary, tariff reform did contribute to a higher price for bread, this would be more than compensated for by the increased employment and revenues for social reform that tariff reform would guarantee.[40] Balfour, who troubled the Tariff Reformers by his continuing disinclination 'to make the position clear and to have an official position' on the food taxes, finally likewise sought to deal directly with the question when he spoke at York on 12 January. In an address in which he came out firmly in support of imperial preference, the principle of protection, and raising revenue so far as was possible by means of indirect rather than direct taxes, Balfour pledged that Unionist tariff policy would not result in any increase in the proportion of the tax burden carried by the poor; it would simply involve a reshuffle of the items on which indirect taxes were paid by them.[41] In the joint manifesto Balfour issued with Joseph Chamberlain on the eve of the first polls, he repeated this pledge, and gave the further assurance that tariff reform would not increase the cost of living of the working classes.

Despite some of his continuing caveats on tariff reform, Balfour's return to the public platform at the end of December, after a month of illness, was the key to the major offensive the Unionists launched in January. The farther the Unionist campaign progressed into January, the more optimistic did Unionists become, and by the date of the first pollings the hopes of many of them were beginning to soar.[42] There is no evidence, however, that Balfour ever came to expect victory, or even wanted it. Hewins, who from his own account saw Balfour regularly from early December onwards, found that the Unionist leader 'did not seem to want to win'. According to Hewins, Balfour 'said it wd. kill him if we did'.[43]

IV

For the Liberals and the Unionists the Lords, the Budget, and tariff reform featured as the 'dominant' issues of the election campaign. For the Labour and Irish Nationalist parties these issues were intertwined with the whole question of the nature and future of their respective alliances with the Liberals.

In effect the decision of the Labour party leadership for the general election was to maintain the alliance with the Liberals, and give priority to producing a majority against the Lords and for the Budget, rather than to any concerted attempt to gain new ground at the expense of the Liberals. The split between the Liberals and Labour that Lloyd George had dreaded was consequently averted, even though Pease and the Liberal party organizers had refused to allow more seats to Labour.

As the Labour leaders perceived it, the issues of the election, and the condition of the party's organization and finances, precluded any major challenge to the Liberals at the polls. On the basic issues of the election, Labour was fundamentally in support of the Liberals, and it would be virtually impossible for Labour candidates to dissociate themselves from the issues that the Liberals gave primacy to. As Philip Snowden put it in the *Labour Leader:* 'It is no use being blind to the fact that a Labour candidate fighting a Tory and a Liberal at this election, in all but a few constituencies, will be at a great disadvantage through being unable to get away from 'the dominating issue' to the Labour programme.'[44] The result was that at the level of policy Labour could do little more than act as a radical appendage of the Liberal party. In addition, Labour was simply not prepared, at the level of organization and finance, to mount a major challenge to the Liberals. By arriving ahead of time, the general election had caught the Labour party only half prepared in the constituencies, with many candidatures insufficiently developed and funded for an immediate election; the dismal showing of Labour in the three-cornered contest at Bermondsey in October had provided the party leaders with a timely warning against attempting too much at the general election; and the judgement of the high court in 1908 in the Osborne case had jeopardized the financial standing of the party by finding illegal the compulsory political levy by which trade unions supported the Labour party. A final consideration the Labour leadership could not ignore was that a concerted Labour challenge to the Liberals would invite retaliation and endanger Labour's hold over the seats it already possessed.

In a series of meetings in November and early December the National Executive Committee of the Labour party consequently agreed considerably to prune the list of approved candidates to seventy-eight, and in all three-cornered contests involving both the Labour and Liberal parties were limited to twenty-seven.[45] In Labour's subsequent election campaign the Lords and the Budget generally featured as prominently as in the Liberal campaign, but Labour was to give far more emphasis than the Liberals to the Osborne judgement of the Law Lords on 21 December, which confirmed the earlier decision of the high court.

Apart from the twenty-seven three-cornered contests, the two parties acted essentially as a combination, and it was Austen Chamberlain's post-election view that this combination proved very much stronger than the Liberal party would have been had the Labour party not existed. 'Many men who would in that case have voted with us', Chamberlain complained, 'voted on this occasion as the Labour Party told them, i.e. for the Liberals.'[46]

For the Irish Nationalists, unlike Labour, there was no question of competing on any scale with the Liberals for the same vote; rather policy issues were of vital importance. Redmond's success in extracting a Home Rule pledge from Asquith meant that the United Irish League felt free to instruct Irish voters in Britain to support Liberal and Labour candidates, but in Ireland itself resentment at the Budget caused the official leadership of the party considerable discomfort, and prompted a direct challenge to the Liberal alliance on the part of William O'Brien, T. M. Healy, and their followers. They formed themselves as the Independent Nationalists, campaigning against the Budget and the restrictions of the Liberal alliance, and contesting nineteen seats.

O'Brien, after a recuperative spell in Italy, had formed the Independent Nationalist party in November 1909. It was based mainly on 'Rebel Cork', O'Brien's stronghold, Limerick and Kerry, but with another major outpost in Tim Healy's Louth. The rebel party's main appeal was to the widespread resentment in Ireland against the Budget but, as the Master of Elibank noted in a 'quite confidential' post-election review of the Irish situation, it also capitalized on O'Brien's role in passing the 'too-successful' Wyndham Land Purchase Act, his aim to secure a 'conciliatory settlement' of the Home Rule question, and the growing sense of disillusionment with 'professional politicians'.[47] The O'Brienites pledged themselves to oppose the Budget in the new Parliament with the object of killing it, and to uphold the policy of independence in the new House of Commons. The Liberal alliance, they insisted, had brought nothing but disaster to Ireland, and until it was ended there could be no hope for Ireland.

Redmond's strategy in this situation was to attempt to focus the election in Ireland entirely on Home Rule on the strength of Asquith's seeming pledges at the Albert Hall to destroy the veto of the Lords and to introduce and pass Home Rule in the new Parliament. For the Nationalists, Redmond repeatedly insisted, there was only one issue in the election: Home Rule. The goal of Home Rule was now immediately obtainable, and by way of the Liberal alliance.[48]

The clash at the polls between the independent and regular Nationalists meant there were more contested elections in Ireland than normal — thirty-seven as against twenty-two in 1906 — and the Irish leaders were consequently less free to intervene actively in the campaigning in Britain. Redmond managed only one speech in England, addressing a packed rally of seven thousand of 'his countrymen' at the Free Trade Hall in Manchester on Sunday 9 January. He then issued a strong appeal to Irishmen in England, Scotland, and Wales to vote for the abolition or limitation of the veto of the Lords, urging that the curbing of the veto would mean Home Rule for Ireland.[49]

The Irish Nationalists and Unionists were alike convinced after the elections that the Irish voters in Britain had faithfully followed Redmond's instructions, and voted everywhere against the Unionists. In Unionist estimates, the Irish vote had given their opponents twenty seats in England and eight in Scotland.[50] From the Unionist standpoint, in short, the Liberal alliance with the Irish Nationalists and Labour had worked all too well for the Liberals in the election, and the challenges to that alliance had few returns for the Unionists. Only four Unionist victories — Bow and Bromley, Camlachie, Cockermouth, and Whitehaven — could be attributed to a Labour challenge to the Liberals.

The immediate question for the future was whether the Liberal alliance with Labour and the Irish Nationalists would hold up in the new Parliament. The election results gave the Irish Nationalists the balance of power in the Commons, and that meant there would be no automatic passage of the Budget through the new House.

V

The polling gave the Liberals 275 seats in the new House of Commons, the Unionists 273, Labour 40, and the Irish Nationalists 82, including 11 Independent Nationalists. The net Unionist gain was 105, fewer than most Unionists had anticipated, and fewer by 63 than what they required for a majority of one in the Commons. It was none the less sufficient to place the Liberal Government in a position of dependence on the Irish Nationalists.

The feature of the election results that immediately impressed contemporaries was the divide between North and South. It was in England south of the Humber-Dee line that the Unionists made the massive bulk of their gains and found their most concentrated support, winning 192 seats, 78 per cent of their total.[51] In the North of England, Scotland and Wales Unionist gains were minimal. 'Never before', Blewett has commented, 'had one half of the nation moved so violently in one direction, while the other half remained almost stationary.'[52] In the South, outside of London, the Liberal defences crumbled before the Unionist onslaught at the polls; in the North, Scotland, and Wales, they were barely dented.

The other notable feature of the results that particularly impressed contemporaries was that Unionist gains were more in county than in borough seats. All told, the Unionists captured 71 new county seats, virtually sweeping the counties in the South, and lost 11 they had previously held. In the boroughs, the Unionists registered 56 gains and 11 losses.

Observers on all sides had little hesitation in giving class-related interpretations to the distinctive features of the results in Britain, particularly England and Scotland. Ramsay MacDonald commented: 'Never before have the rich as a class ranged themselves so completely on one side as they have done this time.' He added: 'Loafing and industry were never so well divided.'[53] For the *Manchester Guardian* what had happened was that the industrial and working-class towns and regions of Britain had voted, with few exceptions, for the House of Commons and free trade, and the market towns, watering-places, cathedral cities, and landlord-influenced areas of the South had thrown their support to the House of Lords and protection.[54] For *The Times* what in fact had happened was that the 'violent' appeals of the anti-Unionists to 'class prejudice and class jealousy' had worked in many of the boroughs, but had carried little weight in the counties, for in them 'the classes know each other, and the poorer can judge the wealthier by a daily knowledge of their lives and acts'.[55]

The geographic cleavage between North and South, and the concentration of Liberal and Labour strength in England in the boroughs rather than in the counties, was also taken to represent the reassertion in English politics of older divisions between town and country. As the special correspondent of *The Times* put it, the revival of an old and radical controversy between free trade and protection had revived the old radical difference between town and country, formerly well known in English politics.[56]

To a significant extent, as Blewett has shown, the cleavages revealed by the election results were indeed between urban, industrial, and working-class England on the one side, and rural, suburban, and middle-class England on the other.[57] The Unionists, to be sure, attracted considerable support in certain industrial and working-class areas, most notably in the Midlands, where the Chamberlain influence proved enormously powerful, and in the North the Liberals retained significant middle-class support. In Lancashire, J. A. Spender reported to Bryce in America, 'the business and middle classes are voting with us against Tariff Reform of any kind'.[58] But Blewett's tables indicate that: 'The swing [to the Unionists] in the predominantly middle-class, rural, and urban-rural constituencies was distinctly above average; in the mixed-class constituencies average; and in the predominantly working-class and mining constituencies distinctly below average.'[59]

The greatest disappointments to the Unionists were London, Lancashire, and Scotland, which pre-election forecasts had pinpointed as the areas most likely to prove pivotal to the outcome of the election. In London the Unionists made a net gain of 11 seats, giving them a total of 33 out of the 62 London seats, below even their minimum expectations; in Lancashire they made only 6 gains, leaving the anti-Unionists with 39 of Lancashire's 57 seats; and in Scotland the Unionists won 5 seats, but also managed to lose 5, meaning that Scotland was again to be represented in the House of Commons by 61 Liberal and Labour MPs and only 11 Unionists.

In seeking to explain their over-all failure to make satisfactory progress in the borough constituencies, and particularly their failure to penetrate working-class constituencies in
London and the North, Unionists were virtually unanimous
in pointing to their inability in the campaign to convince the
working classes that tariff reform was in their better interests.
Contrary to expectations, the special correspondent of *The
Times* commented, tariff reform had even failed to carry on
any scale the constituencies in which unemployment was
severe.[60] This failure to make tariff reform attractive to the
working classes was widely attributed to two main sets of
factors — the old obstacle of the food taxes, and the positive
counter-appeal of the Liberals and free trade, notably the
Budget itself and the attack on the Lords. 'In the North',
the special correspondent of *The Times* found, 'Free Trade
has been helped by the agitation against the Lords, and a
widespread popularity of the Budget.'[61] In London, again,
Austen Chamberlain attributed the containment of the
Unionists to the popularity of the Budget and the unpopularity of the Lords and the landlords, but he thought tariff
reform was likely to attract many more voters at the next
election. In London, he reported to Balfour, electors told the
Unionist canvassers: 'Yes, we want Tariff Reform, but we
want the Budget (i.e. the land taxes) too. We'll have the
Budget first, and we'll have Tariff Reform next time.'[62]

Where the Unionists had succeeded beyond their most
optimistic expectations was in the counties, notably in the
southern half of England. Basically, what Liberals had to
explain to themselves was their massive loss of support
among rural labourers, as well as the middle classes, in the
southern half of England.

Ultimately, Liberals found it easier to explain the loss of
suburbia than they did the loss of the vote of the rural
labourers. Suburbia, they accepted, was lost as the price of
winning the votes of the working classes; this was not inevitable, but it had happened.[63] The rural districts were rather
more difficult to explain. Liberals did not accept that the
farmers had suddenly converted to tariff reform; they had
been protectionist for generations. It was no doubt true, the
Manchester Guardian granted, that many more farmers had

voted in January 1910 than in January 1906, when they had been apathetic, but the real Liberal loss had been among the agricultural labourers.[64] Technically, as some Liberals saw it, they should have retained the vote of the agricultural labourers, largely because of old-age pensions. But, as Spender put it to Bryce, tariff reform had 'got an unexpected hold of agricultural labourers', partly in response to the land taxes of the Budget: 'The doctrine has this time been preached as pure agrarian protection and the landlords and farmers have taken the labourers with them to the poll on the ground that the Govt. is 'taxing land' and hitting the countryside whereas the other party proposes to help agriculture and restore much prosperity by keeping out foreign food-stuffs.'[65] Spender added that there had been 'real intimidation in the country-side', and Liberals generally fell back on the explanation that the rural districts had experienced a real tightening of the old 'feudal screw'.

For all the Liberal disappointment at the result of the elections, and their extensive losses in suburbia and rural England, Liberals such as Spender fully recognized that they had done very much better in January 1910 than they would have done a year previously. 'If we had gone to the country then', Spender wrote to Bryce, 'we should have been out by a majority of not less than 100. Since then we have been steadily recovering thanks to the Budget.' He added: 'For this Lloyd George deserves much credit, since he showed real grit and courage in making a new departure at a very un-promising moment.'[66]

Lloyd George's own feeling on the election results was that: 'I do not know what possesses people to go about talking as if we were beaten. We've won this election. The other side are just frightening us into it.'[67] The point the Unionists made was that the election, by giving the balance of power in the Commons to the Irish Nationalists, had not produced a majority for the Budget, and it was soon to become evident that it was by no means certain that the Budget would again pass the House.

The over-all result of the election greatly disappointed the Liberals, as it did also the Unionists, who now seriously doubted whether they could win the second election everyone anticipated.[68] Almost everything would depend on whether the Liberals faltered in their dealings with the Irish Nationalists on the Budget, the Lords, and Home Rule.

X. The Passage of the Budget

I

The essence of the situation after the general election was
that the Liberal Government, which was without 'guarantees'
from the Crown for dealing with the Lords and which did not
find itself in the position to ask for any, believed it was
committed by Asquith's statement in the Commons on 2
December to secure the enactment of the Budget as its first
legislative act, and that Redmond and his Irish Nationalist
supporters, who commanded the balance of power between
the parties in the Commons and who were hostile to several
provisions in the Budget, were not prepared to allow the
passage of the Budget through the new House until they had
been satisfied on the issue of the Lords. The position adopted
by Redmond was that of 'no veto, no Budget'. The situation
was further complicated by the Cabinet's flirtation with the
idea of proceeding with a reformist solution to the problem
of the Lords, which outraged many of their own supporters
in the Commons, who were also appalled to learn that the
Government was without guarantees. It was not until the
middle of April that the Cabinet was able to devise a formula
on the Lords that enabled it to go ahead and reintroduce the
Budget in the Commons in the knowledge that it would be
carried.

It was universally recognized throughout the crisis months
of February to April that the worst disaster that might befall
the Government would be for Redmond to carry out his
ultimate threat, and combine with the Unionists to defeat
the Budget in the Commons. Such an eventuality would
seem to justify the Lords in rejecting the Budget in the first
instance, and would deprive the Liberals of any momentum
for a second general election. But such an eventuality was no
more desired by Redmond than by the Government, and for
that very reason Balfour always believed that Redmond
would never block the passage of the Budget. As Balfour

told the King on 15 February, he was convinced that Redmond's 'threats will prove more formidable than his actions, and that he will not destroy a Government from whose legislation he expects so much'.[1] The Government was rather less confident, and refused to call Redmond's bluff, if bluff it ever was. At the same time, as Blewett has observed, the Cabinet was highly sensitive to any suggestion of a surrender to the Irish.[2]

In virtually inching its way to the attainment of a formula that would allow for the passage of the Budget, the Cabinet went through four distinguishable phases in its deliberations and negotiations. In the first, from the first meeting of the Cabinet on 10 February to the King's Speech on 21 February, ministers decided that, regardless of Redmond's stand on 'no veto, no Budget', the Government would take the Budget before it confronted the Lords, and within the Cabinet the supporters of a reformist solution to the Lords showed themselves to be in a majority over the committed vetoists. In the second phase, between the King's Speech and the acceptance of Asquith's motion for the time of the Commons on 28 February, the Cabinet, shaken by the response of its own supporters to the announcement that the Government was without guarantees and the suggestions that it was contemplating the reform of the Lords, retreated on two fronts. To the Redmondites it conceded that it would not reintroduce the Budget until the Government's proposed resolutions on the Lords had gone up to the peers; and to the Radicals in the Commons and the country it conceded that the Government should deal with the veto of the Lords in the first instance, leaving reform to a later date. The Cabinet was still far from meeting Redmond's demand that the issue of the Lords should have been basically settled before the Budget was reintroduced, and in the third phase, extending throughout March, Lloyd George sought to save the Budget by negotiating with both the Redmond and O'Brien factions of the Irish Nationalists on concessions to Ireland in the Budget itself, and the Cabinet meanwhile produced its resolutions on the Lords and survived an attempt by Grey to salvage the cause of House of Lords reform. In the final phase, Lloyd George's negotiations on Budget concessions ran into major difficulties among both the Irish and his own colleagues and were finally abandoned by him; what saved the situation was the decision announced by Asquith in the Commons on 14 April that the Government would not recommend a dissolution on the issue of the Lords 'except under such conditions as will secure that in the new Parliament the judgement of the people as expressed in the election will be carried into law'.[3] The Government was consequently able to proceed with the Budget, basically unaltered, before the matter of the Lords had reached its crisis point; and the Redmondites were able to vote for the Budget in the knowledge that when the crisis point was reached the Government would ask for guarantees before dissolving.

II

By the last week in February, when the Commons debated the King's Speech, the main contending positions had been staked out, and definition given to the over-all situation.

On 21 February Asquith announced in the Commons that the Government was without guarantees, and suggested that he would not ask for any until a crisis with the House of Lords had been reached. Within the Cabinet a powerful combination, headed by Grey, a consistent advocate of a reformed Upper House, had emerged in favour of a reformist approach to the problem of the Lords. It included in its ranks Haldane, Crewe, Runciman, McKenna, Samuel, and Churchill, and even Lloyd George appeared 'very bitten with the reform idea'.[4] The idea was that by focusing on the reform of the composition of the Upper House, and by coupling it with some system of joint sittings to resolve deadlocks between the two Houses, in preference to any attempt to carry the Campbell-Bannerman plan for a suspensory veto, the Liberals might counter the allegation that they were intent on establishing a single chamber system of government, and in so doing restore their appeal among 'moderate' middle-class voters for the second general election that everyone anticipated.[5] The reformist approach was strongly opposed by Harcourt, supported by Pentland and Loreburn, as likely to disenchant otherwise committed

Liberal voters, and the King's Speech was in the nature of a stop-gap compromise between the two factions.[6] Apart from Harcourt, who was prepared to put the settlement of grievances before the voting of taxes, the Cabinet was unanimous that its own credibility required that the Budget should be carried as the Government's first legislative act.[7] After much hair-splitting the Cabinet none the less agreed, in order to help meet Redmond's requirement that the Irish Nationalists would have to see and approve the Government's plans for the Lords before they would vote for the Budget, that the Commons should discuss the Government's proposed resolutions on the Lords before it passed the Budget.[8] This procedure, announced by Asquith on 21 February, was intended as a substantial concession to the Irish insistence on the primacy of the Lords, but without basically infringing the Government's insistence on the primacy of finance.

In the Commons many of the Government's own supporters were greatly dismayed by the announcement that the Government was without guarantees, and they were outraged by the suggestions in the King's Speech that the Cabinet had abandoned the Campbell-Bannerman plan for a suspensory veto in favour of the reform of the Lords. As the Cabinet was made to recognize, the Liberal back-benchers were no more willing to see any retreat on the issue of the veto of the Lords than were the Irish Nationalists.[9] In the press, moreover, the *Manchester Guardian* declared its 'alarm' at the Government's apparent 'change of front' over its policy for the Lords, and the *Nation* stressed that the electorate had never been consulted on the reform of the Lords.[10]

Even before the King's Speech, Redmond and T. P. O'Connor had made abundantly clear the basic position of the bulk of the Irish Nationalists. In a letter to Morley, read to the Cabinet on 10 February, O'Connor stated that it was 'a certain fact' that the Irish party would vote against the Budget 'unless they were assured that the passing of a Bill dealing with the veto of the House of Lords was guaranteed during the present year'.[11] On the night of 10 February this threat was repeated and made public by Redmond in a speech at the Gresham Hotel, Dublin. Redmond added that he was prepared to subordinate every other question, including the possibility of concessions in the Budget, to the one question of Home Rule.[12] He was determined that this time the Irish Nationalists should use their pivotal position in the Commons to ultimately force the passage of a Home Rule Bill, though he appreciated that he was by no means master of the situation. By the end of February the O'Brienites, on his flank, were already showing themselves interested in negotiating support for the Government in return for concessions to Ireland on the Budget, and he could anyhow not afford to overplay his hand in attempting to force the Government into a policy and procedure on the Lords that would clear the way for Home Rule. The realization of Redmond's ultimate threat, the overthrow of the Government, would not bring Home Rule any the nearer.

Unlike the Irish, the Labour party, which would hold the balance between the major parties should the Irish abstain, was positively in favour of the Budget and anxious that it should pass. Together with some Liberal back-benchers, however, the Labour party joined the Irish Nationalists in suggesting that, in the absence of guarantees, the withholding of the Budget might prove the most effective weapon left to the Government for forcing the capitulation of the Lords. As George Barnes, the newly elected chairman of the Labour party, declared on 22 February, he could see no reason why the House should surrender the weapon of redress before supply.[13]

The position of the Unionist leaders, stated in private rather than public but none the less an open secret, was that they would do nothing immediately. Balfour refused to be panicked into producing a scheme for the reform of the House of Lords; he would not seek to unseat the Government before urgent matters of supply had been dealt with; and he certainly would not help the Government to carry the 'People's Budget'. In response to an inquiry from Edward VII, who was 'round-tablish' on both the Budget and the Lords, Balfour indicated to the King in mid-February that it would be 'impossible' for the Unionists 'to do otherwise than vote against the Budget as a whole, or, if they came up for separate discussion, those taxes to which they have taken such strong exception both in Parliament and in the country'. For tactical reasons, the Unionists could not be expected 'to vote black where they had before voted white', and even abstention was too high a price to ask. As to the Lords, Balfour advised the King that he doubted 'whether the times are yet ripe' for any joint Unionist-Liberal endeavour to settle the future of the Upper House.[14] Balfour's attitude was clearly to allow the Government and the Irish Nationalists to seek their own salvation on the fate of the Budget in the Commons, and to await developments on the question of the Lords.

In the week of the King's Speech the Government's relations with Redmond came near to breaking-point. Although shaken by the critical reactions to the King's Speech, particularly among the Liberal rank and file, the Government held firm to its decision to carry the Budget as its first legislative act. To withhold it as a means of coercing the Lords seemed to ministers to smack too much of subordinating pressing national interests to party ends, and of being seen to accept the dictates of Redmond and the Irish Nationalists. Moreover, Churchill was convinced that holding back the Budget would hardly prove an effective weapon against the Lords. His consistent theme was that the Lords would be only too pleased to see the Budget further delayed. The Budget, in short, might give the Irish some hold over the Government; it would not give the Government any hold over the Lords.

In a speech which 'followed exactly the suggestions of his colleagues', Churchill duly advised the Commons on 22 February that any attempt to use the Budget as a lever to carry a Veto Bill was likely to prove wholly ineffective, and to go further, and refuse supply, would be to 'bring our system of civilised society to abrupt and complete chaos', exposing its authors to 'a sweeping and blinding catastrophe'.[15] For all that, the Cabinet was later to show itself prepared to curtail the effective duration of supply for the Civil Service and Revenue Departments.

The Cabinet's determination, as confirmed by Churchill, to carry the Budget before any bill or resolutions on the Lords had gone to the peers for a response, brought the relations between the Cabinet and Redmond virtually to breaking-point. Redmond demanded assurances of guarantees for the passage of a Veto Bill, and these assurances the Cabinet declined to give.

When Redmond saw the Master of Elibank, the new Liberal Chief Whip, on 24 February he told him:

... unless Government promised us
(1) To introduce veto resolutions in both Houses at once.
(2) If resolutions rejected or hung up in Lords, to at once ask King for guarantees.
(3) To postpone introduction of Budget in any case until after the foregoing—
unless we receive these promises, we could not support Liberal in St. George's-in-the-East election ...
Further, we would feel bound to vote against the Government and oppose them consistently in the House of Commons.[16]

Redmond had given what the Cabinet understood as an ultimatum.

The situation was now critical, and at its meetings on 25 and 26 February the Cabinet discussed the possibility of resignation, though only to reject the suggestion. Instead, the Cabinet adopted a firm line in response to Redmond's 'exorbitant demands' and instructed the Master of Elibank to inform Redmond that 'they were not prepared to give any such assurances, and that he must act on his responsibility as they would on theirs'.[17] At the same time the Cabinet made a procedural concession to the Irish by agreeing to submit the Lords resolutions to the peers, and it also moved to work out a formula to reassure the Radicals and the Irish that the possibility of reform of the Lords did not entail betrayal of the vetoist cause. At its meeting on 26 February the Cabinet clutched on to the proposals Haldane had devised to 'reconcile the conflicting views re Hereditary v. Elected Peers'.

Haldane's basic idea was that in point of time the carrying of any reform proposals of the Government would be subordinated to its veto proposals, though both proposals could be put forward simultaneously. It was this formula for 'veto first' that the Cabinet approved for Asquith's statement to the Commons on 28 February, and Haldane's fuller proposals were referred to a Cabinet Committee on the Lords.[18] Two men remained distinctly unhappy: Harcourt, who would have no truck with reform, and Grey, who recognized that the reformist advance in the Cabinet had now been checked, and who spoke of resigning.[19]

As Carrington summed up the situation at the week-end, it was 'critical in the extreme but not at this moment desperate'.[20] Among Liberals in the Commons, and Liberal organizations in the country, the reputation of the Cabinet had nosedived, and Asquith himself was extremely unpopular. 'In a week', the Master of Elibank afterwards recalled, 'the Prime Minister's prestige fell to so low an ebb that at one moment I despaired of his ever recovering it.'[21] In the new House of Commons the Government's majorities had shrunk to minuscule proportions compared to the old. On 24 February Irish abstention on a tariff reform amendment to the Address had reduced the Government's majority to 31. The next day, in the division on an amendment calling for urgent action to save the hops industry, Acland-Hood had to keep some of his men back from voting until he knew that the Irish were not voting against the Government, threatening it with defeat.[22]

But, as Carrington sensed at the week-end, the Government was in the process of turning a crucial corner. He correctly anticipated that the Government would succeed on Monday in carrying the motion asking for the time of the House for supply up to Easter, largely because the Unionists wanted to avoid forcing the Government out immediately. He also believed that the check given the reformists would begin reviving the party's spirits.[23]

On Monday 28 February Asquith rose in a crowded Commons to explain the Government's intentions and proposed plan of operation for the House. The whole period up to Easter would be given over to supply and necessary financial business; after Easter the Government would present its proposals on the relations between the two Houses. These would be embodied, in the first instance, in the form of resolutions affirming the need to exclude the Lords from finance and to limit the veto of the Upper House. It would be made plain, Asquith added, that these changes contemplated the subsequent creation of a democratic Second Chamber. The Prime Minister then declared, amidst cheers, that once the Commons had agreed to the Lords resolutions, they would be submitted to the peers so as to bring the main issue to a trial at the earliest possible moment. The Government, he insisted, regarded the legal limitation of the Lords' veto as its paramount duty, and he hinted at the possibility of securing guarantees.[24] Later in the debate Lloyd George, in response to leading questions from Redmond, indicated that the Budget would not be taken until after the Commons had passed the Lords resolutions and suggested more explicitly than Asquith that ultimately guarantees would be asked for.[25]

These announcements were welcomed by the Irish Nationalists and the Radicals as a change of front on the part of the Government, and the atmosphere of the House was transformed. More, the Government's motion for the time of the House was carried without a division. The Irish were deliberating in a committee room as to how they should now act when the motion was put from the chair, and the Unionist leaders had earlier decided to hang back from forcing a division for fear of putting the Government out before essential supplies had been voted.[26] 'The Unionists ran away from the crisis yesterday', Hewins commented curtly in his diary for 1 March. 'They said it was patriotism but it was really fright.'[27] According to Carrington's diary: 'The wild young Tories are very angry at being so feebly led.' The immediate crisis, everyone appreciated, was now over: ' . . . and so there is peace till Easter', Carrington sighed with relief in his diary.[28]

In the letter Churchill wrote to the King, as one of his duties in his new post as Home Secretary in reporting parliamentary proceedings to the monarch, he asked Edward VII not to attribute the Government's concessions of 28 February to 'a weak surrender' to the Irish Nationalists. He pointed out: 'If Mr. Redmond's words have carried weight, it is not because he held the power of altering the balance of voting strength in the House of Commons but because the counsels which he urged were in full harmony with the views of by far the greater part of the Ministerial majority.'[29] This was an essential factor in the situation, as Churchill's letters to the King had consistently stressed.[30] By seeming to retreat on the issue of the Lords, the Government was antagonizing a large group in its own party in the Commons, and with the ever present prospect of another general election in mind that was recognized as fatal.

To a large extent, as was pointed out by the 'Political Notes' of *The Times*, written by Arthur Pole Nicholson, the parliamentary correspondent who prided himself on his ability to get 'the secrets of a Liberal Ministry for an Opposition newspaper', the 'compromise' arrived at on 28 February involved two sets of compromises. The one, over the actual content of the Government's policy towards the Lords, 'was a compromise with the Liberal Party and not with the Nationalists'. The other, over procedure, including the 'promise' of guarantees before the Government went to the country, was with the Irish Nationalists.[31] But ultimately, the Radicals and the Irish Nationalists were at one: they were determined to prevent a 'betrayal' over the Lords, and acted together to prevent one.[32]

In the final analysis, what weighed most with the Cabinet was not whether the Government would be forced out — and it was anyhow clear that the Unionists would not seek to force it out before Easter — but whether the Liberal Party would be in a strong position to contest the second general election in the year. The reformists in the Cabinet had urged that a 'Single-Chamber policy' would prove unacceptable to the country; in the last week of February, the Radicals in the Commons and in the country had made it clear that a fundamental backsliding on the Lords would tear the party apart and make defeat certain. 'Members were declining to stand for their seats in the event of a General Election', the Master of Elibank recalled, 'and, as evidence that these groups were not led by mere irresponsibles, I have only to mention names such as Simon, Percy Alden, the Buxtons, and many old Parliamentary hands from the North, to show the seriousness of the movement.'[33] 'The fighting spirit of the party is still strong', C. P. Scott advised Churchill on 24 February, 'but if they are not strongly led & speedily it will evaporate, & we may whistle for our North of England majorities.'[34] When the Cabinet considered resignation on 25 February, Carrington wrote despairingly in his diary: 'Many openly say they cannot stand again: and if we go to the country at once, with trade reviving, no battle cry with the Lords, and on a policy of funk we shall be "snowed under".'[35]

On 28 February both the Government and the Opposition purchased time. In February, neither Asquith nor Balfour had shown themselves willing to take a strong lead; it suited both their styles to allow the situation to develop. It remained to be seen what they and their immediate colleagues would come up with, in response to the pressures upon them, by mid-April, when the moment for decision was scheduled to arrive.

III

In March, before the Easter recess, the Commons concerned itself with temporary borrowing and supply; the Lords debated Rosebery's resolutions for reform; the Cabinet worked out its policy for its resolutions on the Lords; and Lloyd George negotiated with both factions of the Irish Nationalists on Budget concessions. Immediately after the recess, Asquith moved the Government's Lords resolutions in the Commons, and the Cabinet survived Grey's renewed threat to disrupt it over the issue of reform.

The feature of the proceedings in the Commons on supply was the Government's limitation, on 10 March, of the vote on account to £8,000,000, enough for only about six weeks instead of the customary four to five months. Austen Chamberlain was one who was quick to appreciate the significance of this move. Supply by vote on account would expire in mid or late May, precisely when the Government 'expect in some way to have brought matters with the Lords to a crisis upon which they will resign, or to have been beaten in the Commons on their Budget'. In the latter instance, as everyone recognized, the Liberals, together with the Irish and Labour, would be in the position to deny a Unionist Government the means to carry on business or pay old-age pensions until after another general election, and thereby force a dissolution. But in the former instance, as Austen Chamberlain perceived, the Liberals and their allies might use their control of supply actually to prevent a dissolution by a minority Unionist Government, by denying it the money to run the country for the duration of a general election. A dissolution, in other words, might only be had on Liberal terms.[36] After Asquith's intimation in the Commons on 14 April that he would not dissolve on the Lords issue without contingent guarantees, Balfour concluded that the main purpose behind the Government's limiting essential supply had indeed been 'to prevent a dissolution by their opponents'.[37]

At one stage Sandars entertained the suspicion, and some Radicals the hope, that the Government even planned to use control of supply to entirely avert the need for a second general election. It was Sandars's supposedly informed anticipation that the Government would 'pick their quarrel with the Lords when the opportunity suits them', that Asquith would then demand immediate guarantees and when the King refused he would resign. The King would call in Balfour, who would find himself without the money to carry on, and unable to dissolve Parliament with 'an empty exchequer'. Asquith would again be sent for and would say to the King: 'I told you so. The only possible Government at this juncture is mine, and I must repeat my demand for those guarantees which will enable me to give effect to the decision of the House of Commons as represented by the passage of the Veto resolutions.' Asquith would then get the guarantees he wanted, and escape the general election he dreaded.[38]

There is not a shred of evidence that Asquith ever contemplated exploiting control of supply to extract immediate guarantees. To the contrary, he told Crewe on 8 April: 'I remain of the opinion which I have held throughout – that in this Parliament we cannot advise, and therefore cannot ask for, anything.' But he added that 'the real question' was whether 'we shall only advise a dissolution on the terms of what are called "contingent guarantees" '.[39] It was in the event of the King initially refusing contingent guarantees, if asked for, that the Cabinet might want to be in the position to deny essential supply to a Unionist government for the duration of a second general election, and in this way to seek to force a dissolution on Liberal terms. How far the Cabinet as a whole thought along these lines when, on 9 March, it unanimously agreed to limit supply by vote on account is unclear; at that juncture it had not even thrashed out its fundamental policy on guarantees. Basically it seems that the Cabinet was taking out an insurance policy for contingencies. Control of supply might prove a useful weapon in a variety of circumstances.

Redmond and his supporters welcomed the limitation of supply, but there still remained a considerable gap between what they demanded and what the Cabinet had conceded or seemed prepared to concede. Redmond wanted the peers to respond to the Government's plans for the Lords and thereby force the question of guarantees before the Commons ever voted on the Budget; the Cabinet, on the other hand, remained determined to carry the Budget before confronting the Lords, for that would lead either to resignation or dissolution. On 8 March Lloyd George advised Redmond that the Government would take the Budget in the interval between the veto resolutions passing the Commons and being considered by the Lords. He then told Redmond that if the Irish Nationalists would agree to the Budget going through in this way 'he would be prepared practically to give us any amendments in the Budget that we wished', including, so Redmond understood, the omission of the whiskey duty. 'Of course,' Redmond reported to Dillon, 'he made it clear he was speaking only for himself, but this is the price he personally would be willing to pay for getting the Budget through before the Veto question caused a resignation or a dissolution. He said he believed he could get the Cabinet to agree to these terms.' Lloyd George further informed Redmond that through the Master of Elibank he was in touch with O'Brien and Healy, who were offering to support the Government in return for major concessions on the Budget. Redmond's response was that he stood by 'no veto, no Budget', but at the same time he felt that it was his duty to consider the offer carefully, and required more time to do so. 'To be quite candid with you', Redmond informed Dillon, 'I do not trust Lloyd George in this matter. I do not believe he could get the cabinet to agree to these terms; but I felt bound to, at any rate, say that I would carefully consider them; and I

am far from saying that, if they could be carried out, they
ought not to be accepted.'[40]

What is evident from this exchange, and others before
them, is that the idea of making concessions in the Budget to
Ireland was being canvassed by Lloyd George, not Redmond.
Even though the Cabinet had at its first meeting after the
general election declared against Lloyd George's proposal
that the Government should drop the whiskey tax in the
effort to save the Budget, the Chancellor had suggested the
possibility of Budget concessions to Redmond and T. P.
O'Connor when he had met them on 12 February, and again
to Redmond and Dillon on 21 February, but he could get no
undertaking from the Irish leaders that they would support
the Budget in return for concessions.[41] Redmond certainly
wanted changes in the Budget, and from all accounts was
under strong pressure from Irish publicans, brewers and the
whiskey trade to secure them, but he always suspected that
any concessions he could get from the Cabinet would be
in the nature of a compromise, and that they would be
insufficient to silence the O'Brienites.[42] More important,
he was convinced in his own mind that the veto came first,
and was not inclined to weaken his hand with regard to his
basic demand for guarantees for the sake of Budget concessions. 'Don't make the mistake of thinking R's attitude due
to Budget', T. P. O'Connor was to remind the Master of
Elibank on 22 March.[43] When Redmond and Dillon did urge
the case for Budget concessions, they did so on the ground
that modifications were necessary to make it possible for the
Irish to 'heartily support' the Budget after the question of
guarantees had been decided.[44] When Lloyd George raised
the possibility of Budget concessions he was, by contrast,
manœuvring to make possible the passage of the Budget
through the Commons before the confrontation with the
Lords was reached. If the Cabinet was determined that the
passage of the Budget must be the Government's first major
legislative act, then bartering with the Irish on the Budget
seemed to Lloyd George the obvious tack to take to avert the
politically disastrous outcome of being defeated on the
Budget. By making contact with O'Brien and Healy, Lloyd
George was attempting to undermine Redmond's resolve on

'no veto, no Budget' and to get him to do what he had so far stubbornly refused to do: negotiate on the Budget itself. The threat Lloyd George ultimately held over Redmond was that of major desertions from his own ranks to vote with the O'Brienites and the Government for a suitably modified Budget.

Lloyd George's negotiations with O'Brien did not get very far, and they ended in bitter recriminations. They first met at the home of Sir Hudson Kearley on 9 March, and again on 23 March, when Lloyd George virtually gave notice to O'Brien that their negotiation was stillborn.[45] By then Lloyd George had succeeded in drawing Redmond into direct negotiations on Budget concessions, which was his main purpose.

The first meeting with O'Brien, revealed in the press in the next week, had its desired effect when, in a speech at Liverpool on 20 March, Redmond signalled his willingness to discuss the Budget itself and to consider holding up only the final stage of the Budget in the Commons until the Lords had indicated its stance on the veto resolutions.[46] The next day Lloyd George asked the Cabinet for leave to approach Redmond and 'to say he would like a definite reply as to his attitude towards our Budget, and that he had played long enough with us'.[47] Later the same day Lloyd George, accompanied by Birrell and the Master of Elibank, met Redmond and Dillon, and explored the ways and means by which the Budget might be made acceptable to Ireland. No agreements or bargains of any sort were struck, but from the report back to the Cabinet Pease gained the impression that: 'The obvious desire was on the part of the Nationalists to find a way for supporting the Govmt. on the budget.' Redmond and Dillon were, in fact, under intense pressure to reach a bargain with the Government over the Budget. Apart from Lloyd George's negotiation with O'Brien, they had been approached by the Labour party to allow the Budget through, they had consistently been warned that it would be as fatal to Ireland as to the Government for the Irish to defeat the Budget, and they had throughout been advised by O'Connor that they would have to accept the priority that the Government gave to the Budget over the Lords.[48] Whatever the considerations that impelled the Irish leaders to meet with

Lloyd George on 21 March, they were now involved in serious negotiations over Budget concessions.

At its meeting on 23 March the Cabinet duly discussed Redmond's requirements relating to whiskey, the brewers, stamps, and the land valuation and increment duty. The Cabinet agreed to authorize the Government draftsman to prepare alterations in the provisions for the stamp and increment duties, and Asquith advised the King: 'It is clear that the increased spirit duty — to which the Irish take special exception — will have to be dropped next year, as it has checked consumption and brought in a diminished revenue.'[49]

Where the Cabinet remained firm was in its determination to carry the Budget through the Commons before the Lords had responded to the Government's veto proposals. But what Asquith raised at the meeting of 23 March was whether the Cabinet might decide in advance what its policy would be in the event of the Lords hanging up or rejecting the veto resolutions. If the Cabinet was resolved to secure guarantees, that resolution could presumably be communicated to Redmond.

What Asquith wanted to know from the Cabinet on 23 March was its opinion 'on what guarantees he should seek, or what he should say when pressed'. If the Budget was rejected, the Government would have to go out, but if the Budget was passed and the Lords would not consider the veto resolutions, what, he asked, was the Government to do then? As he saw it, there were three courses open to the Government: it could resign, dissolve, or seek guarantees, not for the present Parliament, but if again returned after a general election. Lloyd George, according to Pease, now in the Cabinet, suggested deferring any decision until the position actually arose, and in this the Cabinet concurred.[50]

Lloyd George's calculations in securing the deferment of the question of guarantees are not immediately clear. It seems likely, though, that his discussions with Redmond on 21 March, and the Cabinet's response to them, encouraged him to believe that Budget concessions could be negotiated to provide the basis for Irish support for the passage of the Budget; certainly it was a possibility worth pursuing. It also seems likely that he reckoned it was still premature to push the Cabinet on the potentially disruptive question of guarantees, given that the Government's veto resolutions had not yet been discussed in the Commons.

Those resolutions, three in number, had been tabled in the Commons on 21 March. The first proposed to disable the Lords from rejecting or amending a money bill; the second to replace the absolute veto of the Lords over ordinary legislation with a suspensory veto; and the third to limit the duration of a Parliament to five years. To Grey's chagrin, the reform of the Lords did not feature in the resolutions, and over the Easter recess he was again to threaten resignation and with that the break-up of the Cabinet.

On Easter Friday, 25 March, Grey wrote to Asquith that he thought it was best that he resigned. The Government's resolutions were due to be debated and voted upon in the Commons immediately after Easter, and Grey was certain that: 'For the C.B. resolution I cannot vote at all, except as preparatory to reconstitution and as a means of carrying it.' If he remained in the Cabinet and voted for the resolution, he would have to explain his vote in the Commons, and that would cause more trouble for the Government than his resignation. He therefore preferred to resign, and if he could do so alone would press Asquith to allow him to go.[51] To ensure that he would not indeed be isolated, Grey conveyed the contents of the letter to Runciman, who promptly wrote to McKenna. Runciman said he thought Asquith still imagined that Grey was isolated, and he consequently proposed to make it plain to the Prime Minister that this was not the case.[52] McKenna likewise responded 'that if Grey goes out I go too'.[53]

As before, Haldane emerged as the 'peacemaker' when the Cabinet met for the first time after the Easter recess on 30 March, suggesting a bill that would 'meet both sections'.[54] His formula, accepted by the Cabinet at its meetings on 4 and 6 April, was to include in the preamble to the Government's draft Parliament Bill a statement that 'it is intended to substitute for the House of Lords as it at present exists a Second Chamber constituted on a popular instead of hereditary basis', and a clause which affirmed that nothing in the Bill should 'diminish or qualify the existing rights and privileges of the House of Commons'.[55] No attempt, in other words, would be made to prevent the Commons from in future repealing the restrictions on the veto of the Upper House. This was enough to placate Grey, who refrained from making his threatened 'explanation' in the Commons debates on the Government's resolutions, although Haldane aroused Harcourt's ire with a speech in the House that suggested that the veto resolutions and the reconstitution of the Second Chamber were parts of an 'indivisible policy'.[56]

On Easter Tuesday, 29 March, Asquith had moved in the Commons that the House go into committee on the Government's Lords resolutions, and after four days of debate the House duly approved the motion, sixty-seven Irish Nationalists, including Healy, voting with the Government. In supporting the resolutions, Redmond reiterated that if the Lords rejected them, the Prime Minister should at once ask the Crown for a promise that peers would be created, and if he was refused he should go to the country without delay and armed with every weapon that was of value to him in the contest.[57] The Budget, in other words, should be held back. The Cabinet, however, at its meeting on 30 March, unanimously agreed that its duty was to obtain a 'prompt decision' by the Commons on the 'long-delayed' Budget for 1909/10, and it accordingly resolved to curtail the debate in the Commons on the Lords resolutions to the week ending 16 April, and to proceed at once thereafter with the Budget.[58] As Pease recorded in his diary: 'Govmt. declined to accept Redmond's dictation as to how appeal should be made to suit Nationalists party pretensions to become the leaders of radical party.'[59]

As Carrington saw the matter, Redmond was in fact now running the risk of antagonizing the Radicals in the Commons by appearing unduly demanding in his negotiations with the Government. On 1 April he entered in his diary: 'Our extreme men putting great pressure on Redmond, and we have put him in the same difficulty as he hoped to get us into. He doesn't mind having a quarrel with the Govt. but he doesn't want a row with our extreme men, whom he hoped to get on his side. Altogether the sky is clearing, and the mistakes at the end of Feby. are being forgotten.'

With the Budget now firmly scheduled to be reintroduced in April, it remained to be seen whether Redmond and the Government would finally fall apart, or come to an arrangement that would permit the passage of the Budget.

IV

In the first weeks of April the Government's Lords resolutions passed easily through the Commons and, until 14 April, Asquith simply side-stepped all questions in the House about what the Government planned to do after the resolutions had finally been approved by the Commons. He told his questioners to 'wait and see' what would happen next. Public speculation, the deliberations in the Cabinet, and negotiations between the Government and the Irish Nationalists, none the less narrowed in their main focus to a consideration of two points: whether the Budget would be fundamentally altered to suit the Irish, and whether the Cabinet would decide and make known in advance of any action by the Lords on the Government's veto proposals if it would ask the King for so-called 'contingent guarantees'.

Redmond and the Irish Nationalists were still far from being squared, and the constraints on the offers that might be made to them were tightening rather than loosening. The Government was committed to passing the Budget before confronting the Lords; the Radicals in the Commons, as well as the more fastidious among ministers, resented the idea of retreating on its contents; and the whole notion of committing the Government to a request for guarantees in advance of action by the Lords troubled a good many Liberals, especially within the Cabinet.

In this situation, Redmond's speech at Tipperary on 3 April was highly significant. Directing his remarks both against O'Brien and towards the Government, Redmond stated that if the only question had been that of securing amendments to the Budget, the whole difficulty between the Irish and the Government would have been resolved long ago. The crucial fact, for Redmond, was that the Budget provided the Irish with their 'one great weapon' to force ministers to stand by their speeches. If the Irish party was assured that guarantees would be asked for on the rejection of the veto resolutions by the Lords, and if in the event of guarantees being refused the Budget was held back, then the Irish party could quite easily discuss concessions on the Budget so as to make it tolerable to Ireland.[60]

The pivot on which everything truly revolved, the 'Political Notes' of *The Times* had already observed on 1 April, was the question of guarantees; if that was dealt with to the satisfaction of Redmond, he and his party would have gained their main point. As reported by the 'Political Notes', Redmond desired that if the Government's veto proposals had not been finally dealt with in the Lords before the third reading of the Budget in the Commons, the Prime Minister should make an explicit statement that if the veto proposals were rejected he would ask for the exercise of the royal prerogative to create peers, and, failing to obtain them, resign office. The 'Political Notes' added that it was thought unlikely that this desire of Redmond's would be met.[61]

The intimations of the 'Political Notes' made a great deal of sense. The Budget was important for the leverage it gave Redmond over the Government; it was not of vital importance for putting pressure on the Crown and the Lords. The Government's control of supply was what counted in the latter regard. Despite certain statements in Redmond's Tipperary speech, made perhaps for the sake of form, the real question was not whether the Government would hold the Budget back, for that had effectively become a political impossibility for the Government. The real question related to the terms on which the Irish Nationalists might allow the passage of the Budget before the final issue with the Lords was joined.

Unfortunately, the exact content of Lloyd George's negotiations with Redmond in early April is not known. What is evident is that when they met after Redmond's Tipperary speech they had a furious clash. On 5 April, according to Hobhouse's diary, there was 'a quarrel of a personal nature when Ll.G. told Redmond in round terms that he might go to the deuce', and the Master of Elibank confirms that the two had 'a very angry difference of opinion'.[62] According to the 'Political Notes' of *The Times*, Redmond had formulated seven conditions which the Irish

Nationalists required should be fulfilled as the price for the passage of the Budget through the Commons, and that Lloyd George indicated his personal willingness to concede four of these conditions, but not the remaining three. Lloyd George was reported as prepared to concede that the increased whiskey duty should not run beyond the 1909/10 fiscal year, but refused to allow that Ireland should be relieved from the new brewery licence duties on the ground that this would involve differential legislation between Great Britain and Ireland.[63]

In the same week that he had his wrangle with Redmond, Lloyd George finally reached the conclusion that Budget concessions would be insufficient in themselves to ensure Irish Nationalist support for the Budget. Whatever concessions were made on the Budget, Redmond, it seems, still hung back from giving a firm assurance that the Nationalists would support the Budget on the third reading.[64] What was becoming obvious to Lloyd George, as well as to Asquith, was that nothing short of a Cabinet decision to request contingent guarantees would satisfy Redmond, but what was equally obvious was that such a decision would be strongly resisted by Morley, who wanted neither the reform of the Lords nor the creation of new peers to abolish the absolute veto of the Lords, and by several others. On 8 April Asquith put it to Crewe that the 'real question' had become whether the Cabinet could make up its mind, and convey to the Irish, that in the event of the Lords rejecting the veto resolutions, the Government would only advise a dissolution on the terms of contingent guarantees.[65]

All concerned recognized that, with the Commons debates on the veto resolutions drawing to an end, the Cabinet meetings in the week beginning Monday 11 April would be crucial, and on the Friday beforehand Harcourt, Churchill, and Lloyd George began their campaigns to persuade the Cabinet to decide for contingent guarantees. In a memorandum circulated on 8 April, Harcourt urged the case for contingent guarantees, not as a means of squaring Redmond, but as a means of rallying the party's fighting forces. What he wanted was for the Prime Minister to make in the Commons a 'full statement' that if the Government was again returned at the next general election, it would require from the King an assurance that if necessary he would create sufficient peers to pass the Parliament Bill into law. 'Any less effective action', Harcourt contended, 'would afford small hope of our attaining a majority in the next Parliament for our policy of the limitation of the Veto.'[66] That same day Churchill, acting on Lloyd George's behalf as well as his own, saw Morley and 'beseeched' him 'to agree about squaring Redmond by creation of peers, contingent on victory at next election'. If the Cabinet declined on Monday to decide for contingent guarantees, Churchill warned Morley with 'great firmness', then he and the Chancellor of the Exchequer would resign.[67]

That Lloyd George was now determined to try and secure a decision for guarantees was confirmed on the Sunday, when he sent for Masterman, who told his wife afterwards that he had never before seen such a change: 'The clouds had lifted and George at that moment was more or less decided in favour of demanding guarantees, and resigning if the demand were not granted.' When Masterman breakfasted with Lloyd George next moring, he found him 'still more emphatic in that direction, but very despairing of getting his way'.[68] This did not mean that Lloyd George had abandoned his attempt to secure Budget concessions for Ireland; what it did mean was that he was no longer restricted to asking for Budget concessions.

The Cabinet meetings of 11, 12, and 13 April proved decisive. At the first two meetings, ministers were at 'sixes and sevens'. Grey and several others were 'emphatically opposed' to giving way on the whiskey tax, and Morley took a 'strong line' against demanding guarantees.[69] Lloyd George, at first, stood out for dropping the whiskey tax, despite the 'general outburst of disapproval' at this course, and eventually, according to Hobhouse, 'said it was impossible for him to stay, his word was pledged; W. Churchill said the same and they took an almost formal leave of the Cabinet'.[70] At this juncture, according to the Master of Elibank's own account, confirmed by Hobhouse, the Master intervened and advised Lloyd George to abandon his effort to drop the whiskey tax and to focus on the demand for guarantees, which was what really concerned the Irish.[71] Whether acting on the Master's advice, or his own tactical instincts, Lloyd George did an about-turn at the Cabinet meeting of 13 April and indicated that he was prepared to leave the whiskey tax untouched. Then, according to Masterman: 'Amid the joy and astonishment . . . caused by this refusal to be dictated to by the Irish he immediately and dramatically challenged them on the question of guarantees . . . '[72]

The main outlines of what happened at the meeting of 13 April are reasonably clear. Asquith, apparently, opened with a statement in favour of retaining the whiskey tax. In his note of the proceedings, Runciman indicates that Asquith insisted that if the Budget was to be passed under guillotine, it would have to remain unchanged. Labour and the Radicals, he further pointed out, were against changing the Budget, and held that guarantees overrode everything. He believed the Irish 'will probably have to say ditto'.[73]

According to Masterman, Churchill prepared to speak next, when Lloyd George passed him a note to keep quiet, and that he was going to abandon his efforts to repeal the whiskey tax.[74] Then, according to Pease: 'Lloyd George said he was prepared to subordinate his own views, & allow whiskey duty to be reduced to secure Irish support for his budget, if we made our position clear in regard to conditional guarantees being secured.' This dramatic stand for guarantees had an immediate snowball effect. Pease himself joined in, and urged the necessity for an immediate decision for contingent guarantees, not so much to satisfy the Irish, as the party. Without guarantees, he contended, 'we should be regarded as failures'. According to Pease's diary, Birrell, Churchill, and Carrington followed with statements in the same sense.[75]

At the week-end, Morley had understood that what Lloyd George and Churchill wanted was a decision to warn the King and to advise the Irish in confidence that the Government would require guarantees if again returned at the next general election; the Cabinet was now deciding that 'conditional guarantees' should be secured before the general election, and that the decision should be made public. On procedure, what Lloyd George recommended was that when the Lords finally rejected the Government's veto proposals, the Cabinet should approach the King for guarantees. If, as was likely, the King said, 'I cannot without another election', the Cabinet should not resign but should accept a dissolution on the basis of contingent guarantees, namely 'if we get a substantial majority (not 30 or 40) he will create peers'. In the meantime, when the Budget was reintroduced on Monday, the Prime Minister was to tell the Commons: 'If the Lords fail to accept our policy we shall immediately tender advice to the Crown we are not in a position to give statutory effect to policy during this Parliament and we shall either resign or advise a dissolution but only under such conditions in the next Parliament as will ensure that the judgement of the people as expressed at the election shall be passed into law.'[76] Asquith's report to the King of the Cabinet's discussions, and his statement to the Commons next day, accurately reflected Lloyd George's recommendations. Whether by design, or by an uncanny ability to sense and seize the advantage at the critical moment, Lloyd George had left his major play to the very last minute, but on 13 April he effectively dictated what the Cabinet would both do and say.

In his letter afterwards to the King, Asquith reported that ministers had come to the conclusion that to purchase the Irish vote by means of a concession on the whiskey duty was 'a discreditable transaction, which they could not defend', and that consequently when the Budget was reintroduced on Monday the Irish Nationalists might combine with the Unionists to defeat the Government. He also reported that, if the Budget was carried and the Lords rejected or laid aside the veto resolutions:

They came to the conclusion that, in that event, it would be their duty at once to tender advice to the Crown as to the necessary steps — whether by the exercise of the prerogative, or by a referendum ad hoc, or otherwise — to be taken to ensure that the policy, approved by the House of Commons by large majorities, shall be given statutory effect in this Parliament. If they find that they were not in the position to accomplish that object, they would then either resign office, or advise a dissolution of Parliament, but in no case would they feel able to advise a dissolution, except under such conditions as would secure that in the new Parliament the judgement of the people as expressed at the election, would be carried into law.[77]

The Cabinet, in short, might ask for an exercise of the royal prerogative in the current Parliament, but in any event, Liberal ministers would only advise a dissolution on terms of contingent guarantees.

The Irish and the Commons remained to be informed of the Cabinet's decision. Asquith himself saw Redmond, and afterwards let it out that the Irish leader 'admitted that he had been completely outmanœuvred, as he had been made to declare that all he cared about was Home Rule whereas his real object was remission of whiskey tax'.[78] On 14 April, immediately after the Commons had approved the veto resolutions on report by majorities of about a hundred, Asquith introduced in the House the Parliament Bill founded on the resolutions and indicated the Government's decision on guarantees. His statement, according to *The Times* report, was received on the Government side 'with ecstatic transports of approval'.[79] The Irish Nationalists seemed no less pleased. 'You fellows have done us', Redmond 'cheerfully' told Masterman afterwards. 'If we vote you out now it is on whiskey, where we shall get no sympathy from the priests or the British Radicals.'[80]

Redmond's Irish Nationalists made no attempt to vote the Government out on the Budget when it was reintroduced in the Commons the next week. On Monday 18 April, when Asquith moved a guillotine resolution allotting time to the various stages of the reintroduced Budget, Redmond announced that the Nationalists regarded the merits or demerits of the Budget as trivial when compared to the abolition of the Lords' veto, and that after the Prime Minister's statement his party was unanimously agreed to actively and enthusiastically support the Government.[81] The next day Budget resolutions were introduced, and the Budget, somewhat amended to ensure the exemption of the purely agricultural value of land from the new land taxes, finally passed its third reading in the Commons on 27 April, the Irish Nationalists voting with the Government.

Ministers were almost euphoric at the final outcome. At the 'very cheery happy' Cabinet meeting of 20 April Asquith was positively 'radiant', there were congratulations all round on securing the support of the Irish without having made concessions of 'a spirituous nature', and Lloyd George was warmly congratulated 'before the whole cabinet' on the fact that he had a surplus of £2,900,000 despite 'all the chaos to his budget proposals created by the Lords'.[82]

Among Unionists the attitude was that Asquith had surrendered more completely to Redmond than they had ever anticipated or thought necessary. On 18 April Austen Chamberlain wrote to his father: 'I am still astonished at the completeness and abjectness of Asquith's surrender, for I am convinced that Redmond would not have voted against him. He has eaten unnecessary dirt. I suppose the appetite grows!'[83]

The conclusion is none the less inescapable that, at the end, the Cabinet did well not to attempt to call Redmond's bluff, if bluff it ever was, or to have backed down on the Budget as a means to purchasing his support. In one direction, the earlier decision to proceed in the first instance on the Lords by way of resolutions was a master-stroke; it gave the Cabinet time in which to explore the situation and to work towards a consensus within its own ranks. In another direction, it restricted the Cabinet's options by intensifying the constraints upon it. The longer the Cabinet delayed the Budget, the less easy it became for it to produce a damp squib at the end, or for Redmond to allow any bluff on his part to be called.

For the Cabinet to have given way on the Budget, rather than to have gone for guarantees, might conceivably have failed in the end to satisfy Redmond, despite the reports that his own rank and file were intent on getting rid of the whiskey tax, and might well have blunted the morale of the Liberal rank and file. The idea of Budget concessions was never popular among the Radicals. Indeed, according to Hobhouse, the Master of Elibank firmly advised Lloyd George that if he chose to resign over the Cabinet's refusal to give way on the whiskey duty, he would 'find no support amongst the advanced section of Liberals'. By contrast, as Harcourt and Pease impressed upon the Cabinet in April, an immediate decision for guarantees would do more than square Redmond; it would ignite the enthusiasm of the Liberal rank and file and guarantee the party's morale for the next general election. Throughout the Cabinet's deliberations between February and April, a healthy concern for the requirements of the next general election was never missing.

What is perhaps surprising is Lloyd George's pertinacity in pursuing the tactic of Budget concessions, appearing to change his ground only at the very end. His main concern throughout was to avoid defeat in the Commons on the Budget, and the consequent resignation of the Government on the Budget rather than the veto. So long as the Cabinet was determined to attempt to pass the Budget first, and so long as he seriously doubted whether the Cabinet would ever agree to decide for guarantees in advance of action by the Lords on the Government's veto proposals, he was politically obliged to attempt to reach a bargain with the Irish on the Budget itself. According to Masterman, when the Cabinet did decide for guarantees, Lloyd George appeared 'dazed' at its 'incredible *volte face*'. What was never in doubt was that Lloyd George would ultimately stand firm for guarantees. Indeed, it was Runciman's estimate at the end of March that Lloyd George and Churchill were deliberately allowing the situation to develop 'until it is considered to be right' before demanding guarantees in conjunction with the Radicals and the Irish. When Asquith refused, Runciman predicted, the cry would go forth that he should give way to someone who would go to the King for guarantees, and Lloyd George and Churchill would resign rather than associate themselves with the Prime Minister's 'craven Whiggery'.[84]

As events proved, Runciman's estimate was partly right. Lloyd George did leave his stand for guarantees until precisely the right tactical moment. Where Runciman was badly wrong in his prediction was that Asquith would stand out against a decision on guarantees until 'a decisive issue' with the Lords was reached. In April 1910, as in the Cabinet's deliberations on the Budget a year previously, Asquith's political instincts proved more radical than some on the right wing of his Cabinet expected, but ultimately they trusted in his judgement and accepted the lead he gave them.

V

After the general election of January 1910 it was taken for

granted that, whatever else the Unionists and the Lords might do, the peers would accept the Budget if it was again passed by the Commons. On Thursday 28 April the Lords duly passed the Budget through all its stages in the course of a single sitting. The next day the Budget was given the royal assent. Exactly one year after Lloyd George had introduced his proposals in the Commons, the 'People's Budget' had finally become law.

One consequence of the Cabinet's decision to postpone taking the Budget until after Easter was that the financial year 1909/10 ended before the Budget for the year had been enacted, requiring the passage in March of the Treasury (Temporary Borrowing) Bill empowering the Government to borrow to meet current expenditure, and further suspending the Sinking Fund. The financial position on 31 March, as announced in the Commons by Lloyd George in his Budget statement on 19 April, was that expenditure for the year was £157,945,000 and actual receipts £131,697,000, leaving a deficit of £26,248,000. This deficit would be more than made up by the collection of £30,036,000 in arrears once the Budget had been enacted, giving a total revenue of £161,733,000. This total was short by £857,000 of the overall estimate Lloyd George had given the Commons the previous April, but an estimated £950,000 had been lost as a consequence of the failure to pass the Budget during the 1909/10 fiscal year.

Among individual sets of taxes, the receipts from the spirit duties were a staggering £2,800,000 down on Lloyd George's original estimate, 'a decline which he attributed to forestalments, trading with low revenues of stock as a consequence of 'uncertainty' about the fate of the Budget, and a startling diminution in consumption, which he estimated at between 20 and 25 per cent. To partially offset the decline in receipts from the spirit duties, the yield from the death duties was substantially higher than the original estimate. The actual yield from the death duties at 31 March 1910 was £21,766,000, as against an estimate of £21,450,000, and arrears remaining to be collected were £1,380,000. Receipts from stamps were £171,000 short of their estimate, but the whole of the new taxation had been lost. Actual receipts and arrears on the income tax, including supertax, amounted to £36,750,000, against the original estimate of £37,400,000, and the loss due to the rejection of the Budget was £350,000. The Post Office receipts were £23,030,000, against Lloyd George's estimate of £22,400,000; the Suez Canal receipts £1,269,000, against £1,166,000; and the miscellaneous receipts £1,687,000, against £1,394,000. Nothing had yet been collected from the land value duties, the additional liquor licences, and the new motor car licences.

Once all arrears had been collected, and after deducting payments to local authorities and the Road Board, the Government would be left with a balance of £2,962,000. Had £1,300,000 not been lost on stamps, income tax and interest charges as a result of the rejection of the Budget, the surplus would have been over £4,000,000. There was a certain artificiality to these figures given the substantial reductions in the contributions to the Sinking Fund; the Budget itself had provided for the diversion of £3,500,000 from the Sinking Fund, and a further £2,700,000 had been suspended by the Treasury (Temporary Borrowing) Act. The fact, none the less, was that the country's finances had escaped the Lords' rejection of the Budget relatively undamaged; no other fiscal system, Lloyd George proclaimed, could have borne so triumphantly so severe a strain.[85] The true revenue producing potential of the 'People's Budget' was still somewhat hidden by the special factors that operated in 1909/10; it would become more evident in the years immediately ahead.

XI. Impact of the Budget

I

In its provisions the 'People's Budget' had ranged far and wide, and its ramifications were to reach even wider. Much of importance flowed from it — the modernization of the British system of taxation, the financing of the social-service state, the defeat of tariff reform, the destruction of the absolute veto of the House of Lords, and the plunge towards civil war in Ireland. It was to have a significant influence on almost everything it touched, either directly or indirectly.

Because of the political controversies to which the 'People's Budget' gave rise, or brought to a point of decision, it was to have a far-reaching impact on politics, and generally served the Liberals well. Even though it failed to prevent major Unionist gains among middle-class voters in England, it greatly assisted the Liberals in retaining the active support of working-class voters in two general elections; it certainly went far to assist the Liberals in 'dishing' both the House of Lords and the Tariff Reformers; and it did much to restore the vitality and sense of purpose of the Liberal party itself.

The rejection of the Budget by the Lords was the key event that made possible the Parliament Act of 1911, which placed statutory limits on the powers of the Upper House. Without the rejection of the Budget the Liberals might well never have managed to work up a successful 'cry' against the Lords. As it was, the anti-Lords agitation that followed the rejection of the Budget served the Liberals for the two general elections that were required, in the event, to secure the limitation of the powers of the Upper House.

The second general election of 1910, contested in December, sealed the fate of the Upper House. In an election dominated by the issue of the Lords, in a way the first had not been, the Liberals and their allies retained their majority in the Commons. The Liberals returned with 272 seats, Labour with 42, and the Irish Nationalists with 84, as against

272 for the Unionists, leaving the balance of forces in the Commons essentially unchanged. The Commons duly passed the Parliament Bill through all its stages by 15 May 1911, and on 10 August the Lords, under the threat of a prompt and large creation of peers, accepted its provisions. The Liberals had finally succeeded in curbing the powers of the Lords.

For tariff reform, as it proved, the first general election of 1910 had been the decisive setback. In a belated endeavour to avert defeat in the second general election, the Unionist leaders in November adopted proposals for a referendum to settle disputes between the Lords and the Commons on matters of 'great gravity'. At the Albert Hall on 29 November Balfour effectively jettisoned tariff reform as an immediate issue in the election by announcing that he was prepared to submit the principles of tariff reform to a referendum. By having the Budget rejected in the Lords Balfour had given the Tariff Reformers the opportunity to prove their claim that they could sweep the country; their failure in the January elections to outbid the attractions offered by the 'People's Budget' prompted Balfour more or less to abandon tariff reform for the December elections. The 'People's Budget' had in fact gone far to help preserve the system of free trade.

For the Liberal party itself the 'People's Budget' performed two fundamental tasks. It enabled the Liberals to consolidate their hold over the working-class vote at a juncture when that hold was being threatened both by a sustained campaign by the Tariff Reformers to win working-class support and by the assertiveness of the Labour party. Simultaneously it restored the morale and sense of purpose of the Liberal rank and file.

By producing a 'People's Budget' Lloyd George not only blunted, but thwarted, the drive of the Tariff Reformers to capture industrial England, and contributed directly to the containment of the Labour party by seriously hampering its ability to differentiate itself clearly from Liberalism. This was achieved at some loss, notably the high wastage of conservative-minded Liberal MPs at the end of the 1909 session, and the considerable erosion of middle-class and rural support for the Liberals in much of England in the general election of January 1910. Though these losses caused the Government to falter temporarily over the issue of the Lords, they did not prove unacceptable, and they intensified rather than curbed the radicalism of the Liberal back-benchers. So far from seeking to restrain the Government, the back-benchers positively urged a forward policy, particularly on the Lords and on the land.

As an instrument of fiscal and social policy, the 'People's Budget' achieved a rather more mixed record than it did in its immediate impact in the political sphere. It proved enormously successful as an instrument for raising revenue, it performed the task of providing the finance required for old-age pensions and the launching of national health and unemployment insurance, but its impact on the over-all distribution of taxation was limited, and individual taxes, with the exception of the duty on spirits, proved frankly disappointing as instruments of social policy. The land value duties signally failed either to produce much revenue or to force a large supply of cheap building land on to the market, and the licence duties did nothing to force the pace of reduction in the number of public houses.

From the revenue standpoint, the 'People's Budget', with the exception of the land value duties, proved an unqualified success. No additions to taxation were required until 1914, despite considerable increases in expenditure. In every year between 1910 and 1914 Lloyd George achieved a surplus, with the taxes of the 'People's Budget' consistently bringing in more than he had estimated. In 1911/12 his realized surplus was £6,545,000, the greatest on record. Exchequer receipts totalled £185,090,000, exceeding the estimate by £3,469,000. The surplus on the revenue side, Lloyd George explained in the Commons in his Budget speech of 2 April 1912, was due to exceptionally good trade and the fact that, apart from the land value duties, the new taxes he had introduced in 1909 'have not only come up to the expectation of the Government, but have actually exceeded it'. In 1911/12 the new taxes had produced £23,900,000, of which £8,000,000 came from 'indulgences and luxuries', namely the liquor and licence duties, tobacco and motor-cars,

£4,900,000 from the increased income tax, £3,000,000 from the supertax, and £6,300,000 from the increased death duties.[1] In the next year the new taxes produced £25,655,000, which, Lloyd George proudly announced, was '£3,300,000 above the estimate we formed of their ultimate yield when they had reached maturity — and they have not yet reached that!'[2] In 1913/14 Exchequer receipts totalled £198,243,000, of which the new taxes contributed £27,215,000. As *The Economist* had commented on 20 May 1911: 'Mr. Lloyd George may stand on record as the author of the most successful Budget, from the revenue producing point of view, which the financial historian of this, or, perhaps, any other, country can recall in times of peace.'

How far the 'People's Budget' had gone to promote the redistribution of the burden of taxation between classes was another question. In this respect its immediate achievement was more limited. According to Exchequer classification, the proportion between direct and indirect taxation stood at 57.6 to 42.4 per cent in 1912/13, as against 52.6 to 47.4 per cent in 1908/9, and 50.3 to 49.7 per cent in 1905/6. During the period of Liberal finance 1906–14 the movement towards increasing the proportion of direct to indirect taxation was clear and distinct, but the conclusion reached by Herbert Samuel in 1919 in an address to the Royal Statistical Society on 'The Taxation of the Various Classes of the People' was that Liberal finance had not in fact even succeeded in completely equalizing the burden of taxation between classes in proportion to income. '(T)he British system of taxation', he asserted, 'is regressive in the lower stages; the classes with the smallest incomes pay a larger proportion of them in contributions to the revenue than the classes immediately above them. This inequality was very marked in the first period (1903/4) we have had under consideration. It had been redressed a little, but only a little, during the decade before the war.'

The statistics that Samuel put forward indicated that between 1906 and 1914 the percentage of income paid in imperial taxation by the working classes had been reduced slightly, that it had also been reduced slightly for earned incomes up to £2,000, and that it had been considerably increased for larger incomes and unearned incomes over £500. Samuel, who left out of his calculations the stamp and licence duties on the ground that they had no clearly definable relation to the income of the individual, gave the following figures for 1903/4 and 1913/14:[3]

| Income | Total Taxation as Percentage of Income | | | |
| | 1903/4 | | 1913/14 | |
£	Earned	Unearned	Earned	Unearned
50	9.1	9.1	8.7	8.7
100	6.2	6.2	6.0	6.0
150	5.0	5.0	4.9	4.9
200	5.6	7.8	4.8	7.0
500	6.6	8.8	5.8	9.9
1,000	7.4	10.3	6.6	12.2
2,000	6.6	9.8	5.8	12.0
5,000	5.6	9.6	6.8	12.4
10,000	5.1	9.5	8.1	15.1
20,000	4.9	10.0	8.3	16.0
50,000	4.8	10.2	8.4	18.1

In 1927 the Colwyn Committee on National Debt and Taxation confirmed and adopted, with some adjustments, Samuel's figures.[4]

The meaning of Samuel's figures was clear enough. The poorest sections in the community, with family incomes of only £1 a week, were grossly over-taxed in proportion to their income. By 1913/14 the working classes generally still paid a higher proportion of their income in taxation than many, perhaps the majority, in the income tax paying class. 'Such regression', Samuel commented, 'is the consequence of relying for revenue to so large an extent as we do upon the taxation of alcohol, tobacco, tea, and sugar, and of the fact that the consumption of these articles is larger in proportion to income among the poorer classes.' In so far as the burden of taxation on the working classes had been lightened during the decade of Liberal finance this was due to Asquith's reduction of the tea and sugar duties. As a consequence, however, of the spirit and tobacco duties of the 'People's Budget' the main effect of Liberal finance had been not so much to reduce the burden of taxation on the working classes as it had been to transfer a larger part of the burden from 'necessaries' to what were deemed 'luxuries'. From Samuel's figures it is evident that it was not the working classes but the middle-class income tax payers with earned incomes up to £2,000 who proved the primary beneficiaries of Liberal attempts to reduce the burden of taxation for certain groups in the community. The white-collar, small-business, and professional middle classes gained, in this respect, the most from Liberal finance between 1906 and 1914. The significant increases in rates of taxation in proportion to income applied to larger incomes over £5,000 and the holders of mainly unearned income.

The main benefit gained by the lower classes from Liberal finance in the decade before World War I, and particularly from the 'People's Budget', was in the financing of old-age pensions and the state's contribution to national health and unemployment insurance, introduced in 1911. Old-age pensions were paid for entirely by taxation, and the state's contribution to health and unemployment insurance amounted to roughly a quarter of the revenue needed to finance the schemes. The health insurance scheme required weekly contributions for all wage-earners at the rates of 4*d*. from the employee, 3*d*. from the employer, and 2*d*. from the state, while the unemployment insurance scheme required for all workers covered a weekly contribution of 2½*d*. from both the employer and the employee with a state subsidy of approximately 1⅔*d*.

To the very limited extent that Liberal finance promoted a redistribution of income between classes, this was the achievement mainly of old-age pensions. The impact of health and unemployment insurance on income distribution between classes was probably fairly minimal, despite Lloyd George's claim that wage-earners were getting 9*d*. for their 4*d*. contribution to health insurance. The compulsory insurance contributions were, in effect, another form of taxation, and it is the consensus among economists that such levies are almost entirely regressive in their incidence, in that the employer contributions are effectively either taken out of wages or passed on to the consumer.[5] As surely as new tariffs, in other words, the insurance contributions considerably increased the incidence of taxation for the lower classes in proportion to income, with the important difference that direct contributions firmly established the contractual right of wage-earners to the benefits they received.

The 'People's Budget' was fashioned as an instrument of social reform not only in that it would raise the revenue required for social reform, apart from insurance contributions, more by way of regular direct taxes than by indirect taxation, but also in that particular taxes, notably the land value and licensing duties, were intended to promote certain social ends as well as raise revenue. Both the land value and the licensing duties did little to achieve the social objectives expected of them. The land value duties, indeed, proved positively counter-productive in dealing with the housing problem as well as a dismal failure from the revenue producing standpoint.

The position at the end of the 1913/14 fiscal year, when Lloyd George sought to secure a series of amendments to the land value clauses of the Finance (1909/10) Act of 1910, was that the land value duties, not including the mineral rights duty, had produced a mere £612,787, and the valuation itself, which was still incomplete, had cost over £2,000,000. The increment duty had raised £57,434; the reversion duty, £151,287; and the undeveloped land duty, £404,066. The mineral rights duty, which was distinct from the genuine land value duties, had raised £1,561,741.

There was no question by 1914 that the land value duties had run into considerable difficulties, some of which Lloyd George sought to overcome in the Revenue Bill of 1914. To begin with, the valuation itself had proved cumbersome and slow, to the chagrin of the land taxers in the Commons who were anxious to use the valuation to establish site value rating. By 31 July 1914 about 79 per cent of the total area and about 86 per cent of the total number of hereditaments in Great Britain had been given provisional valuations, and about 60 per cent of these had become final.[6] In 1914, in fact, a large number of provisional valuations were not served on owners as a consequence of adverse legal decisions, and much of the more difficult work of valuation in the city centres still remained to be done.

Edgar Harper, who was appointed as Chief Valuer to the Board of Inland Revenue in 1911, attributed the slow progress of the valuation to a wide range of factors. These included the recruitment and training of a staff, which by 1914 numbered almost 5,000; the old and complicated systems of tenure; the necessity of assessing and collecting the land value duties, notably the undeveloped land duty, which diverted the Valuation Office from its main task of making the valuation; and the complicated requirements of the valuation, which entailed the ascertainment of four, and sometimes five, values for each hereditament — gross value, full site value, total value, assessable site value, and in the case of agricultural land, the value of the land for agricultural purposes where that value was different from the site value.[7] In Harper's view the requirement for ascertaining a series of values in order to determine site value was 'an altogether needless complication': 'It would have been far simpler — and more accurate — to arrive at the unimproved land value, as valuers always can, by comparison with the sales and lettings of similar land in the vicinity.'[8]

Another factor that became important in retarding the valuation, and which was stressed by Percy Thompson, a commissioner of the Inland Revenue in the evidence he gave to the Select Committee on Land Values in 1919, was the 'prolonged and organised opposition' to the valuation, which led to a mass of legal and technical points being raised against it.[9] This was a factor that hindered not only the valuation itself, but also the assessment and collection of the land value duties. A large amount of litigation was entered into against the valuation and the assessment of the duties, and several important decisions of the courts went against the Board of Inland Revenue or otherwise created difficulties that necessitated amending legislation. By early 1914 the assessment and collection of the undeveloped land duty had been wholly suspended, and that of the increment and reversion duties partially suspended, as a consequence of judicial decisions.[10]

In a memorandum prepared for the Cabinet in December 1913 on 'The Rating of Site Values', Lloyd George stated that: 'During the last ten years, and especially as a result of the further knowledge gained from the discussions upon the valuation under the Finance Act (1909/10), 1910, the rating of site values is no longer regarded so much as a means of raising fresh revenue as a means whereby a stimulus can be given to the better use of land for productive purposes, whether such land be used for building or for agricultural purposes.'[11] By December 1913 there was a widespread agreement that the imperial taxes on land values had not only not succeeded in raising much by way of revenue, but had also largely failed to promote 'the better use of land for productive purposes', and had proved positively counter-productive in helping to resolve the housing problem. For the five years before 1909 the average annual increase in the number of houses in Great Britain was 117,000; for the five years after it was 70,000. The general consensus, supported by the Land Enquiry Committee set up by Lloyd George in 1912, was that the land value duties of the 'People's Budget' had had 'a considerable effect in checking house building'.[12]

In the evidence he gave before the Select Committee on Land Values in 1919, Percy Thompson contended that the undeveloped land duty had failed to achieve its object of taxing land which was ripe for building, but which was held up for other purposes. Because of the exemptions and allowances granted under the Finance (1909/10) Act of 1910, notably the exemptions of land used for business purposes and land occupied together with a dwelling-house, and the allowance for expenditure on roads and sewers, land ripe for building in practice often escaped the duty, and the tendency was for the duty to fall chiefly on land round towns and cities that was ripening for building, but was not yet required for building purposes.[13] In short, the undeveloped land duty had apparently done little to force land ripe for building on to the market. The increment value duty, for its part, was generally deemed to have positively retarded house building by making landowners reluctant to sell and by taxing the profits of builders, even if the profits taxed were mainly speculative. 'Profits from the development of land', Paul Wilding has pointed out, 'had provided a sure source of income for the speculative builder, and in a way, a kind of subsidy to house building.'[14] It was widely held, however, that it was the collective impact of the land value duties, more so than any single duty, that had served to give a decisive check to house-building and investment in building. As the Housing Committee of the Surveyor's Institution contended, the land value duties, the exaggerated controversy that had accompanied their enactment, and the fear that greater exactions were likely to follow, all combined to create an atmosphere of uncertainty which caused investors and capitalists to fight shy of house property as an investment. It also influenced mortgagees to review their security, and in many instances to revise their terms: 'Great inconvenience was thus caused to those who had been conducting this industry on borrowed capital and the holding back of financial help made it impossible for building operations of this type to be continued.'[15]

The critics of the 'People's Budget' undoubtedly exaggerated the impact of the land value duties on house-building. As was pointed out by the Land Enquiry Committee, the Inland Revenue, and also by the Liverpool and District Association of House Builders in the report it gave to the Reconstruction Ministry in 1917, many more fundamental factors operated in the years 1910 to 1914 to check house building, including the increases in the costs of materials and labour and the positive attractions of other forms of investment due to the increased yield from gilt-edged securities.[16] None the less, the general consensus by 1914 was that the land value duties, in their existing form and as interpreted by the courts, had operated to hinder rather than assist house-building, notably for the working classes, where there was a real shortage and where the profits to the builder were small.

It was in the countryside, rather than in the towns, that the 'People's Budget' appeared to have generated an increased supply of land for sale. On 3 January 1914 the *Estates Gazette,* in its annual review of land and property sales, commented that: 'Not for many generations has there been so enormous a dispersal piecemeal of landed estates as in 1911, 1912 and 1913 . . . and the supply of ancestral acres in the provinces is apparently unlimited.' This development the *Estates Gazette* attributed in large part to 'the inroads on capital caused by frenzied legislative finance'. It found that agricultural land sold freely all over the country at high prices on old rents, principally for occupation, but that 'investors have not been prominent'. F. M. L. Thompson has, however, made the point that the enactment of the 'People's Budget' proved more the occasion than the cause for the disposal of ancestral acres in the provinces. The scares of 1909 gave self-justification for a course which had long seemed wise for great landowners to sell part of their family estates in order to clear off debts and increase income by making alternative investments.[17]

Unlike the land value duties, the new licence duties proved highly productive of additional revenue. In 1912/13 the liquor licence duties raised £4,595,203 as against £2,176,463 in 1908/9. The new rates, in other words, had somewhat more than doubled the revenue from the licence duties. What particularly outraged 'the trade' was that the yield from retail licences proved consistently higher than had originally been estimated, and that the promised new valuation and reconsideration of the scale of duties in the light of the new valuation was never forthcoming. 'The trade' was thus being 'unfairly' taxed even by the standards Lloyd George had set in 1909. The sense of grievance was strongest among London brewers, who firmly contested that London had been unfairly discriminated against by the new duties for public houses and beerhouses. In a statement issued on behalf of the London brewers in 1914, it was pointed out that the average payment for an 'on' licence in London had jumped from £28 to £87, a threefold increase, as against a rise in the average payment for the rest of the United Kingdom from £14 to £26, a less than twofold increase. In practice, though, the average payment for the rest of Great Britain was over £30; it was the special terms given to Ireland that had considerably reduced the average for the United Kingdom as a whole. In Ireland the increase in the average payment for an 'on' licence was marginal only, from £8 to £9.[18]

London brewers were undoubtedly hard hit by the 'People's Budget', at least in its initial impact. Because of over-capitalization they were already experiencing difficulties by 1909; the new licence duties, in the assessment of D. M. Knox, made their position 'very perilous'. In the 'boom' period 1896–1902, as Knox has demonstrated in his study of the development of the tied house system in London, brewers had purchased London public houses at prices far and above the true value of the premises or the trade done. From 1903 onwards public-house values fell dramatically, and the brewery companies were forced to begin depreciating the book values of their licensed properties. It was at this juncture that the licence duties of the 'People's Budget' struck them, causing a further depreciation in the values of public houses by reducing net profit after taxation.[19]

In their over-all impact, the new licence duties provoked not so much a 'slaughter' of licensed premises as a 'watering down' of their values. In fact, after the passage of the 'People's Budget' there was a slowing down rather than a speeding up of the rate at which the number of 'on' licences were being reduced, primarily because magistrates became less zealous in refusing licences under the terms of the Licensing Act of 1904. In England and Wales, the highest rate of refusals to renew 'on' licences was achieved in the first four years of the Liberal Government, reaching 1,325 refusals in 1909. Thereafter there was a steady decline in the number of refusals, dropping to 857 refusals in 1914. Except for the year 1911, when 444 'on' licences were allowed to lapse, no increase in the number of lapsed licences followed on the passage of the Budget.[20] If it was the anticipation of magistrates after 1909 that financial pressure would force the rate of 'voluntary' closures, that anticipation was never realized.

In practice, what served to bolster the brewing trade after the passage of the Budget was the reversal of the downward trend in beer consumption. In 1910, for the first year since 1899, beer consumption and output rose, and in 1911, helped by an exceptionally hot summer, output increased to nearly 35,000,000 barrels, 2,000,000 more than in 1909. In 1912 output declined slightly, but as seen by the brewing industry the tide had clearly turned.[21] In 1913 and 1914 there was a good deal of talk in brewing and stock exchange circles about 'the brewing revival', and brewing shares again came to be recommended as a good investment.[22]

The increase in beer output and sales was in part complementary to the decline in the consumption of spirits in response to the new spirit duty of the 'People's Budget'.

In 1908 the total quantity of spirits consumed in the United Kingdom, including imports, was 38,000,000 proof gallons; by 1910 it had dropped to 29,000,000 gallons. Thereafter consumption levelled out at about 30,500,000 gallons.[23] The revenue raised from spirits, apart from the abnormally low returns for 1909/10, was none the less measurably higher as a consequence of Lloyd George's increased duty. In 1908/9 the duty on spirits had produced £21,417,508; in 1910/11 spirits raised £23,049,690 and in 1912/13 £22,599,286.[24] From Lloyd George's standpoint, the new duty on spirits had proved an ideal liquor tax; it had both increased revenue and significantly reduced the consumption of spirits. 'I think it may be said', he asserted in the Commons in 1913, 'that in more than one respect this is one of the most successful taxes ever imposed on the community.'[25]

Despite its many limitations in practice, the 'People's Budget' was an important milestone in the history of British taxation, and together with Harcourt's reform of the death duties and Asquith's differentiation between earned and unearned income for income tax purposes it helped to establish the basic structure for modern progressive direct taxation in Britain. As the *Liberal Magazine* had put it in May 1909, Lloyd George's Budget was not an isolated phenomenon, but was one of a series of measures. The *Liberal Magazine* had further suggested that it would require at least one more major measure of taxation reform, and probably a succession of complementary budgets, 'to complete the formed design of social reconstruction which we call Social Reform'. In 1914 Lloyd George sought to complete the basic design by providing for the reconstruction of local taxation and finance, including, as a follow-up to the 'People's Budget', the introduction of site value rating.

In June 1914, in the face of opposition to Lloyd George's proposals from a 'cave' of important and wealthy Liberal MPs, the Government withdrew from the Budget for 1914/15 the provisions for the reform of local taxation and finance. This retreat raised the fundamental question of whether Lloyd George had finally pushed beyond the limits that the Liberal party was prepared to go in adopting policies of fiscal and social reform.

II

The significance of the 'People's Budget' for the Liberal party
and Liberal policy in the longer term depended on how far
Liberals would be prepared to go in exploiting the opportunities it had created. By the end of 1911 the immediate opportunities the Budget opened up had been taken full advantage
of; the powers of the House of Lords had been curbed, and
national insurance had been enacted. The Parliament Act,
however, had the effect of diverting the Government's attention away from the social policies pursued between 1908 and
1911. With the Lords no longer providing a permanent
obstruction to the 'sectional' items in the Liberal programme,
the Government proceeded to attempt to enact some of the
more traditional Liberal measures, notably Irish Home Rule
and Welsh Disestablishment, but the Lords had no compunc-
tion about employing its suspensory veto to hold these
measures up. The Lords now had a power to delay that had
been legitimatized in law, and it duly proceeded to use that
power. The result, for the Government, was a new period of
apparent impotence and of declining electoral support. It was
in 1914, in the attempt to restore its standing for the general
election due in the next year, that the Government returned
to the attempt to pursue some of the reform possibilities
created by the 'People's Budget'.

The political situation at the beginning of 1914 was remini-
scent in many essentials of the situation at the beginning of
1909. 'Sectional' items in the Liberal programme that generated more antagonism and indifference than they did mass
popular support were being blocked by the Lords; the Land
Values Group was chafing at the lack of evident progress in
securing site value rating; the Government found itself
obliged to sanction large increases in naval expenditure; and
by-elections had been causing concern, with the Liberals
having lost eleven seats to the Unionists since 1910, and in
several instances lost ground to the Labour party, even
though two seats were won from Labour.[26]

In 1914, as in 1909, a budget provided the Liberal Government with its main device for promoting reform, and the
primary reform purpose of Lloyd George's Budget for

1914/15 was to secure the introduction of site value rating, and to reorganize the relations between imperial and local taxation for the benefit of ratepayers, particularly ratepayers who improved their property and those in poor districts.

Lloyd George's proposal for site value rating constituted the urban aspect of his land campaign, launched in 1913, and was intended as the follow-up to the land valuation provisions of the 'People's Budget'. The land valuation that was being secured under the terms of the Finance (1909/10) Act of 1910, with certain amendments to overcome the legal and technical problems encountered in the valuation, was to provide the basis for the introduction of site value rating, with the view to taking some of the pressure of rates off improvements. Lloyd George's proposal for expanding and restructuring the system of Exchequer grants to local authorities was also designed to relieve improvements as well as the more hard-pressed rating areas.

The scheme for reorganizing the relations between imperial and local finance that Lloyd George presented to the Commons in his Budget speech of 4 May, and which he had carried at great haste through a bemused and over-burdened Cabinet, provided for additional Exchequer grants to local authorities totalling £11,000,000 in a full year, equal to a relief on average of 9*d*. in the £ on rates, and for temporary grants of £2,500,000 in 1914/15 so as to bring the scheme within the compass of his current Budget. The operation of the new scheme for grants, including the distribution of the temporary grants, was made conditional on the passage of the Government's proposals for a national system of valuation which would separate site value and improvement value for the purposes of favouring improvements in the relief to be afforded to rates and for the purposes of site value rating. Lloyd George, who said he did not think it would prove 'a very considerable task' to adapt the land valuation of the 'People's Budget' for the purposes of local taxation, made it clear that the Government had no intention of transferring the whole burden of rates to sites, but made it equally clear that: 'We do intend that the taxation of site value shall henceforth form an integral part of the system of local taxation.'

For financing the new grants to local authorities and greatly increased naval estimates, Lloyd George resorted entirely to recommending increases in direct taxation, notably in income tax, supertax, and death duties. As he proudly told the Commons, under his proposals direct taxation would now become responsible for somewhat more than 60 per cent of over-all taxation. They embodied several of the principles on which he had been defeated in the Cabinet in 1909. What he proposed was a graduated income tax, which remained at 9*d*. in the £ for earned incomes under £1,000, increased to 10½*d*. in the £ for earned incomes between £1,000 and £1,500, to 1*s*. between £1,500 and £2,000, to 1*s*. 2*d*. between £2,000 and £2,500, and to 1*s*. 4*d*. as the general rate for earned incomes over £2,500 and for unearned incomes. Incomes over £3,000 were to be subjected to a graduated supertax. With regard to death duties, rates were to be increased on estates over £60,000 and the settlement estate duty was to be abolished. In future settled property was to pay estate duty when it passed on after death as if the property was not settled.[27]

Lloyd George's taxation proposals in May 1914 were directed even more pointedly than the provisions of the 'People's Budget' at the people he liked to call 'the rich'. The increases in the income tax rates for earned incomes were estimated to bring in a mere £330,000 in 1914/15, the increase in the general rate £5,120,000, the increased scale for the supertax £2,500,000, with a normal yield thereafter of £4,500,000, and the revised death duties £800,000 in 1914/15, and £3,000,000 thereafter.

At first, partly because of the complexity of the proposals, the Budget did not stir major opposition, and *The Times* even bestowed muted praise on it on 5 and 6 May for taxing the rich for the benefit of the poor. On 5 May Churchill wrote to his wife: 'The Budget has been less ill received than I expected, but we still have to hear the squeals of the wealthy. The Tory party do not evidently relish fighting their battle.'[28] But what did emerge in June was a major 'cave' against the Budget within the Liberal party itself. The 'cave', organized by Sir Richard Holt, a Liverpool shipowner, numbered about 40 MPs, mainly wealthy. Lloyd George, though 'disgusted with these rich men', became distinctly worried about the Budget's apparent unpopularity in Liberal circles.[29] He found, moreover, that he had badly under-estimated the procedural difficulties his proposals involved. The passage of his rating reforms would require a highly unpopular autumn sitting, which his Cabinet colleagues were not prepared to tolerate; under the terms of the Provisional Collection of Taxes Act of 1913 the Finance Bill would have to become law before it would have been possible to secure the passage of legislation authorizing the new system of Exchequer grants; Harper at the Inland Revenue advised that it would be out of the question to distribute the temporary grants for 1914/15 on any basis other than existing rateable value; and in the Commons the Unionists planned to challenge the constitutionality of tacking what they alleged was a Local Government Bill on to a Finance Bill.[30] On 22 June, at a midday meeting, the Cabinet decided to abandon the tem-porary grants, to deduct a penny from the proposed increase in the general rate of the income tax, and to postpone the section of the Finance Bill dealing with permanent grants, and the measures for valuation and rating reform, until later in the year and the next year. These changes were made, so Asquith informed the King, 'in view of the exigencies of time, and of the objections taken by influential supporters of the Government to the Chancellor of the Exchequer's proposals as introduced by him'.[31] They were announced in the Commons that afternoon, after Speaker Lowther, in response to Unionist questions, had given his opinion that 'it would be desirable if possible to return to the older practice of confining the Finance Bill to the imposition of taxes, the arrangements for dealing with the National Debt and so forth'.[32] On the next day McKenna told Riddell: 'The whole thing has been a shocking muddle.'[33]

From that muddle the cause of site value rating never recovered. Because of the war the Government did not pro-ceed with its plans for the reorganization of local taxation and finance, and the land value duties of the 'People's Budget' were themselves to become victims of the war. The original valuation was indefinitely delayed, and most builders' associations attacked the land value duties as likely to retard reconstruction after the war. Part of the understanding between Lloyd George and the Unionists for the maintenance of his Coalition Government after the war was that the land value duties should be abolished. In 1920 Lloyd George's Government duly repealed them, and the revenue collected was repaid to those who had contributed to it. The repeal was opposed by the Independent Liberals, Labour, and some Coalition Liberals, with the former making great play of Lloyd George's pre-war assertions in favour of land value taxation.

It has been suggested that the Government's retreat in June 1914 on local finance and taxation was a disaster not simply for the cause of site value rating, but for the New Liberalism. For Bentley Gilbert, the land programme had historically been the most significant project of the New Liberalism, and as seen by him Lloyd George's 'defeat' in 1914 on local finance and site value rating constituted a clear indication that 'the limits of his party's tolerance for social and economic change' had been reached. He concludes:

> Possibly then the budget debacle of 1914 marked the end of the new Liberalism. Lloyd George's highly personal commitment to land reform was too advanced for the backbench stalwarts of his party, while its young radicals demanded something less eccentric and more anti-capitalist. Furthermore, the very small team that had driven Liberal reform forward, that had put together the budget of 1909, health and unemployment insurance, had broken up. Churchill was lost. Masterman had died politically. Lloyd George was beleaguered and alone in the summer of 1914. He tried to put his party on a new track and failed.[34]

The 'cave' against the Budget for 1914/15 was certainly more serious, as well as more effective, than the earlier 'cave' against the land value duties of the 'People's Budget'. It was initially a protest against the procedure whereby Lloyd George proposed to vote money for grants to local authorities before Parliament had ever seen and approved the actual scheme by which those grants were to be distributed, but the objections of the 'cave' to the Budget ran well beyond its provisions for local finance and taxation, including the projected introduction of site value rating. Opposition to site value rating was by no means the heart of the revolt. The fundamental complaint of the 'cave' was against massive increases in government expenditure, and the taxation that such increases necessitated. As such the 'cave' was not simply a cabal of rich Liberals against a set of new taxes that seemed to strike at the rich particularly, but a reaction of traditional Gladstonians against what they saw as profligate finance and wasteful government expenditure. It included in its ranks Radicals of the stamp of David Mason, MP for Coventry, who had consistently campaigned against large new expenditures for armaments. Members of the 'cave' repeatedly complained in their speeches in the Commons of the remarkable way in which national expenditure had increased under a Liberal Government. In his speech in the Commons on 22 June, Holt gave it as his opinion that government expenditure had increased more rapidly than national wealth and income, and he pointed specifically to heavy expenditure on armaments and on social reforms that were 'costing a great deal more than we were originally led to believe they would'.[35] 'We spend up to the hilt,' Mason protested, 'and we proceed gaily with our increased taxation.'[36] What the members of the 'cave' insisted was that their opposition to the Budget for 1914/15 was not 'animated by any desire to get a reduction of the taxes which press upon themselves', and the penny taken off the general rate of the income tax, a concession for the benefit of the well-to-do, was insufficient to reconcile many of them to the Budget. On 7 July the Holt group abstained from voting against a Unionist amendment to the Government's motion to curtail debate on the Finance Bill, and the Government's majority on the amendment fell to a mere twenty-three. The abstention of 7 July caused far more antagonism to the 'cave' among advanced Liberals than the earlier stand against the proposals for local grants precisely because it underlined that the fundamental protest of the Holt group was against the over-all direction and method of Liberal finance and taxation as conducted by Lloyd George.

As seen by Carrington, the Holt 'cave' was 'a clique of rich men determined to read a lesson to L. George by resisting a budget which taxes them'.[37] The fact was that the social reform policies and finance of the New Liberalism had progressed beyond the limits that many orthodox, mainly 'business', Liberals were finding themselves able to accept.

As Walter Long put it to Bonar Law in 1912, 'Lloyd George had lost popularity with the business Liberal' primarily because he was moving too fast for them.[38]

The 'cave' against the Budget for 1914/15, and the Government's subsequent retreat on site value rating and the reorganization of local finance, was undoubtedly a major set-back for both the Government and Lloyd George. Lloyd George's own planning for the next general election had focused on directing the electorate's attention to the land question and away from Ulster and Home Rule, on which the Unionists were concentrating. The Tory strategy, Lloyd George had told Percy Illingworth, the Liberal Chief Whip, soon after he had launched his land campaign, was 'to talk Ulster to the exclusion of land', and he had warned: 'If they succeed we are "beat" and beat by superior generalship.'[39] Lloyd George's own 'generalship' over the Budget for 1914/15 had proved highly deficient, and his plans for reorganizing local finance and for presenting to the electorate a dynamic and comprehensive programme for land reform, rural as well as urban, had been thrown into disarray. None the less, it should not be concluded from this that the New Liberalism, and particularly its policies with regard to finance and the land, had been repudiated by the Liberal party itself.

Despite the protests of the Holt group, and the Government's temporary retreat on the reorganization of local finance and taxation, what the Budget for 1914/15 indicated was that the fiscal strategy of the New Liberalism was still basically intact. Liberal finance, as even the amended Budget demonstrated, was moving towards a fully graduated income tax, and the official Liberal agenda for future taxation reform included a major streamlining of the income tax along progressive lines. As Asquith informed the Commons on 25 June at the end of the second reading debate of the Finance Bill, the time had come for a thorough inquiry into the income tax 'with a view to simplification and greater equity'.[40] Again, despite the set-back of June 1914, the reorganization and extension of Exchequer grants to local authorities, and the introduction of site value rating, remained an integral part of the official Liberal programme. They had been temporarily postponed, not repudiated. Certainly, there

was little sense among advanced Liberals that the retreat on
the Budget for 1914/15 represented a decisive check for the
policies of the New Liberalism. They saw the move as a change
of plan, which some of them even welcomed, and not as a
change of policy, and they took the abstentions of 7 July as
the opportunity to put pressure on the conservative elements
in the party that were retarding the pace of social progress
under Liberal auspices. 'We have been making it hot for the
money-bag cave-dwellers during the last week', Christopher
Addison commented in his diary on 13 July, 'and I hear their
constituents have now taken a hand. Good job!'[41]

III

This study has sought to demonstrate that the fiscal policy
of the Liberal Governments after 1905 was fundamental to
Liberal strategy for enabling their party to become a party
of social reform without simultaneously antagonizing its mass
support among the middle classes. The achievement of this
goal, difficult in itself, was made all the more difficult by the
fact that the Liberals had taken office at a time when middle-
class resentment at the 'pampering' of the working classes
was already strongly evident and when the Tariff Reformers
offered the alternative of raising large new revenues without
recourse to massive increases in direct taxation. It was to be
even further complicated by a temporary slump in trade
between 1907 and 1910, and by the need to finance large new
expenditures for the navy. Under the Liberals, imperial
government expenditure rose dramatically from an actual
expenditure of £139,400,000 in 1906/7 to an estimated
expenditure of £206,000,000 for 1914/15, when for the
first time, in peace or even in war, the Budget for the year
provided for an expenditure of over £200,000,000. In the
same period the direct taxes were considerably increased,
and the proportion of direct to indirect taxation rose from
51.4 per cent to over 60 per cent. Yet in 1914, as a consequence of the Liberal determination to reassure the bulk of
the middle classes, the large majority of income tax-payers
were less heavily taxed, even after Lloyd George's Budget
for 1914/15, than they had been when the Liberals assumed

office, when the income tax, as yet undifferentiated, had stood at 1s. in the £.

In their taxation policy, the Liberals often looked upon themselves as disinterested agents promoting both greater equity in the country's taxation system and a sense of shared responsibility for the requirements of the community. An important component in Liberalism was the sense that it represented a disinterested principle of government, seeking to establish a just balance in society and to promote the national interest rather than the narrow interest of a particular class. As Michael Freeden has emphasized, the theorists of the New Liberalism positively rejected the identification of a social reform policy with a working-class policy but conceived of social reform as catering to national social needs.[42] They looked to achieve an impartial approach to social reform and taxation, and one method of emphasizing that Liberal social and taxation policy was not simply a working-class policy was by providing taxation relief for hard-pressed sections of the middle class and by ensuring, through increased taxes on the 'luxuries' of the working classes and employee contributions to national insurance, that the working classes themselves shared responsibility for the financing of social reform. As Lloyd George put it on 11 December 1911, in response to a Unionist amendment to reduce the duty on tea grown in the British Empire, the sense of responsibility for the expenditure for the year should be distributed over the whole community.

I have never had any sympathy with the idea that someone has got to be exempt because he is earning a small amount. It ought to be more or less the sort of principle which you have got in a place of worship, where everyone is supposed to contribute something, however trifling, because they feel they have a kind of interest in the common work that is going on, and there ought to be the same common interest in the work of the Empire, and one way of realising that is to get every section of the community to contribute. The only principle I would lay down would be that they ought to contribute in proportion to their means.[43]

It was on the latter principle that the Liberal Government justified its considerable increases in taxation of the wealthy, making it, in the opinion of Alfred Emmott, 'easier for a camel to pass through the eye of a needle than for a rich man to remain in the Liberal party'.[44] None the less, many wealthy Liberals remained firmly attached to the party. Some, like Sir John Brunner and Sir Alfred Mond, did so because they positively believed in the principles of the New Liberalism.

Considerations of equity and shared responsibility provided Liberal taxation policy with some of its guiding principles, but immediate political considerations had greatly influenced the actual content of Lloyd George's 'People's Budget' and his Budget proposals for 1914/15. Both Budgets sought to couple a positive appeal to working-class voters with reassurances to the bulk of income tax payers, and thereby to help hold the Liberal party together as a party of both the middle and the working classes, which was itself essential if the party was to preserve its character as a 'national party', working for the interests of the community as a whole.

Given that Liberal finance between 1906 and 1914 succeeded in protecting the majority of income tax-payers from large increases in taxation, and in fact provided them with a measure of tax relief, what was troubling to many Liberals were the signs, particularly evident in the general elections of 1910, that the middle classes, most notably in England, had not been reassured and were deserting the Liberals for the Unionist party. In the general elections of 1910, and in by-elections thereafter, the main erosion of Liberal support was not to Labour on the left but to the Unionist party on the right, especially among the middle classes. In 1910 the losses sustained among the middle classes had in effect been accepted by the Liberal leadership as the necessary price for the retention of mass working-class support, and for the maintenance of the Liberal party's own dynamic as a party of reform, and the leadership never thereafter lost sight of the fact that the party was heavily dependent on working-class support. For the Liberal leadership it was a major political priority to keep that support, but at the same time it remained anxious to contain losses to the party among the middle classes. Lloyd George particularly, as is evident from his land campaign, was also determined to restore the appeal of Liberalism in rural areas. In his Budget proposals for 1914/15 Lloyd George reflected the Government's continuing concern to reassure the bulk of the middle classes, in that he resisted suggestions that he should help 'free the breakfast-table' of onerous taxation by reducing the duties on tea and sugar, in that the rate of income tax was not increased for incomes under £1,000, in that an increased allowance was given for the children of income tax payers with incomes under £500, and in that he granted concessions to unearned incomes under £500.

It has sometimes been suggested that the long-term survival of the Liberal party as a party of government required that it make a more overt appeal to the working classes in its policies than the Liberal Governments of 1905—14 had shown themselves capable. Through the prism of Liberal finance and taxation, particularly as handled by Lloyd George in his 'People's Budget', this study has sought to demonstrate that official Liberal policy went a long way in the attempt to adjust itself to working-class needs and interests and in taxing wealth, but that it also reflected a determination to reassure the bulk of middle-class income tax payers that social welfare measures would not despoil them. Lloyd George was himself strongly conscious of the political need for the Liberal party to engage the active support of the working classes, but it was as inconceivable to him as it was to his colleagues in the Government to permit a fundamental divorce between Liberalism and the middle classes.

Liberal concern to contain its losses among the middle classes placed obvious restraints on Liberal social and fiscal policy, but as Lloyd George demonstrated in his 'People's Budget' this by no means prevented Liberalism from making a powerful appeal to the working classes, and there is no real evidence by 1914 that such constraints had stifled the forward advance of Liberal policy.

The point has been made by Ross McKibbin and Martin Petter that Liberal social policy was not in itself sufficient to ensure Liberalism's continued ability to mobilize working-class support in the face of Labour's desire to promote its own support and representation.[45] In the general election of January 1910, the 'People's Budget' had served to enable the Liberals to 'contain' Labour, but even then Lloyd George had shown himself willing to forgo a strict policy of containment in order to avert a split between Liberalism and Labour, for he firmly believed that such a split would prove a catastrophe for the Liberal party. By 1914 he was even more convinced on this point; consequently he impressed on Ramsay MacDonald that a split between the Liberals and Labour at the next general election would lead to disaster for both parties.[46] 'From the point of view of a prospective general election in 1915,' P. F. Clarke has written, 'the importance of the electoral understanding between the Liberal and Labour parties can hardly be overestimated. Nothing could damage the Liberal party — and the Labour party — so seriously as the effect of three-cornered contests.'[47] It was in this respect that the Liberal party faced its main crisis on the left in 1914.

Abbreviations

S.P.	Strachey Papers in the House of Lords Library
T.C.	Trinity College Library, Dublin

Unless otherwise stated, London is the place of publication for books referred to in the notes and the bibliography.

Notes

I. Introduction

1. P. F. Clarke, *Lancashire and the New Liberalism* (1971), 343—64 and 398—9.
2. Ibid. 25, 293, 309, and 393—407.
3. N. Blewett, *The Peers, the Parties and the People: The General Elections of 1910* (1972), 400—8.
4. D. A. Hamer, *Liberal Politics in the Age of Gladstone and Rosebery* (Oxford, 1972), 329.
5. H. V. Emy, *Liberals, Radicals and Social Politics 1892—1914* (1973), ix.
6. B. B. Gilbert, 'David Lloyd George: The Reform of British Land-Holding and the Budget of 1914', *H. J.* XXI (1978), 141.
7. C. F. G. Masterman, 'Politics in Transition', *Nineteenth Century and After,* CCCLXXI (Jan. 1908).
8. Emy, *Social Politics*; Michael Freeden, *The New Liberalism* (Oxford, 1978).
9. Ibid. 134—45.
10. See C. J. Wrigley, *David Lloyd George and the British Labour Movement* (Hassocks, 1976), 26.
11. John Grigg suggests that Lloyd George was initially anxious to avoid a policy 'of aggressively taxing the native rich'. See Grigg, *Lloyd George: The People's Champion 1902—11* (1978), 171.
12. Blewett, *General Elections of 1910,* 395—408.
13. Samuel to Gladstone, 22 Jan. 1910, B. L. Add. MS. 45992.
14. Emy, *Social Politics,* 274—5.
15. Winston Churchill to his wife, 4 May 1914, in R. S. Churchill, *Winston S. Churchill* (1966—7), Companion Vol. II, Pt. 3, 1975.
16. A. J. A. Morris, *C. P. Trevelyan 1870—1958* (Belfast, 1977), 149.
17. *Report of the Select Committee on Land Values* (Cmd. 556 of 1920), 17.
18. J. R. Hay, 'British Government Finance 1906—14' (unpublished Oxford B. Litt. thesis, 1970), 306—7, and *The Origins of the Liberal Welfare Reforms 1906—1914* (1975), 50—9.
19. S. J. Hurwitz, *State Intervention in Great Britain* (New York, 1949), 12—13.
20. *Statistical Society of London Journal,* LXXXII (1920), 176—7; *Report of the Committee on National Debt and Taxation* (Cmd. 2800 of 1927), 94—5.

II. Public Finance and Liberal Politics

1. Quoted in Hamer, *Liberal Politics,* 328.
2. *Nineteenth Century and After,* CCCLXXI (Jan. 1908).
3. Hamer, *Liberal Politics,* 222; J. W. McKail and Guy Wyndham, *The Life and Letters of George Wyndham* (2 vols., 1925), II, 537—9.
4. A. T. Peacock and J. Wiseman, *The Growth of Public Expenditure in the United Kingdom* (Priceton, N. J., 1961), 164.
5. Quoted in H. V. Emy, 'The Impact of Financial Policy on English Party Politics Before 1914', *H.J.* XV (1972), 103—31.

6. *The Times*, 7, 9, and 10 Jan. 1902.

7. See H. C. G. Matthew, *The Liberal Imperialists* (Oxford, 1973), 255.

8. J. Amery, *Joseph Chamberlain and the Tariff Reform Campaign* (Vols. V and VI of *The Life of Joseph Chamberlain*, 1969), V, 267—9.

9. Ibid. 465—6.

10. Ibid. 468 and 893.

11. N. Blewett, 'Free Fooders, Balfourites, Whole Hoggers: Factionalism within the Unionist Party, 1906—10', *H.J.* XI (1968), 95—124; R. A. Rempel, *Unionists Divided* (Newton Abbot, 1972), chap. 6.

12. Quoted in P. Fraser, *Joseph Chamberlain* (1966), 275—6.

13. D. Porter, 'The Unionist Tariff Reformers' (unpublished Manchester University Ph. D. thesis, 1976), 118—19.

14. Quoted in K. Young, *Balfour* (1963), 220.

15. For Chamberlain and an early election see Amery, *Chamberlain*, VI, 662—4.

16. A. K. Russell, *Liberal Landslide* (Newton Abbot, 1973), 182.

17. Asquith quoted in Matthew, *Liberal Imperialists*, 100.

18. Hamer, *Liberal Politics*, 322; R. R. James, *The British Revolution* (2 vols., 1976—7), II, 121.

19. B. B. Gilbert, *The Evolution of National Insurance in Great Britain* (1966), 202 n.

20. Russell, *Landslide*, 65—77.

21 Quoted, ibid. 115.

22. Emy, *Social Politics*, chaps. 3 and 4.

23. See J. R. Hay, 'British Government Finance 1906—14' (unpublished Oxford B. Litt. thesis, 1970), which includes much useful detailed information on government finance in the period, including the relations between central and local government finance.

24. See S. Webb, *The London Programme* (1891); and J. F. Oakeshott, 'A Democratic Budget', Fabian Tract No. 39.

25. Freeden, *Liberalism*, 145—50.

26. H. Samuel, *Liberalism* (1902), 188.

27. See F. Shehab, *Progressive Taxation* (1953), 199—206.

28. See Freeden, *Liberalism*, 130—1.

29. Samuel, *Liberalism*, 185.

30. B. Mallet, *British Budgets 1887—1913* (1913), 77—94.

31. For voters see Russell, *Landslide*, 15—21; and Blewett, *General Elections of 1910*, 359.

32. S.H.L. M.2.68.

33. A. L. Bowley and J. Stamp, *Three Studies on the National Income* (1938), 7—13.

34. Ibid.

35. J. A. Hobson, *The Economics of Distribution* (1903), chap. 10.

36. See E. P. Lawrence, *Henry George in the British Isles* (East Lansing, Michigan, 1957), 78 and 103—6.

37. See M. Barker, *Gladstone and Radicalism* (Hassocks, 1975), 7 and 39—40.

38. See A. J. Peacock, 'Land Reform 1880—1919' (unpublished University of Southampton M.A. thesis, 1962).

39. *First Report of the Royal Commission on the Housing of the Working Classes* (Cmd. 4402 of 1884—5), 42.

40. For the falling in of leases see the speech by T. J. Macnamara in the House of Commons, 27 Mar. 1903, *H.C.D.* 4th Ser., CXX, 470—81; and E. Gauldie, *Cruel Habitations* (1974), 166.

41. See R. Douglas, *Land, People and Politics* (1976), chap. 7; and Morris, *Trevelyan*, 55.

42. 'Separate Report on Urban Rating and Site Values', *Final Report of the Royal Commission on Local Taxation* (Cmd. 638 of 1901).
43. B.L. Add. MS. 41231, ff. 37—42.
44. For an analysis of the reservations among Liberals about land reform see H. J. Perkin, 'Land Reform and Class Conflict in Victorian Britain' in J. Butt and I. F. Clarke (eds.), *The Victorians and Social Protest* (1973), 177—217.
45. Quoted in Matthew, *Liberal Imperialists*, 256.
46. *H.C.D.* 4th Ser., CLXXII, 1191—2.
47. Hamilton Diary, 2 Feb. and 1 Mar. 1906, B.L. Add. MS. 48683.
48. For discussions of Edwardian Radicalism see Emy, Freeden, and also A. J. A. Morris, *Radicalism Against War, 1906—1914* (1972), and Morris (ed.), *Edwardian Radicalism 1900—1914* (1974).
49. *Land Values,* Feb. 1906; and also Ping-Ti Ho, 'Land and State in Great Britain, 1873—1910' (unpublished Columbia University Ph.D. dissertation, 1952), 156.
50. Morris, *Trevelyan,* 77.
51. B.L. Add. MS. 41231, ff. 45—6.
52. For London see P. Thompson, *Socialists, Liberals and Labour* (1967), 180—3.
53. *Nation,* 1 Feb. and 18 Apr. 1908.

III. Asquith's Inheritance

1. A.P. 10, ff. 200—1.
2. *The Times,* 7 Apr. 1908.
3. Quoted in J. Wilson, *CB: A Life of Sir Henry Campbell-Bannerman* (1973), 501.
4. J. Morley, *Recollections* (2 vols., 1917), II, 197.
5. Campbell-Bannerman quoted in J. A. Spender, *The Life of the Right Hon. Sir Henry Campbell-Bannerman* (2 vols., 1923), II, 97.
6. For a detailed study of the Liberal-Labour pact see F. Bealey and H. Pelling, *Labour and Politics 1900—1906* (1958), chap. 6.
7. D. Gwynn, *John Redmond* (1932), 115; Russell, *Landslide,* 33.
8. Haldane, *An Autobiography* (1929), 171.
9. Quoted in Lord Newton, *Lord Lansdowne* (1929), 354—5.
10. McKail and Wyndham, *Wyndham,* II, 643.
11. Newton, *Lansdowne,* 359.
12. For Liberal hopes on licensing and education see J. A. Spender to Bryce, 9 Mar. 1908, B.P. UB. 22.
13. Ibid.
14. B.D., 18 Jan. 1908.
15. Bod. Lib. MS. Eng. Hist. c. 655, ff. 26—7.
16. See Kenneth O. Morgan, *Wales in British Politics* (Cardiff, 1970 ed.), 235—8.
17. Morley, *Recollections,* II, 226—7.
18. S. Koss, *Nonconformity in Modern British Politics* (1975), 79—84.
19. Lord Esher, *Journals and Letters* (2 vols., ed. M. Brett, 1934), II. 263; and A. G. Gardiner, *Prophets, Priests and Kings* (1908), 27.
20. Margot Asquith, *Autobiography* (2 vols., 1920—2), II, 57.
21. J. A. Spender and Cyril Asquith, *Life of Herbert Henry Asquith, Lord Oxford and Asquith* (2 vols., 1932), I, 161.
22. Ponsonby Diary, Jan. 1907, Bod. Lib. MS. Eng. Hist. c. 653.
23. Ilbert to Bryce, 12 Mar. 1908, B.P. 13, ff. 132—5.

24. Spender, *Life, Journalism and Politics* (1927), 155.
25. Gardiner, *Prophets*, 31–2.
26. Esher, *Journals*, II, 303–4.
27. Haldane to his mother, 17 Mar. 1908, N.L.S. MS. 5979; H.D. 72.
28. Esher, *Journals*, II, 303–4.
29. C. P. Scott, *Political Diaries* (ed. T. Wilson, 1970), 30–1.
30. John Grigg, *Lloyd George: The People's Champion 1902–1911* (1978), 21–52.
31. *Aberdeen Daily Journal*, 14 Nov. 1903; H. du Parcq, *Lloyd George* (4 vols., 1912–13), III, 423.
32. *Newcastle Daily Leader*, 6 Apr. 1903.
33. R. C. K. Ensor, 'Permeation', in M. Cole (ed.), *The Webbs and Their Work* (1949); Kenneth O. Morgan, *Lloyd George* (1974), 59.
34. *Review of Reviews*, Jan. 1906.
35. *Croydon Times*, 6 Jan. 1906.
36. W. Beveridge, *Power and Influence* (1953), 73.
37. Austen Chamberlain, *Politics From Inside* (1936), 87.
38. Lucy Masterman, *C. F. G. Masterman* (1939), 175.
39. *Sheffield Independent*, 30 Aug. 1907.
40. Spender, *Life*, 158.
41. E.D., 28 Jan. 1910.
42. Gardiner, *Prophets*, 156.
43. *Review of Reviews*, Oct. 1904.
44. *Nation*, 18 Apr. 1908.
45. Ibid.
46. H.D. 76.
47. Churchill, *Churchill*, Companion Vol. II, Pt. 2, 754–6.
48. E.D., 22 Mar. 1908.
49. Spender, *Life*, 165.
50. See introduction by E. David to *Inside Asquith's Cabinet* (1977).
51. See K. D. Brown, 'The New Liberalism of C. F. G. Masterman' in Brown (ed.), *Essays in Anti-Labour History* (1974), and Brown *John Burns* (1978).
52. P.D., 5 June 1908.
53. Jenkins, *Mr. Balfour's Poodle* (1954), 59.

IV. Lloyd George at the Treasury

1. D. M. Cregier, *Bounder From Wales* (Columbia, Mo., 1976), 121.
2. C. Mallet, *Mr. Lloyd George: A Study* (1930), 34.
3. H.D. 72.
4. P.D., 30 Oct. 1908.
5. G. Riddell, *More Pages From My Diary, 1908–1914* (1934), 107–8.
6. Gardiner, *Prophets*, 158.
7. Masterman, *Masterman*, 129–130.
8. Riddell, *Diary*, 107–8.
9. H. Du Parq, *Life of Lloyd George*, III, 524.
10. H. Roseveare, *The Treasury* (New York, 1969), 230.
11. Oxford and Asquith, *Memories and Reflections* (2 vols., 1928), I, 252.
12. Ibid. 254; Roseveare, *Treasury*, 222.
13. H.D. 73; Murray to Rosebery, 31 Dec. 1908, N.L.S. MS. 10049.
14. A. Fitzroy, *Memoirs* (2 vols., 1925), I, 390.
15. H.D. 72.

16. M. F. Headlam, 'Thomas Little Heath', *Proceedings of the British Academy,* XXVI (1940).
17. Fitzroy, *Memoirs,* I, 400.
18. Headlam, 'Heath'.
19. Roseveare, *Treasury,* 232.
20. T. Heath and P. E. Matheson, 'Lord Chalmers', *Proceedings of the British Academy,* XXV, (1939); W. J. Braithwaite, *Lloyd George's Ambulance Wagon* (ed. H. N. Bunbury, 1957), 36.
21. Ibid. 68.
22. Strachey to Rosebery, 23 July 1908, S.P. S/12/7/12.
23. Chamberlain, *Politics,* 222.
24. Ilbert to Bryce, 11 Aug. 1909, B.P. 13, ff. 176—9.
25. H.P. 576.
26. William George, *My Brother and I* (1958), 220—1.
27. S. Koss, *Lord Haldane* (New York, 1969), 56.
28. H.P. 576.
29. Ibid.
30. Churchill, 'A Note Upon British Military Needs', 27 June 1908, ibid.
31. F. Maurice, *Haldane* (2 vols., 1937—9), I, 230; Churchill, 'A Note Arising Out of the Conversation at the Cabinet Committee on Estimates on the 29th June 1908', 4 July 1908, H.P. 576.
32. Quoted in Morris, *Radicalism Against War,* 84.
33. Esher, *Journals,* II, 325—6.
34. Chamberlain, *Politics,* 126—7.
35. Memorandum of the Cabinet Committee on Old Age Pensions, Apr. 1908, H.P. 575; Lloyd George in the House of Commons, 29 June 1908, *H.C.D.* 4th Ser., CXCI, 394.
36. Ibid. CLXXXVIII, 471—5.
37. Ibid. CXCI, 1789—91.
38. Ibid. 395—6.
39. *The Times,* 4 July 1908.
40. E.D., 3 Apr. 1909.
41. *H.C.D.* 4th Ser., CLXXXIX, 818.
42. Memorandum by Lord Cromer on the position of the Unionist Free Traders, Dec. 1908, P.R.O. F.O. 633/18.
43. Joseph Chamberlain to Mrs Endicott, 30 Jan. 1906, MS. Chamberlain AC 1/8/8/30; J. Chamberlain to Deakin, 16 May 1906, JC 21/2/44.
44. Amery, *Chamberlain,* VI, 903—4.
45. *H.C.D.* 4th Ser., CLVII, 520—9.
46. Cromer memorandum on Unionist Free Traders, Dec. 1908, P.R.O. F.O. 633/18.
47. W. A. S. Hewins, *Apologia of an Imperialist* (2 vols., 1929), chaps. 7 and 9.
48. Hewins to Balfour, 13 May 1907, B.L. Add. MS. 49779, ff. 85—97.
49. *The Times,* 15 Nov. 1907.
50. Bonar Law to Deakin, 17 Jan. 1908, MS. Bonar Law 18/8/6.
51. Balfour to Selborne, 6 Mar. 1908, MS. Selborne 1, ff. 68—79.
52. Cecil to Cromer, 10 Feb. 1908, P.R.O. F.O. 633/18.
53. Strachey to Elliot, 18 Jan. 1908, S.P. S/16/2/4.
54. *Spectator,* 9 and 30 May 1908.
55. Asquith to Strachey, 9 May 1908, S.P. S/11/6/5.
56. *The Times,* 21 Nov. 1908.
57. Haldane to Asquith, 9 Aug. 1908, A.P. 11, ff. 162—5.
58. B. Mallet, *Budgets,* 493.

59. S.H.L. M.2.68.
60. *The Times,* 11 Mar. 1906.
61. S.H.L. M.2.68.
62. Samuel, *Liberalism,* 190—1.
63. 'Notes on the Incidence of Taxation in the United Kingdom', Mar. 1907, P.R.O. CAB 37/87.
64. 'The Amount of Imperial and Local Taxation Falling Upon a Typical Working-Class Family', P.R.O. T1/72/27.
65. *H.C.D.* 4th Ser., CLXXXVIII, 450.
66. McKenna to Asquith, 17 Dec. 1906, P.R.O. T/172/22; Papers on Income Tax Reform, 26 Mar. 1907, P.R.O. T/171/3.
67. Conspectus of the Budget of 1907—8 written for the King, and Fritz Ponsonby to Sir Edward Hamilton, 19 Apr. 1907, P.R.O. T/171/3.
68. McKenna to Asquith, 'Report on Income Tax Committee', 17 Dec. 1906, P.R.O. T/172/22.
69. *Report of the Select Committee on Income Tax* (Cmd. 365 of 1906).
70. W. Blain, 'Supertax', 26 Feb. 1907, P.R.O. CAB. 37/87.
71. For design of Valuation Bill see Brown, *Burns,* 141.
72. See W. S. Robson, 'Valuation Bill: Memorandum', Sept. 1908, H.P. 576; J. Burns, 'Valuation Bill', 10 Oct. 1908, P.R.O. CAB. 37/95.
73. Morris, *Trevelyan,* 77.
74. *H.C.D.* 4th Ser., CXCIV, 320.
75. C. L. Davies to Wedgwood, dated 29 Jan. 1906 but in fact 1907, MS. Wedgwood.
76. See T. M. Wood, 10 July 1907, *H.C.D.* 4th Ser., CLXVII, 1673—7.
77. Wedgwood in the House of Commons, 12 May 1908, *H.C.D.* 4th Ser., CLXXXVIII, 1053—6.
78. Robson, 'Valuation Bill: Memorandum', Sept. 1908, H.P. 576.
79. Burns, 'Valuation Bill', 10 Oct. 1908, P.R.O. CAB. 37/95.
80. Special memorandum prepared for the Chancellor of the Exchequer on the taxation of increment value in Frankfort and other German cities, by Bernard Mallet, Oct. 1908, included in papers on *Taxation of Land* (Cmd. 4750 of 1909).
81. R. Wedgwood to J. Wedgwood, 3 Jan. 1909, MS. Wedgwood.
82. *The Times,* 15 Oct. 1908.
83. Riddell, *Diary,* 10.
84. Masterman, *Masterman,* 114.
85. Copy of estimates given to the Chancellor of the Exchequer, 27 Oct. 1908, S.H.L. R.C. Series.
86. H.D. 73—4.
87. P.D., 4 Oct. 1908; Asquith telegram to Lloyd George, 20 Aug. 1908, A.P. 11, ff. 174—5.
88. Masterman, *Masterman,* 112.
89. P.D., 30 Oct. 1908.
90. Midleton to Selborne, 9 Sept. 1908, MS. Selborne 3, ff. 71—4.
91. P.D., 4 Oct. 1908.
92. Haldane to Asquith, 9 Aug. 1908, A.P. 11, ff. 162—5.
93. *Guardian,* 25 Nov. 1908.

V. Preparation of the Budget

1. For the view that Lloyd George designed his Budget for rejection by the

Lords see P. Cambray, *The Game of Politics* (1932), 42–4; G. Dangerfield, *The Strange Death of Liberal England* (1936), 19–20. For the view that the Budget was intended as an alternative to a battle with the Lords see R. Jenkins, *Mr. Balfour's Poodle* (1954), 40–2; C. Cross, *The Liberals in Power 1905–14* (1963), 101–2; P. Rowland, *The Last Liberal Governments: The Promised Land* (1968), 215–21.

2. Lloyd George to William George, 6 May 1908, in George, *Brother*, 220.
3. I.D.
4. Asquith to the King, 9 Dec. 1908, A.P. 5, ff. 71–4.
5. B.D., 11 Dec. 1908.
6. I.D., 29 Mar. 1909.
7. Riddell, *Diary*, 13.
8. Lloyd George to William George, 9 Dec. 1908, George, *Brother*, 222.
9. *Yorkshire Post*, 25 Nov. 1908.
10. Chaplin to Balfour, 5 Apr. 1909, Bod. Lib. MSS. Eng. Hist. c. 757, ff. 159–62.
11. *The Times*, 24 Apr. 1909.
12. Riddell, *Diary*, 10.
13. I.D., 29 Mar. 1909.
14. P.D., 8 Dec. 1908.
15. *The Times*, 12 Dec. 1908.
16. Ibid., 22 Dec. 1908.
17. Churchill to Asquith, 26 and 29 Dec. 1908, in Churchill, *Churchill*, Companion Vol. II., Pt. 2, 860–4.
18. Ibid. 872–3.
19. Ibid. 887.
20. For constitutional issues arising out of the land valuation clauses see Lloyd George, 'The Taxation of Land Values', 13 Mar. 1909, P.R.O. CAB. 37/98/44; I.D., 10 and 15 Mar. 1909.
21. Midleton to Selborne, 6 Nov. 1908, MS. Selborne 3, ff. 86–90.
22. Masterman, *Masterman*, 111.
23. George, *Brother*, 222.
24. *The Economist*, 23 Jan. 1909.
25. Churchill to Asquith, 26 Dec. 1909, and Asquith to Churchill, 11 Jan. 1909, in Churchill, *Churchill*, Companion Vol. II, Pt.2, 860–1 and 869–70.
26. Crewe to Morley, 9 Dec. 1908, C.P. 37.
27. C.D., 5 and 11 Dec. 1908.
28. C.P. 37.
29. Churchill, *Churchill*, Companion Vol. II, Pt. 2, 862–4.
30. Lloyd George to William George, 17 Mar. 1909, in George, *Brother*, 223.
31. Ibid. 222.
32. H.D. 74.
33. Ibid. 77.
34. Ibid.
35. S.H.L. N.17.12.
36. Bradbury to Chalmers, 4 Mar. 1909, S.H.L. R.C. Series.
37. Murray to Rosebery, 31 Dec. 1908, N.L.S. MS. 10049, ff. 265–8.
38. Margot Asquith, *Autobiography* (1962 edition, ed. Mark Bonham Carter), 259.
39. S.H.L. R.C. Series.
40. 'Inland Revenue Account 1908–9', A.P. 22, ff. 139–41.
41. S.H.L. R.C. Series.
42. Ibid.

43. 'Inland Revenue Account 1908–9', with estimates for 1909–10 added, A.P. 22, ff. 139–41.
44. Lloyd George to William George, 19 Dec. 1908, in George, *Brother*, 222.
45. Customs and Excise, Returns of claims received and pensions granted up to 31 Mar. 1909, P.R.O. T1 11134/23733.
46. 'Report upon the Old Age Pensions work for the quarter ended 31st. December 1908', A. J. Tedder, 1 Feb. 1909, P.R.O. T1 10975/2652.
47. *Census of Ireland, 1911, General Report,* 74.
48. 'Old Age Pensions Estimate 1909–10', P.R.O. T1 11134/23733.
49. Ibid.
50. A.P. 5, ff. 75–6.
51. J.A. Spender and C. Asquith, *Life of Lord Oxford and Asquith* (2 vols., 1932), I, 254.
52. Asquith to the King, 24 Feb. 1909, A.P. 5, ff. 86–7; memorandum by Harcourt, 25 Feb. 1909, H.P. 577.
53. Austen Chamberlain to Mrs J. Chamberlain, 24 Mar. 1909, in Chamberlain, *Politics,* 165–8.
54. *H.C.D.* 5th Ser., VIII, 855–61.
55. Quoted in Morris, *Radicalism Against War,* 160.
56. *The Economist,* 22 Feb. 1909.
57. *Observer,* 21 Mar. 1909.
58. Bod. Lib. MSS. Eng. Hist. c. 757, ff. 159–62.
59. Fitzroy, *Memoirs,* I, 376–9.
60. H.D. 76.
61. Estimates, 26 Feb. 1909, S.H.L. R.C. Series.
62. Asquith to the King, 6 Apr. 1909, A.P. 5, ff. 102–3.
63. 'Balance Sheet 1909–10' sent by Murray to Asquith, 7 Apr. 1909, A.P. 22, ff. 127–31.
64. H.D. 76.
65. P.R.O. CAB. 37/96 and 97.
66. 'Taxation of Land Values', 23 Jan. 1909, ibid.; for original letters by Soares and Dickson-Poynder see A.P. 22.
67. 'Taxation of Land Values', 30 Jan. 1909, P.R.O. CAB. 37/97.
68. 'Land Values Bill. Draft Clauses', 24 Feb. 1909, A.P. 99.
69. 'Incidence of the Burden of Land Value Tax', 4 Feb. 1909, H.P. 577.
70. 'Finance Bill. Draft Clauses', 13 Mar. 1909, A.P. 99.
71. 'The Taxation of Land Values', 13 Mar. 1909, ibid.
72. For McKenna's opposition see J. Wedgwood, *Memoirs of a Fighting Life* (1940), 69.
73. Hobhouse to Asquith, n.d., A.P. 92, ff. 100–13.
74. I.D., 10 and 15 Mar. 1909.
75. H.D. 76.
76. 'Finance Bill. Draft Clauses', 13 Mar. 1909, A.P. 99.
77. H.D. 76.
78. T. Jones, *Lloyd George* (1951), 36.
79. 'Income Tax Proposals', 19 Oct. 1908, S.H.L. N. 17.12.
80. Montagu to Asquith, 25 Mar. 1909, A.P. 22, ff. 121–2.
81. Chalmers to Bradbury, 4 Mar. 1909, S.H.L. R.C. Series.
82. Budget Estimates, S.H.L. R.C. Series.
83. Proposals for Stamps, S.H.L. N.17.11; 'Chancellor's Stamp Proposals', 25 Mar. 1909, H.P. 577.
84. Estimates, 26 Feb. 1909, S.H.L. R.C. Series.
85. Memorandum in regard to licence duties, 16 Feb. 1909, H.P. 577.

86. Rowntree and Sherwell, *Taxation of the Liquor Trade* (1908), 503–5.
87. Asquith to the King, 24 Mar. 1909, A.P. 5, ff. 95–6; 'Finance Bill. Draft Clauses', 25 Mar. 1909, A.P. 99.
88. Memorandum in regard to licence duties, 16 Feb. 1909, H.P. 577.
89. Ibid; 'Finance Bill. Draft Clauses', 25 Mar. 1909, A.P. 99.
90. Asquith to the King, 24 Mar. 1909, ibid. 5, ff. 95–6.
91. Runciman to Asquith, 7 Apr. 1909, ibid. 22, ff. 132–5.
92. Chalmers to Lloyd George, 27 Oct. 1908, S.H.L. R.C. Series.
93. Budget Estimates, ibid.
94. 'The Taxation of Land Values', 13 Mar. 1909, A.P. 99.
95. Lloyd George to William George, 17 Dec. 1908, in George, *Brother*, 222; 'Memorandum on Taxation of "Petrol" used by Motor Cars', 24 Mar. 1909, A.P. 22, f. 142.
96. Churchill to Lloyd George, Apr. 1909, in Churchill, *Churchill*, Companion Vol. II, Pt. 2, 885–6; *H.C.D.* 5th Ser., IV, 493–5; J. Harris, *Unemployment and Politics: A Study in English Social Policy 1886–1914* (Oxford, 1972), 340–6.

VI. The Budget in the Cabinet

1. F. Stevenson, *Lloyd George: A Diary* (ed. A. J. P. Taylor, 1971), 322–3.
2. R. Lloyd George, *My Father Lloyd George* (1960), 120.
3. Morley to Crewe, 13 Dec. 1908, C.P. 37; E.D., 30 May 1909.
4. Fitzroy, *Memoirs*, I, 396–9.
5. P.D., 19 Apr. 1909.
6. Harcourt to Runciman, 24 Mar. 1909, R.P. 28.
7. Runciman to Asquith, 7 Apr. 1909, A.P. 22, ff. 132–5.
8. Wedgwood, *Memoirs*, 68–9.
9. B.D., 29 Apr. 1909.
10. Harcourt to Crewe, 7 Apr. 1909, C.P. 17.
11. Fitzmaurice to J. A. Spender, 19 June 1909, B.L. Add. MS. 46389, ff. 171–3.
12. Loreburn to Grey, n.d., quoted in A. S. King, 'Some Aspects of the History of the Liberal Party in Britain 1906–14' (unpublished Oxford D. Phil thesis, 1962), 85.
13. C.D., 29 Apr. 1909.
14. Haldane to Asquith, 9 Aug. 1908, A.P. 11, ff. 162–5.
15. H.D. 78.
16. Fitzroy, *Memoirs*, I, 376–7.
17. 'The Taxation of Land Values', 13 Mar. 1909, A.P. 99.
18. Lloyd George, n.d., Ll.G. C/26/1/2.
19. A.P. 5, ff. 92–4.
20. 'Finance Bill. Draft Clauses', 22 Mar. 1909, ibid. 99.
21. 'Finance Bill. Draft Clauses', 8 Apr. 1909, ibid.
22. Handwritten notes and questions on land taxes, n.d., H.P. 510.
23. 'Finance Bill. Draft Clauses', 8 Apr. 1909, A.P. 99.
24. See draft Finance Bills of 25 Mar. and 8 Apr. 1909, ibid.
25. Typed memorandum, n.d., ibid. 99, ff. 188–9.
26. *H.C.D.* 5th Ser., IV, 523–6.
27. Asquith to the King, 24 May 1909, A.P. 5, ff. 118–19.
28. Memorandum on excise licences, 20 May 1909, ibid. 100.

29. 'Chancellor's Stamp Proposals', 25 Mar. 1909, H.P. 577; Finance Bill Draft Resolutions, 27 Apr. 1909, A.P. 99.
30. Memoranda by Murray and Chalmers, circulated 27 Mar. 1909, H.P. 577.
31. Extracts of letters on a possible increase in the stamp duty on bills of exchange, 25 Mar. 1909, A.P. 99.
32. Harcourt to Crewe, 7 Apr. 1909, C.P. 17.
33. B.D., 1 Apr. 1909.
34. A.P. 5, ff. 102–3.
35. Ibid.; pencil notes by Runciman, n.d., R.P. 30.
36. Montagu to Asquith, 25 Mar. 1909, A.P. 22, ff. 121–2.
37. 'Income Super-Tax', 25 Mar. 1909, P.R.O. CAB. 37/98.
38. Montagu to Asquith, 25 Mar. 1909, A.P. 22, ff. 121–2.
39. Chalmers memorandum, circulated 2 Apr. 1909, H.P. 577.
40. George, *Brother*, 223.
41. 'Finance Bill. Draft Clauses', 8 Apr. 1909, A.P. 99.
42. Murray to Asquith, 7 Apr. 1909, ibid. 22, ff. 127–31.
43. Harcourt to Crewe, 7 Apr. 1909, C.P. 17.
44. Harcourt to Asquith, 12 Apr. 1909, A.P. 22, ff. 136–8.
45. 'Finance Bill. Draft Clauses', 8 Apr. 1909, ibid. 99.
46. Murray to Asquith, 7 Apr. 1909, ibid. 22, ff. 127–31.
47. Asquith to the King, 7 Apr. 1909, ibid. 5, ff. 104–5.
48. Murray to Asquith, 7 Apr. 1909, ibid. 22, ff. 127–31.
49. 'Inland Revenue Account 1908–9' with estimates for 1909–10 added, ibid., ff. 139–41.
50. Murray to Asquith, 7 Apr. 1909, ibid. 22, ff. 127–31.
51. C.P. 17.
52. A.P. 22, ff. 52–5.
53. Ibid., ff. 127–31.
54. Harcourt to Lord Welby, 3 May 1909, H.P. 441.
55. Ibid. 510.
56. P.D., 19 Apr. 1909.
57. P.D.
58. Asquith to the King, 26 Apr. 1909, A.P. 5, ff. 106–7.
59. H. of C. Paper No. 115 of 1909.
60. Finance Bill Draft Resolutions, Inhabited House Duty, 27 Apr. 1909, A.P. 99.
61. Asquith to the King, 26 Apr. 1909, ibid. 5, ff. 106–7; *H.C.D.* 5th Ser., IV, 498–9.
62. Finance Bill Draft Resolutions, Application of Old Sinking Fund, 27 Apr. 1909, A.P. 99.
63. Harcourt to Asquith, 12 Apr. 1909, A.P. 22, ff. 136–8.
64. *The Times*, 30 Apr. 1909.
65. Ibid., 3 May 1909.
66. C.D., 29 Apr. 1909.
67. F. Owen, *Tempestuous Journey* (1954), 170.
68. George, *Brother*, 224.

VII. The Budget in the Commons and the Country

1. Austen Chamberlain to Mrs J. Chamberlain, 9 May 1909, in Chamberlain, *Politics*, 178–80.
2. *H.C.D.* 5th Ser., IV, 472–548.
3. Ibid. 501.

4. Chamberlain, *Politics*, 176—8.
5. *The Times,* 30 Jan. 1909.
6. Ibid. 1 Feb. 1909.
7. Ibid. 29 Apr. 1909.
8. Ibid. 30 Apr. 1909.
9. Samuel to Gladstone, 29 Apr. 1909, B.L. Add. MS. 45992.
10. George, *Brother,* 226.
11. P.D., 20 Apr. 1909.
12. Harcourt to Lord Welby, 3 May 1909, H.P. 441.
13. Lloyd George to William George, 12 July 1909, in George, *Brother,* 227—8.
14. B.L. Add. MS. 46388.
15. *H.C.D.* 5th Ser., VI, 19—42.
16. In 1907 Snowden had written a rather more radical treatise, *The Socialist's Budget.*
17. *H.C.D.* 5th Ser., IV. 1072—84.
18. Ibid. VI, 313—33.
19. For Balfour's speech, ibid. 510—27.
20. Communication from H. Pike Pease, May 1909, National Trade Defence Association, Parliamentary Proceedings, 1909, I.
21. Ibid.
22. *The Times,* 25 June 1909.
23. C.D., 25 June 1909.
24. *Brewers' Journal,* 15 May 1909; *Brewers' Gazette,* 27 May 1909.
25. *Estates Gazette,* 8 May, 5 and 19 June 1909.
26. Bod. Lib. MSS. Eng. Hist. c. 758.
27. *Builder,* 22 May 1909.
28. Ilbert to Bryce, 6 and 7 June 1909, B.P. 13.
29. Asquith to Runciman, n.d. but probably 22 May 1909, R. P. 302.
30. *The Times,* 15 and 16 June 1909.
31. Raphael to Norman, 20 June 1909, MS. Norman.
32. *The Times,* 11 Sept. 1909.
33. Blewett, *General Elections of 1910,* 72.
34. Ibid. 215—18.
35. For the efforts of Wedgwood and the land taxers, see *The Times,* 15 and 16 June 1909.
36. N.L.S. MS. 5981.
37. *The Times,* 24 June 1909.
38. C.D., 26 June 1909; Asquith to the King, 23 June 1909, A.P. 5, f. 126.
39. Ilbert to Bryce, 9 July 1909, B.P. 13.
40. P.D., 16 July 1909.
41. C.D., 11 July 1909.
42. I.D., 15 June 1909.
43. B.L. Add. MS. 46388.
44. H.D. 79.
45. I.D., 13 July 1909.
46. Sir W. Runciman quoted in Blewett, *General Elections of 1910,* 71.
47. *Guardian,* 30 Apr. 1909; *Chronicle* 30 Apr. 1909; *Westminster Gazette* 30 Apr. 1909; *Nation,* 1 May 1909; *Review of Reviews,* May 1909.
48. *The Economist,* 5 June 1909.
49. Snowden in the Commons, 4 May 1909, *H.C.D.* 5th Ser. IV, 1072—84.
50. *Labour Leader,* 7 and 14 May 1909.
51. Quoted in Morris, *Trevelyan,* 80.
52. MS. Norman.

53. Minutes of the fourth meeting of the executive committee of the Budget League, 21 July 1909, ibid.
54. Speeches on the occasion of a dinner given to Norman, 10 Mar. 1910, ibid.
55. Notes of a conference between the editors of various Liberal newspapers and the executive committee of the Budget League, 9 July 1909, ibid.
56. Minutes of the fourth meeting of the executive committee of the Budget League, 21 July 1909, ibid.
57. P.D., 19 July 1909.
58. Churchill to Asquith, 19 July 1909, in Churchill, *Churchill,* Companion Vol. II, Pt. 2, 898–9.
59. Crewe to Asquith, 19 July 1909, C.P. 40.
60. Asquith to the King, 21 July 1909, A.P. 5, f. 134.
61. Carson letter to *The Times,* 2 Aug. 1909.
62. *The Times,* 31 July 1909.
63. Bod. Lib. MSS. Eng. Hist. c. 759, ff. 91–2.
64. For the meeting see A.M. Gollin, *The Observer and J. L Garvin 1908–1914* (1960), 105–6.
65. *Labour Leader,* 15 Oct. 1909.
66. Quoted in Grigg, *People's Champion,* 208–9.
67. Asquith to the King, 30 July and 4 Aug. 1909, A.P. 5, ff. 138–40.
68. *H.C.D.* 5th Ser., IX, 304–14 and 432–9.
69. P.D., 26 Aug. 1909.
70. Masterman, *Masterman,* 140 and 143.
71. George, *Brother,* 230.
72. 'Proposal to allow property owners to be assessed under Schedule D instead of under Schedule A', D. Ll.G., 17 Sept. 1909, H.P. 577.
73. Memorandum on the effect of a minimum licence duty on licences in Ireland, n.d., A.P. 102.
74. O'Connor to Lloyd George, 25 Sept. 1909 and 'Saturday', Ll.G.P. C/6/10/ 1–2.
75. For the Irish negotiations over the licence duties see D. Gwynn, *Life of John Redmond* (1932), 162–5, and see also Redmond to Lloyd George, 31 Aug. 1909, Ll.G.P. C/7/3/1.
76. *The Times,* 18 Sept. 1909.
77. Ibid., 9 and 11 Oct. 1909.
78. P.D., 18 Oct. 1909.
79. E.D., 18 Oct. 1909.
80. *H.C.D.* 5th Ser., XII, 1922–46; F. Dilnot, *The Old Order Changeth: The Passing of Power from the House of Lords* (1911), 92–106.
81. Blewett, *General Elections of 1910,* 214.
82. For statistics on Liberal MPs retiring see ibid., 211–17; Morley to Rosebery, 13 Sept. 1909, N.L.S. 10047, ff. 200–1.
83. *H.C.D.* 5th Ser., XII, 2026–34.
84. Masterman, *Masterman,* 142.
85. *The Times,* 8 and 10 Dec. 1909.
86. Ibid. 2 Dec. 1909.
87. Norman to Asquith, 20 Nov. 1909, MS. Norman.
88. Speeches on the occasion of a dinner given to Norman, 10 Mar. 1910, ibid.
89. Garvin memorandum on campaign literature, 29 Nov. 1909, B.L. Add. MS. 49795.
90. Pease to Norman, 3 Nov. 1909, MS. Norman; Pease to Churchill, 25 Nov., and Churchill to Pease, 26 Nov. 1909, in Churchill, *Churchill,* Companion Vol. II, Pt. 2, 923–4.

91. Budget League expenditure, n.d., MS. Norman.
92. W. Ashley to Sandars, 16 July 1909, Bod. Lib. MSS. Eng. Hist. c. 759, ff. 23–4.
93. Norman to Pease, 29 June 1909, MS. Norman.
94. Draft letter, n.d., MS. Long, Wilts R.O. 947/428.
95. Balfour to Sandars, 6 Aug. 1909, Bod. Lib. MSS. Eng. Hist. c. 759, ff. 72–3.
96. Acland-Hood to Sandars, 8 Aug. 1909, ibid., ff. 74–7.
97. A. E. Pease to J. Pease, 3 Sept. and 14 Dec. 1909, MS. Gainford.
98. I.D., 13 Nov. 1909.
99. For Lloyd George and Keir Hardie see Kenneth O. Morgan, *Keir Hardie* (1975), 228–9; for MacDonald's letter see Blewett, *General Elections of 1910*, 237.

VIII. Rejection

1. Austen Chamberlain to Mrs J. Chamberlain, 20 Sept. 1909 in Chamberlain, *Politics,* 182–3.
2. Garvin to Northcliffe, 5 May 1909, B.L. Unbound MS. LXXXIV.
3. Gollin, *Garvin,* 115–16.
4. B.L. Add. MS. 49765.
5. Jenkins, *Mr. Balfour's Poodle,* 98–100; Blewett, *General Elections of 1910,* 76.
6. John Ramsden, *The Age of Balfour and Baldwin 1902–1940* (1978), 28–9.
7. H. A. Taylor, *Smith of Birkenhead* (1928), 139–40.
8. Young, *Balfour,* 310.
9. Bod. Lib. MSS. Eng. Hist. c. 759, ff. 64–8.
10. Ibid., ff. 74–7.
11. Ibid., ff. 42–4.
12. Ibid., ff. 74–7.
13. Garvin to Northcliffe, 13 Aug. 1909, B.L. Unbound MS. LXXXIV.
14. Bod. Lib. MSS. Eng. Hist. c. 759, ff. 72–3.
15. See previous chapter, p. 193.
16. Gollin, *Garvin,* 117.
17. Bod. Lib. MSS. Eng. Hist. c. 759, ff. 99–100.
18. Chamberlain Papers AC/6/1/72.
19. Lansdowne to Balfour of Burleigh, 2 Oct. 1909, in Newton, *Lansdowne,* 378–9.
20. Lansdowne to Sandars, 11 Aug. 1909, Bod. Lib. MSS. Eng. Hist. c. 759, ff. 99–100.
21. Sandars to Balfour, 8 Aug. 1909, B.L. Add. MS. 49765.
22. Lansdowne to Sandars, 1 Nov. 1909, ibid. 49730.
23. Sandars to Lansdowne, 6 Nov. 1909, ibid.
24. Milner to Lansdowne, 2 Nov. 1909, ibid.
25. Newton, *Lansdowne,* 378–9.
26. Chamberlain, *Politics,* 181–2.
27 Esher, *Journals,* II, 407.
28. Ibid. 410.
29. Gollin, *Garvin,* 169; Young, *Balfour,* 292.
30. Acland-Hood to Balfour, 29 Jan. 1910, B.L. Add. MS. 49771.
31. Newton, *Lansdowne,* 378–9.
32. Sandars to Lansdowne, 6 Nov. 1909, B.L. Add. MS. 49730.
33. Ibid. 49695.

34. Newton, *Lansdowne,* 378–9.
35. *The Times,* 3 Jan. 1910.
36. Montagu to Asquith, Nov. 1909, in S. D. Waley, *Edwin Montagu* (Bombay, 1964), 34.
37. B.L. Add. MS. 49730.
38. Lansdowne to Sandars, 23 Jan. 1910, ibid.
39. N.L.S. MS. ACC. 5666.
40. S.P. S/5/5/12.
41. Strachey to Lord Hugh Cecil, 15 Nov. 1909, ibid., S/4/3/17.
42. Blewett, *General Elections of 1910,* 76–82.
43. Chamberlain, *Politics,* 196–200; Sandars to Balfour, 15 Mar. 1910, B.L. Add. MS. 49766.
44. Chamberlain Papers AC/4/3/1538.
45. *The Times,* 23 Sept. 1909.
46. I.D., 30 Sept. 1909.
47. N.L.S. MS. 5982.
48. I.D., 13 Nov. 1909.
49. P.D., 20 Sept. 1909.
50. Pease to his wife, 8 Sept. 1909, MS. Gainford.
51. P.D., 5 Oct. 1909.
52. Asquith note, 6 Oct. 1909, in Spender and Asquith, *Asquith,* I, 257–8.
53. E.D., 31 Oct. 1909.
54. Asquith to the King, 3 Nov. 1909, A.P. 5, f. 167.
55. Blewett, *General Elections of 1910,* 85–90.
56. I.D., 26 Oct. 1909.
57. Ibid., 13 Nov. 1909.
58. 'The Finance Bill and the Lords', 16 Nov. 1909, A.P. 22, ff. 274–9.
59. Asquith to the King, 17 Nov. 1909, A.P.5, ff. 169–70.
60. Ibid., f. 172.
61. I.D., 24 Nov. 1909.
62. For an amusing account of the collection of customs see L. Guillemard, *Trivial Fond Records* (1937), 54–8.
63. *The Times,* 15 Nov. 1909.
64. *H.L.D.* 5th Ser., IV, 731–50.
65. Ibid. 750–9.
66. Ibid. 821–31.
67. Ibid. 942–5; *The Times,* 25 and 26 Nov. 1909.
68. *H.L.D.* 5th Ser., IV, 1324–42.
69. I.D., 30 Nov. 1909.
70. *The Times,* 3 Dec. 1909.
71. *H.C.D.* 5th Ser., XIII, 546–58.
72. P.D., 2 Dec. 1909.
73. I.D., 2 Dec. 1909.
74. *H.C.D.* 5th Ser., XIII, 558–71.
75. Newton, *Lansdowne,* 383; *H.L.D.* 5th Ser., IV, 1098–101.
76. *The Times,* 4 Dec. 1909.

IX. The Budget Election

1. Blewett, *General Elections of 1910,* chaps. 6, 7, and 18.
2. *Land Values,* Mar. and Apr. 1910.
3. Hobson, 'The General Election: a Sociological Interpretation', *Sociological Review,* III (1910), 105–17.

4. Gwynn, *Redmond,* 166–9.
5. Koss, *Nonconformity,* 102.
6. *The Times,* 29 Dec. 1909.
7. Ibid., 6, 14, 23, and 29 Dec. 1909, and 8 Jan. 1910.
8. Ibid., 11 Dec. 1909.
9. *Guardian,* 18 Feb. 1910.
10. *The Times,* 4, 6, and 7 Dec. 1909.
11. For Cabinet discussions see Esher, *Journals,* II, 423–5, and C. D. 1 Dec. 1909. See also C. C. Weston, 'The Liberal Leadership and the Lords' Veto, 1907–1910', *H.J.* XI (1968), 507–38, and Blewett, *General Elections of 1910,* 91–4.
12. Spender and Asquith, *Asquith,* I, 261.
13. Weston, 'Lords' Veto', 519–21; Churchill to Asquith, 10 Nov. 1909, in Churchill, *Churchill,* Companion Vol. II, Pt. 2, 919.
14. Ibid.
15. C. D., 29 Jan. 1910; Harcourt to Asquith, 26 Jan. 1910, A.P. 12, f. 77.
16. Sandars to Balfour, 3 Feb. 1910, B.L. Add. MS. 49766. See also Harcourt to Asquith, 26 Jan. 1910, A.P. 12, f. 77.
17. *The Times,* 11 Dec. 1909.
18. Ibid., 3 Jan. 1910.
19. Sir Ivor Jennings, *Party Politics* (3 vols., Cambridge, 1960–2), III. 377.
20. E.D., 28 Jan. 1910. See also Harcourt to Asquith, 26 Jan. 1910, A.P. 12, f. 77.
21. Stuart Rendel, *Personal Papers* (1931), 235–6.
22. Spender to Bryce, 3 Feb. 1910, B.P. UB. 22.
23. *Guardian,* 13 Dec. 1909.
24. Ibid., 6, 7, 8, 9, and 13 Dec. 1909.
25. *The Times,* 8 Jan. 1910.
26. See Jenkins, *Asquith,* 203.
27. Chamberlain, *Politics,* 196–200.
28. *The Times,* 7 Jan. 1910.
29. Ibid., 11 Dec. 1909.
30. See Austen Chamberlain at Redditch, and Milner at Huddersfield, *The Times,* 18 Dec. 1909.
31. Ibid., 6 Dec. 1909.
32. Ibid., 29 Dec. 1909.
33. Chamberlain, *Politics,* 196–200.
34. *Observer,* 3 Oct. 1909.
35. *The Times,* 24 and 29 Dec. 1909.
36. Ibid., 31 Dec. 1909.
37. Ibid., 15 Jan. 1910.
38. Webb, *Our Partnership,* 436; Blewett, *General Elections of 1910,* 122.
39. Austen Chamberlain to Balfour, 29 Jan. 1910, Chamberlain, *Politics,* 196–200.
40. *The Times,* 4 Dec. 1909.
41. Ibid., 13 Jan. 1910.
42. MacKail and Wyndham, *Wyndham,* II, 648.
43. Hewins Diary, 20 and 28 Jan. 1910.
44. *Labour Leader,* 17 Dec. 1909.
45. For details see Blewett, *General Elections of 1910,* chap. 12.
46. Chamberlain, *Politics,* 196–200.
47. Memorandum on the Irish situation, 31 Mar. 1910, N.L.S. 8802.
48. *The Times,* 16 Dec. 1909.

49. *Guardian,* 10 Jan. 1910.
50. Blewett, *General Elections of 1910,* 351.
51. Ibid. 381.
52. Ibid. 385.
53. *Labour Leader,* 4 Feb. 1910.
54. *Guardian,* 21 Jan. 1910.
55. *The Times,* 1 Feb. 1910.
56. Ibid., 31 Jan. 1910.
57. Blewett, *General Elections of 1910,* 400.
58. Spender to Bryce, 3 Feb. 1910, B.P. UB 22.
59. Blewett, *General Elections of 1910,* 400.
60. *The Times,* 31 Jan. 1910.
61. Ibid.
62. Chamberlain, *Politics,* 196–200.
63. See Samuel to Gladstone, 22 Jan. 1910, B.L. Add. MS. 45992.
64. *Guardian,* 24 and 28 Jan. 1910.
65. Spender to Bryce, 3 Feb. 1910, B.P. UB 22.
66. Ibid.
67. Masterman, *Masterman,* 152.
68. Joseph Chamberlain to Hewins, 28 Jan. 1910, MS. Hewins 53/212–3.

X. The Passage of the Budget

1. Bod. Lib. MSS. Eng. Hist. c. 760, ff. 47–50.
2. Blewett, *General Elections of 1910,* 147.
3. *H.C.D.* 5th Ser., XVI, 1547–9.
4. Masterman, *Masterman,* 158.
5. Memorandum prepared by Grey on the Upper House, 31 Jan. 1910, A.P.23, ff. 62–4.
6. Harcourt to Asquith, 26 Jan. and 7 Feb. 1910, A.P. 12, ff. 77–8, and 114–15.
7. Harcourt to Asquith, 26 Jan. 1910, ibid.
8. Churchill to Asquith, 18 Feb. 1910, in Churchill, *Churchill,* Companion Vol. II, Pt. 2, 971–2.
9. *The Times,* 24 and 25 Feb. 1910. The role of the Liberal rank and file is emphasized by A. S. King in 'Some Aspects of the Liberal Party 1906–1914'.
10. *Guardian,* 22 Feb. 1910; *Nation,* 26 Feb. 1910.
11. Asquith to the King, 10 Feb. 1910, MS. Asquith 5, ff. 180–1.
12. *Guardian,* 11 Feb. 1910.
13. *H.C.D.* 5th Ser., XIV, 117–24.
14. Balfour Memorandum for the King, 15 Feb. 1910, Bod. Lib. MSS. Eng. Hist. c. 760, ff. 47–50.
15. *H.C.D.* 5th Ser., XIV, 131–9.
16. Gwynn, *Redmond,* 174.
17. Asquith to the King, 25 Feb. 1910, A.P. 5, f. 192.
18. C.D., 26 Feb. 1910.
19. Ibid.; A. C. Murray, *Master and Brother* (1945), 39.
20. C.D., 27 Feb. 1910.
21. Murray, *Master,* 39.
22. C.D., 26 Feb. 1910.
23. Ibid., 27 Feb. 1910.
24. *H.C.D.* 5th Ser., XIV, 591–5.

25. Ibid. 632—7.
26. Austen Chamberlain to Mrs J. Chamberlain, 27 and 28 Feb. 1910, in Chamberlain, *Politics*, 208—14.
27. Hewins Diary 20.
28. C.D., 28 Feb. and 1 Mar. 1910.
29. Churchill to the King, 1 Mar. 1910, in Churchill, *Churchill*, Companion Vol. II, Pt. 2, 982—3.
30. See Churchill to the King, 28 Feb. 1910, in ibid. 978—9.
31. *The Times*, 2 Mar. 1910. For Nicholson's activity in securing Cabinet secrets see Northcliffe Papers, B.L. Uncatalogued 4890/XCIV. When someone told Churchill that Cabinet discussions leaked out, he allegedly replied: 'Yes, it's a Welsh leak!' See Austen Chamberlain to Mrs J. Chamberlain, 8 Mar. 1910, in Chamberlain, *Politics*, 224—5.
32. Murray, *Master*, 41.
33. Ibid.
34. Churchill, *Churchill*, Companion Vol. II, Pt. 2, 977.
35. C.D., 28 Feb. and 1 Mar. 1910.
36. Chamberlain, *Politics*, 231—2.
37. Esher memorandum of conference with Balfour, Lord Knollys and the Archbishop of Canterbury, 27 Apr. 1910, in Esher, *Journals*, II, 456—9.
38. Sandars to Balfour, 16 Apr. 1910, B.L. Add. MS. 49766.
39. C.P. 40.
40. Redmond to Dillon, 8 Mar. 1910, T.C.D. MS. 6748, ff. 445—6.
41. E.D., 11 Feb. 1910; Redmond to Dillon, 12 Feb. 1910, in F.S.L. Lyons, *John Dillon* (1968), 314; Murray, *Master*, 47.
42. Redmond to Dillon, 5 Mar. 1910, T.C.D. MS. 6748, ff. 442—4.
43. N.L.S. MS. 8802.
44. See Dillon to Sir Edward Russell, 12 Mar. 1910, copy in Ll.G.P. C/7/6/1.
45. H.D., 10 Mar. 1910, O'Brien in the Commons, 18 Apr. 1910, *H.C.D.* 5th Ser., XVI, 1739—51.
46. *The Times*, 21 Mar. 1910.
47. P.D., 21 Mar. 1910.
48. Redmond to Dillon, 5 Mar. 1910, T.C.D. MS. 6748; J. Diamond to Dillon, 19 and 21 Mar. 1910, ibid. MS. 6753; O'Connor to Dillon, 7 Mar. 1910, ibid., MS. 6740; O'Connor to Elibank, 22 Mar. 1910, N.L.S. MS. 8802.
49. Asquith to the King, 23 Mar. 1910, A.P., 5, f.202.
50. P.D., 23 Mar. 1910.
51. A.P. 23, f.81.
52. Runciman to McKenna, 27 Mar. 1910, MS. McKenna 3/22.
53. McKenna to Runciman, 28 Mar. 1910, R.P. 35.
54. P.D., 30 Mar. 1910.
55. Asquith to the King, 6 Apr. 1910, A.P. 5, f. 206; copy of draft bill in H.P. 578.
56. Harcourt to Asquith, 14 Apr. 1910, A.P. 23, f. 96.
57. *H.C.D.* 5th Ser., XV, 1198—1208.
58. Asquith to the King, 31 Mar. 1910, A.P., 5, f. 204.
59. P.D., 30 Mar. 1910.
60. *The Times*, 4 Apr. 1910.
61. Ibid., 1 and 5 Apr. 1910.
62. H.D. 86; Murray, *Master*, 47.
63. *The Times*, 12 Apr. 1910.
64. Murray, *Master*, 47.
65. Asquith to Crewe, 8 Apr. 1910, C.P. 40.

66. 'Suggested Procedure on an issue with the House of Lords', 8 Apr. 1910, H.P. 578.
67. Morley to Haldane, 10 Apr. 1910, N.L.S. MS. 5909; Esher to the King, 10 Apr. 1910, in Esher, *Journals,* II, 453—5.
68. Masterman, *Masterman,* 159—60.
69. Ibid.; P.D., 13 Apr. 1910.
70. H.D. 89.
71. Murray, *Master,* 45—6.
72. Masterman, *Masterman,* 161.
73. Runciman note, 'Cabinet of 13 April, 1910', R.P. 39.
74. Masterman, *Masterman,* 161.
75. P.D., 13 Apr. 1910.
76. Runciman note, 'Cabinet of 13 April, 1910', R.P. 39.
77. Asquith to the King, 13 Apr. 1910, A.P. 5, f. 208.
78. H.D. 89.
79. *The Times,* 15 Apr. 1910.
80. Masterman, *Masterman,* 162.
81. *H.C.D.* 5th Ser., XVI, 1759—65.
82. P.D., 20 Apr. 1910.
83. Chamberlain, *Politics,* 254.
84. Runciman to McKenna, 27 Mar. 1910, MS. McKenna 3/22.
85. *H.C.D.* 5th Ser., XVI, 1906—16.

XI. Impact of the Budget

1. *H.C.D.* 5th Ser., XLI, 1060—1.
2. Ibid. LII, 261.
3. *Statistical Society of London Journal,* LXXXII (1920), 176—7.
4. *Report of the Committee on National Debt and Taxation* (Cmd. 2800 of 1927), 94—5.
5. Hay, *Welfare Reforms,* 59.
6. Evidence given by C. J. Howell Thomas, Deputy Chief Valuer of the Board of Inland Revenue, to the Select Committee on Land Values in 1919, *Report of the Select Committee on Land Values* (Cmd. 556 of 1920), 13.
7. Ibid. 42—4.
8. Paper on 'Lloyd George's Land Taxes' delivered by Harper at the International Conference on Land-Value Taxation in Edinburgh, 1929, and reprinted in *Land and Liberty.*
9. *Select Committee on Land Values,* 17.
10. Ibid. for reviews of the judicial decisions relating to the land value duties.
11. 'The Rating of Site Values', 13 Dec. 1913, P.R.O. CAB. 37/118.
12. P. Wilding, 'Towards Exchequer Subsidies For Housing 1906—1914', *Social and Economic Administration,* VI (1972), 13—14.
13. *Select Committee on Land Values,* 17.
14. Wilding, 'Exchequer Subsidies', 14.
15. Report of the Housing Committee of the Surveyors' Institution, October 1917, quoted in an Inland Revenue memorandum on 'Part I. of the Finance Act (1909—10) 1910 in particular in its relation to Housing', Jan. 1918, P.R.O. D.O.35/424.
16. Ibid., and the Report of the Liverpool and District Association of House Builders, 1917, P.R.O. Reco.1/570.
17. F. M. L. Thompson, *English Landed Society in the Nineteenth Century* (1963), 320—6.

18. *Brewing Trade Review,* 1 Dec. 1913 and 1 Aug. 1914.
19. D. M. Knox, 'The Development of the Tied House System in London', *Oxford Economic Papers,* X (1958), 66–83.
20. Licensing Statistics, 1914, *Parliamentary Papers 1914–16,* LIV.
21. For statistics see the *Brewing Trade Review,* 1 Sept. 1913.
22. Ibid.
23. Mallet, *British Budgets 1887–1913,* 480.
24. Ibid. 478.
25. *H.C.D.* 5th Ser., LII, 259.
26. For discussions of the by-elections 1911–14 and their significance see McKibbin, *Labour Party,* 82–5; Roy Gregory, 'Labour in Decline, 1910–14', in K. D. Brown (ed.), *Anti-Labour History,* 105–25; and P. F. Clarke, 'The electoral position of the Liberal and Labour Parties, 1910–1914', *E.H.R.* XC (1978), 828–36.
27. *H.C.D.* 5th Ser., LXII, 85–94.
28. Churchill, *Churchill,* Companion Vol. II, Pt. 3, 1975–6.
29. Riddell, *Diary,* 214–15.
30. For a detailed examination of Lloyd George's mismanagement of the Budget for 1914/15 see B. B. Gilbert, 'David Lloyd George: The Reform of British Landholding and the Budget of 1914', *H.J.* XXI (1978), 117–41.
31. Asquith to the King, 23 June 1914, P.R.O. CAB. 41/35/15.
32. *H.C.D.* 5th Ser., LXIII, 1569–72.
33. Riddell, *Diary,* 215.
34. Gilbert, 'Budget of 1914', 141.
35. *H.C.D.* 5th Ser., LXIII, 1592–7.
36. Ibid. 2083–91.
37. Quoted in King, 'Aspects of Liberal Party', 181.
38. Quoted in Emy, *Social Politics,* 255.
39. Lloyd George to Illingworth, 24 Oct. 1913, in P. Rowland, *The Last Liberal Governments: Unfinished Business 1911–1914* (1971), 225.
40. *H.C.D.* 5th Series., LXIII, 2045–59.
41. Christopher Addison, *Four and a Half Years* (2 vols., 1934), I, 25.
42. Freeden, *Liberalism,* 150–8.
43. *H.C.D.* 5th Ser., XXXII, 1939; quoted in Mallet, *Budgets 1887–1913,* 329.
44. Quoted in Clarke, *Lancashire,* 405.
45. McKibbin, *Labour Party,* chaps. 3 and 4; M. Petter, 'The Progressive Alliance', *History,* LVIII (1973), 45–59.
46. D. Marquand, *Ramsay MacDonald* (1977), 159.
47. Clarke, 'The electoral position of the Liberal and Labour Parties, 1910–1914', 836.

Bibliography

I. Manuscript Collections

Birmingham University Library

Chamberlain Papers
Minutes of the Midland Liberal Federation

Bodleian Library

Asquith Papers
Bryce Papers
Carrington Papers
Harcourt Papers
Milner Papers
Ponsonby Papers
Sandars Papers
Selborne Papers

Brewers' Society

Brewers' Society Papers
National Trade Defence Association Papers

British Library

Balfour Papers
Birrell Papers
Burns Papers
Campbell-Bannerman Papers
Cecil of Chelwood Papers
Herbert Gladstone Papers
Northcliffe Papers
J.A. Spender Papers

Cambridge University Library
Crewe Papers

Churchill College Library

Esher Papers
McKenna Papers

Conservative Party Offices

Minutes of the National Union of Conservative Associations, Cheshire Division (Manchester), and Eastern Provincial Division (Cambridge)

Gloucester Record Office

St. Aldwyn Papers

National Library of Ireland

Redmond Papers

National Library of Scotland

Elibank Papers
Arthur Elliott Papers
Haldane Papers
Robertson Nicoll Papers
Rosebery Papers

Newcastle University Library

Runciman Papers
C. P. Trevelyan Papers

Nuffield College Library

Emmott Papers
Gainford Papers
Mottistone Papers

Public Record Office

Cabinet Papers
Cromer Papers
Grey Papers
Recontruction Ministry Papers
Treasury Papers

Sheffield University Library

Hewins Papers

Somerset House Library

Inland Revenue Papers

Transport House

Minutes of the National Executive of the Labour Party

Trinity College, Dublin, Library

Dillon Papers

Westminster City Libraries

Minutes of the National Society of Conservative Agents

Wiltshire Record Office

Walter Long Papers

Private

Amery Papers in the possession of the Rt. Hon. Julian Amery
Norman Papers in the possession of Lady Burke
Wedgwood Papers in the possession of the Hon. Mrs. H. B. Pease

Guides

Two invaluable published guides to manuscript collections for the twentieth century exist:
C. Hazlehurst and C. Woodland, *A Guide to the Papers of British Cabinet Ministers, 1900–1951* (1974)
C. Cook, *Sources in British Political History, 1900–1951* (4 vols., 1975–7).

II. Official Papers

Parliamentary Debates 1906–14
Parliamentary Papers 1906–14

First Report of the Royal Commission on the Housing of the Working Classes, C. 4402 of 1884–5
Report of the Select Committee on Town Holdings, H. of C. 214 of 1892
Final Report of the Royal Commission on Local Taxation, Cd. 638 of 1901
Report of the Departmental Committee on Local Taxation, Cd. 7315 of 1914
Report of the Select Committee on Land Values, Cmd. 556 of 1920
Report of the Committee on National Debt and Taxation, Cmd. 2800 of 1927
The Rating of Site Values: Report of the Committee of Enquiry, Scottish Home Department, 1952

III. Newspapers and Periodicals

Daily: *The Times*
           Manchester Guardian

Weekly: *Observer*
           The Economist
           Spectator
           Labour Leader
           Nation

Other: *Blackwood's Magazine*
           Contemporary Review
           Fortnightly Review
           Land Values
           Liberal Magazine
           National Review
           Nineteenth Century and After
           Quarterly Review
           Review of Reviews

IV. Reference Works

Annual Register
Dictionary of National Biography

Who's Who
Constitutional Year Book
Liberal Year Book

V. Selected Memoirs and Published Correspondence and Diaries

Chamberlain, A., *Politics From Inside* (1936).
Esher, R. B., *Journals and Letters* (ed. by M. V. Brett, 2 vols., 1934).
Fitzroy, A., *Memoirs* (2 vols., 1925).
George, W., *My Brother and I* (1958).
Hobhouse, C., *Inside Asquith's Cabinet: From the Diaries of Charles Hobhouse* (ed. by E. David, 1977).
Riddell, G., *More Pages From My Diary 1908–1914* (1934).
Webb, B., *Our Partnership* (1948).
Wedgwood, J. C., *Memoirs of a Fighting Life* (1940).

VI. Theses

Hay, J. R., 'British Government Finance 1906–1914' (Oxford B. Litt., 1970).
Ho, Ping-Ti, 'Land and State in Great Britain 1873–1910' (Columbia University Ph.D., 1952).
King, A. S., 'Some Aspects of the History of the Liberal Party in Britain 1906–1914' (Oxford D. Phil., 1962).
Peacock, A. J., 'Land Reform 1880–1914' (Southampton University M.A., 1962).
Porter, D., 'The Unionist Tariff Reformers' (Manchester University Ph.D., 1976).

VII. Selected Secondary Publications

Allyn, E., *Lords Versus Commons: A Century of Conflict and Compromise 1830–1930* (1931).
Blewett, N., *The Peers, the Parties and the People: The General Elections of 1910* (1972).
Brown, K. D., *Essays in Anti-Labour History* (1974).
    John Burns (1978).
Cambray, P. G., *The Game of Politics* (1932).

Churchill, R. S., *Winston S. Churchill* (2 vols., 1966–7).

Clarke, P. F., *Lancashire and the New Liberalism* (1971).

Cross, C., *The Liberals in Power 1905–1914* (1963).

Douglas, R., *Land, People and Politics* (1976).

Emy, H. V., *Liberals, Radicals, and Social Politics 1892–1914* (Cambridge, 1973).

Fraser, P., *Joseph Chamberlain* (1966).
　Lord Esher (1973).

Freeden, M., *The New Liberalism* (Oxford, 1978).

Gilbert, B. B., *The Evolution of National Insurance in Great Britain* (1966).
　'David Lloyd George: Land, the Budget, and Social Reform', *American Historical Review*, LXXXI (1976).
　'David Lloyd George: The Reform of British Landholding and the Budget of 1914', *Historical Journal*, XXI (1978).

Gollin, A. M., *The Observer and J. L. Garvin 1908–1914* (1960).
　Balfour's Burden (1965).

Grigg, J., *The Young Lloyd George* (1973).
　Lloyd George: The People's Champion (1978).

Gwynn, D., *The Life of John Redmond* (1932).

Hamer, D. A., *Liberal Politics in the Age of Gladstone and Rosebery* (Oxford, 1972).

Harris, J., *Unemployment and Politics: A Study in English Social Policy 1886–1914* (Oxford, 1972).

Hay, J. R., *The Origins of the Liberal Welfare Reforms 1906–1914* (1975).

Hazlehurst, C., 'Asquith as Prime Minister', *English Historical Review* LXXXV (1970).

Jenkins, R., *Mr Balfour's Poodle* (1954).
　Asquith (1964).

Koss, S., *Lord Haldane: Scapegoat for Liberalism* (1969).
　Nonconformity in Modern British Politics (1975).
　Asquith (1976).

Lyons, F. S. L., *John Dillon* (1968).

McKibbin, R., *The Evolution of the Labour Party 1910–1924* (Oxford, 1974).

Mallet, B., *British Budgets 1887–1913* (1913).
　British Budgets 1913–1921 (1929).

Masterman, L. B., *C.F.G. Masterman* (1939).

Matthew, H.C.G., *The Liberal Imperialists* (Oxford, 1973).
Morgan, Kenneth O., *Wales in British Politics* (Cardiff, 1970 ed.).
    Lloyd George (1974).
    Keir Hardie: Radical and Socialist (1975).
Murray, A. C., *Master and Brother: Murrays of Elibank* (1945).
Murray, B. K., 'The Politics of the "People's Budget" ', *Historical Journal,* XVI (1973).
    'Lloyd George and the Land: The Issue of Site Value Rating', in J.A. Benyon *et al.* eds., *Studies in Local History: Essays in Honour of Professor Winifred Maxwell* (Cape Town, 1976).
Newton, L. T., *Lord Lansdowne: A Biography* (1929).
Peacock, A. T., and Wiseman, J., *The Growth of Government Expenditure in the United Kingdom* (Princeton, N. J., 1961).
Pelling, H., *Social Geography of British Elections 1885—1910* (1967).
Rees, J. F., *A Short Fiscal and Financial History of England 1815—1918* (1921).
Rempel, R. A., *Unionists Divided* (Newton Abbot, 1972).
Roseveare, H., *The Treasury* (New York, 1969).
Rowland, P., *The Last Liberal Governments* (2 vols., 1968—71).
    Lloyd George (1975).
Russell, A. K., *Liberal Landslide: The General Election of 1906* (Newton Abbot, 1974).
Sabine, B. E. V., *A History of the Income Tax* (1966).
Scheftel, Y., *The Taxation of Land Value* (Boston, 1916).
Searle, G. R., *The Quest for National Efficiency* (1977).
Semmel, B., *Imperialism and Social Reform* (1960).
Shehab, F., *Progressive Taxation* (1953).
Thompson, P., *Socialists, Liberals and Labour: The Struggle for London 1885—1914* (1967).
Weston, C. C., 'The Liberal Leadership and the Lords' Veto, 1907—1911', *Historical Journal,* XI (1968).
Wilson, J., *CB: A Life of Sir Henry Campbell-Bannerman* (1973).
Wrigley, C. J., *David Lloyd George and the British Labour Movement* (Hassocks, 1976).

Index

Acland-Hood, Sir Alexander, 29, 205, 211–14, 217, 249, 268
Addison, Christopher, 310
Alden, Percy, 270
Amery, Julian, 27
Anglo-Boer War, 1, 20, 21, 24, 30, 32, 38, 63, 219
Anson, Sir William, 220
Anti-Socialist Union, 178, 204
Arbuthnot, Gerald, 213
Army, estimates for 1909/10, 82–4, 130
Asquith, Herbert Henry, 55, 120, 121, 123, 127, 180, 182, 205, 220
   early career and characteristics, 63–4
   as Chancellor of Exchequer, 5, 16, 32, 44–8, 78, 81, 85, 87, 91–2, 93, 98–9, 126
   and income tax reform, 5, 16, 45, 78, 98–9, 302, 309
   and land value taxation, 5, 44, 46, 131–2
   and old-age pensions, 48, 85, 92–3, 126
   as Prime Minister: 49, 51; formation of ministry, 62–75
   and Budget 1909/10: 134, 155, 184, 189, 199, 206, 228; aware Lords might reject, 112–16; general support for in Cabinet, 148–50; reports to King on Cabinet deliberations, 152, 153, 158–9, 162; investigates estimates, 164; on Lloyd George's methods, 167; signs of strain during struggle over, 185, 248; concerned by Limehouse speech, 192; licensing clauses in Commons, 195, 201; Irish Nationalist charges re licence duties, 195–8; fate in Lords, 193–4, 224–6, 232–3; in election campaign, 237, 240, 242–4; procedure over after general

election, 261–4, 268, 276, 279; concessions for Ireland, 276, 283–4
   his general election campaign, 237–40, 242–8, 254
   and policy and procedure on constitutional issue following Lords' rejection of Budget, 220, 232–3, 240–3, 261–4, 267–9, 276–9, 281–7
Asquith, Margot, 111, 123
Asquith, Violet, 247

Balfour, Arthur James, 120
   as Unionist leader, 13, 25, 28–30, 88–91, 209–11, 269
   and tariff reform, 25, 28–30, 88–92, 211, 219, 221–2, 250–2, 291
   and education and licensing, 53
   partisan use of Lords, 56–9
   and Dreadnoughts, 129
   and Budget 1909/10: 177, 193, 200, 201; Lords rejection of, 114, 209–23, 225, 231, 233–4, 248
   his election campaign, 248, 250–2
   did not expect to win January 1910 general election, 217–22, 252
   his policy and tactics after general election, 261, 265–6, 271–2
Balfour of Burleigh, 6th Baron, 42, 216, 219, 232
Banbury, Sir Frederick, 177
Barnes, George, 265
Beck, A.C.T., 181
Bellairs, Carlyon, 200
Bertram, Julius, 200
Beveridge, William, 69
Birrell, Augustine, 73, 194, 196, 198, 275, 283
Blain, William, 77, 79, 100–1
Blewett, Neal, 2, 9, 28, 210, 221, 226, 236, 256–7, 262

343

Board of Customs and Excise, 79, 125, 126, 131, 138−9
Board of Inland Revenue, 79−80, 131, 136−8, 297, 299, 306
Boer War (*see* Anglo-Boer War)
Bowley, A.L., 37
Bradbury, John, 79, 123, 127, 137, 171
Braithwaite, W.J., 80
Brewers, and Budget, 179, 187, 222, 300−2
Brewers' Society, 178
British Weekly, 238
Brunner, Sir John, 312
Bryce, James, 81, 183, 246, 257, 259
Budget 1894/5, 15−16, 35−6, 94, 149
Budget 1901/2, 22, 24
Budget 1902/3, 24
Budget 1907/8, 16, 45, 94
Budget 1908/9, 49, 81, 87, 97
Budget 1909/10 ('People's Budget'):
　taxation strategy of, 1, 4−9, 118−19, 148−50, 169−70
　and issue between free trade and tariff reform, 5−6, 8, 12, 14−15, 118−19, 147, 173, 175−6, 222−3, 235, 244, 291
　preparation of: political goals and strategy, 112−21, 146−7; designed by Lloyd George, 121−4; reservations of officials, 12, 122−3, 139, 145−6; revenue and expenditure estimates, 124−31; land value taxes, 131−6; income tax and supertax, 136−8; death duties and stamps, 138; spirits and tobacco, 139; licence duties, 139−43; estimates for new taxes, 136−8, 143−5; policy making in, 145−7
　in Cabinet: general opposition to, 148−51; land value duties, 152−4; licence duties, 154−7; stamps, 157−8; income tax and supertax, 159−61; death duties, 161−2; spirits and tobacco, 162; estimates, 158−9, 162−9; estimates queried, 158−9, 163−6; significance of changes made, 169−70
　in House of Commons: introduced by Lloyd George, 172−3; first reactions to, 173−5; second reading, 175−8; opposition to in country, 178−80; Liberal 'cave' against land taxes, 180−3, 200, 307; changes made in land taxes, 183−5; Liberal response in country, 186−8; end of committee stage of land taxes, 192−3; concessions in direct taxes in committee stage, 195; Irish Nationalist objections to, 177, 195−8; report stage and new estimates, 199; third reading, 199−201; reintroduced and passed, 285
　and rejection by House of Lords: whether intended to provoke, 112−17, 234−5; speculation about, 114−16, 123, 177, 184, 190, 194, 223−6; Unionist decision for, 209−23; Government decision against 'stop-gap' budget in event of, 226−9; rejection, 229−32; response of Commons, 233−4; as election issue, 238, 242, 245
　and January 1910 general election: as issue in, 236−40, 242−5, 249, 252−4; influence on voting, 258−9; meaning of result for, 255, 259−60
　passage after election: differences between Government and Irish Nationalists over procedure on, 240, 261−4, 266, 278; question of concessions for Ireland, 273−6, 279−85; final passage, 285−8
　balance sheet at 31 March 1910, 288−9
　impact and significance of with regard to: politics, 9−12, 290−2, 302−3; revenue, 292; distribution of tax burden, 14−16, 293−5; social reform, 295−6; land, 296−300; liquor trade, 300−2
　see also Lloyd George, and taxes
Budget 1914/15, 3−4, 10−11, 302, 303−10
Budget League, 150, 175, 182, 188−90, 202−4
Budget Protest League, 178, 202, 204−6, 213

Burns, John, 60, 64, 73, 110, 113, 128, 201, 241
 and land valuation, 48, 102, 105, 109
 and Budget, 149, 158
Buxton, Sydney, 40, 73, 131
By-elections: 1908, 60; July 1909, 188; October 1909, 207, 253; 1910–14, 303

Caird, James K., 204
Campbell-Bannerman, Sir Henry, 30, 31, 32, 43, 44, 48, 49
 his legacy to Asquith, 51–62
 his veto plan for Lords, 59, 241, 263–4
Carrington, 1st Earl, 73, 120, 241, 308
 and Budget, 150, 170, 179, 183, 188, 224
 on situation between election and passage of Budget, 268–70, 278, 283
Carson, Sir Edward, 191
Cawdor, 3rd Earl, 232
Cecil, Lord Hugh, 29
Chalmers, Sir Robert, 79–80, 123, 136–8, 144, 158–9, 165, 227
Chamberlain, Austen, 81, 217, 233
 and revenue argument for tariffs, 88
 and Budget, 128, 173, 176–7, 199, 223
 and general election, 236, 250–1, 258
 and post-election situation, 253–4, 271–2, 286
Chamberlain, Joseph, 17, 20, 31, 32, 43, 66, 216
 and tariff reform, 24–7, 87–8, 251
 and Budget, 211, 222, 223
Chamberlain, Mary, 222
Chance, F. W., 181, 200
Chaplin, Henry, 114, 129
Churchill, Winston S., 1, 3, 11, 17, 29, 71–2, 108, 113, 119, 120, 200, 201, 205, 270, 305
 and armed forces estimates 1909/10, 82–4, 128–30
 and social reform, 72, 109–10, 116, 121, 127
 and Budget: 118, 150–1; Lords
  rejection of, 190, 198, 225, 229, 238, 240
 and Budget League, 182, 188–90, 202–4
 his election campaign, 238–40, 245–7
 and House of Lords reform, 241, 263
 and post-election situation, 263, 266, 269–70, 281–3, 287
Clark, William, 79, 171
Clarke, P. F., 1–2, 314
Committee on National Debt and Taxation (Colwyn Committee), 16, 294
Cox, Harold, 181
Crewe, 1st Earl, 72, 73, 120, 190, 263, 272, 281
 and Budget, 131, 148–9, 158, 163, 232
Cromer, 1st Earl, 87, 119, 231
Curran, Pete, 60
Curzon, 1st Baron, 232, 247–8
Customs and Excise (*see* Board of)

Daily Chronicle, 187
Daily Mail, 191
Daily Telegraph, 129
Dalmeny, Lord, 181
Davidson, Sir Arthur, 220
Davies, C. L., 103
Development and Road Improvements Fund, 146, 172, 194, 201–2
Devonshire, 8th Duke of, 28
Dicey, A. V., 221
Dickson-Poynder, Sir John, 132, 180–2
Dilke, Sir Charles, 40, 45
Dillon, John, 273–5
Dreadnoughts: 127–9, 186; payment for, 179, 213, 244

Economist, The, 119, 129, 187, 293
Edgeworth, F. Y., 34
Education, 238, 247
Education Act (1902), 53, 66, 69
Education Bill (1906), 57–8, 61
Edward VII, King, 84
 complaints about Lloyd George's speeches, 70, 192, 199
 anxious for compromise in Budget struggle, 225, 265–6
 and 'guarantees', 220, 240–2

Elibank, Master of, 180, 254, 267–8, 270, 273–5
Emmott, Alfred, 172, 185, 199, 206, 246, 311
Emy, H. V., 2–3, 6, 10
Esher, 2nd Viscount, 62, 84, 217, 220
Estates Gazette, 179, 299
Evans, Sir Samuel, 201

Faber, George, 177
Fabian Socialists, 34
Fitzmaurice, Lord Edmond, 149
Fitzroy, Sir Almeric, 79, 130, 150–1
Fowler, Sir Henry (*see* Wolverhampton)
Free Trade:
  and Liberal party, 18, 30–1, 53, 55
  and ability to provide for increased government expenditure: 48–50, 87–92, 93, 100;
  Budget as a demonstration of, 8, 110, 118–21, 145, 172–3, 176, 222–3, 235
  as election issue, 238–9
  Budget helped preserve, 291
  see also Budget 1909/10, tariff reform
Freeden, M., 6–7, 34, 311
Fuller, J. M., 113

Gardiner, A. G., 62, 64, 70, 71, 77
Garvin, J. L., 129, 203, 209–12, 214
General Elections:
  1900, 32
  1906, 6, 32, 51, 55
  January 1910, 9, 12, 217–21, 226–60, 312
  December 1910, 290–1, 312
George, Henry, 39
Giffen, Sir Robert, 22–3
Gilbert, Bentley, 2–3, 307
Gladstone, Herbert, 53–4, 174
Gladstone, W. E., 23, 139
Glen-Coats, Sir Thomas, 180
Goschen, George, 22
Government expenditure:
  increases in, 1–2, 19–23, 82–6, 292, 303, 310
  attitudes to, 1, 20–1, 27, 32, 76, 308
  see also Budget 1909/10, free trade, tariff reform

Grayson, Victor, 60
Grey, Sir Edward, 55, 73, 110
  and Budget, 148–9, 239
  and post-election situation, 262–3, 268, 271, 277, 278, 282
Grigg, John, 66
Guest, Ivor, 182
Guillemard, Laurence, N., 79, 122, 123, 125, 138–9, 155–6
Guinness and Company, 155

Haldane, R. B., 55, 64–5, 73, 245
  and army estimates 1909/10, 81–4, 130
  and taxation reform, 23, 93
  and Lloyd George, 111, 135, 172
  and Budget, 131, 150, 182, 201, 224, 225
  and Government's House of Lords policy, 241, 263, 267, 277–8
Hamer, D. A., 2–3
Hamilton, Sir Edward, 42, 46, 77–8, 98–9, 101
Harcourt, Lewis, 73, 81–2, 128
  and Budget, 148–9, 154, 158–61, 163, 167–9
  and House of Lords, 263–4, 267, 278, 281–2, 286
Harcourt, Sir William, 15, 35–6, 94, 160, 302
Hardie, James Keir, 207
Harper, Edgar, 297, 306
Harris, Leverton, 86–7
Hawtrey, R. G., 127
Hay, J. R., 14
Healy, Tim, 196, 254, 273–4, 278
Heath, Thomas, 77, 79
Henderson, Arthur, 234
Henry, Charles, 109, 110
Henry, Julia, 110–11
Herbert, Jesse, 60
Hewins, Professor W. A. S., 89–90, 252, 269
Hicks, William Joynson, 192
Hicks-Beach, Sir Michael (*see* St. Aldwyn)
Hobhouse, Charles, 72, 280, 282, 286
  and Lloyd George, 12, 73–4, 76, 78, 122, 150
  and Budget, 123, 131, 134–5, 201
Hobhouse, L. T., 33

Hobson, J. A., 33, 35, 37–8, 237
Holt, Sir Richard, 305, 308
Home Rule, 2, 10, 54, 195, 219–20,
    237–80, 242, 247, 249, 303,
    309
Hopwood, Sir Francis, 78
Horsfall, J. C., 204
House of Lords:
    and Liberal measures, 4, 55–9,
        108
    Budget as a means of circum-
        venting, 49–50, 117–18, 151–3
    and rejection of Budget, 11–14,
        112–17, 184–5, 209–32
    as election issue, 236–40, 242–
        6, 249–50, 252–3
    Government policy towards after
        election, 262–3, 266, 268, 270,
        271, 277–9, 281
    'guarantees' for dealing with, 240–
        2, 261, 263, 269, 276, 279–87
    passes Budget, 288
    Parliament Bill and, 10, 12, 277,
        282, 285, 290–1, 303
Housing and Town Planning Bill, 201
Hurwitz, S. J., 14–15
Hyde Park, land tax demonstration, 190

Ilbert, Courtenay P., 63, 208, 232–3
    and Lloyd George, 81, 206–7
    and Budget, 113, 115, 135, 152,
        183, 185
    partisan assistance to Government
        over Budget rejection, 226–8
Illingworth, Percy, 309
Independent   Irish   Nationalists
    (O'Brienites), 254, 265, 273–5
India Councils Bill, 201
Inland Revenue (*see* Board of)
Ireland:
    licence duties and, 142, 177, 196–
        8, 281, 300
    plunge towards civil war in, 290
    see also Irish Nationalists, Indepen-
        dent Irish Nationalists
Irish Land Bill (1909), 194, 196, 201
Irish Land Purchase Act (1902), 254
Irish Nationalists:
    and Liberal alliance, 54, 58,
        254–5
    opposition to Budget, 177, 195–
        8, 200, 234

election demands and campaign,
    238, 254–5
and balance of power in Commons,
    10, 12, 217, 219, 225, 256,
    259–60
conditions and negotiations for
    passage of Budget, 261–3, 264–
    5, 268–70, 273–6, 279–81, 285

James, 1st Baron James of Hereford,
    232
Jenkins, Roy, 75, 112, 210
Jennings, Sir Ivor, 245
Jessel, H. M., 178
Joint Committee for the Taxation of
    Ground Rents and Values, 41

Kearley, Sir Hudson, 73, 275
Kennedy judgement, 140
Knollys,   1st   Viscount,   220,   240
Knox, D. M., 300

Labour Exchanges Bill, 201
Labour Leader, 187, 253
Labour party:
    and relations with Liberal party, 2,
        5–6, 9, 49, 53–4, 60, 206–7,
        252–4, 313–14
    and Budget, 176, 187, 195, 234,
        291
    and January 1910 general election,
        237, 252–5
    and post-election situation, 265,
        275, 283
Land   Enquiry   Committee,   298–9
Land taxation (see taxes)
Land Taxes Protest Committee, 178
Land Values, 47, 236–8
Land Values (Scotland) Bill, 48, 58, 101
Land   Values   Group,   46–50,   303
Lansdowne, 5th Marquess of, 56–9,
    236
    and Budget 13, 116, 191, 209,
        215–21, 225, 229–30, 231
Law,   Andrew   Bonar,   90,   176–7,
    250, 309
League for the Taxation of Land Values,
    182
Lewis, Herbert, 135
Liberal   Imperialists,   30,   31,   54–5

Liberal League, 181
Liberal Magazine, 5, 302
Liberal Party:
  nature of class support for: 2–3,
    17–19, 61, 183, 206–7, 236–9,
    256–9, 290; taxation strategy
    and, 4–16, 109–10, 132, 310–
    13
  coalition nature of, 17–19, 51–5,
    56–7
  as party of social reform, 1–11,
    31–44, 51–2, 58, 61, 93,
    302–10
  and relations with Labour, 2,
    5–6, 9, 49, 53–4, 60, 206–7,
    252–4, 313–14
  division in Anglo-Boer War, 30–1
  revival 1903–6, 31–2, 52–5
  difficulties by 1908, 48–50, 51–2,
    55–62, 75
  programme obstructed by Lords
    during 1908, 107–8, 120
  and Budget, 146–7, 174, 178,
    180–3, 186–8, 206–7, 290–
    2, 302–3
  and January 1910 general election,
    236–48, 255–9
  and post-election situation, 262,
    268–9, 270–1, 286
  and Budget 1914/15, 302–10
  see also New Liberalism, Radicals
Liberty and Property Defence League,
  178
Licence duties (*see* taxes)
Licensed Victuallers' National Defence
  League, 178
Licensed Victuallers' Central Protection
  Society, 178
Licensing Act (1904), 53, 67
Licensing Bill (1908), 59, 107–8,
  118
Liverpool and District Association
  of House Builders, 299
Lloyd George, David, 2, 64, 98, 108,
  187, 189, 200, 205, 221, 292,
  293, 295, 297, 298, 313
  made Chancellor of Exchequer, 64–
    71, 75
  as administrator: 68–9, 76–80,
    167;
    relations with officials, 76–81,
    122–4
  and social reform, 7, 66–9, 71,

    109–10, 119–20, 172, 146–7,
    295, 311
  and free trade, 66, 69, 110, 118–
    21, 145, 172–3
  and armed services estimates 1909/
    10, 81–4, 127–30
  and Labour party, 8–9, 206–7,
    291, 314
  goals and strategy in Budget, 5–7,
    112–21, 146–7
  and Budget estimates, 124–30,
    143–5, 158–9, 162–3, 199;
    challenged on, 163–6, 177
  his Budget proposals: land value
    duties, 106–7, 131–6, 152–4;
    income tax and supertax, 136–
    8, 159–61; licence duties, 139–
    40, 154–7; stamps, 138, 157–
    8; spirits and tobacco, 162;
    difficulties with Cabinet col-
    leagues over, 110–11, 135–6,
    148–51, 175, 185, 201
  and Budget in Commons and
    country: Budget speech, 170–3;
    pleased with reactions to, 174–
    5; procedural proposals, 175,
    184; determined to retain land
    valuation, 183–5; speeches at
    Limehouse and Newcastle,
    190–2, 198–9, 206, 209, 211,
    213; negotiations with Irish
    Nationalists over licence duties,
    195–8; triumph in Commons,
    201; and Budget League, 202–4
  and rejection of Budget by Lords:
    possibility considered by, 114–
    16; first suggestions he would
    welcome, 194, 198–9; suggested
    he had planned, 232; against
    'stop-gap' Budget in event of,
    237
  and January 1910 general election:
    anxious for agreement with
    Labour, 206–7; his election
    campaign, 236–40, 244–6; and
    results, 259
  and negotiations with Irish Nationa-
    lists on Budget concessions, 262,
    271, 273–6, 279–81
  and guarantees and final passage of
    Budget, 269, 276, 281–4, 285–
    7, 289
  and Revenue Bill, 1914, 296

and Budget 1914/15, 302—10
and repeal of land value duties, 307
see also Budget 1909/10
London Municipal Reform League, 40—1
Long, Walter, 110, 178, 202, 205, 309
Lords (*see* House of)
Loreburn, 1st Baron, 73, 131, 149, 208, 230, 263
Lough, Thomas, 182
Lytton, 2nd Earl, 232

MacDonald, Ramsay, 53—4, 207, 256, 314
McKenna, Reginald, 69, 72—3, 98—9, 125, 127—30, 131, 186, 263, 277, 306
and Budget, 134, 149
McKibbin, Ross, 313
Macnamara, Dr. T. J., 43
Mallet, Bernard, 94—8, 106
Mallet, Charles, 76
Manchester Guardian, 65, 75, 111, 186, 240, 247, 256, 258, 264
Mason, A. E. W., 200
Mason, David, 308
Massingham, H. W., 116
Masterman, C. F. G., 6, 17—19, 61, 69, 73—4, 77, 117—18, 189, 194, 201, 282, 283, 287
Masterman, Lucy, 201
Merriman, John X., 52
Middle Classes Defence Organisation, 178
Midleton, 1st Earl, 110, 117
Mill, J. S., 34, 39
Milner, 1st Viscount, 36, 216
Mond, Sir Alfred, 312
Money, Chiozza, 47, 96—7, 182
Monkswell, Lord, 41
Montagu, Edwin, 159, 220
Montgomery, W. E., 178
Mooney, J. J., 198
Morley, John, 52, 64—5, 120, 128, 148, 200, 241, 264, 281—3
Morning Post, 194
Mowatt, Sir Francis, 77, 81
Murray, Sir George, 12, 77—80, 122—3, 137, 157, 164—6, 216, 227—8

Nation, 49, 62, 71, 116, 187, 264
National insurance, 3, 109, 119, 172, 295, 303
National Liberal Federation, 203
National Trade Defence Association, 178
Navy, 2, 4, 124—5, 127—30, 249, 303, 310
New Liberalism, 3, 6—8, 11, 31—44, 64, 307—11
Newton, 2nd Baron, 234
Nicholson, Arthur Pole, 270
Nicoll, Robertson, 221, 238
Nonconformists, 17—18, 31, 53, 57, 238, 246
Norman, Sir Henry, 181—2, 189—90, 202—3
Northcliffe, 1st Baron, 191, 210—11

Oakeshott, J. F., 34
O'Brien, William, 254, 262, 273—5, 279
Observer, 129, 194, 203, 250
O'Connor, T. P., 54, 196—7, 264, 274—5
Old-age pensions, 1—3, 26—7, 31, 48, 59, 68, 87, 90—2, 200, 259, 295
estimated cost of, 82, 84—6, 124—7
Osborne judgement, 253
Owen, Frank, 171

Parliament Bill, 10, 12, 277, 282, 285, 290—1, 303
Partington, Oswald, 188
Paulton, J. M., 181
Pease, Sir Alfred, 206
Pease, Jack, 74, 76, 111, 199
and Budget, 149, 184, 201
and Budget League, 182, 189, 203—4
and possible election, 115, 194, 224—5
and Labour, 207, 252
on post-election situation, 275—6, 278, 283, 286
Pentland, 1st Baron (formerly John Sinclair), 73, 263

Perks Sir Robert, 181, 200
Petter, M., 313
Ponsonby, Arthur, 60, 63
Pretyman, E. G., 177
Primrose, Sir Henry, 98, 100–1
Provisional Collection of Taxes Act, 306

Radicals (including 'advanced' Liberals), 11, 39–40, 46–7, 61
   and post-election situation, 262, 267, 269, 270, 272, 278–9, 283, 286–7
   and Budget 1914/15, 308–10
Ramsden, John, 210
Raphael, H. H., 181
Reconstruction Ministry, 299
Redmond, John, 54
   and negotiations with Lloyd George re licence duties, 195–8
   and January 1910 general election, 238, 254–5
   and demands and negotiations for allowing passage of Budget, 261–5, 266–7, 269, 273–81, 285–6
Relugas compact, 55
Rempel, Richard, 28
Rendel, S., 246
Revenue Bill, 1914, 296
Riddell, George, 77, 108, 113, 114, 306
Ridley, 2nd Viscount, 114
Ridsdale, E. A., 200
Ripon, 1st Marquess, 73
   plan for Lords, 241
Ritchie, C. T., 25
Road Board and Fund, 202, 209
Robson, W. S., 102, 105–6, 131, 201, 226
Rosebery, 5th Earl, 54, 78, 123, 181, 231, 271
Rothschild, 1st Baron, 158, 178
Rowntree, Joseph, 108, 139
Rowntree, Seebohm, 66
Royal Commission on Local Taxation, 42–3
Royal Statistical Society, 293
Runciman, Sir Walter, 186
Runciman, Walter, 72, 225, 246, 263, 277, 287
   and Budget, 143, 163–4, 167
Russell, A. K., 30

St. Aldwyn, 1st Viscount (formerly Sir Michael Hicks-Beach), 22–4, 218–20, 232
Salisbury, 3rd Marquess, 21, 25
Samuel, Herbert, 35, 263
   and burden of taxation, 16, 96–7, 293–5
   and Budget, 174, 201
Sandars, Jack, 191, 242, 272
   and decision to reject Budget, 210–17, 220
Schuster, Sir Felix, 178, 186
Scott, C. P., 270
Seeley, J. E. B., 29
Select Committee on Income Tax (1906), 45
Select Committee on Land Values (1919), 13, 297–8
Sherwell, Arthur, 139
Simon, John, 226–7
Sinking Fund, 162, 168, 199, 288–9
Smith, F. E., 174, 211, 250
Smith, Goldwin, 52
Snowden, Philip, 176, 253
Soares, E. J., 132
Socialism and Socialists, 34, 39, 181,
   Budget linked to 13, 166–7, 216, 249–50
   see also Fabian Socialists
South Africa Bill, 201
Spectator, 91, 217
Spender, Harold, 190
Spender, J. A., 63, 70, 73, 86, 109, 185, 246, 257, 259
Stair, A., 124, 130
Standard, 194
Stead, W. T., 68, 71
Stevenson, Frances, 148
Strachey, St. Loe, 91–2, 221
Supply, limitation of, 271–3
Surveyor's Institution, 179, 299
Sutherland, J. E., 48

Taff Vale, 41
Tariff reform and Tariff Reformers, 25–6, 114–15, 205
   and Unionist party, 28–30, 90–1, 215–16, 221
   and challenge to Liberals, 4–6, 20, 30–2, 43–4, 60–1, 111, 121, 147
   and taxation and revenue, 1, 24–7, 33, 87–90, 92, 119, 222, 250

and food taxes, 7, 25–6, 66, 119, 244–5, 251–2, 258
and Budget: 119–21, 149, 176, 290–2; rejection of by Lords, 12–14, 115, 211, 221–2, 235
as election issue, 243–5, 249–52, 258
and unemployment, 27, 250–1
Tariff Reform League, 178, 204
Taxes and taxation:
structure of by 1908, 89–90, 93–8
distribution of burden, 5, 7, 11, 14–16, 36–8, 95–9, 169–70, 173, 293–5, 310–13
direct vs. indirect, 1, 7, 10, 15, 17, 22–4, 33, 44, 79, 93, 293
levels of tolerance of, 21–3, 89–90
to finance social reform, 2–4, 17, 19, 26–7, 32, 35–6, 68, 88–90, 92–3, 98, 109, 116, 119–20, 172, 236, 292, 295–6
New Liberalism and, 5, 6, 23, 33–4
Joseph Chamberlain's scheme of, 25–6
death duties: 33, 35, 46, 94, 305; and Budget, 124–5, 138, 143, 161–3, 165, 167, 168–9, 177, 195, 199, 229, 288, 293
income tax and supertax: 10, 33, 35–7, 45, 89–90, 93–4, 98–101, 305–6, 309; and Budget, 5, 124–5, 136–8, 143–5, 159–63, 164–5, 168, 177, 195, 226, 229, 289, 293, 302
land value taxation: campaign for, 33, 38–44, 46–8, 101–7, 303; and Budget, 5, 9, 14, 117–18, 131–6, 143–5, 149–50, 152–4, 163, 168, 177, 179, 180–5, 188, 192–3, 199, 200, 214–15, 239, 285, 292, 296–300; and Budget 1914/15, 304–10
licence duties, 45, 95; and Budget, 4–5, 9, 107–8, 118, 139–43, 145, 154–7, 163, 165, 167–8, 177, 179, 195–8, 201, 281, 285, 289, 292, 300–1
stamp duties and Budget, 124–5, 138, 143, 157–8, 162–3, 164–6, 168, 177, 199, 288

spirit duty, 95; and Budget, 139, 143, 162, 168, 187, 195–6, 199, 273–4, 276, 281–3, 285, 288, 292, 301–2
tobacco duty: 10, 95; and Budget, 15, 139, 162, 168, 187, 195, 292
motor car licences and petrol tax, 169, 202
corn duty, 25
sugar duty, 87, 97
Tedder, A. J., 124
Temperance reform, 2, 107–8, 238
Times, The, 52, 115, 170, 173–4, 178, 181, 183, 209, 231, 233, 256–8, 270, 280, 285, 305
Thompson, F.M.L., 300
Thompson, Percy, 13, 297–8
Thorne, Will, 185
Thring, Arthur, 133, 163, 185
Trades Disputes Bill, 58
Treasury, 5, 76–9, 81, 117, 123
Treasury (Temporary Borrowing) Bill, 288–9
Trevelyan, C. P., 11, 43, 48, 188
Tweedmouth, 2nd Baron, 72

Unionist Free Traders, 28–9, 87, 91–2
and Budget rejection, 215, 223
Unionist party:
tariff reform and, 24–30, 90–1, 215–16, 221
and basis of taxation, 1, 22, 45, 86–92
and Navy, 128–9, 186, 249
and partisan use of Lords, 55–8, 107–8
and Budget, 11–12, 173–4, 176–8, 191–3; rejection of, 13–14, 208–23
and January 1910 general election, 248–52, 255–8
and post-election situation, 265–6, 269, 270–1, 288
and December 1910 general election, 290–1
United Kingdom Alliance, 108
Ure, Alexander, 104, 131, 200, 203

Webb, Sidney, 34
Wedgwood, J., 47, 102–3, 107
Wedgwood, R., 107

Welsh Disestablishment, 10, 224, 237–8, 303
Westminster Gazette, 187
Whitbread, Samuel, 181, 200
Whitley, J. H., 46
Whittaker, Sir Thomas, 174, 181

Wilding, Paul, 298
Winterton, 6th Earl, 185
Wolverhampton, 1st Viscount (formerly Sir Henry Fowler), 19, 73, 148
Wyndham, George, 19, 56–7, 254